SAINTS' LIVES AND BIBLE STORIES FOR THE STAGE

The Other Voice in Early Modern Europe:
The Toronto Series, 7

The Other Voice in
Early Modern Europe:
The Toronto Series

SERIES EDITORS Margaret L. King *and* Albert Rabil, Jr.

Recent Publications in the Series

1
MADRE MARÍA ROSA
Journey of Five Capuchin Nuns
Edited and translated by Sarah E. Owens
2009

2
GIOVAN BATTISTA ANDREINI
Love in the Mirror
Edited and translated by Jon R. Snyder
2009

3
RAYMOND DE SABANAC AND SIMONE ZANACCHI
Two Women of the Great Schism: The Revelations *of Constance de Rabastens by Raymond de Sabanac and* Life of the Blessed Ursulina of Parma *by Simone Zanacchi*
Edited and translated by Renate Blumenfeld-Kosinski and Bruce L. Venarde
2010

4
OLIVA SABUCO DE NANTES BARRERA
The True Medicine
Edited and translated by Gianna Pomata
2010

5
LOUISE-GENEVIÈVE GILLOT DE SAINCTONGE
Dramatizing Dido, Circe, and Griselda
Edited and translated by Janet Levarie Smarr
2010

6
PERNETTE DU GUILLET
Complete Poems
Edited by Karen Simroth James
Translated by Marta Rijn Finch
2010

Saints' Lives and Bible Stories for the Stage

ANTONIA PULCI

~

Edited by

ELISSA B. WEAVER

Translated by

JAMES WYATT COOK

Iter Inc.
Centre for Reformation and Renaissance Studies
Toronto
2010

Iter: Gateway to the Middle Ages and Renaissance
Tel: 416/978-7074   Fax: 416/978-1668
Email: iter@utoronto.ca   Web: www.itergateway.org

CRRS Publications, Centre for Reformation and Renaissance Studies
Victoria University in the University of Toronto
Toronto, Ontario M5S 1K7 Canada
Tel: 416/585-4465   Fax: 416/585-4430
Email: crrs.publications@utoronto.ca   Web: www.crrs.ca

© 2010 Iter Inc. & the Centre for Reformation and Renaissance Studies
All Rights Reserved
Printed in Canada

We thank the Gladys Kriebel Delmas Foundation for a generous grant of start-up funds for The Other Voice, Toronto Series, a portion of which supports the publication of this volume.

Iter and the Centre for Reformation and Renaissance Studies gratefully acknowledge the generous support of James E. Rabil, in memory of Scottie W. Rabil, toward the publication of this book.

"The Play of Saint Francis," "The Play of Saint Domitilla," "The Play of Saint Guglielma," and "The Play of the Prodigal Son" used with permission from Cook, James Wyatt, and Barbara Collier Cook, eds. *Florentine Drama for Convent and Festival: Seven Sacred Plays*. Chicago: University of Chicago Press, 1996. The Other Voice in Early Modern Europe. © 1996 by The University of Chicago. All rights reserved.

Library and Archives Canada Cataloguing in Publication
Pulci, Antonia, 1452–1501
Saints' lives and Bible stories for the stage / Antonia Pulci ; edited by Elissa B. Weaver ; translated by James Wyatt Cook.
(The other voice in early modern Europe : the Toronto series ; 7)
Translated from the Italian.
Co-published by: Centre for Reformation and Renaissance Studies.
Text in Italian with English translation.
Includes bibliographical references and index.

Contents: La rappresentazione di Santa Domitilla = The play of Saint Domitilla — La rappresentazione di Santa Guglielma = The play of Saint Guglielma — La rappresentazione di San Francesco = The play of Saint Francis — La rappresentazione del figliuol prodigo = The play of the prodigal son — La rappresentazione della distruzione di Saul e il pianto di Davit = The play of the destruction of Saul and the lament of David.
Issued also in electronic format.
ISBN 978-0-7727-2073-3

I. Weaver, Elissa, 1940– II. Cook, James Wyatt, 1932– III. Victoria University (Toronto, Ont.). Centre for Reformation and Renaissance Studies IV. Iter Inc V. Title. VI. Series: Other voice in early modern Europe. Toronto series ; 7

PQ4630.P8A2 2010
852'.3   C2010-905508-X

Cover: Attributed to Ridolfo del Ghirlandaio (Florence 1483–1561). Portrait of a Woman (The Nun), 1510 circa, cm. 65 x 48, oil on panel. Florence, Galleria degli Uffizi, Inv. 1890, n. 8380

Cover design: Maureen Morin, Information Technology Services, University of Toronto Libraries
Typesetting and production: Iter Inc.

Contents

Acknowledgments	ix
Editor's Introduction	1
Texts and Translations	67
La Rappresentazione di Santa Domitilla	68
The Play of Saint Domitilla	69
La Rappresentazione di Santa Guglielma	144
The Play of Saint Guglielma	145
La Rappresentazione di San Francesco	230
The Play of Saint Francis	231
La Rappresentazione del figliuol prodigo	308
The Play of the Prodigal Son	309
La Rappresentazione della distruzione di Saul e il pianto di Davit	362
The Play of the Destruction of Saul and the Lament of David	363
Endnotes	444
Appendix 1: Inventory of the Tanini house in Via de' Leoni	463
Appendix 2: Letter from Jacopa Tanini, widow of Francesco Tanini to Clarice Orsini, wife of Lorenzo de' Medici, 25 April 1475	468
Appendix 3: Fra Antonio Dolciati's Introductory Letter of Dedication of his *Esposizione della Regola di Sant'Agostino* (Detailed explanation of the Rule of Saint Augustine) to the nuns of the convent founded by Antonia Tanini	470
Editor's Bibliography	478
Index	493

Acknowledgments

It is likely that my work on this edition, and especially on the introduction, would never have come to a conclusion, were it not for the friendly reminders and insistent pleas from Al Rabil. I have enjoyed the work too much to let go easily; there was always (and is still) so much to be discovered in the rich collections of the Florentine archives and libraries about Antonia Tanini, her family and that of her husband Bernardo Pulci, and their life together; so much too to learn about her education, the plays she wrote, and the history of their composition and publication. I owe it all to Al's encouragement, his patience, and his guidance, that this book finally goes to press. *Grazie infinite.* I thank Jim Cook too, with whom it has been a pleasure to work, and who was always incredibly patient as I went over again and again the Italian texts and his elegant English pentameters; I thank him too for agreeing to add rhymes here and there to emulate the rhythms of Antonia Pulci's verse, and for redoing lines of the translation as I revisited and continued to correct my Italian edition. All this he did most congenially, no matter how busy his professional and personal life. *Grazie infinite.*

Many are the friends and colleagues who have graciously offered me their time and expertise; among them I owe a very special debt of gratitude to Nerida Newbigin, who knows more about early Italian theater than I ever will. Nerida read through the entire manuscript carefully, catching its glaring errors and making many useful suggestions for its improvement; she checked my scansion of the poetry throughout, helped solve some of the thornier problems of Pulci's syntax and its rendering in English, and she even contributed a few rhymes of her own to the translation. Francesco Bruni applied his immense expertise to the Italian texts and resolved some of the remaining metrical and syntactical difficulties; he greatly improved the punctuation of the plays, insisting on the importance of pauses (and so, more commas) in the syntax of these theatrical texts. Two colleagues whom I saw frequently in the Florentine archives, Sharon Strocchia and Brenda Preyer, shared with me their vast knowledge of fifteenth-century manuscript hands, finances, maps, homes, and furnishings. Riccardo Bruscagli helped me understand how the Prodigal Son lost his money in a game of cards. Finally, my friend and colleague Paolo Cherchi has always willingly shared his erudition with me, and I have called on him more often and for more advice than I can here enumerate. *A tutti, grazie infinite.*

I wish also to thank my dear friend Gabriella Zarri for her hospitality and company in Florence during my research trips, and Philippe Schmitter, who, with his usual enthusiasm for all things Tuscan, explored the Mugello region with me in search of the country homes of the Tanini and Pulci families.

Most of my research has been carried out in the Biblioteca Nazionale Centrale and the Archivio di Stato in Florence, and in Chicago at the Regenstein Library of the University of Chicago and at the Newberry Library. I wish to thank the directors and staffs of those marvelously rich institutions for the privilege of working there, and especially Paul Gehl, the Custodian of the John M. Wing Foundation on the History of Printing at the Newberry Library, for his generous assistance and his friendship.

James Cook dedicates his English translations to his granddaughters, Shaina Anne and Jamie Isabel Cook, who were born as we worked on this edition. I dedicate my work to the memory of my mother, Florina Weaver, neé Rebuffoni (1913–2008), who at ninety-five left this world much too soon.

Antonia Pulci (1452/54–1501)

Donna colta e pia, anch' ella poetò in materia religiosa, componendo drammi sacri ...per i quali le spetta nella storia letteraria un posto tra i principali quattrocentisti scrittori di rime e rappresentazioni sacre.

A cultivated and pious woman, she too wrote religious poetry, sacred drama, ...for which she deserves a place in literary history among the principal fifteenth-century authors of poetry and *sacre rappresentazioni*.

(Francesco Flamini, 1888)

...era vedova e in casa di sua madre, madonna Jacopa, e del suo fratello Nicolò Tanini, nella superiora parte di quella si aveva religiosamente e poveramente ordinata una cameretta con el suo oratorio e più libri devoti, e in quella, standosi quasi sempre sola, dì e notte si essercitava in orazioni e sacre lezioni...

...a widow, in the house of her mother, Madonna Jacopa, and her brother Niccolò Tanini, on the upper floor she had set up a small room, a poor and spiritual place, with an oratory and many devotional books, and there, almost always alone, day and night she dedicated herself to prayer and reading religious works...

(Fra Antonio Dolciati, 19 August 1528)[a]

---

a. In the Florentine calendar the new year began on 25 March, the feast of the Incarnation, and this system prevailed until 1750. In the interest of readability, for the period 1 January through 24 March I have modernized the dates in the text; in the footnotes I provide both the date on the document and the modern equivalent. I have left unchanged dates found in secondary sources, whose validity I have not been able to confirm. I use abbreviations for references to the Florentine institutions most often cited, the Florentine Archivio di Stato (ASF) and Biblioteca Nazionale Centrale (BNCF).

The Other Voice

Antonia Pulci is, if not the first, certainly one of the first women writers to have sent her work to press, and this is not her only claim to our attention.[1] She belonged to the industrious Florentine merchant class, to a family that rose economically and socially in the fifteenth century, and she married into the noble Pulci family, a trajectory shared by prosperous members of her class; but what is unusual is that she married into a family that included three of the most important literary figures in Florence of the time, Luca, Luigi and Bernardo Pulci (four, if we include, Mariotto Davanzati, the husband of their sister Lisa), and she brought to that brilliant, but financially strapped family, more than the value of her dowry. Somewhere along the way, either at home, in a nearby convent, or at a neighborhood public school, she had learned to read and write in the vernacular, at a level of attainment that was exceptional for any woman at the time, certainly for any of her class.[2] However, it was probably as a member of her

---

1. Her published miracle play, the *Rappresentazione di Santa Domitilla*, bears the date 1483 following the title. It was included in the anthology of religious plays published in Florence without indication of date or publisher but attributed to the press of Antonio Miscomini and to the early 1490s. The *Santa Domitilla* is the only play of the collection that is dated, indicating, perhaps, that it was published or slated for publication earlier and then included in the undated collection of plays printed by Antonio Miscomini, who was active in Florence 1481/82–1494. If not the first woman to take her work to press, she shares the distinction only with a learned woman of the upper class, the early humanist writer, Cassandra Fedele, who published her *Oratio pro Bertucio Lamberto* in Modena in 1487 (and again in Venice, 1488; Nuremberg,1489). I thank Diana Robin for this information. According to Virginia Cox, *Women's Writing in Italy 1400–1650* (Baltimore: Johns Hopkins, 2008), it is "an unconscious prejudice that sees publication [by early modern women] as an index of merit"(88), since most prestigious women writers of the upper classes preferred to share their work in manuscript and only with select readers (*passim*). Cox acknowledges that the situation in Florence was quite different from that in the court societies of Italy; yet it is the case that Lucrezia Tornabuoni, Lorenzo de' Medici's mother and Antonia's contemporary, circulated her writing in manuscript.

2. Among Quattrocento Florentine women, only she and Lucrezia Tornabuoni, accomplished authors of vernacular texts, demonstrate such a high level of literacy. For this social class it has been generally thought that the most one finds at the time among women is "semi-literacy," or "partial literacy," like that of Margherita Datini and Alessandra Macinghi Strozzi, who dictated and eventually penned letters in the language of their speech, compelled to do so in order to communicate with distant family members. See the discus-

husband's family that she began to compose dramatic verse; and she soon became known in Florence as one of the most prolific writers of *sacre rappresentazioni*, mystery and miracle plays written in *ottava rima*, one of the most popular vernacular genres in Florence in her lifetime. She is the only known secular woman author of *sacre rappresentazioni*, and at least three of her plays appeared in the first printed anthology of Florentine religious drama (circa 1490–95).[3] Most of her plays had a second edition during her lifetime and were published again and again throughout the sixteenth and early seventeenth century; four have had modern editions. It is an extraordinary success story for a woman of rather humble origins, and it does not end with her literary accomplishments. When she was widowed, she left the social world she knew as a member of the Pulci family but continued her education, studying Latin, reading Scripture, and writing *laude*, religious poems of praise, another of the most popular vernacular literary genres. She became an *ammantellata*, a woman religious living

---

sion of the limited literacy of women of the Florentine merchant class in Ann Crabb, "'If I could write': Margherita Datini and Letter Writing, 1385–1410," *Renaissance Quarterly*, 60:4 (2007), 1170–1206. Judith Bryce, however, has recently shown that this view needs to be revisited and revised, in light of the evidence especially of the many books of devotional readings belonging to women, and evidence of their use, not merely their possession of such books. This and many references to lay women readers, of secular as well as religious texts, suggests that literacy among the women of the Florentine mercantile class was much more widespread than we have acknowledged. See Judith Bryce, "Les livres des Florentines: Reconsidering Women's Literacy in Quattrocento Florence," in *At the Margins: Minority Groups in Premodern Italy*, ed. Stephen J. Milner, (Minneapolis: University of Minnesota Press, 2005), 133–61. It is less surprising in a society in which many women of the mercantile class were readers that literary figures such as Antonia Tanini Pulci and Lucrezia Tornabuoni would emerge.

3. See note 1. The anthology consists of two volumes. Some scholars refer to both volumes as the "Prima raccolta," following Alfredo Cioni, in his *Bibliografia delle sacre rappresentazioni* (Florence: Sansoni Antiquariato, 1961); others, including Anna Maria Testaverde and Anna Maria Evangelista, *Sacre rappresentazioni manoscritte e a stampa conservate nella Biblioteca Nazionale Centrale di Firenze, Inventario* (Florence: Giunta Regionale Toscana Editrice Bibliografica, 1988), call the volume that includes Antonia's plays the "Seconda raccolta." The early bibliographer, Paul Colomb De Batines, *Bibliografia delle antiche rappresentazioni italiane sacre e profane stampate nei secoli XV e XVI* (Florence: La Società Tipografica, 1852), calls it volume 2 of the fifteenth-century *Raccolta*. The distinction is arbitrary. Since recent scholars believe that both volumes were published by Antonio Miscomini, it is often referred to as the Miscomini anthology and that is the term I will use.

in lay society, and she commissioned a chapel dedicated to St. Monica in the church of San Gallo, where she wished to be buried. She purchased property just outside the city walls, a house and some connected buildings, and there she assembled a small group of women, who would become the first sisters in the convent of Santa Maria della Misericordia, which she founded.

The *sacre rappresentazioni* that are known to be hers are the *Rappresentazione di Santa Domitilla (Play of Saint Domitilla)*, the *Rappresentazione di Santa Guglielma (Play of Saint Guglielma)*, the *Rappresentazione di San Francesco (Play of Saint Francis)*, the *Rappresentazione del figliuol prodigo (Play of the Prodigal Son)*, and the *Rappresentazione della distruzione di Saul e il pianto di Davit (Play of the Destruction of Saul and the Lament of David)*. Antonia also wrote a play based on the Biblical story of Joseph, but it is not clear that either of the surviving plays on that subject is hers, and she may be the author of other plays as well—a *Rappresentazione di Santo Antonio Abbate (Play of Saint Anthony Abbot)* has often been attributed to her.[4]

The genre of *sacra rappresentazione* flourished in Tuscany, primarily in Florence in the fifteenth century.[5] The early plays were often performed for religious celebrations in some of the major church-

---

4. Only the plays that can be securely attributed to Antonia Pulci are included in this volume. The two extant Joseph plays are the *Rappresentazione di Joseph, di Jacob e de' fratelli* and the *Rappresentazione di Joseph, figliuol di Jacob*; the latter and the *Rappresentazione di Santo Antonio Abate* were published in the anthology that contains Antonia Pulci's *Santa Domitilla*, *Santa Guglielma*, and *San Francesco* plays, as well as a play written by her husband Bernardo Pulci, the *Rappresentazione di Barlaam e Josafat*; however, unlike the others, these two plays do not include the name of the author.

5. On the Florentine *sacra rappresentazione* much has been written. For some of the most important and useful contributions to its history see Cesare Molinari, *Spettacoli fiorentini del Quattrocento: contributi allo studio delle sacre rappresentazioni* (Venice: Neri Pozza, 1961); Nerida Newbigin, *Feste d'Oltrarno: Plays in Churches in Fifteenth-Century Florence*, 2 vols (Florence: Olschki, 1996); Paola Ventrone, *Gli araldi della commedia: teatro a Firenze nel Rinascimento* (Ospedaletto [Pisa]: Pacini Editore, 1993), "Per una morfologia della sacra rappresentazione fiorentina," in *Teatro e culture della rappresentazione: lo spettacolo in Italia nel Quattrocento*, ed. Raimondo Guarino (Bologna: Il Mulino, 1988), and "La sacra rappresentazione fiorentina: aspetti e problemi," in *Esperienze dello spettacolo religioso nell'Europa del Quattrocento*, ed. M. Chiabò and F. Doglio (Rome: Torre di Orfeo, 1993), 67–99; and the classic study by Alessandro D'Ancona, *Origini del teatro italiano*, 2 vols. (Turin: Loescher, 1971 [rpt. of 2nd ed., 1891]).

es and on public occasions. The most frequent subjects were taken from the Old and New Testament. Toward the end of the century, however, saints' lives became popular subjects of the plays, especially the stories of virgin martyrs, and the genre also admitted romance elements, dangerous adventures, and miraculous interventions, mainly of the Virgin Mary. Antonia Pulci's plays partake of both traditions. She tried her hand at all of these subjects: two of her plays are based on the Old Testament, one on the New Testament, and three are saints' lives, one of which follows the romance tradition. Yet within these well-established parameters, Antonia Pulci's plays display certain characteristics that link them rather closely to her life experiences. She gives considerable emphasis to female characters, she perhaps alludes to members of her family in one play, and she introduces issues that had special appeal to her female readers and audiences, including a very subtle defense of Eve, a prominent feature of the *querelle des femmes* before and after Antonia's time. While the plots of her plays are simple and the stories with one exception quite well-known, her talent lies in their versification and in her ability to enliven the speech of her characters with believable contemporary language and to turn *ottava rima* into an entertaining dramatic form.

Biography

Antonia Pulci, as she is known to modern readers, was born Antonia Tanini, sometime between 1452 and 1454, to Francesco di Antonio di Giannotto Tanini and Jacopa di Torello di Lorenzo Torelli.[6] Antonia's

6. Information about Antonia's mother is from the notarial document that gave her guardianship of the Tanini children following their father's death in 1467: ASF, Notarile antecosimiano 389, notary Andrea di Agnolo da Terranova, dated September 4, 1467, fols. 81r-83r. This and the detailed information that follows regarding Francesco and his family have been gleaned from the Tanini family's tax declarations in the Florentine State Archives for the Quartiere San Giovanni, Gonfalone Leon d'oro, made over the course of the century from 1427 through 1495: Catasto 78, campioni 1427, fols. 535–36; Catasto 407, campioni 1430, fol. 260; Catasto 497, campioni 1433, fol. 273; Catasto 822, portate 1457, fol. 657; Catasto 924, portate 1469, fol. 564; Catasto 1017, portate 1480, fol. 247 and the copy of the 1480 census in Monte Comune 84, fol. 167; the copy of the 1487 census in Monte Comune 86, fol. 1066r; and the 1495 Decima Repubblicana 28, fol. 229v (the *portate* were the original documents compiled by those making their declaration, the *campioni* were redactions made

father's family came to Florence from Scarperia, a town located north of Florence in the region known as the Mugello,[7] and they are first recorded in Florence in the 1427 tax assessment (*catasto*). Jacopa's family was from the Trastevere section of Rome.[8] Francesco had property in and around Scarperia: farmlands, woods, and, in town, three shops where he traded his produce. There were houses on his farms for the laborers and he had a *casa da signore*, presumably his family's country home, just north of Scarperia on the Palagio road. Wheat was his largest crop, but he also grew spelt and other cereals and forage grasses (*grano, panico, segala, spelta, biada*), and he produced and marketed assorted other foodstuffs as well: walnuts, chestnuts, oil, capons, eggs, meat (unspecified in the records, where it is, however, noted that he owned sheep), and wine. And he sold wood.[9]

In the early years of the century Francesco lived in Florence with his family in a rented house,[10] but, as the century wore on, he began to sell off some of his holdings in Scarperia, primarily the shops,

---

by the tax assessors). For Antonia I have also consulted the tax records of her husband Bernardo di Jacopo di Francesco de' Pulci, Quartiere Santa Croce, Gonfalone Carro, ASF, Catasto 1002, campioni 1480/81, fols. 64–65. It appears that Antonia was born between 1452 and 1454. Because the ages found in the tax records were recorded at different times of the year, depending upon when the declarations were filed, and because there were sometimes reasons not to be entirely truthful, these documents can only yield approximate figures. Antonia Tanini's name is not found in the Florentine baptismal records (which begin in 1450); she was either overlooked or, perhaps, baptized in or near Scarperia, the town in the Mugello from which her family originated.

7. Scarperia was founded in 1306 by the Florentines to provide protection to their north. See Emanuele Repetti, *Dizionario geografico fisico-storico della Toscana*, 6 vols. (Florence: Allegrini e Mazzoni, 1833–46), 5: 221b–229b.

8. ASF, Notarile antecosimiano 389, cit., fol. 81r: "Domine Iacope vidue, filie Toreli Laurentii Toreli de regione Transtiveri, civitatis romane, et uxori olim Francisci Antonii Gannocti, civis et mercatoris florentini." I have not been able to trace her in Rome; Roman baptismal documents are not available for this period.

9. All the information about the family's property and business has been gleaned from their tax records of 1427, 1430, 1433, 1457, 1469/70, 1480, and 1487 (see above, n6).

10. Francesco rented a house from Niccolò Lottini, according to the *catasto* of 1427; it was probably in the parish of San Simone, which is adjacent the that of Sant'Apollinare, where he would eventually purchase a house. In a notarial document, ASF Notarile antecosimiano 390, fol. 154r, dated 13 January 1470/71, Niccolò's son Apardo di Niccolò Lottini is said to live in the parish of San Simone.

and in 1465 he bought a house in Via de' Leoni,[11] in central Florence, very near the grain market, which had moved by the early fifteenth century from Orsanmichele to an area adjacent to Palazzo della Signoria, the central government palace (the area called the Loggia del Grano, just east of the Uffizi). The house, which was located in the parish of Sant'Apollinare, still stands today, next to Palazzo Gondi in what is now Piazza San Firenze (Figure 1).[12] The house and all its belongings are described in detail in the inventory made just after Francesco's death in 1467, in which his widow Jacopa was awarded guardianship of the children.[13]

It was a three-storey house with a courtyard, described in the inventory from top to bottom (see Appendix 1).[14] The top floor had one *camera* (that is, a bed-chamber but also a place for various household activities and for receiving guests) and a terrace. On the main floor was the *sala principale* (a large space that served as living, dining, and reception room), the kitchen, female servant's room (*camera della fante*), the main *camera* and an *anticamera* (a small, elaborately decorated room that followed the *camera*, and, like the *camera*, had various uses). On the ground floor was another *camera*, a male servant's room (*camera del famiglio*), and a courtyard.[15] There was also a

11. Via de' Leoni was a narrow street at the time, but in the seventeenth century it was widened in front of the church of San Firenze, the area which is now Piazza San Firenze.

12. The location is specified in the *catasto* records, ASF, Catasto 924, portate del 1469, Tanini, rede di Francesco d'Antonio, fol. 564r. The Tanini house is discussed by Linda Pellecchia in her article on the Gondi palace, "Untimely Death, Unwilling Heirs: The Early History of Giuliano da Sangallo's Unfinished Palace for Giuliano Gondi," *Mitteilungen des Kunsthistorischen Institutes in Florenz*, 47 (2003/1): especially p. 86 and notes 53–55 on pp. 109–10. A small portion of the Tanini house is visible in Pellecchia's figure 3, on p. 81, in figure 9, on p. 87, and it is section V in the plan showing the expansion of the Gondi palace on p. 90.

13. ASF, Notarile antecosimiano 389, fol. 84.

14. My definitions of *camera*, *sala*, and *anticamera*, and my general understanding of the Florentine fifteenth-century household are indebted to Brenda Preyer, whom I thank for her help in translating the inventory of the Tanini household (Appendix 1). I have also consulted her two articles, B. Preyer, "The Florentine *Casa*," and "The *acquaio* (Wall Fountain) and Fireplace in Florence," in *At Home in Renaissance Italy*, ed. M. Afmar-Wollheim and F. Dennis (London: V & A Publications, 2006), 34–49 and 284–87.

15. The courtyard, not noted in the inventory, is mentioned in the document of the sale of the property in 1520, cited by Pellecchia ("Untimely Death, Unwilling Heirs," 109n53): "Unum domum cum palcis salis cameris curia et voltis et terrazzio et aliis suis habituris et

cellar (*volta*), which served as a storage room and contained barrels, a copper basin, and a large funnel for filling them. The furnishings and servants' quarters, the several beds and bed-coverings, the seating areas, daybeds with large overhanging backrests (*capellinai*) and built-in all around benches, a writing desk, chests (some gilded and painted), art work, andirons, tables, chairs, silverware, and kitchen utensils clearly indicate that this was the house of a moderately successful merchant. The main *camera* on each floor had an image of the madonna (the artists are not named): the ones upstairs and on the ground floor are not described but were probably painted images, the one in the main *camera* was in relief (most likely marble or terracotta). The *anticamera* contained figured tapestries on the door and on the walls. The Tanini family home had all the necessary comforts and a few luxury items; and, like most families that had moved to the city from the Tuscan countryside, they kept a country house as well.

Antonia's family of origin became the subject of some confusion in the late nineteenth century, when a prominent literary historian, Francesco Flamini, claimed that those who thought she was a Tanini (among them, the bibliographer Paul Colomb de Batines and Alessandro D'Ancona)[16] were incorrect, and he insisted that she belonged rather to the important Florentine Giannotti family.[17] Since that time and until my return to the archival documents has proved otherwise, this incorrect information was accepted and inhibited any attempts, if there were any, to find out more about her.[18] Flamini's er-

---

pertinentis" (a house with [3] stories, reception rooms, bed-chambers, a court and cellars and a terrace and other rooms and appurtenances).

16. Paul Colomb de Batines, see his *Bibliografia delle antiche rappresentazioni*, 15, and A. D'Ancona, *Origini del teatro italiano*, 1:268.

17. Francesco Flamini, "La vita e le liriche di Bernardo Pulci," *Il Propugnatore*, n.s. 1 (1888), 217–48, and on Antonia, 224–25. On p. 224 he calls her Antonia di Francesco d'Antonio Gianotti, and in a note writes: "Che la moglie di Bernardo fosse dei Tanini è un errore entrato non so come nella storia letteraria, e restatovi poi a lungo" (That the wife of Bernardo was a member of the Tanini family is an error which entered literary history—I know not how—and has long remained there.)

18. Among modern scholars only Eletto Palandri has disagreed with Flamini. He argues that Bernardo Pulci's dedication of his *Passione di Cristo* to Annalena de' Tanini, a nun in the convent of the Murate, is evidence that Antonia belonged to the Tanini family. See E. Palandri, "Rappresentazioni sanfrancescane," *Studi francescani*, 23 (1926), 420.

ror is easy to explain. The earliest tax records and even some notarial documents list Francesco as "Francesco di Antonio di Giannotto dalla Scarperia," some as "Francesco di Antonio Giannocti," transforming the given name of Francesco's grandfather into the Latin genitive, the frequent path to an Italian surname. However, by the mid-fifteenth century, when the family surname was finally established and used with regularity in fiscal and notarial documents, it was to Francesco's great-grandfather Tanino Bozzi that the family turned. Perhaps it was in order to clarify the family's link to cousins who had also come to Florence from Scarperia and who also descended from this ancestor.[19] In fact, archival documents reveal that the two Tanini families in Florence remained in close contact throughout the fifteenth century: Agostino di Lotto Tanini, a paternal cousin, is one of the executors named in Antonia's will. Shortly after Francesco's death in 1467, his heirs filed their tax declaration as "Tanini, eredi di Francesco d'Antonio"(Tanini, hiers of Francesco d'Antonio), and Francesco's elaborate floor tomb in the church of Santa Croce, still visible today (Figure 2) bears the inscription: "*Sep[ulchrum] Francisco Antonii Iannocti de Taninis mercatori ex vrbe in patriam redvcto Ivlivs patri benemerenti fecit. Obiit anno salvtis 1467 die 23 avgvsti*" (Tomb made [paid for] by Giulio for his worthy father Francesco di Antonio di Giannotto Tanini, merchant, brought home [to Florence] from the city [of Rome]. He died on 23 August in the year of salvation 1467).

In the many records left during his lifetime and even shortly after his death Francesco does not use a surname, only a string of patronymics, his father, grandfather, and great grandfather, and sometimes their provenance.[20] Francesco died intestate and in the docu-

---

19. Listed in the same tax district (*gonfalone*) as the family of Francesco d'Antonio Tanini is that of Lotto di Tanino Tanini and his wife Nanna, their sons Agostino, Lorenzo, and Girolamo, ASF, Catasto of 1480, 1015. San Giovanni, Leon d'Oro. Judith Bryce has noted that members of this Tanini family worked for the Medici bank: Lotto di Tanino Tanini became the manager of the Venice branch in 1436, and his son Lorenzo di Lotto Tanini worked in the branch in Bruges: see J. Bryce, "Adjusting the Canon for Later Fifteenth-century Florence: the Case of Antonia Pulci," in *The Renaissance Theatre. Texts, Performance, Design*, ed. Christopher Cairns (Burlington, VT: Ashgate, 1999), 1: 135.

20. According to David Herlihy, Francesco was the most popular baptismal name among Florentine men scrutinized for office between 1450 and 1500, even surpassing Giovanni, the name of Florence's patron saint; and Antonio was the most popular name for a man in the

ment, dated 4 September 1467, which gave his widow guardianship of their children (she was named *curatrice* of Antonia, who was between the ages of 12 and 14, and no longer considered a child, and *tutrice* of the younger children), Jacopa is said to be "uxori olim Francisci Antonii Gannocti, civis et mercatoris florentini."[21] From 1469 on, however, the family is listed in Florentine tax records and in other notarial documents as Tanini, and Antonia uses that surname in the three redactions of her will filed in 1501.[22]

Having ascertained that Tanini was the family name, I have found many documents that refer to Francesco's family and to his daughter Antonia, or "Antonina," as her father called her when he first registered her name among the *bocche* (list of household members) in his 1457 tax declaration, and as her brother Niccolò referred to her in his tax declaration of 1469 ('Ntonina).

From the archival records, primarily the tax declarations (*catasti*), I have been able to sketch a fairly detailed picture of the

---

1427 Catasto (4,767 occurrences; Francesco was seventh then, occurring 1,442 times): see David Herlihy, "Tuscan Names, 1200–1530," *Renaissance Quarterly*, 41:4, 1988, 573n and 575. Francesco must have found it necessary to use a third patronymic and, often, the indication of the family's place of origin to distinguish himself from others named Francesco di Antonio. On Florentine surnames see Anthony Molho, "Names, Memory, Public Identity in Late Medieval Florence," in Giovanni Capelli and Patricia Rubin, eds. *Art, Memory and Family in Renaissance Florence* (Cambridge: Cambridge University Press, 2000), 238–50. There is also a brief discussion of surnames in Christiane Klapisch-Zuber,"The Name 'Remade': The Transmission of Given Names in Florence in the Fourteenth and Fifteenth Centuries," in *Women, Family, and Ritual in Renaissance Italy*, trans. Lydia G. Cochrane (Chicago: University of Chicago Press, 1985), 283–309, especially 285–86. This study was originally published as "Le nom 'refait': La transmission des prenoms à Florence (XIV–XVIe siècles)," *L'Homme*, 20:4 (1980), 77–104.

21. ASF, Notarile antecosimiano 389, notary Andrea di Agnolo da Terranova, dated September 4, 1467, fol. 81r.

22. ASF, Notarile antecosimiano 9535, *protocolli del notaio* 1499–1506. In the entry for "suora m[onn]a Antonia di Francesco Tanini," there are copies of the three versions of her will, dated 19 July, 16 August, and 2 September 1501, (notary 379: Giovanni di Domenico di Bartolo da Tizzana). The first two wills refer to her as "Antonia vedova di Bernardo di Jacopo de' Pulci e figlia di Francesco di Antonio de' Tanini," while the third introduces an error referring to her father as "Francesco di Piero de' Tanini." The wills are on fols. 66r-67v, 70v, and 72v–74r.

growth of Antonia's family.²³ Francesco's name first appears in the 1427 *catasto*; he was nineteen-years old, unmarried, and living with his mother, Monna Tita, of forty-three, and his nineteen-year old sister Gita. By 1430 Francesco was also supporting his one-year old natural child, Giulio, who was born in Rome. In 1447 he married Jacopa, also from Rome and younger than Giulio, when she was about fifteen years old and he thirty-nine. The couple had their first child, a daughter, Girolama, the following year, 1448. Antonia was the next born, sometime between 1452 and 1454, and there followed Niccolò in 1461, Costanza in 1463, and Cornelia in 1464.²⁴ In that same year Francesco had a second illegitimate child, Lisabetta. The next year, 1465, Jacopa bore another daughter, whom they named Tita (after his mother who had died sometime before 1457),²⁵ and in 1466, the year before Francesco's death, their last daughter, Lucrezia, was born.

So many daughters and only one legitimate son made life difficult for Jacopa after Francesco's death, even though the family had made considerable economic progress over the years. As their legal guardian, Jacopa accepted the obligation of assuring the children of their inheritance, which in the case of the daughters meant providing their dowries; Niccolò, their legitimate son, was his father's only heir.²⁶ The eighteenth-century historian, Giuseppe Richa, who included a brief biography of Antonia Tanini in his history of Florentine religious

---

23. The names and approximate ages of family members have been gleaned from the archival documents mentioned above, n6.

24. Florence, Archivio dell'Opera di Santa Maria del Fiore, Battesimi. In the database of baptisms there is a record, dated 19 January 1463/64, for a Cornelia Antonia di Francesco d'Antonio, registered as belonging to the parish (*popolo*) of San Simone, very likely this girl, since Francesco had not yet bought his house in the parish of Sant'Apollinare and was renting a house that belonged to Niccolò Lottini, whose residence was in the parish of San Simone, a church just up the street from Sant'Apollinare in the direction of Santa Croce (see above, n10).

25. On the Florentine practice of naming a child after a recently deceased sibling or other relative, known as "to remake" (*rifare*) the deceased, see Christiane Klapisch-Zuber, "The Name 'Remade,'" 299–303.

26. ASF, Notarile antecosimiano 389, fols 81r–88v and 92r.

institutions, claims that four of the Tanini women married, one in Pisa and three in Florence.[27]

Antonia's older sister Girolama, married a Florentine, Roberto Visdomini, sometime before 1467, with a dowry that included a house just north of Scarperia;[28] she died in 1468. In 1475 Jacopa, then a widow, wrote to Clarice Orsini, the wife of Lorenzo de' Medici, thanking her for all she and the Medici family had done for her "poor daughters"("queste mie povere fanciulle"), which almost certainly meant helping her to place in appropriate marriages and convents some of the daughters who were still with her at home (see Figures 3a and 3b and Appendix 2).[29] Clarice Orsini was betrothed to Lorenzo in 1468, and their marriage took place on the second of June, 1469. Antonia and Bernardo Pulci married in 1470, shortly after Clarice's arrival in Florence, and Lorenzo's young wife may well have been a party to that arrangement and perhaps intervened on behalf of Cornelia and Lucrezia as well. In 1475, when Jacopa wrote to thank Clarice for helping her daughters, Costanza would have been twelve, Cornelia eleven, Tita ten, and Lucrezia nine. Francesco's illegitimate daughter Lisabetta would also have been eleven. Clarice may have helped place Cornelia, Lucrezia, and Lisabetta, since only Costanza and Tita were still listed as belonging to their brother's household in 1480, and Tita still in 1487. In 1470 when Antonia married there were yet five daughters

27. Giuseppe Richa, *Notizie istoriche delle chiese fiorentine* (Florence: Stamperia di Pietro Gaetano Viviani, 1757), vol. 5: 249–57, 263–64 (10 vols., 1754–62). On pp. 249–50, Richa, citing from a work by a contemporary and friend of Antonia's, fra Antonio Dolciati, writes: "Francesco Tanini Cittadino Fiorentino ebbe per Moglie Donna Iacopa da Roma, dalla quale nacque un Figlio mastio per nome Niccolò, che ancor oggi vive, ed ebbe sei Figliole femmine, delle quali ne furono maritate tre in Firenze, ed una in Pisa con Persone di eguale condizione. Una di queste tre si chiamò Antonia, la quale fu moglie di Bernardo de' Pulci Gentiluomo Fiorentino, con cui visse in somma pace anni 17, dopo dei quali Bernardo passò ad altra vita…" (Francesco Tanini, a Florentine citizen, married lady Jacopa from Rome, who gave birth to a son named Niccolò, who is still alive, and six daughters, three of whom married in Florence and one in Pisa to persons of equal social condition. One of these three was named Antonia, who was the wife of Bernardo de' Pulci, a Florentine gentleman with whom she lived contentedly for seventeen years, and then Bernardo passed on to another life…).

28. ASF, *Catasto* 924, the 1469 *portate* of the heirs of Francesco d'Antonio Tanini, 564r.

29. ASF, Medici Avanti Principato (MAP), LXXX, fol. 132r-v. The text and my English translation are provided in Appendix 2.

to take care of, and we know that one more would marry in Florence and another in Pisa. One of the three remaining sisters must be Suor Annalena de' Tanini, who professed at the prestigious Benedictine convent of Santissima Annunziata, known as "Le Murate,"[30] and to whom Bernardo Pulci dedicated a poem on the Passion of Christ.[31]

30. "Le Murate" (lit.,"the walled women"), situated on the Via Ghibellina, was one of the oldest and most prestigious convents in Florence. It was also one of the largest, which at the end of the fifteenth century housed around two hundred women. On this convent, see Saundra Weddle, "'Women in wolves' mouths': Nuns' Reputations, Enclosure and Architecture at the Convent of Le Murate in Florence," in *Architecture and the Politics of Gender in Early Modern Europe*, ed. Hellen Hills (Burlington, VT: Ashgate, 2003), 115–29, and "Enclosing Le Murate: The Ideology of Enclosure and the Architecture of a Florentine Convent, 1390–1597" (Ph.D diss., Cornell University, May 1997), which includes an edition of the convent's Chronicle (translation forthcoming in this series). See also Kate (K. J. P.) Lowe, "Female Strategies for Success in a Male-ordered World: the Benedictine Convent of Le Murate in Florence in the Fifteenth and Sixteenth Centuries," *Studies in Church History*, 27 (1990), 209–21, and her study of the convent's chronicle, *Nuns' Chronicles and Convent Culture in Renaissance and Counter-Reformation Italy* (Cambridge: Cambridge University Press, 2003). Sharon Strocchia in *Nuns and Nunneries in Renaissance Florence* (Baltimore: Johns Hopkins, 2009) discusses the Murate throughout, and she has studied specific aspects of convent life at the Murate in her articles "Naming a Nun: Spiritual Exemplars and Corporate Identity in Florentine Convents, 1450–1530" in *Society and Individual in Renaissance Florence*, ed. William J. Connell (Berkeley: University of California Press, 2002), 215–40, especially, 230–34, and "Taken into Custody: Girls and Convent Guardianship in Renaissance Florence," *Renaissance Studies* 17.2 (2003), 177–200, especially, 191–92. See also Richa, *Notizie istoriche*, 2: 79–112.

31. Bernardo Pulci, *Passione del nostro Signor Gesù Cristo*, published posthumously, undated and without indication of the publisher, but in Florence, probably by Antonio Miscomini, ca. 1489–90. The dedication (fols. 1r-4r) begins: "Bernardo Pulci fiorentino alla devota in Christi suora Annalena de Tanini nel monasterio delle Murate" (1r). (Bernardo Pulci, Florentine, to Sister Annalena de' Tanini, vowed to Christ, in the convent of the Murate). Bernardo mentions having attended Suor Annalena's religious profession, which would seem to indicate that she was Antonia's very close relative, probably her sister: "…contempla che gli è morto colui al quale tu fusti desponsata e, essendo io presente, dal suo vicario lo anello e la corona virginale ricevesti …" (fol. 2r) (…consider well that he died, the one to whom you were espoused, and, in my presence, from his vicar you received the ring and virginal crown.…). Don Eletto Palandri suggests that this Annalena Tanini might have been "figlia d'una cugina carnale di lei [Antonia]," the daughter of a female cousin and blood relative of Antonia's ("Rappresentazioni francescane," 420). Palandri's was just a speculation, which seems to me unlikely. If she were the daughter of a female cousin, one who was presumably married, it seems little likely that the daughter's surname would be Tanini;

In the same letter to Clarice Orsini, Jacopa asked for assistance in settling her dispute with the city over taxes, which she claimed were imposed on property that was not hers. After Francesco's death it cannot have been easy for Jacopa to care for her large family, but she had taken on the responsibility of guardianship and she seems to have successfully enlisted the help of a powerful Medici connection, Lorenzo de' Medici's wife, an Orsini and a Roman like herself.[32] Jacopa's son Niccolò, Francesco's heir, was only six at his father's death; Giulio, Francesco's illegitimate son, then in his late thirties, remained close to the family;[33] he served as one of the administrators and a guarantor (*fudeiussore*) of the inheritance, and for a while also as Jacopa's *mundualdus*, or legal representative.[34] Giulio paid for his father's elegant tomb in Santa Croce.

Francesco made deposits in the Florentine dowry fund for his daughters. Luigi Pulci, in a letter written to Lorenzo de' Medici on 27 February 1471, asks his patron to help his brother Bernardo who was having a problem getting Antonia's dowry from the Monte, the Florentine dowry investment fund.[35] Costanza and Tita are listed in

---

and I find no girl who fits the description among the offspring of the other Tanini family in Florence at the time.

32. The Roman connection, however, was probably not the primary reason Jacopa turned to Clarice for help. As Judith Bryce has pointed out, the Tanini family had long had Medici connections: there were Tanini family members who worked for the Medici bank in their Venice and Bruges branches. See above, n19.

33. He is listed among the *bocche* in their 1469 tax declarations.

34. ASF, Notarile antecosimiano 389, fols. 81r and 86r. At first her *mundualdus* was Francesco di Ranieri Tosigni, but two months later Giulio took on that responsibility (fol. 88v). In Florence at the time women had to have male representatives for any legal act.

35. Luigi Pulci, *Letter* XVII, 27 February 1470/71, published in Pulci, *Morgante e lettere*, ed. Domenico De Robertis (Florence: Sansoni, 1962), 964: "Il mio povero Bernardo so che ha bisogno d'aiuto da te al Monte per la sua dote." (I know that my poor Bernardo needs your help at the Monte for his dowry). The Florentine Monte delle doti has been studied by Julius Kirshner and Anthony Molho: see J. Kirshner, "Pursuing honor while avoiding sin: the Monte delle doti of Florence," *Studi Senesi*, 87 (1977), 175–256; J. Kirshner and A. Molho, "The Dowry Fund and the Marriage Market in Early Quattrocento Florence," *Journal of Modern History* 50 (1978), 403–38, and Anthony Molho, *Marriage Alliance in Late Medieval Florence* (Cambridge, MA: Harvard University Press, 1994). The problems one might encounter in attempting to collect a Monte dowry are discussed by Julius Kirshner in "The Morning After: Collecting Monte Dowries in Renaissance Florence" in *From Florence to the*

the family's 1480 tax records as having each a dowry of one thousand florins, quite a good dowry at that time (Lorenzo de' Medici listed his daughters in the same years as having dowries of one thousand florins).[36] The dowry Antonia brought to her marriage with Bernardo Pulci must have been the same; it was returned to her after her husband's death, but not immediately, according to Fra Antonio Dolciati, Antonia's friend and early biographer.[37] Dolciati wrote that it took several years following Bernardo's death for Antonia to recover her dowry, with which, he claims, she paid for the house and property that would be the site of Santa Maria della Misericordia, the convent she founded.[38]

Mediterranean and Beyond: Essays in Honor of Anthony Molho, ed. Diogo Ramada Curto, Eric R. Dursteler, Julius Kirshner and Francesca Trivellato (Florence: Leo S. Olschki, 2009), 29–61. It is likely that Bernardo's problem was owing to his family's financial difficulties, to which the brothers allude in their 1470 tax declaration, Catasto 911, fols. 499r–500v (their account books were still in the hands of the creditors of Luca Pulci and their financial advisers, 500r).

36. ASF, Catasto 1016, portate 1480 San Giovanni, Leon d'Oro, fol. 474v. Lorenzo claims dowries for his four daughters of one thousand two hundred *fiorini di sigillo*, the equivalent of one thousand *fiorini d'oro larghi* (see Guid'Antonio Zanetti, *Nuova raccolta delle monete e zecchi d'Italia* (Bologna: Per L. dalla Volpe, 1775–89), especially the section intitled "Del fiorino di sigillo della repubblica fiorentina." Parte prima, 249–74). Lorenzo was surely not truthful but wanting to underplay his family's extravagance for the public record.

37. On Antonio Dolciati (6 Sept.1476–1530), see the entry, written by Raffaella Zaccaria, in the *Dizionario biografico degli Italiani*, vol. 40 (Rome: Istituto della Enciclopedia italiana Treccani, 1991), 433–35. In the "Pistola de l'auctore," dated 1528, the dedication of his treatise on the Augustinian Rule, *De tribus regulis S. Augustini* or *Esposizione della Regula di S. Agostino* (Florence, Biblioteca Laurenziana, ms. Gaddi 132, fols. 2r–4v), Dolciati remembers Antonia fondly and describes her life as a widow and founder of the Augustinian convent of which he was governor. I have transcribed and translated the "Pistola" in Appendix 3.

38. Bernardo in his will, dated 7 February 1487/88 (ASF, Notarile antecosimiano 7220, ser Antonio di Niccolò Ferrini, fasc. 8, fols. 13r–14r), bequeathed to Antonia one thousand two hundred *fiorini di sigillo*, the exact amount, it seems, of her dowry (13v). Giuseppe Baccini, in his study of the Pulci brothers, discusses Bernardo's will, but he does not mention the money; he writes that Bernardo made Antonia his universal heir and left her three properties in the Mugello, called Il Palagio, Vignamore and another referred to as "a Montici," which she sold to Piero di Francesco Bettini in 1490 for a thousand florins ("I poeti fratelli Pulci nel Mugello e il *Driadeo d'amore*," *Giotto* 2 [1903]: 358). Baccini cites as his source Bettini's tax declaration of 1495, so perhaps he had not seen the will. These properties may have been given to her in lieu of her dowry money. Dolciati writes ("Pistola de l'auctore," fol. 3v)

The noble Pulci family was in serious financial difficulty at the time of Bernardo's marriage to Antonia. Bernardo's father Jacopo first and then his brother Luca had led them into debt, to the point that in late 1464 or early 1465, the brothers had to leave Florence for their country estate in the Mugello because of this disgrace.[39] Bernardo, Luca, and Luigi Pulci were well-known members of the cultural elite, all writers, and closely associated with the Medicis. Lucrezia Tornabuoni, the wife of Piero de' Medici, and Lorenzo's mother, was especially fond of Luigi, who dedicated his poem, the *Morgante*, to her, claiming that it was at her instigation that he undertook the project.[40] All three Pulci brothers wrote verse in praise of the Medicis, especially Lorenzo, and they successfully interceded with Lorenzo for their return to Florence in 1466 and employment. Luca made more bad investments and died in disgrace in 1470.[41] Bernardo and Luigi shared responsibility for the family their brother left behind, a pregnant wife,

---

that Antonia, when she reacquired her dowry, bought with it the house and property that would become her convent of Santa Maria della Misericordia. The convent was sold in 1558 for 800 *scudi*, according to Giuseppe Richa, *Notizie istoriche*, 5: 255.

39. On the Pulci family, see Guglielmo Volpi, "Luigi Pulci. Studio biografico." *Giornale storico della letteratura italiana* 22 (1893), 1–63; Carlo Carnesecchi, "Per la biografia di Luigi Pulci," *Archivio storico italiano* 17 (1896): 371–79; Paolo Orvieto, "Luigi Pulci" in *Storia della letteratura italiana* (Rome: Salerno Editrice, 1996), 3: 405–55; and Stefano Carrai, *Le Muse dei Pulci* (Naples: Guida, 1985). Little has been written specifically on Bernardo's life aside from Francesco Flamini's "La vita e le liriche di Bernardo Pulci"(see above, n17); some details have been added by Giuseppe Baccini in "I poeti fratelli Pulci nel Mugello," and Armando Verde has provided several letters and other new documents regarding Bernardo's years as provveditore of the Studio in Pisa in *Lo Studio fiorentino 1473–1503 ricerche e documenti*, 5 vols. (Florence: Olschki, 1973–94), 2: 752 and 4, pt. 2: 468, 725–26, and *passim*.

40. The poem, a humorous epic-chivalric poem in twenty-eight cantari of narrative octaves, was, according to the wishes of Lucrezia Tornabuoni, to celebrate Charlemagne, the legendary re-founder of Florence following the city's destruction by the Goths. However, for most of the poem, Pulci makes fun of Charlemagne (Carlo Magno), an old fool easily duped by the traitor Gano and given to irrational judgments.

41. Stefano Carrai, in *Le Muse dei Pulci*, corrects a number of inaccuracies in the literature on the Pulci family. He cites (p. 9, n.10) the research of Paola Benazzi, who in her dissertation on Luca Pulci, directed by Domenico De Robertis (Florence, Facoltà di Lettere, 1972–73), casts doubt on the legend that Luca died in debtors' prison (*le Stinche*), since his name does not appear in the official list of prisoners in those years.

a son and a daughter; Bernardo and Antonia cared for Luca's son Raffaello.[42]

While there may have been other reasons for Antonia's betrothal to Bernardo, her dowry and his great financial need precisely at this time must have played a role. The couple may have met before their marriage was arranged. Both families had holdings along the Sieve River in the Mugello and both lived in central Florence.[43] Antonia and Bernardo seem to have been well suited to one another. Both held strong religious sentiments; and Antonia's intelligence and high degree of literacy must have appealed to Bernardo, who at the time of their marriage was already a well respected writer. He was known in Florence in his youth for his lyric poetry, for his translation with commentary of Virgil's *Eclogues*, and later for religious verse.[44] Certainly for Antonia's family her marriage into the old nobility represented an important social advancement.[45] The couple married in 1470 when Antonia was seventeen or eighteen years old, Bernardo thirty-two.

---

42. ASF, Catasto 911, Santa Croce, Carro, campioni 1469, fol. 499, the entry for the heirs of Jacopo Pulci and Catasto 1002, Santa Croce, Carro, campioni 1480, Part I, fols. 64–65, the entry for Bernardo di Jacopo di Francesco de' Pulci, and Part II, fol. 309, the entry for Luigi di Jacopo di Francesco de' Pulci. In 1480 Bernardo indicated that Raffaello was sixteen years old and was working at the shop of a relative in the silk industry.

43. Members of the family of Jacopo Nasi may also have provided a connection between the Pulci and the Tanini families: Gerolamo di Lotto Tanini, Antonia's cousin, was married to Lena di Jacopo Nasi, and Lena's brother Giovanni rented a house in Florence to the Pulci brothers, which they mention in their 1451 tax declaration (see Gaetano Volpi, "Luigi Pulci. Studio biografico," 5).

44. Bernardo first published Virgil's eclogues with the Miscomini press on 28 February 1481/82, however, the translation is thought to have been made much earlier, before 1465, according to Paolo Orvieto (P. Orvieto, "Lorenzo de' Medici e l'umanesimo toscano del secondo Quattrocento," in *Storia della letteratura italiana*, [Salerno Editrice], 3: 318); before 1464 according to Susanna Villari ("Una bucolica 'Elegantissimamente composta': Il volgarizzamento delle egloghe virgiliane di Bernardo Pulci,"in *Filologia umanistica per Gianvito Resta*, ed. Vincenzo Fera and Giacomo Ferraú [Padua: Editrice Antenore, 1997], 3: 1878). See also Emilio Giorgi "Le piú antiche bucoliche volgari," *Giornale storico della letteratura italiana* 66 (1915), 140–41. The first known editions of Bernardo's religious verse are from 1489–90.

45. The family had earlier arranged the marriage of the eldest daughter, Girolama, to a member of the noble Visdomini family.

Antonia and Bernardo were childless, and in a letter written to Lorenzo de' Medici in 1473 Bernardo appealed for help to convince his reluctant brother Luigi to marry, since he and his wife had no hope of having children.[46] In Bernardo's tax records of 1480 he wrote that his wife Antonia had been ill for seven years. This is possibly true but perhaps exaggerated, since such statements were often a ploy for getting one's taxes reduced. If Antonia was ill, she was not too indisposed to write: the first edition of her *Play of Saint Domitilla* bears the date 1483 following the title (see Figure 4).[47]

A Family of Writers

Nothing is known of Antonia's early education, but she would have learned at least the rudiments of reading and writing in the vernacular at home from her mother Jacopa, who was literate, as we know from her autograph letter to Clarice Orsini (Figure 3 and Appendix 2).[48] Her verse dramas demonstrate a high level of literacy and of literary achievement, which she most likely acquired in the Pulci household; she wrote in a genre practiced as well by her husband, and the language of at least one of her plays seems indebted to the chivalric poetry of Bernardo's brothers. In the Pulci household Antonia would have had access to texts unlikely to have belonged to her own family; no books are mentioned in the inventory of their home (Appendix 1).

Bernardo, after his return to Florence from the Mugello in 1466, traveled to Sicily (1466), and, after his marriage to Antonia, to Camerino (1472) and to Rome (1474), perhaps on business for the Medici family. He was named *camerario*, a financial administrator, for the Mugello region in 1477, and in 1481 he was appointed *Provveditore degli Ufficiali*, the administrative officer of the Studio, the Florentine

---

46. The letter, dated 27 October 1473, is published in *Lettere di Luigi Pulci a Lorenzo il Magnifico e ad altri*, ed. Salvatore Bongi, second edition, enlarged (Lucca: Tipografia Guasti, 1886), 176–80. Luigi married Lucrezia degli Albizi, probably in 1473 (see D. De Robertis, *Morgante e lettere*, liii).

47. The date follows the title of the play only in the undated Miscomini anthology. See above, n1.

48. She might have been educated in a local convent or attended a neighborhood public school, but I have found no documentation for this.

University, a position he held until his death in 1488.[49] The *Provveditore* was the representative in Pisa of the five officials of the Studio, who resided in Florence. He handled the hiring of professors, kept accounts, and reported the day to day business in Pisa to the officials, personally and by letter. Armando Verde, who studied the Florentine Studio, speculates that, as Bernardo's wife, Antonia may have attended university lectures.[50]

Among Bernardo's literary works is at least one *sacra rappresentazione*, the *Rappresentazione di Barlaam e Josafat (Play of Barlaam and Josafat)*, also published in the early Miscomini anthology.[51] There, it follows Antonia's Saint Domitilla play and precedes her Saint Guglielma; other plays too have been attributed to Bernardo.[52] Besides

49. F. Flamini, "La vita e le liriche di B. Pulci," 231–40.

50. A.Verde, *Lo Studio fiorentino*, 3, pt. 1: 76–77. Verde (see above, n39) cites many documents regarding Bernardo's position as *Provveditore degli Ufficiali* of the Studio in Florence and Pisa (1481–88). Verde, in vol. 4, pt.2, includes many letters to and from Bernardo in his capacity as *Provveditore*. Francesco Flamini, "Vita e liriche di Bernardo Pulci," in notes on 235–39, published three of Bernardo's letters to the officials of the Studio.

51. His is probably the *Rappresentazione di Barlaam e Josafat* that was performed by the Compagnia della Purificazione at San Marco in 1474. See Nerida Newbigin, "'Word Made Flesh': The *Rappresentazioni* of Mysteries and Miracles in Fifteenth-Century Florence," in *Christianity and the Renaissance: Image and Religious Imagination in the Quattrocento*, ed. Timothy Verdon and John Henderson (Syracuse: Syracuse University Press, 1994; rpt. of 1990), 368, and her *Feste d'oltrarno: Plays in Churches in Fifteenth-Century Florence* (Florence: Olschki, 1996), 1, 142. On this play see also Georges Ulysse, "Un Couple d'écrivains: les sacre rappresentazioni de Bernardo et Antonia Pulci," in *Les femmes écrivains en Italie au Moyen Âge et à la Renaissance*, ed. G. Ulysse (Aix-en-Provence: Publications de l'Université de Provençe, 1994), 177–96; Sophie Stallini, "Du religieux au politique: la *Sacra Rappresentazione* chez Antonia et Bernardo Pulci," *Arzanà. Cahier de littérature médiévale italienne*, 11 (2005), (special issue *La poésie politique dans l'Italie médiévale*, ed. Anna Fontes Baratto, Marina Marietti and Claude Perrus), 327–76; and Gianni Cicali, "L'occultamento del principe. Lorenzo il Magnifico e il *Barlaam e Josafat* di Bernardo Pulci," *Quaderni d'Italianistica* 27:2 (2006), 57–70.

52. Often the anonymous *Rappresentazione dell'Angelo Raffaello e Tobia*. Antonia alludes to the story of Tobia in her *Rappresentazione di Santa Guglielma* (oct. 27, lines 5–6), and in Antonia's parish church of Sant'Apollinare (San Pulinare) the story was depicted in the decoration of the Sacchetti Chapel (Richa, *Notizie istoriche*, 2, 119: "entrando a man ritta viene tavola antica dell'Arcangiolo Raffaello con istoriette di Tobbía dipinte nella predella." (as you enter on the right hand side you come upon an ancient painting of the Archangel Raphael, and in small on the predella episodes of the story of Tobias).

his lyric poetry and his vernacular edition of Virgil's eclogues, he was also the author of religious poems on the Passion and Resurrection of Christ, on the life of the Virgin Mary, and on Mary Magdalen.[53]

As Domenico De Robertis has written, "the Muses were at home in the Pulci household ("le Muse dai Pulci ci stavano a casa").[54] Of the brothers, Luigi (1432–1484) is the most famous. His romance epic, *Il Morgante*, the story in *ottava rima* of Orlando, his adventures with the giant Morgante, and his death at Roncisvalle, is Luigi Pulci's undisputed masterpiece; and he also wrote sonnets, many varieties of popular poetry, parodies, a novella, and, following a career of humorous sacrilegious verse, an apparently sincere poem of confession.[55] Luigi collaborated with his brother Luca on another narrative poem of adventure, entitled *Ciriffo calvaneo*. Luca Pulci (1431–1470), the eldest of the brothers, was also known for his *Pìstole*, an imitation in *terzine* (tercets) of Ovid's *Heroides*, and the *Driadeo d'Amore*, a mythological poem that tells the story of the origin of the two rivers in the Mugello region, the Sieve and the Lora, at whose confluence lay the Pulci family's country home known as "Il Palagio." Lisa, one of the two Pulci sisters, in 1452 married the poet Mariotto di Arrigo Davanzati (before 1406–after 1470), known for his *canzoni*, sonnets, and a *capitolo* in *terza rima* on friendship that he entered in the Certame Coronario, the celebrated Florentine poetry contest held in 1441; and their son Bartolomeo is known to have versified a famous Florentine short story, the *Grasso legnaiuolo* (The Fat Woodcarver). Only Costanza, who in 1453 married Tedice di Ludovico Villani, has left no evidence of literary activity. As a member of the Pulci family Antonia was surrounded by writers and very likely encouraged by them, or at least by Bernardo. The family's connection to the Medici, and especially to Lucrezia Tornabuoni (1425–1482), Lorenzo's mother and the

---

53. The *Passione di Cristo*, the *Resurrezione di Cristo*, *Il pianto di Maria Maddalena*, and the *Vita della gloriosa Vergine Maria*. There is a brief discussion of these poems in F. Flamini, "Vita e liriche," 244–46. For the *Passione*, dedicated to a Tanini nun, undoubtedly Antonia's sister, see above, n31.

54. Domenico De Robertis, *Pulci Morgante e lettere* (Florence: Sansoni, 1962), L.

55. There is an excellent English translation: *Morgante. The Epic Adventures of Orlando and His Giant Friend Morgante*, trans. Joseph Tusiani, introduction and notes by Edoardo A. Lèbano (Bloomington and Indianapolis: Indiana University Press, 1998).

author of narrative poems on religious topics similar to those of Antonia's plays, may also have proved an inspiration to Antonia's work.[56] Even before she married, Antonia Tanini lived in close proximity to writers and to the Florentine book industry in all its sectors. Paper sellers, printers, copyists, and booksellers were located in and around the Canto dei Cartolari (the 'bookseller's corner'), which lay between the Tanini house and the Badia Fiorentina. The Tanini family's next-door neighbor to the north was Franco Sacchetti, the grandson of the famous Trecento author and a writer himself.

The Pulci family members were among the first to take advantage of the newly established Florentine printing industry, which began operations in 1471. Studies of the Florentine presses in the fifteenth century and catalogues of incunables yield approximately 25 works published during the lifetime of the Pulci family writers, 60 by the end of the century;[57] and the interest in their work continued throughout the sixteenth century and beyond.[58] Antonia's plays seem to have had two editions each by the end of the century, amounting to ten or twelve publications; of these, seven are extant today. Her works

56. Lucrezia Tornabuoni wrote *laude* and narrative poetry. See *Le laudi di Lucrezia de' Medici*, ed. G. Volpi (Pistoia: Flori, 1900), her *Poemetti sacri*, ed. Fulvio Pezzarossa (Florence: Olschki, 1978), and *Sacred Narratives*, ed. and trans. Jane Tylus (Chicago: University of Chicago Press, 2001). See also J. Bryce , "Adjusting the Canon," 136–37.

57. To arrive at these approximate numbers I have consulted bibliographies, incunable catalogues, the catalogues of several libraries, principally, the Florentine Biblioteca Nazionale and the British Library, and the studies of early printing in Florence by Roberto Ridolfi, *La stampa in Firenze nel secolo XV* (Florence: Olschki, 1958), Dennis Rhodes, *Gli annali tipografici fiorentini del XV secolo* (Florence: Olschki, 1988), and his catalogue *La stampa a Firenze 1471-1550, omaggio a Roberto Ridolfi*, ed. Dennis Rhodes (Florence: Olschki, 1984), Paolo Trovato, "Il libro in Toscana nell'età di Lorenzo," in *L'ordine dei tipografi. Lettori, stampatori, correttori tra Quattro e Cinquecento* (Rome: Bulzoni Editore, 1998), 49–89, and *Edizioni fiorentine del Quattrocento e primo Cinquecento in Trivulziana: Biblioteca Trivulziana, 25 gennaio-10 marzo 2002*, catalogue of an exhibition, curated by Adolfo Tura (Milan: Comune di Milano, 2001), containing in appendix essays on Florentine books by L. Boninger, "I primi passi della stampa a Firenze: nuovi documenti d'archivio" (67–75), and G. Bertoli, "Per la biografia di Bartolomeo de' Libri." (77–83)

58. The Pulci poets seem to have worked with most of the presses in operation in Florence, with the early German printers, Nicolaus Laurentii (Niccolò Tedesco) and Johannes Petri, with the press in the convent of San Jacopo di Ripoli, with Antonio Miscomini, Francesco Bonaccorsi, Bartolomeo de' Libri, Francesco di Dino, Lorenzo Morgiani and others.

were published repeatedly in the sixteenth and seventeenth centuries, especially the two plays with female protagonists.[59]

Antonio Miscomini, a northern Italian printer working in Florence, who today is generally thought to have published the anthology in which Antonia's and Bernardo's plays first appeared, was also the printer responsible for the first edition of Luca Pulci's *Pistole,* of Bernardo Pulci's translation of Virgil's *Eclogues,* and Luigi Pulci's *La Giostra di Lorenzo de' Medici* (the Joust of Lorenzo de' Medici), all of which appeared in the same period, in February and March of 1482. Since Antonia Pulci's *Play of St. Domitilla* is dated 1483 on its first page in the anthology, we might want to rethink the date of 1490–95, generally given by print historians as the approximate date of the two volumes attributed to the Miscomini press.[60] In the three plays that are definitely Antonia's, following the title, she is named as the author and as the wife of Bernardo Pulci:

> INCOMINCIA La rapresentatione di san
> cta Domitilla uergine facta & compo
> sta in uersi per mona Antonia
> dōna di Bernardo pulci lāno
> MCCCCLXXXIII.

[Here begins the play of Saint Domitilla virgin, written and versified by lady Antonia, wife of Bernardo Pulci in the year 1483 (Figure 4)].[61]

The first page of the *Play of St. Guglielma* notes simply that it was "written by lady Antonia, wife of Bernardo Pulci," as does the *Play*

---

59. In my study of Italian convent theater I speculate that the demand came largely from nuns who needed, perhaps preferred, such plays for their convent theater productions (see Elissa Weaver, *Convent Theatre in Early Modern Italy: Spiritual Fun and Learning for Women* [Cambridge: Cambridge University Press, 2002], 54, 99–104, 126, and the accompanying notes).

60. E. Palandri, "Rappresentazioni sanfrancescani," 481, suggests that her plays must have been written between 1480 and 1488, when Bernardo died. Palandri claims that she couldn't have written them before 1480 because she was very ill; however, his evidence, and that of others who make this claim, is based on the not entirely reliable statement about her ill health that Bernardo made in his 1480 tax declarations and on the fact that the couple was childless.

61. This is the first play in the volume, and the title appears on fol. a_1.

of St. Francis (Figures 5–6).⁶² Bernardo died in February of 1488, and, since Antonia is said in these titles to be his wife and not his widow, it is clear that her plays must have been set in type before his death, even if, and this is not at all certain, the publication of the entire anthology did not occur until later.

These three plays written by Antonia were published again during her lifetime. According to Nerida Newbigin, who has carefully examined the type fonts and the woodcuts used, the second edition of the *Play of St. Domitilla* was Miscomini's (Figure 7), but the others, the *Play of St. Guglielma* (Figures 8a, b) and the *Play of San Francesco* (Figures 9a, b), were the work of Bartolomeo de' Libri (Bartolomeo di Francesco, called "de' Libri"), a priest and publisher who collaborated with Antonio Miscomini and whose workshop specialized in religious books.⁶³ Antonia's play, the *Destruction of Saul and the Lament of David*, was also published by Bartolomeo de' Libri, as is clear from the style of the volume, the woodcuts, and the type font (Figures 10a, b).⁶⁴ The earliest extant edition of her *Play of the Prodigal Son* is from the mid-sixteenth century, but there must have been a fifteenth-century edition, since Fra Antonio Dolciati mentions having seen this play together with others, including the Saul and David play, as early as 1492.⁶⁵ A Prodigal Son play written by Castellano Castellani, which was published in the very early years of the sixteenth century, opens with a scene that seems to have been inspired by Pulci's play.⁶⁶

62. COMINCIA LA RAPRESENTATIONE / DI SANCTA GVGLIELMA COMPO / STA PER MONA ANTONIA DON / NA DI BERNARDO PVLCI (g¹); RAPRESENTATIONE DI SANCTO / FRANCESCO COMPOSTA PER / MONA ANTONIA DONNA / DI BERNARDO PVLCI (n¹). (Here begins the Play of Saint Guglielma, written by Lady Antonia, wife of Bernardo Pulci; the Play of Saint Francis, written by lady Antonia, wife of Bernardo Pulci.)

63. Nerida Newbigin, "Plays, Printing and Publishing, 1485–1500: Florentine *sacre rappresentazioni*," *La Bibliofilia* 90 (1988), 269–96.

64. Ibid., 275 n.9.

65. A. Dolciati, "Pistola," 3v.

66. Nerida Newbigin claims that the two plays are independent of one another (N. Newbigin, *Nuovo corpus di sacre rappresentazioni del Quattrocento*, [Bologna: Commissione per i testi di lingua, 1983], 32). Both, however, begin in a rather unusual manner, with a card game, and Dolciati claims to have seen this play before 1492 ("Pistola," 3v, and see discussion below); as Newbigin notes, Castellani's play has been dated to around 1496 (see Giovanni Ponte in *Attorno al Savonarola: Castellano Castellani e la sacra rappresentazione in Firenze*

Fra Antonia Dolciati is the author of a brief account of the life of Antonia Tanini after she was widowed, which is included in the dedicatory letter of his treatise on the Rule of Saint Augustine, the *Esposizione della Regola di Sant'Agostino* (see Appendix 3).[67] The letter is dated 19 August 1528. In his dedication of the work to the nuns of Santa Maria della Misericordia, the convent Antonia founded in her will, Dolciati remembers Antonia fondly as his "mother and spiritual teacher" ("madre e maestra nella via di Dio," 3r). She had hired him, when he was a student at the cathedral school, to teach her the Latin of the breviary, and he credited her with persuading him of his religious vocation, for which he, then Francesco Dolciati, took Fra Antonio as his religious name in homage to her. In his brief outline of Antonia's life as a widow, Dolciati praises her for her strong religious faith and also for her exceptional literary talent. He mentions her beautiful *laude* (religious poems of praise), and in particular one, the *Corpo di Cristo* (Body of Christ), of which she gave him an autograph manuscript,[68] and he remembers having seen some of her plays:

> She also composed many beautiful and devout plays, on Joseph, on David and Saul, on the Prodigal Son, and many others which I do not now recall, since it has been more than thirty-six years since I've seen them.[69]

---

tra '400 e '500, [Genoa: Pagano, 1969], 14). I base my conjecture on this dating, which is, however, only approximate and cannot be confirmed.

67. Florence, Biblioteca Laurenziana, manuscript Gaddi 132 (see above, n37). My transcription and translation of the letter of dedication (the "Pistola") are found in Appendix 3.

68. There are two anonymous *laude* on that subject in early editions: *O Cristo, ver uomo e Dio*, a *ballata* of six stanzas with a two-line refrain composed of a *settenario* (a seven-syllable line) followed by an *endecasillabo* (an eleven-syllable line), originally published in Florence, in an undated edition, but circa 1480; and *O corpo sacro del nostro Signore*, a *ballata* composed of four stanzas and a two-line refrain, both *endecasillabi*, also published in Florence, circa 1489. They have been published in the collection *Laude spirituali di Feo Belcari, di Lorenzo de' Medici, di Francesco D'Albizzo, di Castellano Castellani e di altri comprese nelle quattro più antiche raccolte* (Florence: Molini e Cecchi, 1863), 35 and 103.

69. A. Dolciati, "Pistola," 3v: "Compose *etiam* molte belle e devote rapresentazioni, di Joseph, di David e Saul del figliuolo prodigo e assai altre delle quali ora non mi ricordo, emperoché sono più di trentasei anni non le ho vedute."

Thirty-six years earlier would have been 1492, and since Dolciati's reference is so specific, I believe we can on his word posit 1492 as the date *ante quem* of her dramatic compositions. We may also conclude that they were probably written in the 1480s, and at least three, but perhaps all of them, before early 1488.

Bernardo died on February 8, 1488, and was buried in Santa Croce.[70] In his will, written the day before his death, he made Antonia his sole heir.[71] She inherited the three properties in the Mugello near Cavallina that Bernardo had gotten in the division with Luigi of their inheritance: one known as 'Il Palagio,' another 'Vignamore' and the third 'Montici.'[72] Antonia sold them on April 14, 1489 to Piero di Francesco Bettini for a thousand florins.[73]

We owe information about the last years of Antonia's life to Dolciati and also to the eighteenth-century Jesuit, Giuseppe Richa, author of a magnificent history of Florentine churches. Richa includes the story of the founding and dissolution of Antonia's convent in his discussion of the Florentine religious house of San Clemente, where the nuns of her convent, Santa Maria della Misericordia, moved several decades after its founding.[74] Richa claims that his information on Antonia Tanini was gleaned from an old "rituale" written by Fra Dolciati, which seems to be Dolciati's study of the Rule of Saint Augustine;[75] however, some details in Richa's account differ slightly from those in the copy of Dolciati's work that I have consulted, and

---

70. Salvatore Bongi, *Le lettere di Luigi Pulci*, ("Avventenza," 21n4), citing his source as the "Libro mortuorio della Grascia" (ASF), writes "1487 (1488) 8 di Febraio/ Bernardo Pulci riposto in S. Croce." (In 1487 [1488]), on 8 February, Bernardo Pulci, buried at Santa Croce). His death was also registered in the deliberations of the officials of the Studio: "Bernardus Jacobi de pulcis provisor officialium studij obiit die 8 februarij 1487 (1488)" (Bernardo di Jacopo de' Pulci, *Provveditore degli Ufficiali* [administrative officer] of the Studio [University], died on 8 February 1487 [1488]). (F. Flamini, "Vita e liriche," 239n).

71. See above, n38.

72. For these details of Bernardo's will, see Giuseppe Baccini, "I poeti fratelli Pulci in Mugello": 358.

73. The sale was notarized by ser Giovanni da Romena and the purchase appears in Piero di Francesco Bettini's tax declaration (the *portata*) of 1490, according to Baccini, "I poeti fratelli Pulci," 358.

74. G. Richa, *Notizie istoriche*, 5: 249–57, 263–64.

75. For Dolciati's work, see above, n37.

Richa also includes much information not provided by Dolciati, especially regarding the history of the convent in the early decades of the sixteenth century. He may have been using a different copy of Dolciati's work, or, and I find it likely, he had other sources as well that he does not name.

According to Dolciati, soon after Bernardo's death Antonia returned to live with her mother and brother in the upstairs floor of the family's home in Via de' Leoni. There she studied the Scriptures and followed ascetic practices of penance: she slept on a straw mattress, wore a hair shirt, and practiced self-flagellation[76] Antonia took frequent communion at the church of San Gallo and there received the religious habit of an Augustinian *ammantellata* from Fra Mariano da Genazzano, a preacher famous at the time for his elegant and erudite sermons.[77] It was there, according to Dolciati, that Antonia commissioned a chapel to be dedicated to Saint Monica, which she paid for with her own money, and where she wished to be buried. Sometime later, Dolciati explains, Antonia, no longer wanted to live among secular persons, and she gathered together a group of like-minded women with the intention of founding a convent. They lived for a time at the Dominican convent of San Vincenzo, known as Annalena.[78] Later Antonia rented a house and some property ("casa e orto"), perhaps the first location of her convent, or the permanent location which she first rented and then purchased. What is clear is that she was prioress of her convent, Santa Maria della Misericordia, by November 1500 and that by July 1501, when she wrote the first draft of her will, she owned the convent property.[79]

---

76. A. Dolciati, "Pistola," 3r.

77. Fra Mariano received lavish praise for his oratorial skills from Poliziano. He was dear to the Medici and a purported enemy of Fra Girolamo Savonarola. See David Gutiérrez, "Testi e note su Mariano da Genazzano," *Analecta Augustiniana*, 32 (1969), 117–204. The biography by David Perini, *Un emulo di fra Savonarola fra Mariano da Genazzano* (Rome: Tipografia dell'Unione Editrice, 1917), surpassed now by Gutiérrez, is still useful. For some of his sermons, see Zelina Zafarana, "Per una storia religiosa di Firenze nel Quattrocento. Una raccolta privata di prediche," *Studi medievali*, ser. 3, 9:2 (1968), 1017–1113. On Pulci and Fra Mariano, see Judith Bryce "Adjusting the Canon," 140.

78. Called Annalena for its foundress Annalena Malatesta.

79. ASF, Corporazioni religiose soppresse dal governo francese, 100. Sant'Orsola, Vol. 125. This volume contains an unnumbered notebook belonging to Francesco di Tommaso Ac-

Richa claims that Antonia bought from Domenico Alamanni the property on which to locate her convent; it was outside the Gate of San Gallo, across from the convent of Lapo in Borgo di San Marco on the old road to Fiesole. She and her nuns moved into the new convent on Berlingaccio (the Thursday before Ash Wednesday) in 1501.[80] In her will, the final version of which was dated 2 September 1501, Antonia left money to the convent and also for the chapel dedicated to Saint Monica in the church of San Gallo.[81] She stipulated in the will that, if her convent did not succeed at all, or if it had a short life, a hundred florins each were to be given instead to the convents of

---

carigi, dated 1497–1505. On fol. 44v we find the following note, dated 1500: "Suor Antonia, figliuola di Francesco Tanini, priora del munistero di Santa Maria Madre di Misericordia, de' avere a dì 19 di novembre, F[iorini] tre e mezo larghi d'oro in oro e per lei dal bancho di Ridolfo di Filippo Strozzi, dissono per conto di pigione di casa e orto." (Sister Antonia, daughter of Francesco Tanini, prioress of the convent of Santa Maria Madre di Misericordia, must have three and a half gold Florins credited to her account on 19 November by the bank of Ridolfo di Filippo Strozzi; they said it was to pay the rent of a house and garden). I thank Sharon Strocchia for this information, which proves that Antonia was already prioress of her convent in the fall of 1500. For the three redactions of Antonia's will, see above, n22.

80. Dolciati and Richa do not agree on this point. According to Fra Antonio Dolciati, Antonia and her convent sisters entered the convent "el dì di Berlingaccio nel 1501, che fu quello anno a dì 18 di febraio"(A. Dolciati, "Pistola,"3v; see Appendix 3, p. 473); in that same document he continues to say that she would die on 21 September of that same year; and, in fact, she died in 1501. While we would expect Dolciati to be using the Florentine calendar *ab incarnazione*, in which the year did not end until 24 March, and indicate the year as 1500, he has clearly rendered that year as 1501. Richa, on the other hand, writes that they moved into their convent, which they purchased from Domenico Alamanni, on Berlingaccio, 26 February 1500 ("il dì 26 febbraro del 1500, giovedì giorno di Berlingaccio," G. Richa, *Notizie istoriche*, 5: 250). Berlingaccio fell on 26 February in 1499/1500, so it would seem that he too has rendered the date of 1499 *ab incarnazione* in his document as 1500. The source for dating Berlingaccio is Adriano Capelli, *Cronologia, cronografia e calendario perpetuo*, 5th ed. rev. (Milan: Hoelpi, 1983). Since Dolciati was writing only 27 years after Pulci's death and Richa, who, though he says he is quoting from a document written by Dolciati, is writing two centuries later, we should, I think, trust the dates that Dolciati gives in his "Pistola". The document cited in n79 above indicates that Pulci was Prioress of Santa Maria della Misericordia already in the fall of 1500 and that she was paying rent; it would seem that she first rented a place for her small community before they were able to move to the property outside the walls.

81. Her will was drawn up three times in 1501, on 19 July, 16 August , and for the last time on 2 September, by the Florentine notary Giovanni di Domenico di Bartolomeo da Tizzana. See above, n22.

Annalena and to the Murate. Antonia Tanini died either on 21 or 26 September 1501 and was buried according to her wishes in the chapel she had built.[82] Unfortunately, the church of San Gallo, just outside the city gate, was among the buildings destroyed in 1529 in advance of the seige of imperial troops, in order to deprive the besiegers of anything useful.[83] The convent of Santa Maria della Misericordia, also called the "Assunta" in its few surviving documents, remained in its original location outside the city walls until 1538, when the nuns, for whom the space was no longer adequate, moved into the city to the convent of San Clemente, just inside the Gate of San Gallo, where some of them were already living.[84] Richa claims that they brought with them a most venerable (*divotissimo*) crucifix that had been in their interior church and which had belonged to their foundress.[85] The original convent was sold by the nuns in 1558 to the Fanciulle della Concezione for 800 *scudi*; these women stayed only a short time and the property was sold again.[86]

Richa's account includes a description of the buildings of Antonia's convent, which were apparently still intact in the eighteenth century, church and convent with dormitory, cells, and workrooms. There was a painting of the Madonna in the church on the high altar that he claims to be in the manner of Ghirlandaio (he does not

---

82. According to A. Dolciati ("Pistola,"3v, and Appendix 3, p. 473), Antonia died on 21 September 1501; however Richa (*Notizie istoriche*, 5: 250) gives the date of her death to be Sunday, 26 September 1501.

83. John Najemy, *A History of Florence, 1200–1575* (Oxford: Blackwell Publishing, 2006), 454. See also G. Richa, *Notizie istoriche*, 1, 265–66.

84. ASF, Corporazioni religiose soppresse dal governo francese, 125, fol. 9, dated 15 marzo 1537/38. The entry reads: "Monache e capitolo del monasterio della misericordia observanti dell'ordine di S[an]c[t]o Augustino fuori della porta a San Ghallo, come per la strectza del luogho, dette monache sono necessitate venire ad habitare in Firenze e max[ime] perché è stato concesso loro San Chimenti presso a San Roccho dentro a decta porta dove di già la parte di loro hanno incominciato ad habitare" (The nuns and chapter of the convent of the Misericordia, outside the Gate of San Gallo, observants of the order of Saint Augustine, will have to move to Florence, both because those nuns need larger quarters and especially because they have been given San Clemente, near San Rocco, inside the Gate, where some of them have already taken up residence). See also G. Richa, *Notizie istoriche*, 5: 253–54.

85. G. Richa, *Notizie istoriche*, 5, 263–64.

86. Ibid., 5, 254–55.

say which Ghirlandaio), and he mentions that there was a grille high on the wall through which the nuns heard mass. He lists the artwork found in the convent: a fresco of the Pietà in the dormitory, by a painter he calls simply Maestro Antonio (who received at least two payments in the amount of 27 *scudi* for his work); at the top of a stairway in the convent there was a fresco of the Virgin of the Annunciation, with the donor nun, thought to be a portrait of Antonia Tanini, kneeling at her feet; in one room there was a fresco of the Crucifixion with several saints of the Augustinian order; and above a doorway was the convent's namesake and protectress, the Madonna della Misericordia, a terracotta tondo by Luca della Robbia of the Madonna protecting beneath her large mantle a group of nuns on one side and of lay women on the other, all kneeling.[87] Unfortunately, the convent buildings no longer exist, and I have not been able to locate any of the artwork mentioned by Richa. Moreover, there are very few documents relating to Antonia's convent in the Florentine archives; of these there are some

---

87. Ibid., 5, 255: "Convento con Dormentorio, Celle, Officine, ec. Vi è la Chiesa con le grate in alto per sentire la Messa, nelle pareti veggonsi tuttavia le Croci fatte nella Sacra di essa con all'Altar Maggiore una tavola di nostra Donna dipinta della maniera del Grillandaio. In cima di una Scala si vede l'immagine della Nunziata colorita a fresco in una lunetta, con appiè della medesima tavola una Monaca genuflessa, la quale credesi essere il ritratto della Fondatrice. In una Stanza àvvi pure dipinto a fresco un Crocifisso con alquanti Santi dell'ordine Agostiniano, e similmente nel Dormentorio vi è una Pietà, della qual dipintura se ne trova ricordo nei Libri di Entrata e Uscita segnato A, a pag. 46. Che dice 'adì 3 di Marzo 1507. Danari dati a Maestro Antonio dipintore per la Pietà fatta in Dormentorio scudi 18 adì 5 detto scudi 9 dati al medesimo.' E per fine sopra una Porta si vede un tondo di terra cotta invetriata, lavoro di Luca della Robbia, che vi effigiò nostra Signora, che tiene sotto il Manto da una parte le Monache, e dall'altra le Secolari genuflesse." (Convent with dormitory, cells, workrooms, etc. There is a church with a grille high on the wall [through which] to hear mass; on the walls we still see the crosses put there when it was consecrated; on the main altar [there is] a representation of Our Lady, painted in the manner of Ghirlandaio. At the top of the stairway one sees the frescoed image of the Virgin of the Annunciation in a lunette, and at the foot of the painting [there is] a kneeling nun, thought to be the portrait of the foundress. In one room we also find a frescoed crucifixion with several saints of the Augustinian order, and, similarly, in the dormitory there is a Pietà, a painting that is mentioned in the financial record books [sic], marked A, on page 46, where it says 'on 3 March 1507 [1508], paid to the painter Mastro Antonio for the Pietà in the dormitory 18 ducats [and] 9 ducats again to him on the 5th.' And lastly, above a door we see a round terracotta, the work of Luca della Robbia, in which he made an image of Our Lady who has under her mantle on one side the nuns and on the other secular women, all kneeling).

dating from the early sixteenth century in the hand of Fra Antonio Dolciati, who, as prior of San Gallo, served also as the convent's *direttore*, or governor, and for a while kept their records, which today are found with those of San Clemente.[88]

The Plays

The anthology in which Antonia first published her plays may have been intended for an audience of readers, and it seems that the individual plays also circulated separately, perhaps the better for use in performance.[89] These characteristics and the lack of a dedication in either of the two volumes of the anthology suggest that the publication aimed at a wide pool of consumers; and, as Paolo Trovato and others have argued, local consumers, since Florence had little access to other markets, having to use for exports land routes which were expensive and slow.[90] Large sectors of the Florentine population had achieved a significant level of literacy, and, judging from the many religious plays that were published in the last decade of the fifteenth century and in the early years of the sixteenth, there must have been a local demand for them. We can assume, I believe, that they were bought by some to be read as devotional texts, and also by others to be performed, by confraternities in churches and oratories or for civic celebrations, and by nuns in convent theater.[91] We know that one of the plays in the

---

88. In 1532 Dolciati, then prior of San Gallo, was asked to straighten out the accounts of the convent of Santa Maria della Misericordia, which was under the supervision of his Augustinian house. The sister who was the recorder that year, Sister Serafina, was confused by the records and needed assistance. To his accounts Dolciati added a note saying that he had done his best, but the problems were not entirely resolvable, since Sister Monica, the previous convent recorder, who had held that office since the convent's founding, had died of the plague and all earlier records had been burned (ASF, Corporazioni religiose soppresse dal governo francese, 125, entry for 14 September 1532, fol. 9).

89. Several of the anthologies held by the Florentine Biblioteca Nazionale have been reconstructed from copies of individual plays.

90. Paolo Trovato, "Il libro in Toscana nell'età di Lorenzo," in *L'ordine dei tipografi. Lettori, stampatori, correttori tra Quattro e Cinquecento* (Rome: Bulzoni, 1998), 49–89.

91. Local convent theater has been documented as early as the last decade of the fifteenth century. Richard Trexler reports that theatrical performances by young boys at the convent of Santa Caterina al Monte in San Gaggio, just north of Florence, common in the past,

anthology, whether intended or not for convent theater, was read and performed by nuns: a copy of the *Santa Domitilla* at the Florentine Biblioteca Nazionale Centrale contains the names of convent women entered in the margins of the text alongside the parts they played (Figures 11a, b). There are eleven or twelve names: suor Maria Angelica; suor Maria Gostanza (both are mentioned again as Maria Angelica and Gostanza); others, given without title, are Jacopa, Ottavia, Innocenza, Lodovica, Dorotea, Filippa, Pace, Maria Vincenza, Anna and Maria Anna (the latter two may refer to the same person), novices perhaps, or the title of *suor* may have been omitted in order to fit the names easily into the book's margins.[92]

Antonia's plays were short texts, averaging around a hundred octaves each, and they were sold unbound in small quarto pamphlets of eight to twenty-four leaves. Those in the Miscomini anthology, the first editions of her St. Domitilla, St. Guglielma, and St. Francis plays were unadorned but generously printed in a single column per page. The second editions of the same plays and the Saul and David play, also incunables, were illustrated with woodcuts and printed in double columns (Figures 4–11).

The structure of the plays varies according to the source, as we shall see below, but all begin with a prologue delivered by an angel, who is depicted bearing a lily, like the angel of the Annunciation, in a woodcut on the opening page of many of the early editions. The prologue invokes divine help in telling the story and often provides a very brief summary of it. This is the case in all of Antonia Pulci's extant plays except the *Prodigal Son*, where the author simply indicates

---

were avoided by the Savonarolan boys during the Carnivals of 1496-98. See his "Florentine Theater, 1280-1500. A Checklist of Performances and Institutions," *Forum Italicum* 14 (1980), 471.

92. It seems likely that the demand for her plays was owing, at least in part, to the growing convent population of those years and the tradition in the convents of performing plays at Carnival time and for important convent festivities, such as the clothing ceremony and profession. According to the bibliographer Colomb de Batines (*Bibliografia delle antiche rappresentazioni italiane*, 15–16), this play had been printed at least fifteen times by 1602. See Weaver, *Convent Theatre*, Ch. 2, "The Convent Theatre Tradition," and also 99–104, 126, and the accompanying notes. The many references to 'taking the veil' in the play would suggest, at the very least, the appropriateness of this play for the festivities connected with a convent 'veiling' ceremony (see note 8 to the Italian text of the *Santa Domitilla* play).

that the source of the story is the well-known parable of the Gospel. Despite their presentation by an angel, the language of the prologues implies that the speaker is the author, for example, "And, Virgin Mary, you, elect in heaven/… /Inflame and set alight my fantasy/… /So that, unfraught with peril, my small boat / Can reach the harbor, …" (*St. Francis*, 2. 1–6), or the opening of the *Prodigal Son*, where it is said that the Redeemer "to Heav'n, / Summoned us" (15–16).[93] The angel returns at the end of the play to dismiss the audience with the *licenza*, the envoy, and in this case speaks as a messenger from heaven, for example, in the *St. Domitilla*, by referring to the audience as you who are "in this blind world where you're entangled all" (106.5) or, in the *St. Guglielma*, "O you who wander in this wayward wood,/ This mortal life where nothing is secure" (106.1–2).[94]

Another characteristic of Antonia Pulci's plays that is perfectly in keeping with the tradition as it developed in Tuscany is their disregard for temporal and spatial realism. Much time can pass in the imagined story between octaves; and between octaves the scene can shift from one place to another. Some of these incongruities could be overcome in the performance of the play as the action shifted from one *luogo deputato* to another. The *luogo deputato*, or 'appointed place,' was the term used to indicate where the action is performed; there could be many *luoghi*, and the term could refer to different small stages or to designated locations in the performance space: in a church, piazza, refectory, courtyard, or in a simple curtained stage.[95] The movement

---

93. "E tu, vergine eletta in ciel Maria,/ … / accendi e infiamma la mia fantasia/ … / acciò che in porto la barchetta mia / arrivar possa sanza alcun periglio" (*San Francesco*, 2. 1–6); "al ciel per tua pietà ci revocasti," (*Figliuol prodigo*, 1.6).

94. "nel mondo cieco, dove involti siete" (*Santa Domitilla*, 106.5); "O voi che siete in questa selva errante,/ vita mortal dove non è fidanza"(*Santa Guglielma*, 106.1–2).

95. I have found two places in the stage directions which seem to refer specifically to the performance space. In the *Rappresentazione del figliuol prodigo*, the stage direction just before octave 41 reads "El figliuol prodigo, *uscendo fuori* tutto stracciato, dice da sé," where "uscendo fuori," literally "coming out," can mean making a stage entrance. In the *Distruzione di Saul e il pianto di Davit*, preceding octave 33 we read "E partonsi con assai romore e strepito di trombe e, giunti al *luogo diputato*, Gionatas segue," where the place to which the characters arrive is called the "luogo diputato," the appointed space, ambiguous here perhaps, but it is the technical term used to indicate the performance space of miracle and mystery plays (italics mine).

of the audience, or only of their eyes and attention, to a different *luogo deputato* could simulate the change in geography in the story and the passing of time in the action.[96] It seems obvious, however, that a realistic depiction of time and space was not a concern of the authors of early mystery and miracle plays, at least not in the late fifteenth century before classical theater became the tradition to emulate.

The verse form typical of the genre of *sacra rappresentazione* was *ottava rima*, or octaves, eight-line stanzas composed of *endecasillabi*, eleven-syllable lines,[97] of three pairs of alternating rhymes followed by a rhymed couplet (ABABABCC). Antonia Pulci's verse seems to flow easily from her pen. She varies her diction, including her rhyme words, which are simple but never repetitive, and are often carefully chosen to lay emphasis on the important notions expressed in the octave. She also exhibits a facility in representing conversations, frequently enlivening them by dividing up the lines of an octave, sharing them between and among her characters. With the final couplet she often closes a discussion (see, e.g., *St. Domitilla*, octaves 6, 7, 35, 43, 65).

The Play of St. Domitilla

The *St. Domitilla* appears first in the early anthology. It dramatizes the story of Flavia Domitilla, a Roman noblewoman, niece of Emperor Domitian (81–96 CE) and virgin martyr. She has always been associated with Saints Nereus and Achilleus, the two Christian servants who converted her to Christianity, convinced her of the superiority of virginity to marriage, and who were martyred and buried with her. The Church celebrates her feast on May 7th, that of Nereus and Achilleus, instead, on May 12th.[98]

---

96. On the movement of action from one *luogo deputato* to another and its spatial and temporal implications, see C. Molinari, *Spettacoli fiorentini del Quattrocento*, 77–78.

97. It is a common oversimplification to call an *endecasillabo* an eleven-syllable line. It may have ten, eleven, or twelve syllables depending upon whether the word in rhyme position is an oxytone (accented on the final syllable), paroxytone (accented on the next last syllable), or proparoxytone (accented on the third from last syllable). The final accent in an *endecasillabo* falls invariably on the line's tenth syllable.

98. See *Acta Sanctorum, Mai*, II and III (Paris, 1866), 13: 132–33; 14: 4–16.

Pulci's account of Domitilla's life may be derived from more than one early hagiographical account. A brief version is found in the *Legenda aurea* of Jacobus de Voragine (widely circulated in manuscript and published in Italian translation in 1475); there Domitilla's story is told together with that of Nereus and Achilleus. Other versions of this martyr's tale were available to Antonia, several written in the fourteenth and fifteenth centuries, in Latin and in the vernacular language, in prose and in verse.[99] Pulci may have known the *Vita di Santa Domitilla vergine e martire con l'ufficio proprio della di lei festività* (the life of Saint Domitilla virgin and martyr with the office proper for her feast day), written by Giovanni dalle Celle (ca. 1310–1396), a monk of the Benedictine community of Vallombrosa.[100] According to Emanuela Carney, she almost certainly was familiar with a longer version of the life of Saint Domitilla that appeared in a hagiographical collection written by the Milanese humanist Boninus Mombritius (b. 1424), published in 1480, the *Sanctuarium seu Vitae Sanctorum*

---

99. "Saints Nereus and Achilleus" in Jacobus de Voragine, *The Golden Legend. Readings on the Saints*, trans. William Granger Ryan (Princeton: Princeton University Press, 1993), 1: 308–99. Jacobus de Voragine, bishop of Genoa, wrote his hagiographical collection, known as the *Legenda Aurea*, between 1260 and 1263. By Antonia's time there had been a number of vernacular manuscript versions of the saint's life, and the *Legenda aurea* was printed in Niccolò Manerbi's new Italian translation in 1475. For a discussion of the sources of the life of Saint Domitilla and of the two Roman women by that name, see Emanuela Carney, "Antonia Pulci's *Rappresentazione di Santa Domitilla* and the Defense of Virginity in Quattrocento Florence," in *Scenes from Italian Convent Life: An Anthology of Theatrical Texts and Contexts*, ed. Elissa Weaver (Ravenna, Italy: Longo Editore, 2009), 19–21. See the census of the extant manuscripts transmitting the legend of Domitilla in the *Biblioteca agiografica italiana (BAI): repertorio di testi e manoscritti, secoli XIII–XV*, ed. Jacques Dalarun et al., (Florence: Edizioni del Galluzzo, 2003), 2: 201–3; most of the manuscripts of the life of Saint Domitilla cited here are of Tuscan origin.

100. Judith Bryce suggests that this *Vita* by Giovanni dalle Celle is a possible source for Pulci's *Rappresentazione di Santa Domitilla* that should be investigated in "'Or altra via mi convien cercare': Marriage, Salvation, and Sanctity in Antonia Tanini Pulci's *Rappresentazione di Santa Guglielma*," in *Theatre, Opera, and Performance in Italy from the Fifteenth Century to the Present: Essays in Honour of Richard Andrews*, ed. Brian Richardson, Simon Gilson, and Catherine Keen (Leeds: The Society for Italian Studies, 2004), 37 n24. A list of works written by Giovanni dalle Celle appears in Giovanni dalle Celle, Luigi Marsili, *Lettere*, ed. Francesco Giambonini, (Florence: Olschki, 1991), I: 179, n1.

(Sanctuary or lives of the saints).[101] Indeed, all of the scenes in the play that are not in the *Golden Legend* are presented in detail by Mombritius (e.g., the servants' conversion of Domitilla, Domitilla's healing of the blind and the mute, Aureliano's dancing and death, etc.). As Carney rightly claims, Pulci's version often includes language that is the close Italian equivalent of the Latin of Mombritius. Many elements of the speech of the servants in their praise of virginity and in Domitilla's responses are in Mombritius' account, for example, Domitilla's recollection of her mother's suffering because of her father's jealousy: "Scio matrem meam passam patrem meum zelotipum et hac iniuria per longa tempora fatigatam," (426: 9–10), which in Pulci is "Ben mi ricorda che la madre mia/ sostenne molte pene tutti gli anni / della suo vita sol per gelosia / del suo marito con sì gravi affanni"(20. 1–4); and "O quam beata est sancta uirginitas ... et est deo amabilis et omnibus angelis cara (426: 30–31), in Pulci's version "Santa verginità quanto se' degna, / diletta a Dio e agli angeli cara" (23. 1–2). It is unclear how much Latin Antonia knew at the time, but Carney argues that Bernardo, who translated Virgil's eclogues, could easily have served as her interpreter. In her article Carney studies the development of the legend of Saint Domitilla beginning with the early historical sources, but she concentrates on the central issue developed in the play, the superiority of virginity over marriage; she demonstrates that Antonia was very familiar with the arguments of the Church Fathers on the subject, especially those of Jerome and Ambrose, and that she borrows heavily from Jerome's defense of virginity in his letters and in his treatise *Against Helvidius* for the scene in which Domitilla's two servants point out to her the disadvantages, indeed the miseries of matrimony and the high value God places on virginity (octaves 11–30).[102] All of

---

101. E. Carney, "Antonia Pulci's *Rappresentazione di Santa Domitilla*," 19. Mombritius' work has a modern edition: Boninus Mombritius, *Sanctuarium seu Vitae Sanctorum*, (Hildesheim: Georg Olms Verlag, 1978); for the life of Saint Domitilla, 1: 424–28.

102. Ibid., 25–27. Carney sites especially Jerome's Letter 108 (to Eustochium), his treatise *Against Helvidius*, and Ambrose in his *Concerning Virgins*, who express arguments against marriage and in favor of virginity, arguments that were commonly repeated by preachers in Pulci's time, such as Giovanni Dominici (see his *Regola del governo di cura familiare*, ed. D. Salvi [Florence: Garinei, 1860]).

these arguments are present in Mombritius' text, but it is possible that both he and Antonia Pulci found them in another source.[103]

Domitilla's story follows the typical virgin martyr plot: a Christian maiden, betrothed to a pagan, takes a vow of virginity, refuses to marry and to adore idols; she is unmoved by attempts to change her mind, and is condemned; miracles surround her martyrdom, and others are converted by her example.[104] The action of the play shifts back and forth among four *luoghi*, the Emperor's palace, Aureliano's home, Domitilla's home, and the island of Ponza, where Domitilla and her servants are imprisoned. These four *luoghi deputati* could be represented on a single elaborate stage, on four small stages, or on a simple curtained stage with various *fori*, or openings, over which *polizze*, signs, indicate the space represented, the sort of stage depicted in the woodcut of the Lyons (1493) edition of Terence (Figure 12). The beheading of the servants Nereus and Achileus, the death by fire of Domitilla and of her two friends (not named in the play, but known in the tradition as Euphrosina and Theodora), and the death of Aurelianus by dancing are reported either in the stage directions or in the speech of a character and would, therefore, seem to take place off stage. Nerida Newbigin, in an article on the performance of virgin martyr plays, explains some of the ways in which such actions were portrayed on stage, but, in this case, the text clearly offers

103. In the Sienese comedy entitled *Ortensio*, performed in Siena by the Accademia degli Intronati for the Grand Duke of Tuscany in 1561, there is a reference to a "Libro delle vergini" containing the life of St.Domitilla. A serving girl says she will borrow a copy of that book of virgins so that her mistress can read the life of Domitilla to her before they go off to attend a performance of a "rappresentazione" (play) of Saint Domitilla. That the book is no better identified is evidence of the abundance of such books and the continued popularity of the genre of virgin martyr stories. I thank Nerida Newbigin for sending me this reference. Though the author of the play is not mentioned, it is likely that the play to which it refers is Antonia Pulci's *Rappresentazione di Santa Domitilla*, which was printed many times in the sixteenth century, surely for the purpose of performance.

104. See Judith Wogan-Browne for a synthesis of the typical virgin martyr story and its standard variations, in "Saint's Lives and the Female Reader," *Forum for Modern Language Studies*, 27 (1991), 314–32, cited by Nerida Newbigin, "Agata, Apollonia, and Other Martyred Virgins: Did Florentines Really See These Plays Performed?" *European Medieval Drama 1997* (Proceedings of the Second International Conference on "Aspects of European Medieval Drama," Camerino, 4–6 July 1997), 181–82, ed. S. Higgins, 2 vols. (Camerino: Centro Audiovisivi e Stampa Università di Camerino, 1998) 1: 175–97.

a way to avoid the complicated staging that these examples of torture and death would necessitate.[105]

As Georges Ulysse argues in his perceptive reading of the play, the conflict that is the center of the action is that of marriage versus virginity and not, as we might expect, between the Christian and the pagan faiths. Aureliano is a kind suitor, the Emperor a well-meaning uncle, and both use reasonable arguments in their effort to persuade Domitilla to marry.[106] Domitilla is immoveable, having been instead convinced by the arguments against marriage, presented by her servants and confirmed by her memory of her mother's suffering from her father's jealousy. She is persuaded by the arguments in favor of virginity, that it is the greatest virtue, most prized in heaven, and that as a virgin she marries Christ, a kind and compassionate spouse who will never leave her and who will celebrate her in heaven (octaves 24–25).

Pulci's Domitilla and her other heroines, as we shall see, win their battles through perseverence and prayer, but they also rely on their wits. Domitilla wins her argument with the Emperor, telling him he hasn't read his pagan books well, for, if he had, he would see that even his religion exalts virginity, venerating the chaste goddess Diana and holding in high regard the Sibyls, the heroine Camilla and the vestal virgins (44–57). When he cannot rebut her point he answers in anger that he has the power to free her or to put her to death ("Misera, non sa' tu ch'i' ho potenza/ di liberarti e di farti morire! 58.1–2) and sends her off to punishment and eventually death on the island of Ponza. This too is a victory for Domitilla, who wants nothing more than to join her heavenly Bridegroom.

The Play of St. Guglielma

The *Play of St. Guglielma* follows that of *St. Domitilla* in the Miscomini anthology. While St. Domitilla is a virgin martyr, St. Guglielma is a wife. Guglielma's story is that of an unjustly persecuted faithful wife. An English princess, married to a Hungarian king who has recently converted to Christianity, she is falsely accused of infidelity and

---

105. Newbigin,, "Agata, Apollonia, and Other Martyred Virgins," especially 183–88.

106. Georges Ulysse, "Un Couple d'écrivains," 185.

condemned to death, but she survives and prospers because of her constancy and her faith; through divine intervention she receives the power of healing, and in the end is vindicated and leaves the world for a hermitage, together with her persecutors, her husband and his brother, whom she has forgiven. The protagonists are nobles, a typical feature of the romance tradition to which this story belongs; so too the perils, peregrinations, abrupt reversals of fortune, miraculous interventions, recognition and final reunion of the couple, all features of a genre known to the West first in the early Greek romances.[107] Guglielma's very different story shares, however, with Domitilla's the message that virginity is a higher calling than matrimony. Guglielma preferred to remain a virgin, but marries out of obedience to her parents; when she is abandoned, alone and afraid, she laments her decision, but in the end turns adversity into advantage and her marriage into a religious vocation of penance and prayer. With this play and the *St. Domitilla*, Antonia Pulci addresses both vocations available to women of her time, marriage and the convent; she does not deny that both have value and can lead to salvation, though she argues that virginity is the better way, and marriage is fraught with danger. She also shows, and this was obvious in fifteenth-century Italy, that a woman alone cannot survive in the dangerous world of men; her only refuge, beyond miraculous intervention, is in the religious life, in Guglielma's case the convent and the hermitage. The dangers of matrimony are reviewed in great detail in the episode of Domitilla's conversion (childbirth, deformed children, ungrateful ones, cruel and unfaithful

---

107. On Greek romances, see Arthur R. Heiserman, *The Novel Before the Novel: Essays and Discussions about the Beginnings of Prose Fiction in the West* (Chicago: University of Chicago Press, 1977). On the medieval romance traditions to which the story of Guglielma belongs see Alessandro D'Ancona, *Origini del teatro italiano*, (Turin: Loescher, 1891, 2nd ed. rev. and enl.), I, 436, and, especially, the introduction to his edition of the play in *Sacre rappresentazioni dei secoli XIV, XV e XVI* (Florence: Successori Le Monnier, 1872), 3.199–208. For Luigi Banfi, Apollo Lumini, and others (few critics accord the play much attention) the romance element in this play prevails over the religious motif (see L Banfi, Introduction, *Sacre Rappresentazioni del Quattocento* [Turin: UTET, 1963], 26; A Lumini, *Le sacre rappresentazioni italiane* [Palermo: Tipografia di Pietro Montaina e comp., 1877], 197). Georges Ulysse, in disagreement with that view, argues that religion in the play is important and is given a human dimension, expressed in the affectionate relationship Guglielma has with her parents and her husband (G. Ulysse, "Un Couple d'écrivains," 184).

husbands, etc.) and they are presented directly through the example of Guglielma's life.

The Church does not acknowledge a Saint Guglielma, but in fifteenth-century Italy her legend was popular and many prose versions of it survive.[108] The story of Saint Guglielma is a variant of the medieval narratives of the "accused queen," known as the "Empress of Rome" and also as the "Crescentia" legend, after two of the most famous examples of the topos; only the specific context, names and places are changed.[109] Yet despite the shared story, as Nancy Black, who has studied the tradition explains, each reprise of the legend can convey a different message and must be understood in "its textual, artistic, and social context."[110] The social and religious context which gave rise to the prose legend of St. Guglielma in Northern Italy, though near in time, seems far removed from that of Florence when Antonia Pulci chose to dramatize the story. When Pulci rewrote the prose legend as a *sacra rappresentazione*, she also transformed its message.

The legend of St. Guglielma, unknown outside of Italy, enjoyed great popularity in the fifteenth century. Recently, scholars have

---

108. Barbara Newman has studied the cult of St. Guglielma which still lives in the town of Brunate above Como, though the saint is not recognized by the Church. See her article, "The Heretic Saint: Guglielma of Bohemia, Milan, and Brunate," *Church History* 74 (2005/1), 1–38. Anna Pullia's undergraduate dissertation at the University of Florence "Due Guglielme per una drammaturga. Guglielma d'Ungheria e Guglielma la Boema nell'ottica teatrale di Antonia Pulci" (Tesi di laurea, University of Florence, 2005) documents the wide diffusion of the legend in northern Italy, provides detailed descriptions of nine exemplars, all written in the vernacular and, in an appendix, an edition of the version of the legend redacted ("composta et ampliada") by Andrea Bono, the abbot of San Giorgio in Venice, based on the Marciana Library manuscript, Ital. V, 41. See also *Biblioteca agiografica italiana*, 2: 394–95, for a list of manuscripts of the legend.

109. See Nancy B. Black, *Medieval Narratives of Accused Queens* (Gainesville: University Press of Florida, 2003). Alessandro D'Ancona illustrated this tradition and its major variants in the introduction to his edition of Pulci's play; see his *Sacre rappresentazioni dei secoli XVI, XV e XVI*, 3: 199–208. Barbara Newman, in her discussion of the cult of Saint Guglielma, refers to the tradition of the "calumniated wife," a more inclusive category to which the "accused queen" tradition belongs ("The Heretic Saint,"24), and which would include the legends of Costanza, Genovefa, Ines, Hildegard, and other popular medieval variants, and, among the religious plays of Antonia Pulci's time, the stories of Saint Uliva, Stella, and Rosana.

110. N. Black, *Medieval Narratives*, 6.

shown that the explanation lies in the connection of this legend with the story of Guglielma of Milan (c.1210–1281), a charismatic woman, reputed to have come to Italy from Bohemia and venerated as a living saint.[111] The cult that formed around her and flourished after her death was later condemned as heretical (among other things, her followers thought she was the incarnation of the Holy Spirit), her most famous disciples were condemned and burned, and her body, buried at the Cistercian abbey of Chiaravalle, was exhumed and burned.[112] Barbara Newman has shown that the cult of St. Guglielma is still alive today in a small mountain town north of Como, but her story has been transformed and she is remembered not as the heretical Guglielma but as the accused queen of popular legend, St. Guglielma of Hungary. Newman traces the continued devotion to Guglielma of Milan and the preservation of her memory to the devotion to her of members of the powerful Visconti family.[113] Dávid Falvay argues that the followers of the heretical cult promoted the legend of Saint Guglielma of Hungary in order to preserve in this surreptitious way, the memory of Guglielma of Milan.[114]

The legend of St. Guglielma of Hungary emerges in Northern Italy in the 1420s. The earliest prose version known was written by a Ferrarese friar, Antonio Bonfadini (d. 1428).[115] In all the extant versions of the prose legend Guglielma is falsely accused and condemned twice. The first time it is her brother-in-law who attempts to seduce her when the King is away on a pilgrimage to the Holy

---

111. B. Newman, "The Heretic Saint," *passim*. Dávid Falvay, "A Lady Wandering in a Faraway Land: The Central European Queen/Princess Motif in Italian Heretical Cults," *Annual of Medieval Studies at CEU* 8 (2002), 157–79; "Santa Guglielma, regina d'Ungheria: Culto di una pseudo-santa d'Ungheria in Italia, *Nuova Corvina: Rivista di Italianistica* 9 (2001), 116–22; and "Szent Erzsébet, Szent Vilma és a magyar királyi származás mint toposz Itáliában (Saint Elizabeth, Saint Guglielma and the Hungarian Royal Origin as a Topos in Italy, with English summary), Aetas (2008/1): 64–76. See also Anna Pullia, "Due Guglielme," *passim*.

112. B. Newman, "The Heretic Saint," 5.

113. Ibid., 17–23.

114. For the studies of D. Falvay, see above, n111.

115. Antonio Bonfadini's work, *L'istoria de Santa Gulielma fiola delo re dangalterra, et moglie delo Re dungaria*, is known today in *Vite di S. Guglielma regina d' Ungheria e di S. Eufrasia vergine romana*, ed. Giuseppe Ferraro, "Scelta di curiosità letteraria inedite o rare dal secolo XIII al XVII," 159 (Bologna: G. Romagnoli, 1878), 1–67.

Land. She refuses him and he seeks revenge accusing her to the king of infidelity. The king condemns her to be executed by fire, but she is freed by the executioners who recognize her innocence. She flees, and, lost in a forest, she encounters the King of France. She is taken to the court where, her real identity unknown, she becomes the governess of his newborn son. There she is once again the object of the attentions of a courtier and the victim of his revenge. The seneschal wants to marry her, and, when she declines, he strangles the child in her care and accuses her of the murder. She is again condemned to death by fire and is again freed, this time through the intervention of the Blessed Virgin, who, in response to Guglielma's prayer, sends two angels to accompany her to safety. The main lines of the story are the same in all of the manuscripts, except for the ending which exhibits two variants: one in which the protagonists end their lives in Hungary building churches and monasteries and performing other charitable works, and another in which both husband and wife leave the world to live out their lives in religious institutions they have founded. Antonia Pulci's play presents a third alternative, in which husband, wife, and brother-in-law leave the world to live the ascetic life of hermits; this and some other significant differences between Pulci's version and the prose legend are the subject of a recent study by Judith Bryce.[116]

Undoubtedly, it was in the interest of streamlining the plot of her play that Pulci eliminated the second trial of the protagonist; and there was no need for another, since the message, that an innocent woman is in peril in an evil world, has been firmly established through the first episode. It is also likely that Pulci as she dramatized the story kept in mind the exigencies of performance. The plot is complex even without this episode and requires many scene changes: from the English to the Hungarian court, to the queen's quarters where the attempted seduction occurs, the scene of the King's return just outside the city, the site of the execution, a wilderness, a port, a convent, and then a return to the Hungarian court (the final departure for a hermit-

---

116. Judith Bryce, "'Or altra via mi convïen cercare': Marriage, Salvation, and Sanctity," cited above, n100.

age in the wilderness is announced in the final stage direction but not dramatized).[117]

There are many minor differences between the prose legend and Pulci's version of the Saint Guglielma story, some simply inherent in the process of transforming a narrative account into dramatic form. One of the most interesting characteristics of the prose legend is the attention it gives to motivating the actions of characters. In the play the interest is shifted to the actions themselves; their motivation is left to the words exchanged in conversation and, presumably, to the interpretation of the actors, whose gestures and their meaning are sometimes suggested in the stage directions. Pulci also adds minor characters, such as the underserving poor asking for alms (there is a similar scene also in her *Play of St. Francis*),[118] and, as Bryce has pointed out, this introduces an element of everyday life in Florence and also provides comic relief.[119] Another reference to contemporary life, humorous in the way it interrupts the serious story, is the request made by the king's messenger who offers the innkeeper a florin and more for something quick to eat, and asks if he has any partridge, cockerel or squab; the innkeeper says that he has and that he'll throw in the wine too (32.1–4). Such touches of realism were typical of the Florentine *sacra rappresentazione*, and Pulci's recourse to them shows that she knew well how to involve her listeners and readers in a sacred story by appealing to their common experiences.

Pulci's other major innovation, the ending in which the protagonists leave the world to live as hermits, is reminiscent of the conclusion of Bernardo Pulci's *Rappresentazione di Barlaam e Josafat*, in which Josafat, when he becomes king, immediately renounces his rule in favor of a baron, and retreats to the desert to join there his holy

---

117. I agree with Nerida Newbigin that "stage direction" is not the best way to refer to what in Italian is called the *didascalia*, which often performs, as in this case, a narrative function." See N. Newbigin, "Agata, Apollonia, and Other Martyred Virgins,"187–88.

118. *Santa Guglielma*, octave 19; *San Francesco*, octaves 4–5, and especially 36–37; and see also Bernardo Pulci's *Barlaam e Josafat*, 16–18. See the discussion of this topos as a reflection of city life in Florence by Franco Cardini, "La figura di Francesco d'Assisi nella *Rappresentazione di Sancto Francesco* di Antonia Pulci," in *Il Francescanesimo e il teatro medievale*. Atti del convegno nazionale di studi, San Miniato, 1982 (Castelfiorentino: Società storica della Valdelsa, 1984), 203.

119. Judith Bryce, "'Or altra via mi convïen cercare': Marriage, Salvation, and Sanctity," 27.

teacher Barlaam. Both plays conclude with this message of *contemptus mundi*, but the ending of Antonia's play makes a statement about marriage as well. As Judith Bryce argues, with the new ending of the play, Antonia Pulci shows that her protagonist has fulfilled "a married woman's aspirations to perfection."[120] She had desired the more perfect vocation of virginity, but in obedience to her parents she entered the marriage, and as obedient and faithful wife, she persevered, constant in the face of adversity, and in the end she secured not only her own salvation but that of her husband and his brother as well.

The St. Guglielma play has met with greater success than the others Pulci wrote, largely, I think, because of the appeal of the romance plot, with its dangers, supernatural interventions, surprise encounters, and reversals of fate. It had many early editions, twenty-six by 1604, according to the bibliographer Paul Colomb de Batines, and it was anthologized in the nineteenth and twentieth centuries.[121]

The Play of St. Francis

Pulci's *St. Francis*, which survives in only three early editions, was clearly less popular with its contemporaries than the *St. Guglielma* or the *St. Domitilla*; however, it has received considerable attention from modern critics, largely because of the interest in the protagonist.[122]

---

120. Ibid., 31–32.

121. Paul Colomb de Batines, *Bibliografia delle antiche rappresentazioni*, 17–18. Pulci's *St. Domitilla* was second in popularity to the *Santa Guglielma* with fifteen known editions during the same period. See above, n92. A. D'Ancona, *Sacre rappresentazioni*, 3: 199–234; Luigi Banfi, ed., *Sacre rappresentazioni del Quattrocento*, 537–81; *Sacre rappresentazioni fiorentine del Quattrocento*, ed. Ponte, Giovanni (Milan: Marzorati Editore, 1974), 69–98; Anna Pullia has also edited the play, which she includes in "Due Guglielme," 95–135.

122. It has been studied by Eletto Palandri, O.F.M., "Rappresentazioni sanfrancescane," *Studi francescani*, n.s. 12 (23) (luglio-dicembre 1926), 417–30; Mario Ferrigni, "San Francesco e il teatro," *Nuova Antologia*, 258, series 7, (March 1928), 207–10; Franco Cardini, "La figura di Francesco d'Assisi nella *Rappresentatione di Sancto Francesco* di Antonia Pulci," in *Il Francescanesimo e il teatro medievale*. Atti del convegno nazionale di studi, San Miniato, 1982 (Castelfiorentino: Società storica della Valdelsa, 1984), 195–207, and in the same volume, Andrea Mancini, "Francesco nella lauda e nella sacra rappresentazione," 135–47. Georges Ulysse discusses the play in "Un couple d'écrivans," 186–87. E. Palandri in "Rappresentazioni sanfrancescane," 439–67, also published the play, and it has been published again by Paolo Toschi, *L'antico dramma sacro italiano* (Florence: Libreria Editrice Fiorentina, 1926),

Franco Cardini, in his study of the play, asserts that St. Francis was not a popular subject of the arts in late fifteenth- and early sixteenth-century Florence; his fame had been eclipsed in the fifteenth century and recovered fully only in the nineteenth.[123] The first edition of the play appeared in the Miscomini anthology; there was a second edition shortly thereafter, published, it seems, by Bartolomeo de' Libri, and a third Florentine edition (publisher unknown) appeared in 1559. We cannot know why Antonia Pulci would choose to write a play about St. Francis, but I would like to speculate that this choice was related to her biography. Both Antonia's father and her husband were buried in the Franciscan church of Santa Croce, and St. Francis was her father's patron saint. If Francis of Assisi was not widely represented in the arts in Florence in the fifteenth century, he was certainly known in the famous cycle of his life painted by Giotto in Santa Croce (after 1317), and he was remembered well in the names of Florentines. According to David Herlihy, Francesco was the most popular man's name among Florentines scrutinized for office between 1450 and 1500, even surpassing Giovanni, the name of Florence's patron saint.[124] And the biographical references, in my opinion, do not end here.

The *Play of St. Francis* is based on the legends of the life of the saint, which had wide circulation in many forms. Antonia probably knew the *Legenda maior* of Saint Bonaventure, perhaps in the vernacular translation by Domenico Cavalca, as Cardini suggests;[125] and she almost certainly used the popular compilation of legends known as the *Fioretti*, from which she seems to have taken the story of the visit of Jacopa da Settesoli, a Roman friend of St. Francis.[126] She also

---

2: 655–96, and by Erhard Lommatzsch, *Beiträge zur älteren Italianischen Volksdictung untersuchungen und texte* (Berlin: Akademie Verlag, 1963), 17/4: 212–33.

123. F. Cardini, "La figura di Francesco d'Assisi," 195–96.

124. See above, n20.

125. F. Cardini, "La figura di Francesco d'Assisi," 206. Cardini cites G. Paci, "Domenico Cavalca, volgarizzatore della Legenda maior," *Italia francescana* 44 (1969), 322–28.

126. E. Palandri, "Rappresentazioni sanfrancescane," 422–30, documents how closely Pulci follows Buonaventura's life of St. Francis for the first 64 octaves and the *Fioretti* for the remainder of the play. For Jacopa da Settesoli, see Èdouard d'Alençon, *Frère Jacqueline, recherches historiques sur Jacopa de Settesoli, l'amie de Saint-François*, Paris: Société et Librairie Saint-François d'Assise, 1927 and Rome: Postulation Générale des f.f. m.m. Capucins, 1927.

undoubtedly knew Giotto's fresco cycle painted in the Bardi Chapel of the church of Santa Croce.

Pulci chose from among the many legends of the life of St. Francis only a very few, owing to the limitations of the dramatic genre. The play opens with Francis, the merchant, working at his *banco*, a scene that would have been familiar to Pulci and her Florentine audience; Francis is busy and turns away a beggar, but then repents. There follow scenes at the church of San Damiano where Francis speaks to the crucifix and the city center in the piazza where he renounces all earthly possessions and is disinherited by his father; then the action moves to his home where he is first imprisoned by his father, then freed by his mother. The next series of episodes are dedicated to Francis's mission: he acquires disciples, the first of whom is Bernardo (di Quintavalle), he then appeals to the Pope to approve his Rule, sets out to convert the Sultan in far away Babylon (i.e. Egypt), and returns to found a religious house at La Verna, where he receives the stigmata. The play ends at the church of Santa Maria degli Angeli, where Francis dies surrounded by his followers and aided by his Roman friend, Jacopa da Settesoli. These are among the most famous episodes of the saint's life, and the playwright uses them to convey religious messages that characterize all her work: the importance of charity, of conversion (of oneself and others), and of renunciation of the world, the theme of *contemptus mundi* that we have seen also in St. Domitilla's embrace of virginity and martyrdom and in St. Guglielma's withdrawal to a hermitage. Franco Cardini stresses the mercantile context of the play and the way the story speaks to its audience of Florentine merchants and artisans about the need to engage in charity and not to be so caught up in the material world.[127] I agree, but would add that the playwright very likely also envisioned an audience of convent women and male clerics, perhaps especially Franciscans, to whom she addressed her message of *contemptus mundi*.

The conflict between Francis and his father, then Francis and the pope, and later between Francis and the Saracens at the Sultan's

---

127. F. Cardini, "La figura di Francesco d'Assisi," 200–03 and G. Ulysse, "Un Couple d'écrivains," 186–87, who suggests that in the conflict between father and son the Florentine merchants would very likely have sided with Francis' father (187).

court are moments that lend themselves to dramatic representation.[128] Francis's conversation with Christ on the crucifix at San Damiano and his reception of the stigmata at La Verna would call for some special effects. There are also two scenes, one at the beginning and another at the end of the play, where Francis takes off his clothes; this gesture too may have been an attention getter, even if simulated, as it probably would have been. A good rendering of these scenes could make the play successful in performance, but on the page the movement from one scene to the next rarely seems well prepared. Were this a text only to be read, I would be inclined to agree with one critic who found the play to be "on the whole pleasing and characterized by a certain variety"("varia ed attraente nell'insieme"), yet "formally weak and poorly put together"("slegata e fiacca nella forma").[129]

I mention above that I consider this play to be autobiographical (in the very limited sense possible at the time), and that Antonia Pulci chose to dramatize the life of St. Francis because it allowed her to pay homage to her father Francesco through the life of his patron saint. I am persuaded of this also because, of the many episodes available to her, Pulci chose to include in the play two that involve characters whose names are those of her husband, Bernardo, and her mother, Jacopa, and indeed Francis's friend, Jacopa da Settesoli, like Antonia's mother, came from Rome. If I am correct, the play makes up in allusion what it lacks in artistic development, and Antonia Pulci's references to her family members are both an homage to them and, as it is a religious play, a prayer for them.

The *Play of the Prodigal Son* and the *Destruction of Saul and the Lament of David* can be attributed to Antonia Pulci on the reliable word of her friend and Latin teacher, Fra Antonio Dolciati.[130] Dolciati in 1528 claimed to have seen the plays thirty-six years earlier, that is, in 1492. A fifteenth-century edition of the Saul and David play has

---

128. G. Ulysse, "Un Couple d'écrivains," 186. On the conflict of Francis and his father, see Richard C. Trexler, *Naked Before the Father: The Renunciation of Francis of Assisi* (New York: Lang, 1989).

129. E. Palandri, "Rappresentazioni sanfrancescane," 422.

130. See above, n69.

survived, but the earliest edition we know today of the Prodigal Son play was published in mid sixteenth century.[131]

The Play of the Prodigal Son

There are three Florentine *sacre rappresentazioni* based on the parable of the Prodigal Son (Lk 15:11–32). Besides Antonia Pulci's play, there is an earlier one, entitled *La festa del vitello sagginato* (the fatted calf play), written by Piero di Mariano Muzi,[132] and a later play by Castellano Castellani, the *Rappresentazione del figliuol prodigo*.[133] The earliest extant manuscript of Muzi's play is known to predate 1464; it

---

131. The earliest edition is without date or publisher. Colomb de Batines thinks it is an early sixteenth-century edition (*Bibliografia delle antiche rappresentazioni*, 18), and Alfredo Cioni suggests 1550 (*Bibliografia delle sacre rappresentazioni*, 138 [in his bibliography it is play number xxx.1]). Colomb de Batines lists fifteen editions between the early sixteenth century and 1606 (18–19), and, according to Cioni, it had sixteen through 1627 (*Bibliografia delle sacre rappresentazioni*, 139–41).

132. Richard Trexler identified Muzi as the custodian of the Compagnia della Purificazione, which, beginning in 1427, met at the Dominican friary of San Marco. See his "Ritual in Florence; Adolescence and Salvation in the Renaissance," in *The Pursuit of Holiness in Late Medieval and Renaissance Religion*, ed. Charles Trinkaus and H. A. Obermann (Leiden: Brill, 1974) 200–64 and esp. 207–08 and 212–15. This information is cited by N. Newbigin, *Nuovo corpus*, 32n2.

133. Nerida Newbigin published Muzi's play, *La festa del vitello sagginato*, in *Nuovo corpus*, 29–55. See her notes on the manuscript tradition (xii-xiv) and her introduction to the play (31-3). I base my analysis on Newbigin's edition. For Castellano Castellani, see Giovanni Ponte, *Attorno al Savonarola. Castellano Castellani e la sacra rappresentazione a Firenze tra Quattro e Cinquecento* (Genoa: Fratelli Pagano Tipografi editori, 1969). Castellani (1461–1519/20), according to Ponte, was vicar of the Bishop of Florence after 1495 and, in 1517, *governatore* of the Compagnia di San Gerolamo della Costa di San Giorgio, the group for which he probably wrote his religious plays, which, Ponte claims, were inspired by the work of both Antonia and Bernardo Pulci (11–12 and 100–25). Ferdinando Neri, "Studi sul teatro antico. Le parabole," *Giornale storico della letteratura italiana*, 65 (1915), 1–14, thought both Muzi and Castellani had used Antonia Pulci's play as the model for their prodigal son plays; he was obviously unaware of the copy of Muzi's play in a Vatican manuscript copied between 1448 and 1464 (see Newbigin, ed., *Nuovo corpus*, note on p. xii). Konrad Eisenbichler treats Castellani's play briefly in his study of three sixteenth-century theatrical versions of the parable, K. Eisenbichler, "From *sacra rappresentazione* to *commedia spirituale*: Three Prodigal Son Plays," *Bibliothèque d'Humanisme et Renaissance*, 45 (1983), 107–13.

was first published by Bartolomeo de' Libri around 1490.[134] Pulci's play according to Dolciati was written by 1492, and Castellani's has been dated 1496–97.[135] The three plays are interrelated. Pulci follows Muzi's play closely, varying its structure only slightly, but rewriting each octave in an entirely new style and with attention, lacking in Muzi's play, to the depiction of human emotions. Pulci also innovated by beginning her play with an entertaining bit of realism, an animated card game, played and lost by the prodigal son. Such a scene, but three times the length, also opens the play by Castellano Castellani, whose action, otherwise, is quite different from that of his two predecessors, and much longer.

While Antonia Pulci clearly based her play on Muzi's, following its structure closely, her innovations are many and significant, beginning with the card game with which she chose to open the action and characterize the protagonist.

Muzi's play begins with a long *annunziazione* (octaves 1–7), which opens with two lines of invocation and closes with four more; in the intervening octaves, an angel narrates the parable that will be the action of the play. Pulci, instead, begins with an *annunziazione* of one octave. She skips the parable, probably because it is well known and will be dramatized in the play; she must have considered it sufficient to announce in the first octave (1ine 8) that the action of the play is taken from the Gospel. In the place of Muzi's resumé Pulci adds five original octaves in which she introduces the prodigal son to her audience, playing cards and gambling, demonstrating his immaturity through this weakness and sin.[136] When he loses, he condemns the cards: "O cursed Ace, you were and you are still / The reason that I suffer so much ill! ("O asso maladetto, in tante pene / fusti sempre

---

134. N. Newbigin, *Nuovo corpus di sacre rappresentazioni*, xi and note 4, 31–33. On the early manuscript, Vatican codex L. VII 266, see Bernard Toscani, ed., *Le laude dei Bianchi* (Florence: Libreria Editrice Fiorentina, 1979), 32.

135. The earliest notice of Castellani as author of religious plays is provided by his letter to Bartolomeo Dei, dated 24 July 1493, which he wrote from Pisa, when he was at the Studio, informing Dei that he had written a play and would bring it to him in Florence.

136. The subject of gambling returns in two other plays, and in both it is presented as a sin characteristic of beggars: in the *St. Francis* (37.6: "…soon, they'll have gambled it away") and in the St. Guglielma (19.5: "You ugly loafer, didn't I see you gambling?").

cagion di farmi stare! 4. 5–6). Both Pulci and Muzi then follow the Biblical account, he beginning in octave 8, she in octave 7. For most of the play Pulci follows Muzi octave for octave, but she generally rewrites each stanza completely. Occasionally her syntax remains close to his, varying only slightly his terms, and in two instances she repeats a line identically (Muzi's 9.2 and 48.1 are Pulci's 8.2 and 58.1). Yet Pulci's language is more nuanced and she endows the characters with believeable human emotions, which are lacking in Muzi's play. Pulci eliminates some of Muzi's octaves and adds some of her own; these changes seem variously motivated, and I will return to them below.

Pulci's revisions of Muzi's text are largely made in the interest of psychological realism, especially in protraying a loving relationship of the father to his sons, and, at the end of the play, of the elder to the younger brother. The opening scene sets the tone that will characterize each play. When the prodigal son first tells his father he wants to leave, Muzi has the father react in anger and with strong language, the son with insensitivity and determination. Pulci rewrites the scene, depicting the father's reaction as one of sadness and worry for his son. Even the son, in her version, asks briefly for forgiveness for having been rude, but we should read this as a ploy, since the son is momentarily worried that his father may not agree to give him his inheritance at once.

Muzi's octave 9:[137]

O figliuol mio, ch'è questo ch m'hai detto?	O my son, what is it that you've told me?
Come ti vuoi dal tuo padre partire	That you want to leave your father
che stai qui meco con tanto diletto	with whom you live so pleasurably
e se' ricco e con ogni bel vestire?	and richly and with beautiful clothes of all sorts?
Deh, statti meco che sie benedetto!	Oh, stay with me where you are so blessed!
Perché stia ben, patito ho gran martire:	I have suffered much to make it good for you:
acciò che tu abbi del mio guadagnato,	in order for you to benefit from my earnings,
insino alla morte io mi son cacciato.	I have worked myself nearly to death.[138]

---

137. In the Newbigin edition, lines 65–72. Newbigin numbers the lines consecutively throughout the play; in my edition of Pulci's plays I number instead the octaves. Here I will cite the passages in Muzi's play as numbered octaves in order to facilitate the comparison with Pulci's text.

138. This literal translation and all others of Muzi's text are mine.

Pulci's corresponding octave 8:

Oimè, che mi di' tu, caro figliuolo?	Oh my, dear son, what are you telling me?
Come ti vuoi dal tuo padre partire?	Why from your father do you desire to part?
Tu m'hai messo nel core un grieve dolo;	*You've set a grievous sorrow in my heart.*
fa' che tal cosa più non t'oda dire.	Don't let me hear you say such things again.
Senza pensare ti vuoi levare a volo?	Without a thought you wish to rise in flight?
Io non lo vo' per nulla acconsentire.	For nothing will I give you my consent.
Pensa, dolce figliuol, di starti meco,	*Consider staying here with me, sweet son,*
ché la mia vita vo' finir con teco.	*I long to be with you 'til my life's done.*

(emphasis mine)

In Muzi's text the father emphasizes the material benefits the son has enjoyed and would be leaving behind; in Pulci's revision, he stresses his love for his son and the great sorrow at his decision to depart (see especially the italicized lines).

In a related innovation, Pulci has the prodigal son, on his return home, think to himself what he will say when he meets his father (43). It is a passage that gives some psychological depth to the character and mitigates the abrupt leap in time and space, as the son moves from far away to home in Muzi's two consecutive octaves. In Pulci's intervening octave we follow the son along the road that takes him home.

Both plays present the misfortunes of the prodigal son through the allegory of the seven capital sins that are his traveling companions. In Muzi's play this occupies three octaves (27–29), in the second of which the seven sins are listed. Pulci develops this scene in nine octaves (28–36), giving each sin an octave of self-presentation, an addition with both a didactic purpose (explication of the sins) and entertainment value (actors would presumably represent the sins, through gestures, voice, and costume). Elsewhere Pulci eliminates the allegorical names Muzi attributes to the father's bookkeeper and servants: Libero Arbitrio (Free Will), his money manager, Speranza (Hope) and Providenza (Providence), his servants. Pulci prefers common nouns and refers to these characters as the accountant (*cassiere*) and servants (*servi*).

Another small but interesting change that Pulci made was to eliminate three octaves of conversation between the elder son and his father after the prodigal son has departed (Muzi: 32–34). In the first two octaves, Muzi has the good son tell his father that he will manage his land for him, keep the books, and deal with the laborers who are used to cheating them:

The elder son to his father:

32
[…]

Con ciaschduno io starò attento	I will take care (in my dealings) with each one
di non far quistion, e non muover lite.	not to disagree nor start an argument.
Del far ragione ne saranno strani,	It will be difficult to get them to agree to terms
però che l'uso è cosí de' villani.	since that's just the way the country folk are.

33

Fatemi dare il libro e iscritture	Have the books and accounts given to me
ched i' son certo ched e' negheranno.	for I am certain they will disagree (with our [accounting)
A dire il vero, hanno le teste dure,	To tell the truth they have hard heads,
e hannoci fatto pur di molto inganno.	and they have cheated us many times.

[…]

The father responds less harshly regarding his debtors:

34
[…]

A far ragione i' sarò sempre intero	I'll always be honest in my business
con misericordia al nostro amico.	showing mercy to a friend.
Se la chiedera\<nno\> sanza ingannare,[139]	If they will ask and not cheat,
el debito lor farò cancellare.	I'll have their debt cancelled.

---

139. This line in Newbigin's edition (271) has "chiedera\<n\>." I have added an "no" as well to the truncated verb, which seems to me necessary for the meter.

This brief exchange is perhaps Muzi's attempt to present the elder son from the beginning as one who is unforgiving, as we will see him at first when the prodigal son returns home. The spiritual connotations of the term "misericordia" (mercy) seem significant in this context. The father's willingness to forgive a debt if the debtor is honest and asks for "misericordia" points to the allegory: God's willingness to pardon the sinner who repents and asks for mercy. Pulci, nevertheless, omits it, substituting an octave in which she depicts the elder son as a kind and willing helper of his father, and she makes no reference to their associates nor any mention of the books or other business details, mercantile concerns which she may have found unnecessary and digressive. She writes:

The elder son:

40

Ciò che tu di' fia fatto volentieri.	What you command, that willingly I'll do,
Lievati, padre, dal cuore ogni doglia:	From your heart, Father, banish every woe,
vo' che tu viva senza alcun pensieri.	Free from all cares I hope that you will live,
Ista' sopra di me di buona voglia;	Burden me then with anything you will;
provisto fia a ciò che fa mestieri.	I shall attend to what needs doing, so
La mente tua d'ogni pensieri spoglia	Set your mind free from all anxiety,
e da te scaccia tanta passiöne	And rid yourself of such great suffering
per non esser di tua morte cagione.	So it will not precipitate your death.

For Pulci he is a good son, and she stresses this from the beginning. Later, his disappointment at the feasting for his wayward brother's return is shown to be the result of incomprehension, not ill will. This change is consistent with Pulci's general process of humanizing the family relationships and imposing psychological realism on their interactions.

Pulci also adds to the conversation between father and repentant son the father's prayer of thanksgiving for his son's return (48), and she gives another octave to the father in which to express his relief and happiness (55). She introduces a second octave to the elder son's complaint that the festivities are being held for his wayward brother, and, in it, to his anger and disappointment she adds his sadness: "With sorrow, by my faith, my heart will break" ("Di doglia, per mia fé, mi scoppia il core" 62.6).

Both plays offer the same interpretation of the parable; however Muzi gives it to the father, as his final speech and as the *licenza* (envoy), or adieu to the audience, in his case the young boys of a confraternity. Pulci has the angel, instead, give voice to the divine wisdom of the proverb, taking this metacritical statement out of the story and giving it to a heavenly messenger. She also adds a final octave in which the angel addresses those in attendance who have contemplated the meaning of the parable, asking them to give thanks to God and to pray that He teach them how to merit eternal glory after this brief life. In both plays the meaning of the parable is said to be that the sinner who truly repents will be forgiven, and that the penitent who humbles himself before God will be exalted (Muzi: 63; Pulci: 70).[140]

For Georges Ulysse, the *Play of the Prodigal Son* is Pulci's best effort. He praises her theatrical sensibility shown in the opening card game, the lively, natural dialogue she attributes to her characters, and her ability to depict their personalities. He finds her work in no way inferior to that of Castellano Castellani, and her expression of emotion and humanity, preferable.[141]

Castellani's play, aside from the opening game of cards, probably suggested to him by the scene in Pulci's play, is a very different rendering of the parable. Rather than rely on allegorical figures to lead the boy astray, Castellani has him encounter several bad companions to whom he regularly falls prey. Bruno, an innkeeper, and some ruffians eat and drink at his expense, win his money at cards, offer him other pleasures for a price, and in the end leave him penniless. The language of the play is colloquial, often obscure jargon, more in the style of Luigi than of Antonia or Bernardo Pulci. The action shifts back and forth between the prodigal son on his escapades and his father and brother working and worrying at home. The son's evil companions turn him away when he has lost all his money and

---

140. For a history of interpretations of this parable, see *Interpretazione e invenzione. La parabola del Figliol Prodigo tra interpretazioni scientifiche e invenzioni artistiche*, ed. Giuseppe Galli (Atti dell'ottavo colloquio sulla interpretazione, Macerata, 17–19 marzo 1986) (Genoa: Mariotti, 1987), especially Vittorio Fusco, "Narrazione e dialogo nella parabola detta del figliol prodigo (Lc 15, 11–32)," 17–67, and Enrico Cattaneo, "L'interpretazione di Lc 15, 11–32 nei Padri della Chiesa," 69–96.

141. G. Ulysse, "Un Couple d'écrivans," 188–91.

his clothes. His suffering is narrated at length and he is given several octaves of lament. Following the happy reunion and the conclusion of the play, a young man with a lyre sings the moral of the parable in sixteen octaves; he repeats with comment and interpretation the main events of the story, insisting upon the great peril to salvation posed by the senses. Castellani's is quite a different explication and dramatic rendering of the parable than either that of Muzi or of Pulci.

The Destruction of Saul and the Lament of David

The final play of this collection, *The Destruction of Saul and the Lament of David*, is almost certainly the play attributed to Antonia Pulci by Fra Antonio Dolciati. There is no other known early play in the Florentine repertory on this subject, and there is also internal evidence in the play that, I believe, argues for Pulci's authorship.

There is an early edition of this play, published during Pulci's lifetime, most likely by Bartolomeo de' Libri.[142] The typeface and woodcuts are like those of the second editions of the *St. Guglielma* and the *St. Francis* plays, also attributed to that publisher (Figures 8–10). The play, typical of the late fifteenth-century *sacre rappresentazioni*, though unlike Pulci's *Prodigal Son Play*, privileges variety and complication over fidelity to the religious story and consistency of message. Based primarily on the Biblical subject that gives the play its title, the actions portrayed also belong to the romance and to the virgin martyr traditions. Indeed this play seems to represent a coming together of many elements we have found earlier in Antonia Pulci's theater.

The principal action of the play is taken from the Old Testament account of the battle between the Hebrews and the Philistines in which Saul's sons are killed and he commits suicide (1 Sam. 31, recounted also in Chron. 10: 10 and 13–14). It includes the report of

142. I have consulted the copy of this edition at the Riccardiana Library in Florence, Ed. R. 686/17. Erhard Lommatzsch published the play in *Beiträge zur älteren Italianischen Volksdictung*, vol. 17, Band IV, 2 teil: *Sacre Rappresentazioni* (Berlin: Akademie Verlag, 1963), 79–97; his edition, which is not error-free, is based on a sixteenth-century Florentine edition of the play, published in 1559, (probably the edition included in the 1559 Florentine anthology of the Giunti). There was another edition, published in Florence by Zanobi Tozi [Tosi] da Prato in 1547. Leone Allacci (in his *Drammaturgia*) mentions an edition of the play published by Bonetti in Siena at the end of the century [1590 or 1600].

Saul's death to David, the execution of the messenger, and David's lament (2 Sam. 1). There follows an account, which seems to be entirely original, of the capture and execution of Saul's wife, a figure who in the Biblical text appears only as a name.[143] In addition to the standard opening announcement (*annunziazione*) and concluding envoy (*licenza*) delivered by an angel, there is another action that serves as a frame for the Biblical story: first Saul at home sends a new governor to his subject city of Beth-Shan (octaves 1–6), while the leader of the Philistines, his enemy, makes plans to take the city and bids farewell to his wife and daughters, promising both his daughter Clareta and the city of Beth-Shan to his captain, if the Philistines are successful in defeating the Hebrews and taking the city (7–17). This scene has all the earmarks of romance: there is a king and his nobles are "barons," his wife and daughter have attendants ("compagne," "damigelle"), and the prize offered to the bravest soldier is marriage to a princess and the rule of a subject city.[144] The scene of adieu is reminiscent of the one in the *St. Guglielma* (25–26) in which the king sets out for the Holy Land, leaving his wife and brother to govern in his absence.[145] In this play the Philistine king turns to the queen and says (14, 1–4):

I' ti lascio lo scetro e 'l segno e 'l regno	My scepter, seal, my realm I leave with you,
e fa' di governarlo con amore.	And please be sure to govern it with love.
Giustizia osservi perch' è 'l primo segno	Rule here with justice; that's the foremost sign,
e sopra tutto fa' d'avere onore!	And, most of all, earn honor for yourself!

---

143. Ahinoam, the wife of Saul, is mentioned only once, in 1 Sam. 14:50: ". . .and the name of Saul's wife was Ahinoam the daughter of Ahimaaz." One of David's wives was also called Ahinoam, and she was captured by the Amalekites but later saved by David (1 Sam. 30: 5, 18). Perhaps the story of this Ahinoam inspired Pulci's episode of the capture and death of Saul's widow. On Saul's wives, see n25 to the Italian text of the play.

144. There is an inconsistency in the text: in octave 18.5–6, and 84.3–6. See notes 16 and 57 to the Italian edition of the play.

145. "I know it is not lawful to desert/ The realm; so you must in my place remain;/With justice and with prudence will you rule;/And when I go, don't find my leaving cruel ("Non è lecito sol lasciar il regno,/ però bisogna che in mio luogo stia;/ reggerai con giustizia e con prudenza/ e non ti pesi questa mia partenza." *Santa Guglielma*, 25.5–8).

Saul too, in octave 27.3–6, leaves his queen in charge of his kingdom in his absence:

Làscioti el regno, e fa' con diligenza	This realm I leave you; rule with diligence
e la giustizia abbi a governare.	And govern justly. Take the scepter here,
Tien qui lo scetro, adopera prudenza,	And, until the time that I once more assume
tanto che nel mie seggio abbia ' tornare;	My throne, employ great prudence, …

These two similar scenes underscore a pattern found from the beginning of the play and throughout, in which the actions of the two kings are juxtaposed as the scene shifts back and forth between them at court and their troops on the battlefield. And indeed the scene changes are many and hard to follow in a reading of the text (I have written additional stage directions for the Italian text and English translation to make the many displacements of the action as clear as possible). The changes of venue could be made more obvious on a stage with clearly defined *luoghi*: the two courts and camps (not always clearly distinct), the city of Beth-Shan (or perhaps just the city gate), the battlefield at Mount Gilboa, David's retreat, and the scene where the execution of Saul's widow takes place. While the proliferation of scene changes and the difficulty of performing them might make one think that the play was written for devotional reading rather than theatrical recitation, there are several scenes in the play that lend themselves very well to performance, a few that could be especially effective on stage, to which I will return.

Pulci has added liberally to the Biblical text, first of all with the introduction of the family of the Philistine king. Clareta, his daughter, has a name that is certainly not Biblical, but is suggestive instead of the romance tradition, and the name of their servant Melino is Italianate (suggestive of Merlino, the sorcerer of the chivalric tradition). If this were not enough innovation in a play that dramatizes a well-known Biblical account, there is also a startling anachronism: the Philistine captains and soldiers are called Turks! Pulci acknowledges this in the stage directions just before octave 77, where she writes "The Turks, that is the Philistines, all fall asleep." ("E turchi, cioè e filistei cascono tutti adormentati.")

The odd names attributed to the enemy king and his soldiers, which seem to be entirely invented, are perhaps intended to suggest Turkish names. The king is called Disnudo, and his captains are Carfase, the "first Turk," and Ginieri, the "second Turk." It is this last name, vaguely reminiscent of Janissary, *giannizzero* in Italian, a Turkish soldier, that suggests the connection.[146] Though it is a jolting anachronism, it comes as no surprise that Pulci would depict the enemy as Turks in this century of Turkish expansion in the Mediterranean, of the fall of Constantinople in 1453, and of the savage destruction of the Venetian colony of Negroponte in 1470 and of Otranto in Southern Italy in 1480. Fear of the Turks was widespread in Italy, and they are represented in Italian literature of the time as cruel and ferocious enemies. Vespasiano da Bisticci, whose bookshop was in the center of Florence, only a few steps from the Tanini family home, wrote a *Lamento d'Italia per la presa d'Otranto fatta dai Turchi nel 1480* (Lament of Italy for the siege of Otranto carried out by the Turks in 1480).[147] The Turks were the "Infidel," whom Pope Pius II in mid-century had hoped to convert and against whom he sought to launch a crusade, against whom preachers of the time railed. Pulci's anachronism is an analogy—the contemporary situation as reenactment or continuation of the Old Testament war of God's people against the infidel—and with it she adds her voice to those of her contemporaries. As we would expect, she shows the enemy to be fierce and cruel in battle, yet she depicts them rather sympathetically in their domestic life. Disnudo and his family are a lot like Saul and his family when they are at home.[148] These domestic court scenes come to her from romance

---

146. I thank the Turkish scholar Ebru Turan for suggesting this possible connection (private communication by email, 28 June 2006). Turan also proposed a possible link between the name Ginieri and Jem, the younger son of Mehmet, the Sultan who conquered Constantinople. Jem (called Zemzeme and Zimzim) was well known in Italy, since he died in Rome in 1494, of poison, it seems, and perhaps at the hand of the Pope on agreement with his brother the Ottoman sultan Bayazid II.

147. Ludovico Frati published the *Lament* at the end of his edition of Bisticci's *Vite* (Bologna: Romagnoli dall'Acqua, 1892–93), 3: 306–25. For Vespasiano, as for many others, especially the preachers, the destruction of Otranto was divine punishment for the sins of Christians and a call to penitence.

148. It is interesting in this connection that one of the episodes she chose to represent in the *San Francesco* was Francis's attempt to convert the Sultan (not surprising, though, since it

literature, but, as we have seen in her other plays, it is a characteristic of her style to emphasize the human qualities of her characters, especially their affectionate family relationships.

Pulci added still more to the Biblical account. In addition to the courtly frame she imposed on the action and the contemporary analogy, Pulci gives voice to characters fleeing from the rout at Beth-Shan and on the battlefield, and she invents the episode of the Hebrew queen's martyrdom. The language she uses to recount the battle reflects the influence of the narrative poems of the Pulci brothers, Luigi and Luca. This is especially noticeable in the language of insults, such as "vile and evil dog"("tristo can villano" 20.4), "evil, wicked dog" ("quel can tristo e rio" 30.4), "villainous dog" ("can fello" 46.3), "villainous cur" ("can villano" 54.8), and "I'd not give a fig for them," ("I' non gli stimo un fico," 53.5), a way of denigrating the enemy typical of the popular *cantare* tradition. Luigi Pulci, for example, in the *Morgante*, commonly refers to the Saracen enemies as "dogs" ("cani"), and his adjectives for them are most often "villainous" ("villano"), "evil" or "wicked" ("tristo" or "fello").

In the Biblical text the traveler who gives David the news of Saul's death claims to have killed the king at the king's own request, because he was seriously wounded, and would not have survived; he insists that he took Saul's crown and his armlet only in order to give them to David (2 Sam.1: 9–10). Pulci makes this character more deserving of the fate he meets at David's hand by portraying him as deceitful, happy to find Saul dead, and hoping to gain favor with David by declaring that it was he who slew the king. On finding Saul's body, the traveler says to himself:

---

was one of the famous episodes of Francis's biography and was depicted in the Bardi Chapel frescoes). In that episode, while she depicts the Saracens as fearful enemies, she portrays the Sultan as a reasonable man, who would like to convert to Christianity, but is afraid of the reaction of his cruel subjects (*St. Francis*, 49–64, see 62–63). She does not go so far as her source, the *Fioretti*, which claims that because of his encounter with Francis, the Sultan eventually converted and was baptized (*Fioretti, di S. Francesco*, chapter 24, "Come santo Francesco convertì alla fede il Soldano di Babilonia," ed. Guido Battelli [Turin: UTET, 1929], 55–57).

51–52

Or vedra' che ventura sarà questa	Now you will see what good luck this may be
e s'i' aricchirò pur qui 'n un tratto.	And see if I'll grow rich here all at once.
I' vo' cavargli questa sopravesta	I shall relieve him of this cloak of his,
e la corona e caminar vie ratto.	And of this crown and hurry on my way.

[…]

So ch'è Davit<te> collo gran<de> isdegno	I know that David harbors great disdain
e, come vedrà questo, tal tinore	So when he sees these, this is what I'll say:
dirò: ch'i' l'abbia morto col mie brando.	With my sword I struck down Saul today.
Gran tesoro daràmmi al mie comando.	Great treasure he will place at my command.

In Pulci's treatment of the scene, David is not fooled and responds in anger, calling the man a "villainous cur" ("can villano" 54.8), a "little thief" ("ladroncello" 58.1) and a "felon" ("felloncello" 58.4). With this new slant to the scene Pulci prepares and justifies David's summary condemnation of the man, which is left ambiguous in the Biblical text.

Pulci's most significant addition to the Biblical story, however, is the account of the death of Saul's wife (69–81). Ahinoam is not named in the play; she is simply called Saul's queen (Reina di Saul), but the playwright identifies her by having her say that she loves Saul's sons, Jonathan, Aminadab [Abinadab], and Melchi [Malchishua], even though they are not hers (octave 28).[149] The episode, while not part of the Biblical account, may have been suggested to Pulci by the passage in 1 Sam. 30:5 in which David's wives, one of whom is also named Ahinoam, are captured by the Amalekites.[150]

The attention the playwright gives to this figure makes her an important protagonist of the play, along with Saul and David. The queen's interrogation by the enemy king, her torture, death, and the miracles that accompany it, follow the familiar pattern of the virgin martyr play. The dialogue, however, in the interrogation scene is among the most lively and realistic that Pulci wrote (see especially octaves 71–73). The rhythm of the queen's language in octave 71 is that of the spoken Florentine vernacular, which we could not capture

---

149. The Bible mentions that Saul has two wives and a concubine (2 Sam. 3:7).

150. However, David, in 1 Sam. 18, saves his wives.

in translation. Responding to Disnudo's demand to know the whereabouts of Saul, she says:

71 (1–4)

A tuo dimanda i' non so dar risposta	I don't know how to answer your demand
né dirti di Saul dove si sia;	Nor tell you where King Saul may be; for sure
per certo è strana questa tuo proposta,	This question that you pose is very strange;
non l'ho veduto po' che gli andò via.	I have not seen him since he went away.

This queen of the Israelites has a heavy Florentine accent, which we hear especially in the use of Florentine forms and speech patterns characteristic of the late Quattrocento: the invariable possessive pronoun "tuo" (3), the apocope, the loss of the final syllable of "poi" in the temporal conjunction "po' che," and the use of "gli" as subject pronoun.[151]

The episode of the arrest, interrogation, and martyrdom of Saul's widow is the part of the play best suited for theatrical perform-

---

151. These characteristics of spoken Florentine appear in all of Pulci's plays, but they are more pronounced in those printed by Bartolomeo de' Libri, a Florentine priest and printer. Antonia Pulci's language in the plays she published with Antonio Miscomini is different enough from her language in Bartolomeo de' Libri's editions to suggest that someone working for Miscomini may have intervened with the intention of distinguishing the poetic text from the spoken language. It is less likely that it was Bartolomeo de' Libri to have added spoken Florentine forms to the texts he printed, though it is certainly possible that he did so inadvertently. Miscomini was born in Modena and worked in Venice before coming to Florence, and, perhaps for that reason, found the spoken Florentine unfamiliar and inappropriate for verse; however, it is more likely that he sought to elevate the language of the poetry he published under the influence of the Florentine humanists of the Medici circle, especially Poliziano and Landino, who found the Florentine vernacular too limited in its lexicon and unpleasant in its sounds. The humanists of the circle of Lorenzo de' Medici turned to the language of the Tuscan Trecento and to Latin for forms with which to improve the literary language, to make it more elegant. Among the important studies of spoken and literary Florentine of the period, which I have consulted, are Guido Ghinassi, *Il volgare letterario nel Quattrocento e le* Stanze *del Poliziano* (Florence: Le Monnier, 1957), Gianfranco Folena's study and edition, *Motti e facezie del Piovano Arlotto* (Milan-Naples: Ricciardi, 1953), Paola Manni, "Ricerca sui tratti fonetici e morfologici del fiorentino quattrocentesco," *Studi di grammatica italiana*, 8 (1979): 115–71, and Mirko Tavoni's chapter "Gli umanisti e il volgare," and the anthology of Florentine texts in his, *Storia della lingua italiana. Il Quattrocento* (Bologna: Il Mulino, 1992), 57–83, 175–205.

ance. Following the animated conversation between Saul's widow and King Disnudo are two scenes of miraculous interventions in which the action on stage is abruptly frozen. The soldiers sent to torture the queen and put her to death remain motionless, as though in a trance, when an angel appears on stage. When the angel leaves, they awaken, unaware of the interruption. In the first of these two scenes, the angel has come in answer to the queen's prayer, but only she acknowledges his presence; he informs her that Saul is dead and that she will receive the palm of martyrdom. In the second scene, after the queen is hanged by her hair from a tree, beaten, and left to die, the angel again appears, this time to take her body away, protecting it from desecration by pagan hands. Once the angel has departed the scene is reanimated and there is general confusion.

The two scenes of suspended animation, the repartee of the queen to her persecutors, and her gruesome torture and death, coming near the end of the action, give the figure of Saul's widow a more dramatic and prominent role in the play than that of either Saul, David, or their enemy Disnudo, to whom is given the concluding scene of the play. Purportedly on the defeat and death of Saul and the sorrow of David, the play is to a greater extent the story of the martyrdom of Saul's widow and a portrayal of female heroism. It is worth noting, and perhaps not unintended, that with this figure of a saintly widow Pulci will have provided examples of female sanctity and heroism for all three of what were then considered the 'stages' of a woman's life, for the virgin with Saint Domitilla, the wife with Saint Guglielma, and now the widow, with Saul's queen.[152] It is a play that seems clearly to belong in the Pulci canon.

It is perhaps going too far to speculate that Pulci wrote this play in her widowhood, but it did not appear in the Miscomini anthology, and the only known fifteenth-century edition almost certainly comes from the press that published the second edition of her *St. Guglielma* and *St. Francis* plays.

---

152. Emanuela Carney, in "Antonia Pulci's *Rappresentazione di Santa Domitilla*," 12–13, suggests that the three plays represent a trilogy on women, distinguished according to their status.

Editions

I have based the Italian text of the *Rappresentazione di Santa Domitilla, the Rappresentazione di Santa Guglielma,* and the *Rappresentazione di San Francesco* on the first known edition of the plays, published in Florence in the late 1480s or the early 1490s and attributed to the printer Antonio Miscomini (Cioni[153] XX n. 1, p. 118; LVIII n. 1, p. 210; and XXXI n. 1, p. 142). In my textual notes I refer to this edition of the three plays as A. All three plays had a second edition in the 1490s. The second edition of *Santa Domitilla* was also published by Miscomini, (Cioni XX n. 2, pp. 118–19), while the second editions of *Santa Guglielma* and *San Francesco* have been attributed to Bartolomeo de' Libri (Cioni LVIII n. 2, p. 210 and XXXI n2, p 143). I call the second editions B, and I have checked the first editions against the second, occasionally correcting errors in A with the version in B. There are copies of these plays in both editions at the Biblioteca Nazionale Centrale of Florence (BNCF). The *Distruzione di Saul e il pianto di Davit* was not included in the Miscomini anthology, and perhaps first appeared in the incunable edition published by Bartolomeo de' Libri; the Biblioteca Riccardiana in Florence owns the only known copy (Cioni XCIIII, n1, p. 276). I have based my text on this edition, which I call A, and I have checked it throughout against the two extant sixteenth-century editions, Florence: Zanobi Tosi da Prato, 1547 and Florence, n. p., 1559 (Cioni XCIIII, n2 and n3, p. 276), both in copies at the BNCF. The *Rappresentazione del figliuol prodigo* almost certainly had a fifteenth-century edition, but none survives. I have based my text on a collation of the three earliest editions, also found at the BNCF: A, an edition lacking typographical information (but 16th c.) and incomplete, interrupted at the end of octave 51 (not in Cioni); B, another which bears no indication of publisher or city but which, according to Cioni, was published ca. 1550 in Florence (Cioni XXX n1, p. 138); and the third, C, published in Florence "Ad istanza de Iacopo Chiti" in 1572 (Cioni XXX n2, p. 138).

Linguistic characteristics of the texts published by Miscomini and those by Bartolomeo de' Libri differ, the latter including elements

---

153. All references numbers to the editions of Pulci's plays are taken from Alfredo Cioni's *Bibliografia delle sacre rappresentazioni* (Florence, Sansoni Antiquariato, 1961).

of spoken Florentine that Miscomini generally eschews, for example, the invariable possessive pronouns *mie, suo,* and *tuo*.[154] Clearly we cannot trust either publisher to have reproduced Antonia Pulci's orthography faithfully.[155]

Note on Editing the Italian Texts

In general I have sought to reproduce the pronunciation rather than the orthography of the original where these do not coincide. I have followed standard procedures for modernizing the orthography of literary texts, and I have corrected obvious errors. My purpose has been to render the texts readable to a modern audience without eliminating important evidence of the culture of the author.

I have resolved abbreviations and the alternation of *u* and *v*, modernized punctuation, the use of diacritical marks and of upper and lower case letters, and I have written *e* or *ed* for *et, &,* and other representations of the conjunction. I introduce the diacritical *i* between *gl* and *a, o,* or *u*; I eliminate the unnecessary *i* following *g* or *c* before *e* and following the group *gn*; and I have regularized the plural of words ending in *–io*. I eliminate the superfluous *h* before *a, o* or *u* and the etymological Latin *h* where it is no longer used today; I add an h where it is used today in forms of the verb *avere*. I substitute *z* or *zi* for the Latin groups *ti* and *cti* and double the consonant *t* in the Latin groups *ct, pt,* and *bt* (except in the case of *nct* where I only eliminate the *c* and *mpt*, which I rewrite as *nt*); I also assimilate *mn* and *bs*, which are rewritten *nn* or *n* and *ss*; and I transcribe *x* as *ss* when intervocalic. I substitute *i* for the Greek graph *y* and *f* for *ph*.

I have left the oscillation of single and double consonants where the author's usage is unclear, making an exception, however, for proper names, which are regularized in order to eliminate confusion; and I have consistently eliminated the doubling of a consonant when

---

154. For these terms and other characteristics of spoken Florentine in fifteenth century, see Paula Manni, "Ricerche sui tratti fonetici e morfologici del fiorentino quattrocentesco," 115–71; on the invariable possessive pronouns, see 131–35. See also *S. Guglielma,* n1.

155. On the many ways a text was altered at the printer's and the many reasons for it, see Paolo Trovato, *Con ogni diligenza corretto. La stampa e le revisioni editoriali dei testi letterari italiani* (1470–1570) (Bologna: Il Mulino, 1991).

it follows a liquid or nasal consonant (e.g. *nanzzi=>nanzi*) and regularized the use of *n* and *m* before labial and labiodental consonants (e.g *impunto=> in punto*) I have joined words that were separated in early texts but no longer today and vice versa, unless doing so misrepresented the sound of an intervening consonant: for example, I have united articulated prepositions where there is a double l; otherwise, I have written them separately. I have eliminated syntactic doubling when to do so does not change the pronunciation (*allei => a lei , ellei=> e lei, essara=> e sarà*, etc.) so as not to encumber the text with marks and spellings unfamiliar to a modern reader; I have conserved *nolla* and *nommi*.

Pulci's texts are characterized by the absorption of the preposition *a* when followed by a word beginning with *a*. I have indicated this with a spaced apostrophe ("Rispondono i servi di Domitilla ' Aureliano," *Santa Domitilla*, 75).

Since the edited texts are theatrical, in order to facilitate the delivery of the lines with the proper rhythm, I have truncated words that occur in mid verse, when, though they were written out in their entirety in the early texts, it is required by the meter. For example: "e con questi baron*i* presto n'andrai," has been rewritten "e con questi baron presto n'andrai," (*Santa Domitilla*, 4.5); "benché 'l partir*e* da te mi duole e spiace;" as "benché 'l partir da te mi duole e spiace;" (idem, 7.3), or "di poi figliuo*li* che nella tua vechieza," as "di poi figliuo' che nella tua vechieza," (idem, 13.5; the italics are mine).

Other transcription issues are indicated and explained in footnotes.

The English translations

The English translations of the plays are by James Wyatt Cook; and, except for the *Destruction of Saul and the Lament of David*, an earlier version appeared in Antonia Pulci, *Florentine Drama for Convent and Festival*, ed. James Wyatt Cook and Barbara Collier Cook (Chicago: University of Chicago Press, 1996). These translations are published here in a new edition; they have been corrected following my suggestions, and in them we have introduced some rhymed couplets in an effort to reproduce occasionally the rhythm of the original.

Many of the endnotes that accompany the Italian editions are linguistic and refer exclusively to the Italian text. Some, however, treat broader issues and can be helpful for reading both the Italian and the English versions of the plays. Only those that pertain to both the Italian and English texts are noted in the English translation, and, in the interest of simplicity, their numbering is keyed to the Italian text (e.g., in the English *Play of St. Domitilla*, notes relevant to the English translation are 1, 7, 17, etc.). The titles of the plays and the names of the characters in the notes (with few exceptions) are given only in Italian.

THE PLAYS OF ANTONIA PULCI

A BILINGUAL PRESENTATION

La rappresentazione di Santa Domitilla

INTERLOCUTORI

PROLOGO
IMPERADORE Domiziano
AURELIANO, nobile romano
[Molti baroni di Aureliano]*
DOMITILLA, nipote dell'Imperatore
NEREO, servo in casa di Domitilla
ARCHILEO, servo in casa di Domitilla
PAPA CLEMENTE
I POVERI
UNO CHE DÀ LA LIMOSINA, della casa di Domitilla
SERVO di Aureliano
SERVI dell'Imperatore
DUE VERGINI, also DONZELLE, compagne di Domitilla
GLI SPOSI delle Compagne di Domitilla
LUSSURIO, fratello di Aureliano
MANIGOLDO
CAVALIERE
ERODE, fratello delle Compagne di Domitilla, cieco sanato
SERVA MUTOLA delle Compagne di Domitilla, sanata
*Accompagnano Aureliano, ma non parlano.

The Play of Saint Domitilla

INTERLOCUTORS

PROLOGUE
EMPEROR Domitian
AURELIANUS, noble Roman [also AURELIAN]
[Many barons of Aurelianus]*
DOMITILLA, niece of the Emperor
NEREUS, servant of Domitilla
ARCHILEUS, servant of Domitilla
POPE CLEMENT
PAUPERS
ONE WHO DISTRIBUTES ALMS at Domitilla's house
SERVANT of Aurelianus
SERVANTS of the Emperor
TWO VIRGINS, also MAIDENS, companions of Domitilla
THE BRIDEGROOMS of the Companions of Domitilla
LUXURIUS, brother of Aurelianus
EXECUTIONER
KNIGHT
HEROD, brother of the Companions of Domitilla, blind man healed by Domitilla
mute MAIDSERVANT delle Compagne di Domitilla, healed by Domitilla

*They accompany Aurelianus but do not speak.

[PROLOGO]

        1
O buon Iesù, per la tua gran potenza,
concedi grazia al mio basso intelletto
sì ch'io possa mostrar per tuo clemenza
la sua storia divota e 'l gran concetto
di Domitilla, pien di sapienza,
che volse verso Idio con puro affetto.
Cristiana essendo, vergine sposata,
secretamente a Dio fu consacrata.

        2
Nipote fu questa vergine detta
del gran Domiziano imperadore;
fuggì lo sposo, essendo giovanetta,
e volse l'alma al suo degno fattore;
e per trovar la via vera e perfetta
da potere abitar col suo Signore,
cercando la corona del martire,
al fin nel fuoco poi volse morire.

Lo IMPERADORE *parla a uno suo barone*[1] *chiamato Aureliano e dice come gli ha dato per donna Domitilla:*

        3
Aurelïan, perch'io t'ho sempre amato
quanto conviensi un buon figliuol diletto,
perch'io t'ho visto onesto e costumato,
sendo dal padre tuo pregato e stretto,
per tua sposa diletta io t'ho donato
una donzella di gentile aspetto,
a me nipote di gran pregio e fama,
che Domitilla per nome si chiama;

[THE PROLOGUE]

1

O good Jesus, by your power great
Grant to my lowly intellect such grace
That through your clemency I can present
The great renown and sacred history
Of Domitilla who, with love most pure
And filled with wisdom, pledged herself to God.
A Christian virgin, having been betrothed,
Was consecrated secretly to God.

2

This virgin whom I spoke about was niece
To great Domitian, the Emperor;
She, still a girl, fled from her plighted groom
And to her worthy maker pledged her soul,
So she might find the true and perfect way
That she could go on dwelling with her Lord,
Seeking the crown of martyrdom at last
She gave herself to perish in the fire.

The EMPEROR *speaks to one of his barons[1] named Aurelianus and says he has given him Domitilla as his wife:*

3

Aurelian, since I have ever loved
You as a good and cherished son deserves,
And found you honorable and well brought up,
Entreated by your father secretly,
I've given you for your belovèd wife
A damsel of a noble mien and mild,
My niece, one greatly valued and renowned,
And she is Domitilla, by her name.

4

la qual per mio rispetto accetterai
e sopra ogni altra cosa amerai quella.
So che lieto e felice ne sarai
perché ella è molto graziosa e bella;
e con questi baron presto n'andrai
con molta festa a casa per vedella.
Pregate e nostri dèi che sien propizi
benignamente a questi isposalizi.

Risponde AURELIANO allo Imperadore e dice:

5

Bench'io non sia di tanta sposa degno,
poi ch'è piaciuto alla tua maestate
benignamente il tuo fedele indegno
acompagnar con la tua nobilitate,
io ti ringrazio col mio basso ingegno.
Signor, sia fatto la tua volontate.
Fate questi baroni aparechiare:
andiàn la nuova sposa a vicitare.[2]

AURELIANO *con molti baroni va a vicitare la sua sposa Domitilla e dice giunto a lei:*

6

Tu sia la ben trovata, o cara sposa,
tu sola se' dolceza del mio core.
O Domitilla, sopra ogni altra cosa
da me amata con perfetto amore,
sappi ch'ogni speranza in te si posa,
che se' di tutte l'altre il vero onore.

Risponde DOMITILLA 'Aureliano:[3]

E tu, mio sposo, il ben venuto sia,
con tutta questa degna compagnia.

4

Accept her, for you owe me this respect,
Beyond all else, too, love her faithfully.
I know that you'll be happy when you do.
For she is very gracious and she's fair,
And with these barons you will quickly go
With great festivity and ask to see
Her at her home; entreat our gods
To kindly sanctify these nuptials.

AURELIANUS *answers the Emperor and says:*

5

Although for such a highborn spouse I am
Unworthy, since your majesty is pleased
So graciously your loyal subject low
To match with your nobility, I thank
You with my humble intellect, my lord,
And may your will be done; these barons—have
Them get prepared at once and let us ride
To pay a visit to my newfound bride.

AURELIANUS *with many barons goes to visit his betrothed Domitilla and on arriving says to her:*

6

I bid you the most happy day, dear spouse,
You only are the sweetness of my heart,
O Domitilla, more than anything
With perfect love you are by me beloved,
Know that my every hope is placed in you,
For, past all others, you are the true prize.

DOMITILLA *answers Aurelianus:*

And welcome here, dear husband mine, are you—
And welcome all your fine companions too.

Qui dopo alquanta festa di suoni e balli AURELIANO *si parte e dice così a Domitilla:*

7

Rimanti, sposa mia, nella tua pace;
io non posso più teco dimorare,
benché 'l partir da te mi duole e spiace;
di rivederti mill'anni mi pare.
S'alcuna cosa ti diletta o piace,
comanda Aurelïan, ché tu 'l puoi fare.

Risponde DOMITILLA *' Aureliano:*

Che posso io più da te, sposo, volere,
se non che tu mi torni a rivedere?

Partito Aureliano, uno servo di Domitilla detto NEREO *dice con l'altro servo chiamato Archileo:*

8

O Archileo, tu sai con quanto amore
la madre di costei, venendo a morte,
essendo ognun di noi suo servidore,
sorella dette a noi questa per sorte,
perché l'amaestrassin nel Signore
Cristo Iesù, ch'è nella eterna corte,
sendo la madre sua e lei cristiana.
Or si congiunge alla legge pagana.

Vanno questi dua servi a Domitilla, partito Aureliano, per convertirla di servare virginità e dicono fra loro. E prima detto ARCHILEO *dice:*

9

Immenso Iddio, dacci tanta forteza
che per tua grazia a te facciàn tornare
costei che la tua legge non appreza;
nolla lasciare in perdimento andare

After some festivity of music and dancing, AURELIANUS *bids farewell, and says to Domitilla:*

7

Remain, my bride, in your tranquility;
I cannot longer linger at your side—
Though parting from you grieves and saddens me;
A thousand years 'twill seem before we meet.
If aught delight or please in any way,
Know you can ask Aurelian, for you may.

DOMITILLA *answers Aurelianus:*

What can I wish from you except, O spouse,
That you'll return to see me at my house?

When Aurelianus has gone, a servant of Domitilla, NEREUS, *says to the other servant, Archileus:*

8

Archileus, you know with what great love
Her mother, as she was about to die,
Since each of us did serve her as a slave,
Made her our sister, as our destiny,
So we would teach her of Lord Jesus Christ
Who reigns in the eternal court, for both
She and her mother Christians were. She now
Intends to marry into the pagan law.

The two servants go to Domitilla, after Aurelianus has left, to convert her to a life of virginity, and the two speak. First the one called ARCHILEUS *says:*

9

O God immense, pray give us such great strength
That by your grace we bring her back to you.
She does not know the value of your law—
And don't let her immortal soul be damned

allo sposo mortal, che con presteza
la sua verginità gli vuol furare.
Benigno Redentor, che intendi e puoi,
fa' che tu guidi questi servi tuoi.

ARCHILEO *rivolto a Nereo dice così:*

10
Nereo, andiàn con l'aiuto di Dio
alla nostra madonna Domitilla,
ché egli è tanto clemente e giusto e pio
forteza ci darà di convertilla
e vorrà contentar nostro desio;
nel cor gli accenderà qualche favilla
del dolce amor che la convertiremo
e di cotanto ben cagion saremo.

Giunti a Domitilla, UNO DI DETTI SERVI *dice così:*

11
Madonna, benché sia presunzione
el servo il suo signore amaestrare,
perch'io ti porto grande affezione
la verità non si convien celare,
la qual credendo, tu sarai cagione
farti felice su nel ciel posare
tra le vergine elette in compagnia,
se vorrai prender la diritta via.

12
O Domitilla, con che vestimenti
adorni il corpo tuo per compiacere
al tuo marito. E se altri ornamenti
facessi all'alma, ancor potresti avere
per isposo Iesù, ch'a' sua serventi
concede il ciel per grazia a possedere,

By mortal spouse who hastens to her bed
To seize her maidenhood without delay.
Redeemer kind, since you know how, and can,
Give guidance to us now to foil his plan.

ARCHILEUS *turns to Nereus and says:*

      10
Nereus, with God's help now let us go
To see our lady Domitilla, for
He's so clement, compassionate, and just,
That to convert her he will give us strength
And he will want to satisfy our wish;
Within her heart a spark of gentle love
Will kindle so that we'll convert her; thus
We shall become the cause of much great good.

Having come before Domitilla, ONE OF THE SAID SERVANTS *says:*

      11
My lady, though it seems presumptuous
To have a servant educate his lord,
Since I feel such great affection for you
It is improper for me to conceal
The truth that, once you believe it, will become
The happy cause of setting you in heaven
Amid the company of chosen virgins,
If you will choose to take the righteous way.

      12
O Domitilla, with what garments you
Array your body to make your spouse rejoice,
But if with other ornaments your soul
You would adorn, then Jesus you could have
To be your spouse, who to his servants grants
That, through his grace, in heaven they may dwell;

el quale è vero Idio, Sposo eternale,
e 'l tuo Aurelïan è uom mortale.

Risponde DOMITILLA *a' servi e dice:*

      13
Io non so qual si sia maggior dolceza
ch'aver marito che sia di te degno
per consumar con lui sua giovaneza,
giovane e ricco e di gentile ingegno,
di poi figliuo' che nella tua vechieza
sien di tua vita bastone e sostegno.
E chi può disprezar le cose certe
per le future, le qual sono incerte?

UNO DE' SERVI *risponde a Domitilla:*

      14
Tu, Domitilla, ha' posto ogni tua cura
nella pompa del mondo sì fallace,
la qual sì come fior passa e non dura;
e cerchi ove non puoi trovar mai pace,
non pensando a colei che presto fura,
quando più il viver ci diletta e piace,
ogni speranza, e nessuno è sì forte
che non vinca costei chiamata Morte.

Segue detto SERVO:

      15
Ciò che tu vedi è in man della fortuna;
tal che fu degno ha poi fatto infelice
costei, con chi non val difesa alcuna;
e però[4] non si può chiamar felice
nessun che vive qui sotto la luna,
se non colui ch'al mondo contradice

He is the true God, an eternal Spouse;
A mortal man is your Aurelianus.

DOMITILLA *answers the servants:*

13
What greater sweetness could be, I don't know,
Than having a husband worthy of one's self
And sharing with one's mate the bloom of youth—
A mate young, rich and with a courteous wit—
Thereafter children, who in one's old age
Will be one's life's support, its staff; and who
Can cease to value certainties? Who would
Exchange them for uncertainties to come?

ONE OF THE SERVANTS *answers Domitilla:*

14
You, Domitilla, have placed your every trust
In the pomp of this false world, which will,
Just like a flower, pass and not endure,
And, where you seek, peace never can be found,
You think not on that one who, just when life
Delights us most—most pleases, quickly steals
Our every hope; but no man's strong enough
To not be conquered by the one named Death,

That SERVANT *continues:*

15
The visible world lies in Fortune' hands.
She, against whom no defense prevails,
Makes men once worthy fall to wretchedness.
And thus no one who lives beneath the moon
Can be called happy, but a person who
Will set his face against the world and turn

volgendo a quel ch'è d'ogni ben cagione.
È cieca e falsa ogni altra opinione.

Risponde DOMITILLA *a' servi:*

16
Qual cosa è più difficil che sprezare
della vita presente le richeze
e non voler tanti piaceri usare,
l'umane pompe e tante gentileze,
per volere altra vita al fin trovare,
la qual di te s'acquista con aspreze,
con tormenti e digiuni e discipline?[5]
Intendale chi può vostre dottrine!

UNO DE' DETTI SERVI *a Domitilla risponde e dice:*

17
Quando sarai congiunta col tuo sposo,
della virginità perderai il nome,
e se ti fia benigno t'è nascoso,
che spesso uom si rallegra e non sa come
ha ' a saper, ché 'l futur sempre è dubioso.[6]
E così si raguaglian queste some:
oggi tu vesti la virginil gonna,
e poi detta sarai femmina e donna.

18
E tu, che non potevi sostenere
che la nobilità tua virginile
fussi sol violata nel pensiere,
la sottometti a un pagan or vile;
e converratti a ogni suo piacere
mutar vita, costumi, modi e stile
e fare ogni suo vil comandamento,
pur che 'l suo desiderio sia contento.

To Him who is the source of every good.
Any opinion else is false and blind.

DOMITILLA *answers the servants:*

      16
What is more difficult than to despise
The riches of this present life and not
Desire to taste the pleasures manifold
Of human splendor, great nobility,
So one can want, at last, another life
That one gains for oneself with torment and
With harshness, fasting, and self-wielded whips?
These doctrines of yours! Who can fathom them?

ONE OF THE SERVANTS *answers and says to Domitilla:*

      17
When you have been united with your spouse,
The title of virginity you'll lose,
And whether or not he'll treat you kindly is
Quite hidden from you, for one's often blithe
But knows not why; the future is unsure.
And so these burdens are weighed side by side:
Now you wear a maiden's gown, but then
You will be called a woman and a wife.

      18
And you, who could not even entertain
The very notion that your virginal
Nobility might be defiled, would bend
Yourself to a base pagan and submit
To every pleasure of his, transform your life,
Your habits, and your manner, and your style;
His every vile commandment you'd perform
So that he'd gratify his appetite.

19

Tutti gli sposi si mostran discreti
quando la donna lor tengon giurata;
voglion parere umili e mansueti
prima che a casa lor l'abbin menata;
però non puoi saper cotal secreti,
se prima un tempo con lui non se' stata.
Sara' pien di paura e di sospetti:
fa' che tu pensi ben di ciò gli effetti.

Risponde DOMITILLA *e dice:*

20

Ben mi ricorda che la madre mia
sostenne molte pene tutti gli anni
della suo vita sol per gelosia
del suo marito con sì gravi affanni;
e s'io credessi seguitar tal via
già mai non vestirei del mondo e panni.
Non credo che 'l mio sposo Aurelïano
questo facessi, perché è molto umano.

UNO DI DETTI SERVI *dice a Domitilla:*

21

Quel ch'io ti parlo spesse volte aviene:
ècci chi tiene amiche o concubine,
e le lor donne con tormenti e pene
batton con molte dure discipline;
per questo molti sdegni si sostiene.
D'ogni cosa si vuol pensare al fine,
alle pene del parto e ' grievi duoli
quando si partoriscono e figliuoli.

22

Alcuna volta ancor nel nascimento
chi nasce muto, attratto o insensato,

                    19
All these husbands put their best foot forward
When their lady is engaged to them;
How humble, then, they wish to seem, and mild
At least until they've led her to their home.
However, secrets like those you can't know,
If you have not first spent some time with him.
You will be filled with fear and full of doubt:
Be sure you think about such outcomes well.

DOMITILLA *answers*:

                    20
My mother suffered, as I well recall,
So many torments throughout all her life;
Because of her husband's jealousy alone
Bore very great distress; and if I were
To think that I would follow such a path,
The garments of the world I'd never don,
Though I don't think my spouse, Aurelian
Would act like this because he is so kind.

ONE OF THE SERVANTS *says to Domitilla*:

                    21
That which I tell you often comes to pass,
Some maintain mistresses or concubines,
And some their ladies batter painfully,
Beat them cruelly with sturdy whips;
Many scornful outbursts, too, wives bear.
One needs to think through all things to their end—
About the pangs of childbirth and the woes
So grievous when the children are brought forth.

                    22
Sometimes, as well, when coming forth, a child
Will be born dumb, deformed, or senseless, whence

onde sente la madre gran tormento,
chi nasce cieco, al mondo disprezato.
Or pensa tu se l'ha' gran pentimento
d'aver cotal figliuol già mai portato.
Alcuna volta la madre morire
fanno e figliuoli innanzi al partorire.

L'ALTRO SERVO *aggiunge e dice:*

23
Santa verginità quanto se' degna,
diletta a Dio e agli angeli cara,
la quale in sempiterno vive e regna
in ciel col suo fattor lucente e chiara!
Quanto è beato chi sotto tua insegna
piglia il camino e questa vita amara
dispreza, la quale è d'affanni piena,
per trovar altra vita più serena.

24
Con penitenza si spegne e peccati,
ma la virginità, poi ch'è perduta,
già mai non può tornar più ne' sua stati.
Misera a quella che questa rifiuta,
ch'ogni altra virtù vince, e tra ' beati
nel sommo ciel con gaudio è ricevuta!
Sì come la reina è la maggiore
di tutte l'altre, questa è 'l vero onore.

25
Getta suave odore apresso a Dio.
Se terrai questa, per sposo arai
un giovane gentil, benigno e pio,
il qual da te non si partirà mai,
cioè, Cristo Iesù, che con disio
delle sue spose in ciel fa festa assai.

The mother will experience great grief;
Some children, those born blind, the world will scorn.
Consider now if you'd have great regret
For ever having borne a child like these.
Sometimes before they're born, some children will
Become the causes of their mothers' deaths.

THE OTHER SERVANT *joins in and says:*

      23
O sacred maidenhood, what worthy joy
You bring to God, and to the angels dear
Who live in heaven for eternity
And with their bright and shining Maker reign!
How blest whoever may, beneath your sign,
That journey undertake, whoever scorns
This bitter life so trouble-filled to find
Another life more tranquil, calm and kind.

      24
With penitence can one atone for sins,
But once virginity is lost, no more
Can it return to its first state again;
Woe unto her who throws it all away!
All other virtues virginity excels;
With joy the saints in heaven welcome it.
And as the queen is greater than the rest,
So is virginity true glory's best.

      25
It wafts a sweet aroma up to God.
If you preserve this, for a spouse you'll have
A noble youth, compassionate and good,
Who will not ever go away from you,
That is Christ Jesus, who, with yearning for
His brides, rejoices greatly in high heav'n.

Qui gaudio certo, qui vero riposo:
beato a chi si volge a tanto sposo.

26
Prendi or di questi dua qual più ti piace:
o questo Aurelïan che de' morire
e lasciar le richezze in contumace,
breve speranza a sì lungo martire;
se vuoi prender Iesù, Sposo verace,
e solo a lui desideri servire,
dolceza senza affanno ch'è infinita,
e ti darà dopo la morte vita.

Risponde DOMITILLA *a' dua servi e dice:*

27
E' mi par già sentire il core aprire,
tanta potenza han le vostre parole;
e quel ch' i' ho dentro non vi so scoprire,
ma d'aver tolto sposo assai mi duole,
perché Iesù desidero servire
e la sua santa legge, e sia che vuole,
fuggendo il mondo e ogni pensier vano,
e vo' lasciar lo sposo Aurelïano.

28
Come potrò delle suo man fuggire?
Ma spero nel mio Dio che col suo aiuto
mi darà tanta forza e tanto ardire
che 'l mio giusto pensier sarà adempiuto;
perché non lascia e sua servi perire
e per isposa di nuovo m'ha 'vuto,[7]
vorrà guardar la mia virginitate,
per la infinita sua somma bontate.

Here certain joy, here true repose—she's blest
Who is devoted to so great a spouse.

26

Whichever of these two most pleases you,
Choose now: take either this Aurelian
Who must die, leave his riches in default,
A fleeting hope for such long suffering;
Or, if you want Jesus the true Spouse,
And your desire is to serve him alone,
He'll give untroubled sweetness infinite
To you, and after death will give you life.

DOMITILLA *answers the two servants and says:*

27

Truly I seem to feel my heart unfold,
Such power your words have, and what within
I feel I can't express, but I'm much grieved
I took a spouse because I wish to serve
Christ Jesus, keep his holy law, do all
He asks of me, fleeing the world and each
Vain thought, and I desire now to renounce
The spouse I'd meant to wed, Aurelian.

28

Yet from his hands how can I flee? But still
I place my trust in God, for with his aid
Such courage and great strength he'll give to me
That my just purposes he will fulfill;
Because he does not let his servants die,
And, since for his new bride he's taken me,
He will watch over my virginity
In his great goodness infinite and high.

29
Fate ch'io sia prestamente velata
e consacrata al mio superno Sposo,[8]
il qual m'ha del suo amor tutta infiammata,
ch'a' sua diletti dà sommo riposo.
Eccomi qui presente apparecchiata[9]
servire al mio Signor giusto e pietoso.
Tu che m'apristi e misurasti el core,
fammi costante nel tuo dolce amore.

UNO DE' DETTI SERVI, *rendendo grazie a Dio, dice così:*

30
Io rendo grazie a te, superno Idio,
che ci hai per tua pietà fatto sì degni
e sì contento el nostro buon desio,
che veggiàn caminar sotto tuo insegni
costei che andava in perdimento rio;
or l'hai rivolta a' tua superni regni.
Quanto la tua bontà per noi si mostra,[10]
poi ch'è disposta a far la voglia nostra.

Vanno QUESTI DUA SERVI *a Papa Clemente e dicono come hanno convertita Domitilla e che lui debba venire a vederla e confortarla:*

31
O reverente in Cristo buon pastore,
intendi perché a te venuti siamo;
che la nipote dello Imperadore
a te parente convertita abbiamo,
benché fussi sposata a grande onore
a quel nobil barone Aurelïano.
Ella non cura il suo sposo lasciare,
ché sua virginità vuol conservare.

Risponde PAPA CLEMENTE *a detti servi e dice:*

29

Arrange for me to take the veil[8] at once
And swear allegiance to my heavenly Spouse,
Who's filled me with the fiery flame of love,
Who brings great peace to all those whom he loves.
Behold me present here and all prepared
To serve my Lord, compassionate and just;
Thou who has opened me and seized my heart,
Oh, make me constant in thy tender love.

ONE OF THE SERVANTS, *giving thanks to God, says:*

30

I render thanks to you, supernal God,
Who mercifully have made us of such worth,
And our good purposes so satisfied
That 'neath your banners we see setting forth
One who was on her way to wicked loss;
Now you've aimed her toward your supernal realms.
How much your goodness you've revealed to us
Since to perform our wish she is resolved.

These TWO SERVANTS *go to Pope Clement, explaining that they have converted Domitilla and that he must come to see her and urge her to be strong:*

31

O Reverend Sir, good shepherd of the Christ,
Pray understand why we have come to you;
For we've converted the Emperor's niece, your kin—
Though she with honor great was soon to wed
The noble cavalier Aurelian.
In truth, she would prefer to take her leave
From that Aurelian, for she desires
To keep inviolate her maidenhood.

POPE CLEMENT *answers the servants and says:*

32

Da parte di Iesù grazie vi rendo,
ch'avete così bene adoperato.
Del dolce fuoco suo tutto m'accendo:
eccomi qui presente apparecchiato.
Mostrato hai, buon Iesù, s'io ben comprendo,
quanto se' giusto a' tuo fedeli e grato;
superno Idio, che bene adoperasti,
poi ch'a te questa vergine chiamasti.

Viene CLEMENTE *a casa Domitilla e giunto a lei dice così:*

33

Quel ver Idio, che incarnò di Maria
e che per noi fu crocifisso e morto,
salvi e mantenga te, figliuola mia,
doniti pace e 'l suo dolce conforto.
Veggoti andar per la diritta via,
la quale al fin ricondurrà a buon porto.
Io ti consacro e dono questo velo,
el qual ti manda il tuo Sposo da cielo.

Vengono MOLTI POVERI *a casa Domitilla per limosina e dicono:*

34

Buona madonna, un povero quatrino
a questo infermo e vecchio che non vede;
un po' di pan e un po' del vostro vino,
per Iesù Cristo che per noi si crede.[11]

DOMITILLA *volta a uno suo di casa dice:*

Fate vestir quel povero meschino
e gli altri poi che son di nostra fede;
di tanti ben che Dio ci ha conceduti,
non gli usando per lui sarien perduti.

32

I thank you on behalf of Jesus, for
You have performed a feat of such great good
That his sweet flame has quite enkindled me;
Behold me present and all ready here.
Good Jesus, as I see it, you have shown
How just and gracious to your flock you are;
Supernal God, the moment that you called
This virgin to you, then all goodness flowed.

POPE CLEMENT *goes to Domitilla's house, and when he arrives he says:*

33

That true God who in Mary took on flesh
And who for us was crucified and died,
My daughter, save and keep you; his sweet peace
And comfort may he give to you as well.
I see you on the straight course setting forth
That leads you to safe harbor in the end.
I consecrate you, give to you this veil—
One that your Spouse sends you from heaven above.

MANY PAUPERS *come to the house of Domitilla for alms and they say:*

34

Good lady, a paltry pittance for this old,
Infirm one who cannot see, a little bread,
A little of your wine for Jesus Christ,
The risen Lord in whom we all believe.

DOMITILLA *turns to one of her house servants:*

Arrange to have that needy wretch attired,
Those others too, since they are of our faith,
For all the wealth that God has granted us
Would be quite lost not given in his name.

QUELLO CHE DÀ LA LIMOSINA *dice a uno povero:*

      35
Tien qui! Fa' che tu prieghi Idio per noi
e per costei che viva in castitate;
partite questi don fra tutti voi
e queste cose non ve le giucate.

Risponde UNO DI DETTI POVERI:

Noi pregheremo Idio co' santi suoi
che riserbin nel ciel tal caritate.

UN ALTRO DI DETTI POVERI *risponde e dice:*

Andianne! Che bisogna più parole?
Promettigli di far quel ch'ella vuole.

UNO SERVO, *sentito Domitilla essere convertita, viene ' Aureliano e dice:*

      36
Aurelïan, tu arai troppo indugiato
a far le noze della cara sposa;
a questi dì m'è stato rivelato
ch'ella è fatta cristiana e sta nascosa.

AURELIANO *dice seco medesimo:*

Miser a me, ch'è quel che m'hai parlato?
Chi arebbe tentato mai tal cosa?
Io voglio ire a veder se fusse il vero,
benché questo di lei non penso o spero.

AURELIANO *va a casa Domitilla e dice a' sua servi:*

THE SERVANT DISTRIBUTING ALMS *says to one of the paupers:*

      35
Take this, see that you pray to God for us,
For her, as well, that chastely she may live;
And, all of you, among you share these gifts,
And do not gamble all of them away.

ONE OF THE PAUPERS *answers:*

We'll pray to God together with his saints
That heaven may reward such charity.

ANOTHER PAUPER *answers and says:*

Let's go from here, why need we parley more?
Promise him to do that which she asks.

A SERVANT, *having heard of Domitilla's conversion, goes to Aurelianus and says:*

      36
Too hesitant you've been, Aurelian,
In marrying this cherished bride of yours,
For someone lately has reported that
She's joined the Christians and now hides away.

AURELIANUS *says to himself:*

Ah woe is me that ever such a thing
Was said, or ever such thing would be tried;
I want to go to see if it's the truth,
Though this I cannot dream or believe of her.

AURELIANUS *goes to the house of Domitilla and says to her servants:*

37

Ditemi presto. I' vengo per vedere
quel che fa oggi Domitilla mia.
La mia venuta gli fate a sapere,
che di vederla sol mio cor desia.

Risponde UNO DE' SERVI DI DOMITILLA ' *Aureliano:*

Noi faremo al presente il tuo volere,
pur che la tua venuta in van non sia;
presto la tua imbasciata gli faremo
e come tu se' qui gli conteremo.

UNO SERVO *va a Domitilla e dice:*

38

Sappi ch'Aurelïano è qua venuto
e dice ch'a lui venga prestamente.
Quel che tu ha' fatto arà forse saputo,
che mi par per dolor fuor della mente.

DOMITILLA *risponde:*

Dite che e passi e 'l tempo arà perduto
e ch'io non vo' parlargli per niente,
ch'i' ho nel cielo un altro sposo preso,
che del suo dolce amor m'ha il cor acceso.

Dice il SERVO ' *Aureliano:*

39

Quel che ti manda Domitilla a dire[12]—
ch'a te non vuol venire, Aurelïano,
non è disposta ' volerti ubbidire,
sì ch'aspettarla t'affatichi in vano,
ch'un altro sposo ell'ha preso a servire—
questo per parte sua t'anunziàno.

                    37
Report at once. For I have come to see
Just what, today, my Domitilla does.
Tell her that I've arrived, because my heart
Only desires that I may meet with her.

ONE OF DOMITILLA'S SERVANTS *responds to Aurelianus:*

Immediately shall we perform your will
So that your coming will not be in vain;
We shall at once your errand undertake
And we shall tell her that you have arrived.

A SERVANT *goes to Domitilla and says:*

                    38
Know that Aurelianus has arrived
And says that you should come to him at once.
Perhaps he's learned about what you have done;
He seems to me beside himself with grief.

DOMITILLA *answers:*

Tell him he's wasted both his steps and time
And that I do not wish to speak to him
At all, for I have found another spouse
In heaven whose sweet love inflames my heart.

The SERVANT *says to Aurelianus:*

                    39
To you this message Domitilla sends,
Aurelian, that she will not come to you—
That to obey you she can't be induced;
Vainly you tire yourself awaiting her,
For she has taken another spouse to serve.
This we report to you on her behalf.

AURELIANO *dice seco medesimo:*

Ecco che sarà ver quel ch'i' ho sentito.
Omè, ch'i' ho carestia di buon partito!

AURELIANO *va allo Imperadore e dice:*

40
Serenissimo e magno Imperadore,
sappi che questa setta de' cristiani,
contro a tua maëstà, contro al tuo onore,
fatto hanno sì con lor consigli vani
che Domitilla mia, caro signore,
Clemente velato ha con le suo mani.
È vergin consecrata al loro Idio,
se non provedi a questo caso rio.

41
I' sono andato a casa per vedella;
non gli ho potuto dire alcuna cosa
ché sta rinchiusa e più non mi favella,
e dice che di Cristo è fatta sposa;
però ti piaccia di mandar per quella,
la quale io amo sopra ogni altra cosa.
Fa' che punito sia chi n'è cagione,
e che mia sposa sia come è ragione.

Lo IMPERADORE *risponde 'Aureliano:*

42
Io ti prometto e giuro, Aurelïano,
pe' nostri dèi ch'io ne farò vendetta:
io disfarò questo popol cristiano,
gente perversa, iniqua e maladetta;
e farò lei di questo pensier vano
forse pentir con la sua falsa setta.

AURELIANUS *says to himself*:

I see that everything I've heard is true;
Alas! My hope for this fine match falls through!

AURELIANUS *goes to the Emperor and says:*

    40
Great Emperor, Your Highness most serene,
This sect of Christians, you should know,
Against your honor and your majesty
Have with their hollow counsels brought to pass
That my dear Domitilla, good my Lord,
Received the veil from Clement, from his hands.
She's now a virgin consecrated to
Their God, unless you set this dire case right.

    41
I went to see her at her house, but I
Could not say anything to her because
She stays within, no more will speak to me,
But says that she's become the bride of Christ.
Be pleased, on that account, to send for her
Whom I adore beyond all else and see
That those responsible are punished and
That, as is proper, she becomes my wife.

The EMPEROR *answers Aurelianus:*

    42
I promise you and swear, Aurelian,
That, by our gods I'll have revenge for this.
I shall destroy this Christian populace,
These wicked people, cursèd and perverse,
And I'll make her, perhaps, with her false sect,
Repent of this preposterous idea.

E volto a' sua servi dice lo IMPERADORE:

Andate, servi mia, presto per quella;
dite che venga a me, ch'io vo' vedella.

Vanno E SERVI *per Domitilla e dicono:*

43
Per parte dello immenso Imperadore
con esso noi, Domitilla, verrai;
d'averlo offeso ha' fatto grande errore,
ma prestamente te ne pentirai.

DOMITILLA *responde:*

Andiàn, ch'io non aprezo il tuo signore,
e manco le minacce che mi fai.

E volta al cielo dice:

O buon Iesù, dove il mio cor si fida,
fammi costante e sia mia scorta e guida.

Lo IMPERADORE *dice a Domitilla venuta innanzi a lui:*

44
O lasso a me, che è quel ch'i' ho sentito?
Nipote mia, che trista fama è questa
che di te hanno e mia orecchi udito?
Oimè, perché mi se' così molesta
e nostri dei e me così ha' schernito?
Questo è lo scambio della tanta festa
ch'io fe' quando nascesti? E sappi come
degna ti feci del mio proprio nome!

And he turns to his servants and says:

Go at once, my servants, fetch her here!
Tell her to come, for I must make things clear.

And the SERVANTS *go to Domitilla and say:*

43

On our exalted Emperor's behalf,
You must now come with us to him because
In giving him offense you've greatly erred,
But instantly you will repent of it.

DOMITILLA *answers:*

Let's go, for I do not esteem your lord,
And threats you make against me have no force.

And she turns to heaven and says:

O Jesus good, my heart believes in thee,
O, make me constant; guide and shepherd me.

When Domitilla comes before him, the EMPEROR *says:*

44

O woe is me! What's this I hear? My niece,
What is this sorrowful news that's reached my ears
About you? Woe, why do you give such grief
To me, and have thus scorned our gods and me?
Is this the way that you repay me for
The celebration I made at your birth?
For well you know how much I honored you
In giving you the name that is my own!

45

Misera a te, per gli sciocchi consigli
de' cristian falsi se' così velata!
Non è più ragionevol che mi apigli.
Sai ch'io non t'ho come nipote amata,
ma come padre e lor più cari figli;
or la mia santa fede hai rinegata.
S'io posso ritrovar quel vecchio mago
che t'ha velata, per mia fé, ne 'l pago!

46

Non hai temuta la indegnazione
de' nostri idei, che cotante richezze
ci han concedute per le lor cagione;
mantengonci felici in tante altezze.
O stolta, con tua falsa opinione,
perché vai tu cercando tante asprezze
a seguir de' cristian le lor dottrine,
vita pien di tormenti e discipline?

DOMITILLA *risponde allo Imperadore:*

47

Quel ch'i' ho fatto, o sommo Imperadore,
per nessuna cagione il vo' negare.
I' ho fuggito il cieco e falso errore
tanto ch'io conosco or le cose chiare;
la vera via m'ha mostra el mio Signore,
per la qual son disposta a caminare
parata sempre al mio Iesù servire,
che pel nostro peccar volse morire.

48

Questa vita presente in che noi siamo,
la qual ti par sì piena di diletti,
non pensi tu quanto poco ci stiamo,
perché sìan tutti alla morte suggetti,

45

Poor wretch, for on the fatuous advice
Of these false Christians have you been thus veiled!
You can no longer rightly turn to me,
For I have loved you, not as uncles do,
But as a father loves his dearest child,
Now you have renounced my sacred faith.
If I can catch that ancient sorcerer
Who veiled you, 'pon my faith, I'll pay him back!

46

You have not feared the indignation of
Our gods, who have for motives of their own,
Conceded us such boundless wealth that they
Support us happy in such eminence.
O foolish girl with your opinion false
O why do you seek out such hardships dire
In following the teachings of these Christians,
A life with torments filled and chastisements?

DOMITILLA *answers the Emperor:*

47

What I have done, O highest Emperor,
I would on no account repudiate;
So far from error blind and false I've fled
That now I clearly know the way of things;
My Lord has shown me now the proper path
On which I am resolved to travel forth,
Ever prepared to serve my Jesus, who
Agreed to die to expiate our sin.

48

This present life in which we find ourselves,
Which seems to you so brimming with delights,
Do you not think about how briefly we
Enjoy it as we're subject, all, to death?

e per far questa fin tutti nasciamo?
Di quel ch'io parlo intendi ben gli effetti:
nel novissimo dì susciteremo,
tutti ne' nostri corpi torneremo.

49

Lingua non è che potessi contare
della virginità la sua grandeza,
la quale io son disposta d'osservare,
e fa' quanto tu puoi con ogni aspreza!
O Imperador, se potessi gustare
di quella immensa gloria la dolceza,
tu lasceresti questi idoli vani
per seguir la mia legge de' cristiani.

Lo IMPERADORE *risponde a Domitilla:*

50

Non so come i' m'ho tanta sofferenza
ch'io non t'uccida al presente con furia!
Ma, poi che ' nostri idèi con pazïenza
hanno passato questa grieve ingiuria,
ch'aran forse di te buona credenza
che torni ancor sotto lor degna curia,
anch'io vo' sopportar la tua pazia,
pur che tu torni alla diritta via.

51

Ma pogniàn[13] che sia ver quel c'hai parlato,
che facilmente in contrario si pruova,
né in alcun nostro libro fu trovato:
vietare il matrimonio. È cosa nuova,
semplice e falso al tutto riprovato
opinion.[14] Che seguitar ti giova
a contradire a' ben della natura,
che vedi che ne parla ogni scrittura?

To reach this end, then, have we all been born?
Of what I speak these will be the effects:
At the final trumpet we shall rise
And to our bodies we shall all return.

      49

The tongue does not exist that could recount
The grandeur of the maidenhood that I've
Resolved to hold in reverence, and you,
O Emperor, whatever you may do
With all severity, if you could taste
The sweetness of that glory measureless,
You would abandon all these idols vain
And follow too this Christian faith of mine.

The EMPEROR *responds to Domitilla:*

      50

Why I have such forbearance, I don't know,
That I don't kill you in my fury now!
But since our gods have borne with patience thus
This grievous injury, perhaps they have
For you good confidence that you will yet
Return unto their worthy court once more,
I also shall endure your madness if
You turn again to tread the righteous path.

      51

Supposing, though, that what you've said were true,
The opposite how easily one can prove;
Never was wedlock, in a book of ours,
Found banned. A false opinion, merely, is that view—
And one disproved and quite rejected, strange.
What good will come if you persist and shun
Fair nature's blessings that are spoken of
In every script on wedlock, as you see?

52

Molto è da farsi di te maraviglia,
la quale ha' ' nostri libri già studiati,
che lodon generar degna famiglia,
onde son molti regni rilevati.
Misera e stolta e più chi ti consiglia,
pescator vil, da tutti disprezati!
Credi a chi t'ama e che non parla in vano,
ed ubidisci al tuo Aurelïano.

DOMITILLA *risponde allo Imperadore:*

53

Mirabile e profondo e gran misterio
contengon le parole che tu ha' detto,
se con vera ragione ha' desiderio
d'intender di tal cosa ben l'effetto.[15]
Pò tutt'adoperar più che 'l tuo imperio[16]
semplice pescator col suo concetto;
col segno della croce ha suscitati
e morti, e sordi e ciechi ha liberati.

54

Più può nel cuor degli uomini operare
el crocifisso che Mercurio o Marte,
quantunche tu gli faccia venerare
da tutte le tue genti in ogni parte;
per loro stessi nulla posson fare,
per man d'uomini finti e fatti ad arte,
tutti imagine false e pien d'inganni
che vi conducono agli eterni danni.

55

O Imperador, tu di' che ' tua poeti
biasimon molto la virginitate;
tu non intendi ben questi secreti,
però non puoi saper la veritate,

52

How very much I am surprised at you
Who have perused and studied well our books
That praise begetting a worthy family
Whence many kingdoms are raised up: O wretch,
O fool!—more those who counsel you,
Vile fisherman by everyone disdained!—
Believe one who loves you, one who speaks not
In vain, and yield to your Aurelian.

DOMITILLA *answers the Emperor:*

53

The words that you have spoken have in them
A mystery—profound, great, wonderful.
If you desire with reason true to grasp
Aright the consequences of such things,
Far more than all your empire can effect,
A simple fisherman with what he taught,
And with the cross's sign has raised the dead,
And set at liberty the deaf and blind.

54

More can the crucifix accomplish in
The hearts of men than Mercury or Mars—
No matter how revered you make them be
Among your people everywhere. They can
Themselves do nothing, nonetheless; for by
Man's hand they're counterfeited and by craft;
They're all false images, and full of tricks
To lead you to your everlasting harm.

55

O Emperor, you say your poets much condemn
Virginity; you do not fully grasp
These secret matters; you cannot, therefore,
Grasp the truth; your words ring false like those

e, come gl'ignoranti e inquïeti,
le tue parole dicon falsitate.
E tua poeti l'hanno posta in cima
sopra l'altre virtù, degna di stima.

56
Quanto è da' vostri savi commendata
questa virtù, che tanto a torto offendi!
La dea Dïana al tempio fu addorata
da' Roman; dunche perché mi riprendi
e vuoi ch'io sia di cotal ben privata,
che quanto più mi di' il cor m'accendi
del dolce amor del mio Sposo eternale,
che mi promette dar vita immortale?

57
Pe' tua poeti ti posso provare
la degnità di ciascuna Sibilla,[17]
che meritorno di profetizare
di Cristo, e quella vergine Camilla,
quanto gli piacque a Turno di essaltare;[18]
di Calidonia si scrive e postilla,[19]
e Claudia, che fra noi tanto si noma;[20]
la vergine vestale amò già Roma.[21]

Lo IMPERADORE *dice a Domitilla:*

58
Misera, non sa' tu ch'i' ho potenza
di liberarti e di farti morire?
Se non ch'io voglio usar la mia clemenza,
io ti farei quel c'hai detto disdire;
ma tu n'arai più lunga penitenza
che non parlerai più con tanto ardire.

The ignorant and afflicted speak; instead,
Upon the very pinnacle of worth
Your poets set virginity above
All other virtues worthy of esteem.

56

How greatly was this virtue—that you err
So wrongfully to offend—exalted by
Your wise men! At her temple Rome adored
Divine Diana, so why do you fault me
And such a virtue want to keep from me?
The more you speak, the more my heart's aflame
With the sweet love of my eternal Spouse
Who's pledged to give immortal life to me.

57

Appealing to your poets I can prove
The dignity of every Sibyl[17] who
Earned the reward of prophesying Christ;
And how much it pleased Turnus to exalt
That virgin Camilla; and praise we find[18]
In rhymes of Calydonia,[19] and of Claudia,[20]
The vestal virgin kept alive in fame
Among us for the love she bore to Rome.

The EMPEROR *says to Domitilla:*

58

Do you not know I have the power, wretch,
Either to set you free or cause your death?
Had I not chosen to show my clemency,
I could make you unsay what you have said;
But you will have such penance for it that
No longer will you speak so daringly.

E volto a' suo servi dice:

Menatela nella isola Pontiana,
poi ch'ella è tanto maladetta e strana!

DOMITILLA *fa orazione a Dio dicendo:*

        59
Immenso Idio, dell'anima mio Sposo,
raguarda il core e la contrizion mia,
che quel ch'i' ho dentro a te non è nascoso;
fa' che l'ancilla tua sempre ti sia
racomandata—io so che se' pietoso—
e falla andar per la diritta via.
Quanto questo tiranno è più crudele,
fammi, Signor, costante e più fedele.

DOMITILLA *rivolta a' sua servi dice:*

        60
O cari servi mia, veduto avete
quanto la crudeltà d'altrui ci offenda,
però con meco Iesù pregherrete
che dal crudo tiranno ci difenda.
Or si vedrà, se voi mi seguirete,
quanto la carità vostra si stenda;
presto arén la corona del martirio
che ci promette il sommo cielo impirio.

Viene UNO SERVO *' Aureliano e dice come ha lasciato Domitilla nell'Isola di Ponzio*[22]:

        61
I' ho lasciato in grande amaritudine
nell'isola tua donna, o signor mio,
dove ella sta co' servi in solitudine
e solo ha volto a Cristo ogni disio;

And he turns to his servants and says:

Confine her on the Pontine Island, for
She has become so cursèd and so strange!

DOMITILLA *says a prayer:*

> 59

Illimitable God, Spouse of my soul,
Upon my heart and my contrition, look,
For what's inside me is not hid from you;
Keep your handmaiden ever in your care;
I know you're merciful, and ask you to
Keep her ever on the righteous path.
The more this tyrant torments me, O Lord,
Make me more constant, faithful to your word.

Turning to her servants, DOMITILLA *says:*

> 60

O my belovèd servants you have seen
How much we're harmed by others' cruelty;
With me entreat, therefore, our Jesus that
He will defend us from this tyrant harsh.
Now we shall see, if you will follow me,
How far your love for me extends, for soon
We shall acquire the crown of martyrs that
Will earn for us the highest realm of heaven.

A servant goes to Aurelianus and says that he had left Domitilla on the Island of Ponza:

> 61

In bitterness surpassing have I left
Your lady on the island, O my lord;
With servants she in solitude remains.
On Christ alone, her every hope is fixed;

attende sol con gran solecitudine
' adorar giorno e notte il loro Iddio.

AURELIANO *dice seco medesimo:*

Io vo' far noto al signor questo caso,
ch'altra speranza a me non è rimaso.

AURELIANO *va allo Imperadore e dice così:*

62
Sappi, principe, immenso Imperadore,
che ostinata è più che fussi mai
la nostra Domitilla nel suo errore,
tanto che convertite ha gente assai;
però di tormentar, caro signore,
piena licenza mi concederai,
con ogni aspreza que' falsi donzelli
ché di cotanto mal cagion son quelli.

Lo IMPERADORE *risponde ' Aureliano:*

63
Io ti do, Aurelian, piena licenza:
fa' di loro e di lei ciò che ti pare.
Se non ch'io volli usar la mia clemenza,
l'ultimo duol gli arei fatto provare.
In te sia posto e nella tua prudenza,
ch'io non so di costei più che mi fare.

E volto a' servi dice:

E voi, servi, ubbidite ' Aurelïano
e non n'abbiate alcun suo detto in vano.

With great fervor she quite devotes herself
To worshiping day and night that God of theirs.

AURELIANUS *says to himself:*

This matter to my lord I must make known,
What hope I have can come from him alone.

AURELIANUS *goes to the Emperor and says:*

62

Great Emperor, O Prince, I'd have you know
How obstinate, and even more than she
Was ever, is our Domitilla still
In error, so much so that many folk
She has converted; therefore, dear lord, grant
Me full authority to punish those
False knaves with every harsh asperity
Who have occasioned such great wickedness.

The EMPEROR *answers Aurelianus:*

63

Aurelian, my full authority
I give you: do your will with them and her.
Had I not chosen to be merciful,
I would have made them feel the final woe.
To you and to your prudence it is left,
For I don't know what more to do with her.

And turning to the servants he says:

And, servants, you obey Aurelian, too;
Don't fail to act, whatever he says to do.

AURELIANO *dice a' servi:*

            64
O fedel servi, andate a que' donzelli
che sono appresso a Domitilla mia;
dite come el signore ha dati quelli
liberamente nella mia balia
e ch'i' ho desiderio di vedelli,
che venghin con voi presto in compagnia.

E SERVI *dicono 'Aureliano:*

Ciò che comandi, Aurelian faremo;
presto dinanzi a te gli meneremo.

UNO SERVO *giunto a Domitilla dice a' sua servi:*

            65
Venite presto, perfidi cristiani,
' Aurelïan, perché 'l signor v'ha dati
liberi ognun di voi nelle sue mani;
fate che siate presto aparechiati,
e forse che de' vostri pensier vani
a questa volta sarete pagati.

Rispondono E SERVI:

Presto faremo ogni suo voler sazio,
pur che ci sia concesso un po' di spazio.

L' UNO SERVO *dice a l'altro:*

            66
Ecco che 'l tempo, dolce fratel mio,
venuto fia d'abandonar la vita,
ma, poi che così piace al nostro Idio,
ringraziar vuolsi sua bontà infinita.

AURELIANUS *says to the servants:*

64

O faithful servants go among those knaves
That are around my Domitilla, and
Explain that my lord's freely given them
Into my power and that I desire
To see them; have them come along with you—
Immediately have them come in company.

The SERVANTS *answer Aurelianus:*

What you command, Aurelian, we'll do.
We shall lead them presently to you.

A SERVANT *comes to Domitilla and says to her menservants:*

65

Come before Aurelian at once,
Perfidious Christians, for into his hands
Our lord has freely given each of you;
See that you quickly get yourselves prepared
And for your unavailing thoughts, perhaps,
You will at this time be repaid in full.

The SERVANTS *answer:*

His every wish we shall at once fulfill,
If he will grant us just a little time.

The one SERVANT *says to the other:*

66

Behold the time has come, sweet brother mine,
To leave behind this life, but as it is
So pleasing to our God, let us give thanks
To Him for goodness infinite, for me,

La morte mi sare' sommo desio,
ma sol mi duol questa crudel partita
da questa sventurata che lasciàno
qui nelle man del crudo Aureliano.

DOMITILLA *a' suo donzelli:*

67
Questo che vuol, dolci mia frate', dire,
che voi fate sì aspro e gran lamento?
Sarebbe mai ch'io dovessi morire?
Nommi celate quel ch'avete drento,
ch'io son contenta mia vita finire
e portar pel mio Sposo ogni tormento.

Rispondono E SERVI *a Domitilla:*

Quel che piace al Signor lodar si vuole,
ma d'avere a lasciarti assai ci duole.

UNO SERVO *dice a Domitilla:*

68
Sappi ch'Aurelian per noi ha mandato,
perché ha licenza dallo Imperadore;
ciascun di noi nelle sue mani ha dato,
e duolci di morir sol per tuo amore.
O Domitilla, fa' che 'l core armato
sia della somma grazia del Signore;
fa' che tu pensi a chi tu se' sposata,
sì che d'Aurelïan non sia ingannata.

UNO ALTRO SERVO *aggiugne e dice:*

69
Cara sorella, con gran diligenza
la tua virginità sappi guardare;

My highest aspiration will be death;
But only for this wretched one whom we
Leave here in cruel Aurelianus' hands
Does this harsh circumstance make me lament.

DOMITILLA *says to her menservants:*

      67

What does this mean, O my sweet brothers dear,
That you are making such harsh and loud lament?
Could it be that I am condemned to die?
From me do not conceal what you within
You feel, for I'm content to end my life
And any torment for my Spouse endure.

The SERVANTS *answer Domitilla:*

On what God wishes we must praise bestow,
But having to leave you fills us full of woe.

A SERVANT *says to Domitilla:*

      68

Know that Aurelian has sent for us
For he has license from the Emperor
Who's given each of us into his hands,
And we are only loath to die for love
Of you. Dear Domitilla, arm your heart
With our Lord's highest grace; take care to think
About that one to whom you have been wed;
And by Aurelian be not misled.

ANOTHER SERVANT *joins in and says:*

      69

Dear sister, with great diligence, take care
That you protect your virginal estate

sostien per quella ogni aspra penitenza,
d'alcun tormento non ti spaventare,
ché d'ogni cosa la divina essenza
nel sommo ciel ti potrà ristorare.
Quanto quaggiù sarai più tormentata
tanto sarai lassù vie più beata.

Dice L'ALTRO SERVO *a Domitilla:*

70
Dilettissima mia, poi ch'a Dio piace
di partirci da te, abbi nel cuore
el tuo Sposo diletto e datti pace
e non ti lamentar pel nostro amore;
con teco resta il tuo Sposo verace
e fia sempre tuo aiuto e difensore,
ch'a' suo buon servi è sì benigno e pio.
Dolce sorella mia, fatti con Dio.

DOMITILLA *dice loro:*

71
Chi in vostro scambio arò, frate' diletti,
che m'avevi[23] sì bene amaestrata,
e dimostrati e luoghi oscuri e stretti
e della santa fé raluminata
con le vostre parole e buon precetti?
E or lasciate questa sventurata
afflitta e sola, senza compagnia,
che non sa più dove si vada o stia!

72
Sì aspra m'è questa crudel partita,
oimè, ch'i' perdo in un punto ogni speme!
Io resto qui come cosa smarrita.
Perché non m'è concesso con voi insieme,
diletti mie frate', perder la vita,

And bear each bitter pang on its account,
Of any torture do not be afraid,
For every thing that holy essence in
The highest heaven can restore to you.
As much as you are tortured here below,
So many more blessings above will God bestow.

The OTHER SERVANT *says to Domitilla:*

      70
My dearest one, since God is pleased to part
Us from you, keep your cherished Spouse within
Your heart; you must resign yourself; you must
Not grieve for love of us; with you will stay
Your rightful Spouse, and he will always be
Your help and your defender, for to his
Good servants he is merciful and kind.
Sweet sister mine, thrive in God's grace divine.

DOMITILLA *says to them:*

      71
Belovèd brothers, who can take your place?
For so well you've instructed me and you've
Explained the darkling places and the strait,
And have made crystal clear the holy faith
With your good precepts and your words and this
Unfortunate woman now you leave alone,
Afflicted, of all company bereft,
She's unsure if she stands, goes right or left!

      72
So harsh is this departure cruel for me!
Alas, for in an instant every hope
I lose; I stand here like a woman lost.
Why has it not been granted me to lose
My life together with you, brothers dear?

che per gran doglia il mio cor forte teme?
Pregate Idio che gli sia di piacere
che con voi muoia, se gli è il suo volere.

UNO DE' DETTI SERVI *dice a Domitilla:*

73

Perdonami se mai alcuna offesa
t'avessi fatto per la mia ignoranza.
Segui col cor sincer questa tua impresa
e nel tuo Sposo abbi ferma speranza,
il qual sarà tuo aiuto e tua difesa.
Or ti bisogna usar la tua costanza;
segui questa tua degna intenzione
e a noi da' la tua benedizione.

AURELIANO, *mandato per dua servi di Domitilla, dice loro:*

74

Acciò che voi sappiate la cagione
perch'io v'ho fatti innanzi a me venire,
sapete quant'io porto affezione
a Domitilla con sommo disire;
se voi saprete con vostro sermone
far che quella mi voglia aconsentire,
sarete per frate' da me tenuti,
con molti benefici e gran tributi.

Rispondono E SERVI *di Domitilla* ' *Aureliano:*

75

Non ti parrebbe, Aurelïan, gran cosa
chi tôr volessi al nostro Imperadore
la sua amata e degna e cara sposa?
Non sare' questo troppo grande errore?
Or pensa quanto più sarebbe odiosa

That's what my heart with utter sorrow fears!
Pray God that he'll be pleased to let me die
With you, if that might be his will for me.

ONE OF THE SERVANTS *says to Domitilla:*

   73

Forgive me if ever, through my ignorance,
I have done any injury to you.
Your business, with a heart sincere, I've done,
So in your Spouse sustain a steady hope,
For he will be your help and your defense.
And on your constancy you now must call;
Pursue your worthy resolution and
Your benediction give to each of us.

AURELIANUS, *having sent for the two menservants of Domitilla, says to them:*

   74

So that you'll understand the reason why
I've made you come before me, be aware
How great a love, with consummate desire,
I feel for Domitilla. If you'll know
How, with your urging, to arrange it so
That she'll choose to consent to me, you shall
Be kept by me as brothers, and with great
Emoluments and many offices.

Domitilla's SERVANTS *answer Aurelianus:*

   75

Would it not seem despicable to you,
Aurelian, should someone wish to steal
Our Emperor's dear and plighted, cherished wife?
Would this not be a sin beyond belief?
How much more hateful it would be to steal

tôr Domitilla a così gran Signore,
al quale è sempre di servir disposta;
però semplice e vana è tua proposta.

AURELIANO *dice a' servi di Domitilla:*

        76
Non è ancor doma questa maladetta,
pessima, iniqua setta de' cristiani!
Poi che la morte vostra vi diletta
ed avete e mia prieghi tutti vani,
io farò far di voi cruda vendetta
e faròvi straziar, ribaldi cani![24]

E volto a' sua servi dice:

Fate che sien battuti e tormentati,
poi che son tanto iniqui e ostinati.

AURELIANO *comanda a' sua servi così dicendo:*

        77
Dinanzi a' nostri dèi po' gli menate
e, se que' non volessino adorare,
la testa a ciaschedun di lor tagliate,
se in questo error voglion perseverare.

Dicono E SERVI *di Aureliano:*

Quel che comanda tua benignitate
presto fatto sarà sanza indugiare.

IL MANIGOLDO *dice:*

Andianne, ch'i' ho già tanto aspettato
ch'io m'ho mezo il guadagno consumato.

Fair Domitilla from such great a Lord
Whom she's resolved to serve eternally.
Thus your proposal's vain and foolish too.

AURELIANUS *says to Domitilla's servants:*

      76

This cursed, evil, wicked Christian sect
Has not been broken yet! Since, then,
You take delight in your own death—since all
My prayers have been addressed to you in vain,
A cruel vengeance I shall take on you,
You dirty dogs, I'll have you torn apart!

And he turns to his servants and says:

See that they're soundly beaten, tortured too,
Since wicked they remain, and obstinate.

AURELIANUS *commands his servants saying:*

      77

Conduct them then before our gods, and if
They do not wish to worship them, cut off
The head of each of them if they insist
On persevering in this error great.

The SERVANTS OF ARELIANUS *answer:*

What you in your beneficence decree,
At once shall be performed in each degree.

The EXECUTIONER *says:*

I've waited long enough; get on with it;
I've halfway spent the fee I've earned for them.

IL CAVALIERE,[25] *menatola dinanzi agl'idoli, dice:*[26]

78
A' nostri idèi rendete riverenza,
se delle nostre man campar volete;
se non ch'io vi darò la penitenza,
se 'l vostro Cristo non rinegherete.

Rispondono e DUA SERVI *di Domitilla al cavalieri:*

Né tu né questi idèi n'aran potenza;
di queste carni sol vi sfamerete.

E volti al cielo dicono a Dio:

L'anima sia di te che la creasti,
Signor, che 'l sangue tuo per noi versasti.

AURELIANO *dice a dua compagne di Domitilla.*[27]

79
Dilettissime mie sorelle care,
io credo vi sia noto in quanta doglia
la mia vita si truovi, in pene amare,
cagion della mia sposa che mia voglia
non vuol seguire, onde io vi vo' pregare
che ciascuna di voi questo far voglia:
d'andare a lei, e con buone parole
veder se quella aconsentir vi vuole.

80
I' ho la testa a' sua donzelli tagliata
e veggo che niente non mi giova,
perché ell'è via più ferma e ostinata
e però vorrei far quest'altra pruova;
io so che insieme con voi s'è allevata,
e facil cosa fia che si rimuova

The KNIGHT[25] *leads them to the idols and says:*

        78

Pay homage to our gods if you expect
To be released from our hands; if you don't
I shall inflict the punishment on you,
If you will not repudiate your Christ.

THE TWO SERVANTS OF DOMITILLA *answer:*

That power neither you nor these gods have;
You'll sate your hunger only on this flesh.

And turning to heaven they say to God:

The soul is for you who its creation willed,
O Lord; for us your holy blood you spilled.

AURELIANUS *says to Domitilla's two female companions:*[27]

        79

O dearest sisters, cherished in my heart,
I think you've seen into what disarray
My life has fallen, and what bitter pain
Because my bride will not perform my will,
Whence I appeal to each of you to grant
My wish and go to her, and with good words
Find out if that one will consent
To acquiesce in what I'd have her do.

        80

I have cut off her servants' heads, and I
Can see that nothing will avail because
Her mind is made up, and she is obstinate,
Yet I would like to try this other way:
I know she has been reared with you, and it
Would be an easy thing for her to be

alle vostre parole e buon consigli,
che piaccia a' nostri dèi ch'ella gli pigli.

81
E perch'io sento il tempo già appressare
de' vostri sposalizi, con voi insieme
io son disposto le mie noze fare
della mia dolce sposa e cara speme,
se voi saprete quella lusingare
e dirgli quanto il suo partir mi preme.

Rispondono le DUE DONZELLE *' Aureliano:*

No' farem volentier quel che ci hai detto,
pur che ne segua qualche buon effetto.

Vanno queste DUE VERGINE *a Domitilla nell'Isola Ponziana e, giunte a lei, dicono così:*

82
Più che cara sorella da noi amata,
per lo infinito amor che ti portiamo,
duolci trovarti afflitta e tribolata
in questo luogo pel consiglio vano
di chi non t'ama, e però ostinata
se' di lasciare il tuo Aurelïano,
giovane, bello, assai ricco e gentile,
ch'un altro non si truova a lui simìle.

83
S'alle nostre parole crederrai,
tu sarai ancor la più felice sposa
che nella città nostra fussi mai;
beata a te, se vorrai far tal cosa.
Vuoi tu finir tua vita in tanti guai
e tanti affanni sanza aver mai posa?

Persuaded by your words and good advice—
Which may it please our gods to have her take.

>   81

And since I see the time already near
For you to wed, together with you I
Intend to celebrate my marriage with
My darling bride, my dear and cherished hope,
If you know how to win her sympathy
And tell her how her leaving crushes me.

The TWO MAIDENS *answer Aurelianus:*

We willingly will do what you have asked,
So that some good result might come of it.

These TWO MAIDENS *go to the Pontine Island to Domitilla, and when they arrive they say:*

>   82

Belovèd sister, more than dear to us,
By the unbounded love we feel for you,
We are distressed to find you suffering,
Afflicted in this place, and obstinate—
All on account of vain advice from folk
Who do not love you, and because you've left
Your young Aurelianus, comely, rich,
And very noble; you'll not find his like.

>   83

If you will heed our words, you can become
Right now the happiest bride who ever was
Within our city, and how blest you'd be
If you'd give your consent to do this thing.
For would you wish to end your life in woes
Surpassing and in troubles harsh? Please do

Vogli al tuo degno sposo aconsentire,
ché molto ben ne potrà ancor seguire.

84
Nella legge di Cristo ancor si dice
che questo matrimonio è giusto e santo,
e questo alcun cristian non contradice;
e che sia ver, Pietro, che amò già tanto
el vostro Idio e fu così felice,
già ebbe sposa, e poi fu in grazia tanto
che per discepol fu da Cristo eletto,
ed è sì grato nel divin cospetto.

Risponde DOMITILLA *alle Vergini:*

85
Non può conoscer ben la veritate
chi 'nanzi agli occhi ha il vel della ignoranza;
questo che dite è ben semplicitate.
Veggo che posto avete ogni speranza
nel mondo, il quale è pien di falsitate,
però parlate con tanta aroganza
a dir ch'io lasci il mio Sposo eternale
per trovar in suo scambio uno uom mortale.

Seguita DOMITILLA:

86
Se voi volete intender per figura,
pensate s'a ciascuna di voi tolto
fussi lo sposo. Vi parrebbe dura
questa partita e dorrestivi molto,
ch'io so che voi gli amate oltre misura:
ogni vostro pensiero a loro è volto.
Tanto più grave a me sare' lasciare
el mio che 'n sempiterno può durare.

Submit and yield to your praiseworthy spouse
Since so much good can still proceed from that.

        84

In Christ's own law is marriage said to be
Both just and holy, and no Christian this
Will contradict; and Peter, it is true,
Who so much loved your God, indeed, and who
Enjoyed great happiness, had wed a wife,
And then remained in such grace Christ chose him
As one of his disciples and he is
Extremely pleasing in the sight of God.

DOMITILLA *answers the Virgins:*

        85

The truth cannot be fully understood
By those whose eyes are veiled by ignorance;
Your words reveal your simplemindedness.
I see that you have set your every hope
In this world full of falsity, of lies;
So arrogance provokes your tongue to say
I must abandon my eternal Spouse
And take a mortal husband in his place.

DOMITILLA *continues:*

        86

If by example you would understand,
Suppose that each of you had had your groom
Snatched from your side. That parting would seem hard
To you, and you would suffer great distress,
For boundless love, I know, you bear to them:
They're at the very center of your thoughts.
How much more grievous would it be for me
To leave my Spouse who will forever live!

87

Non si dimostra in tal modo l'amore
che mi portate a darmi ta' consigli,
a dir ch'io lasci il mio Sposo e Signore
e che Aurelïan, uom mortal, pigli,
per perder quel ch'è sommo Redentore
che ci ha creati e siàn tutti suo figli:
il qual beat'a voi se 'l conoscessi
e s'alle mie parole ancor credessi.[28]

UNA DI DETTE VERGINI *dice a Domitilla:*

88

Se la potenza di questo tuo Idio
è tanta, pe' tua prieghi ci dimostra
che lume renda a Erode, fratel mio,
e similmente a questa serva nostra
renda il parlare, e fia nostro desio
disposto di seguir la legge vostra;
e tutt'a dua nel tuo Idio crederemo
e i nostri sposi morta' lasceremo.[29]

DOMITILLA *fa orazione a Dio dicendo così:*

89

Benigno Idio, se ' mie prieghi son degni,
questa tua serva ti piaccia essaudire;
fa' che l'orazion mia ne' sommi regni,[30]
immenso Sposo, a te possa venire.
Della tua gran potenza mostra e segni:
piacciati a questo cieco gli occhi aprire
e a questa serva render la favella,
che la tua gran potenza mostri quella.

87

You do not in this fashion show the love
You bear me when you give me such advice
And say that I must leave my Spouse and Lord,
And take a mortal man, Aurelian,
And so lose him who is our Savior high,
Who has created us, his children all.
Were you to know him, then you would be blest,
And were my words believed within your breast

ONE OF THESE VIRGINS *says to Domitilla:*

88

If so great is the power of this God
Of yours, reveal it to us with your prayers:
My brother Herod, give him back his sight,
And likewise to this servant girl of ours
The power of speech restore, and our desire
Will be resolved to accept your faith, and both
Of us will in your God believe as well;
Our mortal bridegrooms we shall both forsake.

DOMITILLA *prays to God, saying:*

89

O God beneficent, if these my prayers
Be worthy, be pleased to grant your servant's
Plea to you; let my prayer in the highest realms,
O my Spouse infinite, before you come.
Of your mighty power display the signs:
Be pleased the eyes of this one to unseal,
And make this servant capable of speech,
So your great power may appear in each.

La SERVA MUTOLA, *riaùto il parlare per le orazioni di Domitilla, dice volta al cielo:*

        90

Pe' giusti prieghi, immenso eterno Dio,
di Domitilla ha' degnato mostrare
la tua somma potenza, Signor mio,
che t'è piaciuto rendermi il parlare;
io ti ringrazio quanto più poss'io
e nel tuo nome mi vo' battizare.
Fa' che l'anima mia a te sia volta,
come la lingua mia per grazia ha' sciolta.

IL CIECO ALLUMINATO *per Domitilla dice:*

        91

Figliuol di Dio, o Somma Sapienza,
che per noi morte e passion sentisti,
per la tua carità e gran clemenza
per noi ricomperar qua giù venisti;
ben si dimostra la tua gran potenza
poi ch'al tuo servo indegno gli occhi apristi.
Sendo del vero lume alluminato,
nel tuo nome voglio esser battezato.

Le DUE VERGINI *dicono a Domitilla, veduto*[31] *questi miracoli:*

        92

Dolce sorella, sì mirabil segni
del tuo superno Dio veduto abbiamo,
che ci par esser già ne' sommi regni,
e che tu ci battezi ti preghiamo;
e d'accettarci fa' che non ti sdegni
che vivere e morir teco vogliamo.
O sommo Idio, che i nostri cuori intendi,
della tua carità c'infiamma e accendi.

Her speech recovered in answer to Domitilla's prayers, the MUTE MAIDSERVANT *turns to heaven and says:*

      90

O vast, eternal God, by the just prayers
Of Domitilla have you deigned to show,
My Lord, your power surpassing; you were pleased
To give me now my speech. As much as I
Am able, I give thanks to you, and in
Your name I wish to be baptized. O let
My soul be turned to you, for by your grace
You have my tongue unfettered and set free.

The BLIND MAN, *his sight restored by Domitilla, says:*

      91

O Son of God, O highest Sapience,
Who suffered death and passion for us all,
In loving charity and mercy great
You came to earth that we might be redeemed;
Your mighty power is surely manifest
Since this unworthy servant's eyes you have
Unsealed, so with the true light he might see;
In your name I desire to be baptized.

Having seen these miracles, the TWO VIRGINS *say to Domitilla:*

      92

O sister sweet, such signs miraculous
Of your eternal God we have observed,
We seem already in the highest realms.
Baptize us, we entreat you, and we pray
That you won't scorn to welcome us, for we
Desire to live and then to die with you.
O highest God, you hear our hearts' desire:
Ignite us with your love and with your fire.

AURELIANO, *mandato per gli sposi delle due vergine, dice loro che vadino a sapere quello abbino adoperato con Domitilla:*

93
I' ho le noze al presente ordinate,
però vi priego che in piacer vi sia
d'andare a Domitilla e che intendiate
s'ell'è disposta a far la voglia mia.

Rispondono gli SPOSI *'Aureliano:*

Le nostre mente son sempre parate
sol di far cosa che in piacer vi sia;
no' farén presto quel che t'è in piacere,
pur ch'ella voglia far il tuo volere.

E DUA SPOSI *giunti alle lor donne dicono:*

94
Dilette spose, che vorrà dir questo
che 'l vostro capo è già così velato?[32]
Fateci presto il caso manifesto,
che ci par questo fatto aver sognato.
Aurelïano al suo caso molesto
aspetta quel ch'avete adoperato
con Domitilla e che conclusione,
perch'è rimaso in gran confusione.

Rispondono le VERGINI *a' loro sposi:*

95
El frutto è stato sì maraviglioso
della nostra venuta, o sposi eletti,
e tal misterio a voi non fia nascoso.
Veder potrete e cogitar gli effetti
dello infinito Idio, giusto e pietoso,
che mostra opere degne a' suo suggetti:

AURELIANUS, *having sent for the grooms of the two virgins, tells them to go find out how it has gone with Domitilla:*

93

I have ordained the weddings right away;
Therefore, if you please, I beg you now
To go to Domitilla and inquire
If she is yet prepared to do my will.

The BRIDEGROOMS *answer Aurelianus:*

Our minds are ever ready just to do
Whatever you may wish, and we at once
Shall do whatever pleases you in this
Provided she submits to do your will.

The two BRIDEGROOMS, *having come before their ladies, say:*

94

Belovèd brides, whatever does this mean
That your heads in this fashion are thus veiled?[32]
This circumstance make clear to us at once,
For to us it seems we've dreamed this thing.
Aurelian waits for news of his dispute
With Domitilla and if you've prevailed,
Because in great confusion he's remained.

The VIRGINS *answer their bridegrooms:*

95

Our coming here has borne us such a fruit,
O chosen spouses, that the miracle
And mystery will not be concealed from you.
So you can see and think upon the works
Of God, just, infinite, and merciful,
Who to his subjects shows his worthy works:

sappiate come Erode è aluminato
e questa serva mutola ha parlato.

96
E noi per tal miracoli ci siamo
nella legge di Cristo battezate,
pe' gran misteri che veduti abbiamo,
e questa è la cagione che siàn velate;
però, sposi diletti, vi preghiamo
che in tanto error più non perseveriate.
Aprite gli occhi delle vostre menti
e di credere a lui siate contenti.

E dua SPOSI *convertiti rispondono:*

97
O infinito Amore, o Padre immenso,
che ci hai mostrato per questa tua ancilla
cose sì degne, che quanto più penso
della tua grazia il mio core isfavilla;
tu m'hai del dolce fuoco tutto acceso.
O santissima sposa Domitilla,
batteza noi nel nome del tuo Idio,
ch'a lui servire è volto ogni disio.

UNO SERVO *va ' Aureliano e dice come e dua sposi sono convertiti nella fede di Cristo:*

98
Io ti vorrei, Aureliano, portare
di Domitilla tua miglior novella.
Sappi ch'ell'ha saputo sì ben fare
che quelle che mandasti per vedella
si sono or fatte da lei battezare,
e ' loro sposi convertiti ha quella.

Observe how Herod has received his sight,
And this mute servant girl has spoken, too.

96

And through such miracles are we baptized
Into the Law of Christ by mysteries
Immense that we have seen; this is the cause
Of our now being veiled, and therefore then,
In such great error, cherished bridegrooms dear,
We pray you will no longer persevere.
Unseal the eyes of your intelligence
And be content to place your faith in him.

Converted, the two BRIDEGROOMS *answer:*

97

O boundless Father, O Love infinite,
Who has through this your handmaid shown to us
Such worthy matters that the more I think
About your grace, the more my heart grows bright;
With your sweet fire you've set me all alight.
O Domitilla, bride most sanctified,
Baptize us in the name of your God, for
Our every wish is bent on serving him.

A SERVANT *goes to Aurelianus and tells him that the two bridegrooms have converted to Christianity:*

98

I'd bring you better news, Aurelian,
Of Domitilla, whom you love the best,
But know that she has managed things so well
That those you sent to see her have now been
Baptized by her; their plighted grooms as well
She has converted to the Christian faith.

AURELIANO *volto a' sua servi dice:*

Andate presto e tanto adoperate
che 'n qualche modo qui me la meniate.

Giunti e SERVI, *a Domitilla dicono:*

99
Domitilla, per forza o per amore
con esso noi presto ti metti in via;
così comanda il tuo sposo e signore,
il qual t'aspetta con gran baronia.

DOMITILLA *fa orazione a Dio dicendo:*

O Iesù mio benigno Redentore,
vogli guardar la verginità mia,
e voi, dilette mia, meco verrete,
né minacce e tormenti non temete.

AURELIANO, *venuta Domitilla a lui, così dice:*

100
O Domitilla mia, sommo desire,
a chi t'apreza più che altra cosa
benignamente voglia acconsentire.
Tu se' gentil, perché non se' pietosa,
perché ti giova mia vita finire
in tanti affanni senza aver mai posa?
Comanda e sarà fatto quel che brami.

DOMITILLA *volta a Dio dice:*

Or si vedrà, Signor, quanto tu ami.

AURELIANUS *turns to his servants and says:*

Go quickly and let every effort be
To bring her somehow right back here to me.

The SERVANTS, *having come before Domitilla, say:*

> 99
> By force, O Domitilla, or for love
> Set out upon your way with us at once;
> For thus commands your husband and your lord
> Who waits for you with great baronial pomp.

DOMITILLA *prays to God sayings:*

O Jesus mine, Redeemer tender, kind
Be pleased to shelter my virginity,
And you belovèd friends, set out with me,
Be not afraid of torments or of threats.

Upon Domitilla's arrival, AURELIANUS *says:*

> 100
> O Domitilla, my supreme desire,
> You whom I value, prize above all else,
> I beg you in your kindness to consent.
> You are genteel, why not show mercy then?
> How does it serve you thus to end my life
> In such great torment and no hope of rest?
> Ask only—it will be as you request.

DOMITILLA *turns to God and says:*

Now, Lord, how much you love me we shall see.

Uno SERVO va a Lussurio e dice come Aureliano ballando è cascato morto:[33]

101
Sappi che Domitilla con sua incanti
ha fatto cader morto il tuo fratello,
così ballando con suoni e con canti;
però, vien presto, se tu vuoi vedello.

LUSSURIO, *fratello di Aureliano, dice:*

Se tutti e nostri dèi non sono erranti,
non fia senza vendetta morto quello.
Pigliate questa maga maladetta,
ch'io intendo far di lei cruda vendetta.

LUSSURIO *giunto a Domitilla, dice:*

102
Se' tu quella perversa incantatrice
che m'hai privato del fratel maggiore?
Presto sarai di lui vie più infelice.
Così da parte dello Imperadore
a voi serventi si comanda e dice
che tutte le spogliate a gran furore;
faretegli sentir l'ultimo strazio
nel fuoco acceso sanza alcuno spazio.

DOMITILLA, *rivolta alle sue compagne, dice:*

103
Or si vedrà di noi la gran costanza
e quanta accesa sia la fiamma immensa.
Volgete verso Idio vostra speranza
che presto sarén tutti alla sua mensa.
O buon Iesù, sotto la cui fidanza
la vita a tanto strazio si dispensa,

A SERVANT *goes to Luxurius and says that Aurelianus fell dead while dancing:*[33]

101

Know you that Domitilla with her spells
Has made your brother fall down dead while he
Was dancing thus to instruments and songs.
Therefore come quickly if you want to see him.

LUXURIUS, *Aurelianus' brother, says:*

Unless our gods are all mistaken now,
My brother's death will not go unavenged.
That sorceress accursèd apprehend,
A vengeance cruel upon her I intend.

LUXURIUS, *having come to Domitilla, says:*

102

Are you that perverse sorceress, the one
Who took my elder brother from me now?
More unfortunate than he you soon will be.
So, in the Emperor's name I now command
And order you who serve him—take the women,
Strip them naked with the utmost force;
Make sure they suffer to the very end,
And let them have no respite in the flames.

DOMITILLA *turns to her companions and says:*

103

Now they shall see our steady constancy,
However hot the vast flame burns around.
In God repose your hope, for very soon
We all shall at his holy table be.
O Jesus good, entrusted to your love
We yield our lives by suffering great pain.

tu vedi ben la nostra intenzione,
fa' che non vinca il senso la ragione.

IL CAVALIERE, *menato Domitilla agl'idoli,*[34] *dice prima ch' uccida lei e le compagne:*

          104
Bench'io n'abbia licenza, io non vorrei
sì degna cosa a morte giudicare,
però, se mi prometti a' nostri idei
far sacrificio, io ti farò scampare.

DOMITILLA *risponde al Cavaliere:*

Che pensi tu per questi falsi e rei
ch'i' voglia a tanto Sposo rinunziare?
Sappi che per suo amor morir mi giova.

EL MANIGOLDO *dice:*

Andiànne! Tu sarai presto alla pruova.

DOMITILLA *fa orazione a Dio dicendo così:*

          105
Perdona, Signor mio, a queste ancelle.
Pietà, Signor, di tutti e pensier vani.
Perdona a queste semplicette agnelle,
a' lupi oggi venute nelle mani.
In manus tuas, Signor, ricevi quelle
e gli altri che per noi fatti cristiani.

EL MANIGOLDO, *volendo abruciarle, dice:*

Usciànne![35] Tu m'ha' fatto consumare![36]
Racomandati a me, che t'ho a bruciare.

You very clearly see what we intend,
Lord, let sense not vanquish reason in the end.

The KNIGHT *leads Domitilla before the idols, and, before he kills her and the others, says:*

104
Though I have license for it, I don't wish
To sentence such a worthy one to death,
Therefore, if to our gods you promise me
To offer sacrifice, I'll set you free.

DOMITILLA *answers the Knight:*

Do you imagine that for idols false
And wicked I'd forswear a Spouse so great?
Know you that for his love I'll gladly die.

The EXECUTIONER *says:*

Come on, we'll quickly put you to the test.

DOMITILLA *prays to God saying:*

105
These your handmaids, O my Lord, forgive.
Have mercy, Lord, for all their foolish thoughts.
Forgive these childlike and unworldly lambs
Who on this day have fallen prey to wolves.
Into your hands, O Lord, receive them now,
And all the others whom we've brought to Christ.

The EXECUTIONER, *ready to burn them says:*

Let's move along! You've made me waste my time.
Submit now, I must burn you for this crime.

L'AGNOLO *dà licenza:*

106
O tutti voi che contemplato avete[37]
di Domitilla la divota storia,
all'eterna bontà grazie rendete
che v'amaestri di trovar vittoria
nel mondo cieco, dove involti siete,
come costei ch'alla superna gloria
volse l'anima bella e 'l suo disire,
non curando del mondo alcun martire.

FINIS

The ANGEL *dismisses the audience:*

106

O everyone who has considered well[37]
The sacred story of St. Domitilla,
Give thanks to Eternal Goodness for his grace,
That he may teach you to find victory
In this blind world where you're entangled all,
And be like her, who pledged her lovely soul
To reaching heav'nly glory—her sole desire,
Not heeding the world's torments or its fire.

THE END

La Rappresentazione di Santa Guglielma

INTERLOCUTORI

ANGELO, annunziatore
IL RE d'Ungheria
IL FRATELLO del Re d'Ungheria, detto poi, IL LEBBROSO
IL RE d'Inghilterra
GUGLIELMA, figlia del Re d'Inghilterra
LA REGINA d'Inghilterra
UN CORRIERE
IL SINISCALCO del Re d'Ungheria
UN POVERO
UN ALTRO POVERO
UN ALTRO CORRIERE
UN OSTE
IL PODESTÀ, anche IL RETTORE
LA CAMERIERA di Guglielma
LE SERVE di Guglielma
UN CAVALIERE del Re d'Ungheria
[I compagni del Cavaliere]*
NOSTRA DONNA, la Beata Vergine Maria
DUE ANGELI mandati in aiuto di Guglielma
UN PADRONE di nave
[I compagni del Padrone]*
INFERMO sanato da Guglielma
BADESSA
[Molti poveri ammalati]*
UN SERVO del Re d'Ungheria
IL PRIMO MEDICO
IL SECONDO MEDICO
UN ALTRO SERVO del Re d'Ungheria
I BARONI del Re d'Ungheria
*Non parlano.

The Play of Saint Guglielma

CAST OF CHARACTERS

ANGEL, who announces the play
The KING of Hungary
The BROTHER of the King of Hungary, later called, the LEPER
The KING of England
GUGLIELMA†, daughter of the King of England
The QUEEN of England
A MESSENGER
The SENESCHAL of the King of Hungary
A PAUPER
ANOTHER PAUPER
ANOTHER MESSENGER
AN INNKEEPER
The PODESTÀ, the chief administrative and judicial officer
Guglielma's CHAMBERMAID
Guglielma's MAID SERVANTS
A KNIGHT of the King of Hungary
[The companions of the Knight]*
OUR LADY, the Blessed Virgin Mary
TWO ANGELS, sent in aid of Guglielma
A SHIP'S CAPTAIN
[The companions of the Ship's Captain]*
SICK MAN healed by Guglielma
ABBESS
[Many sick persons]*
A SERVANT of the King of Hungary
THE FIRST DOCTOR
THE SECOND DOCTOR
ANOTHER SERVANT of the King of Hungary
BARONS of the King of Hungary

† Guglielma is pronounced: gu- ʎel- ma [the *gli* is a liquid *l*, not a *g*]
*They gesture, but do not speak.

Comincia la rappresentazione di Santa Guglielma composta per mona Antonia donna di Bernardo Pulci.

*Prima viene l'*ANGELO *' annunziare la festa e dice:*

1

O giusto eterno e sommo Redentore,
che per noi peccator qua giù venisti,
essendo tu del ciel Padre e Signore,
di queste umane spoglie ti vestisti,
e per tua gregge come buon pastore
in croce morte e passion sentisti,
fa' ch'io possa mostrar sol per tua gloria
di Guglielma beata la sua storia.

2

Essendo nuovamente battezato
alla fé di Iesù, il re d'Ungheria
di tôrre sposa fu diliberato
e fe' cercar per ogni signoria;
col gran re d'Inghilterra imparentato
si fu d'una sua figlia eletta e pia,
che fu Guglielma nominata quella,
ornata di costumi, onesta e bella.

3

Questa Guglielma molti lunghi affanni
sostenne, e fu nel mondo peregrina,
e condannata fu con falsi inganni
nel fuoco, e quella Maestà Divina
liberò questa d'ogni insidie e inganni,
perché soccorre chiunche a lei s'inchina.
Benché fussi nel mondo tormentata
sì come Iob al fin fu ristorata.

Here begins the play of Saint Guglielma, written by Mona Antonia, wife of Bernardo Pulci.

First the ANGEL *comes to announce the play:*

1

O Highest Savior, O Eternal Right,
You, for us sinners, came amongst us here,
Though you're the Father of heaven and its Lord—
You still arrayed yourself in human flesh,
And like a shepherd good to save your flock
You died upon the cross and felt its pangs,
Allow me to set forth the lovely story
Of Saint Guglielma here just for your glory.

2

Having been in the faith of Jesus Christ
Baptized of late, the king of Hungary
Decided that he wished to take a wife,
And having searched abroad through every land
With England's mighty king he linked himself
By means of his pious daughter, God's elect,
And she was named Guglielma and was graced
With manners beautiful and habits chaste.

3

This Guglielma many miseries
Long bore, and was a wanderer in the world
And to the fire with fraudulent deceits
She was condemned, whence Majesty divine
Freed her from every peril and from harms,
Because he succors all who turn to him.
Tormented in the world was she, deplored
Like Job, at last like him she was restored.

Il RE *d'Ungheria volto al fratello e a' baroni dice:*

    4
Attendi ben, diletto fratel mio,
e voi, baron, la mia voglia ascoltate:
di tôrre sposa è fermo il mio disio,
e però l'Inghilterra ricercate
d'una che ci dimostra il nostro Idio,
adorna di costumi e d'onestate,
Guglielma detta, del gran re figliuola.

Risponde il FRATELLO *del Re:*

Ubidita sarà la tua parola.

Il fratello del Re e i baroni giunti al Re d'Inghilterra dicono e prima il FRATELLO *del Re:*

    5
La fama, serenissimo signore,
che della figlia tua nel mondo suona,
c'induce a supplicare il tuo valore,
mandati d'Ungheria dalla corona,
che degni acompagnar con puro core
tua cara figlia colla sua persona
qual dono accetto; se 'l consentirai
ancor lieto e felice ne sarai.

Il RE *d'Inghilterra risponde così dicendo:*

    6
I' rendo somme grazie al vostro sire
che degna la mia figlia dimandare,
e di piacere a quello ho gran desire;
ma vo' con la Reina consultare.
Fate Guglielma e lei da noi venire
per poter questo caso essaminare.

The KING of Hungary, addressing his brother and his barons says:

>   4
> Attend me well, belovèd brother mine,
> And all you barons, listen to my will:
> For my desire is fixed to take a spouse,
> In England, therefore, make your inquiries
> Concerning one our God points out to us,
> One graced with chastity, and habits good,
> The great king's child, Guglielma is her name.

The King's BROTHER answers:

All your instructions, sir, shall be obeyed.

The brother of the King and the barons, having come before the King of England, speak to him—first the BROTHER of the King:

>   5
> O Highness most serene, the high renown
> That of your daughter sounds throughout the world
> Induces us, sent here by Hungary's king,
> Your lordship to beseech with heart sincere
> That with sincere heart you'll agree to make
> Your daughter's person a most welcome gift;
> If you'll consent to this, confer that gift,
> For that you will be joyful and content.

The KING of England answers:

>   6
> With utmost gratitude I thank your lord,
> That he should deign to want my daughter's hand,
> And I greatly long to gladden him,
> But first I wish to seek the Queen's advice;
> Let Guglielma and her before us come
> So we can well consider this affair.

E volto a gl'imbasciadori dice:

Assai diletta a noi vostra proposta,
e presto renderem grata risposta.

Venuta la Reina e Guglielma in corte; il RE *dice prima alla Reina:*

7
Dilettissima mia cara consorte,
a noi son d'Ungheria messaggi degni,
mandati dal signor in nostra corte,
e priega ognun di noi che non si sdegni
di dar Guglielma a lui con lieta sorte;
avendo già cercati molti regni,
d'amor sospinto, da buon zelo e fama,
Guglielma nostra sol ricerca e brama.

Il RE *volto a Guglielma dice:*

8
E tu, diletta mia cara figliuola,
se così piace a quel che tutto regge
che da tanto signor eletta sola
nuovamente venuto a nostra legge,
non s'aspetta altro che la tua parola
a dar questa risposta a chi t'elegge.
Fa' che consenta al tuo diletto padre,
e similmente alla tua dolce madre.

GUGLIELMA *risponde al Re suo padre e dice:*

9
Dilettissimo padre e signor mio,
abbi pietà[1] della mia castitate.
Non basta esser promessa al nostro Idio,
eterno Sposo di tal degnitate

And, having turned to the ambassadors, he says:

Of your proposal we are pleased to learn,
And soon a welcome answer we'll return.

Guglielma and the Queen having come into the court, the KING *speaks first to the Queen:*

7

My most belovèd one, my consort dear,
These worthy messengers into our court
By Hungary's lord were sent, and he requests
That we will not object to giving him
Our Guglielma with surpassing joy.
He's searched through many realms for love, indeed,
Urged on by love, by zeal, and fame and seeks
Alone our Guglielma, longs for her.

The KING, *facing Guglielma, speaks thus:*

8

And you, belovèd daughter dear to me,
If that One who rules everything is pleased
That you've been chosen by so great a lord,
One recently converted to our law,
It waits on nothing but your word to give
This answer to that one who's chosen you.
To your belovèd father give consent,
And likewise give it to your mother sweet.

GUGLIELMA *answers her father:*

9

O most belovèd father and my lord:
Take pity on my chastity; does it
Suffice not that I'm promised to our God—
A Spouse eternal of such dignity

al qual servir è volto ogni disio?
Iesù, merzé di mia verginitate!
Io pensai camminar per la tua via;
or non so più quel che di me si fia.

Il RE parla con Guglielma e dice:

10
Che la verginità sia degna cosa
a questo ignun non è che contradica,
ma ben potrai nel mondo essendo sposa
operar verso Idio come pudica.
Al Re alquanto sarai più graziosa
nella fé di Iesù più t'affatica.

La REINA dice a Guglielma:

Se tanti prieghi son degni di grazia,
fa' che tu faccia nostra voglia sazia.

GUGLIELMA consente al padre e alla madre dicendo:

11
Per non esser a voi disubidiente
io voglio a tanti prieghi aconsentire,
benché disposta fussi la mia mente
vergine e casta vivere e morire.
Benigno padre mio, giusto e clemente,
né debbo o posso a te nulla disdire:
se così piace alla tua maestate,
signor, sia fatto la tua volontate.

Il RE fatto chiamare gli ambasciadori:

12
Udite, o cavalier, la mia parola
la qual sia ferma fede per risposta:

My every desire's intent on serving him?
Have mercy, Jesus, on my virginity,
For though I'd thought to walk thy path with thee,
I don't know now what will become of me.

The KING *speaks with Guglielma and says:*

        10

A worthy condition is virginity,
Of course, this no one will deny, but you,
When in the world you are a wife, can, like
A modest woman, well behave toward God.
The more you strive in the faith of Jesus Christ,
That much more pleasing to the king you'll be.

The QUEEN *says to Guglielma:*

If many, many prayers deserve reward
Be sure that you discharge our will in this.

GUGLIELMA *consents to her father and mother, saying:*

        11

To not be disobedient to you,
I wish to yield to prayers so pressing, yet
My mind had been resolved to be a maid,
A virgin chaste to live and chaste to die.
My kindly father, merciful and just,
For that I can't refuse you, and should not,
If it's so pleasing to your majesty,
My lord, then let your will be done by me.

The KING *having called the ambassadors:*

        12

O barons, hear the words I utter now
Which give our answer in the best of faith:

benché Guglielma, a noi diletta, sola
di servir a Giesù fussi disposta,
pur volendo ubidir come figliuola,
benigna a' nostri prieghi al fin s'accosta.
Al Re scrivete la sentenzia nostra,
e Guglielma prendete omai per vostra.

Gli ambasciadori rispondono al Re ringraziandolo; e prima parla el FRATELLO *del Re:*

13
Quanto conviensi a noi, grazie immortale
si rende a te da parte del signore,
di sì gran don, di tanta sposa, e tale
magnificenza, con allegro core.

E volti a Guglielma gli danno certi doni dicendo:

Guglielma, a cui null'altra al mondo equale,
accetta questi don per nostro amore.

Il RE *volto a' sua servi dice:*

Fate vestir costei di ricche veste
e ordinate molti balli e feste.

Gli ambasciadori dicono al Re come hanno lettere dal Re d'Ungheria e prima viene UNO CORRIERE *con dette lettere:*

14
Lettere abbiam dal Re di tal tenore
il qual si raccomanda a tua clemenza;
la sposa aspetta sol con lieto cuore
e però ci costrigne alla partenza.

Although Guglielma, our delight, had been
Solely resolved on serving Jesus Christ,
Because an obedient daughter she would be,
She kindly has acceded to our prayers
At last. Write our pronouncement to your king,
And take Guglielma now to be your own.

The ambassadors answer the King, thanking him, and first the King of Hungary's BROTHER says:

13

For this agreement, our unending thanks
We render to you on our lord's behalf
For such a fine gift of so great a spouse—
Such generosity—with joyful hearts.

And turning to GUGLIELMA, they give her certain gifts, saying:

Guglielma, whom none equals in the world,
For our devotion, please accept these gifts.

The KING says to his servants:

Make sure that she's attired in rich array!
Order feasts and dances for this day!

The ambassadors tell the King that they have letters from the King of Hungary, and first a MESSENGER with the said letters enters:

14

We've letters from the king to this effect
To your grace, first, does he commend himself;
With joyful heart he longs but for his bride.
And this obliges us to take our leave.

Risponde il RE:

Guglielma ha ' ubidire² il suo signore:
a voi sia dato di partir licenza.
Quanto gli par, di lei disponga e quando:
sorella e figlia a voi la raccomando.

GUGLIELMA, *udendo che aveva a partirsi, dice al padre e alla madre inginocchiata:*

15
Come potrò da voi far dipartita,
dolce mio padre, o mia madre diletta?
Se mai v'avessi offeso alla mia vita,
priegovi che da voi sia benedetta.
Colui che è Somma Carità infinita
mi mostri la sua via vera e perfetta;
forteza, del mio cor fidanza e luce,
tu m'accompagna e sia mia scorta e duce.

La REINA *benedicendo Guglielma dice:*

16
Benedetta sia tu, figliuola mia.
Fa' ch'allo sposo tuo sia reverente,
in parlar saggia, in fatti onesta e pia,
a' minor tutti benigna e clemente.

Il RE *aggiunge e dice:*

Ricordati di noi dove tu sia,
e nella carità sarai fervente;
fa' che tu viva nel timor di Dio.

GUGLIELMA *risponde:*

Così fia fatto, padre e signor mio.

The KING *of England answers:*

Guglielma's duty is to obey her lord.
We give you license to depart. Let him
Direct her when and as he will. Take her
Into your care as child and sister too.

GUGLIELMA, *hearing that she had to depart, on her knees says to her father and mother:*

15

How am I able to depart from you,
My father sweet, O cherished mother mine?
If ever I have caused you any grief,
I pray you, give me blessing. Let that One
Who is surpassing, who is boundless love
Show me his way so perfect and so true.
O my heart's fortitude and faithful guide,
Escort me, light my way, with me abide.

The QUEEN, *blessing Guglielma says:*

16

O, my daughter, may you blessèd be,
Be sure that you're respectful to your spouse;
Be wise in speech, in actions chaste, devout,
To all your subjects, merciful and kind.

The KING *joins in and says:*

Remember us wherever you may be,
In charity be zealous, and be sure
That in the fear of God you live your life.

GUGLIELMA *answers:*

So shall I do, my father and my lord.

Giunti apresso al Re d'Ungheria con la sposa, il RE *viene incontro a Guglielma e presala per mano dice:*

17
Dolceza del mio cor, diletta sposa,
per mille volte ben venuta sia;
ogni mio desiderio in te si posa,
sommo riposo della vita mia.
Domanda se ti piace alcuna cosa:
ogni mia possa è nella tua balia.

Risponde GUGLIELMA *al marito:*

Altro non vo' se non ch'io chiego grazia
ch'i' facci, signor mio, tua voglia sazia.

Qui si fa festa e, fornite le noze, il RE *dice, volto a Guglielma e a' baroni, che si facci limosine e a' templi si vada a render grazia a Dio:*

18
Poi che fornite son di celebrare
le nostre noze e lieti sposalizi,
conviensi e sacri templi visitare
con degne offerte e con divini ufizi,
e a' servi di Dio offerte dare
acciò che questi giorni sien propizi.
Queste richeze son ben di fortuna:
al mondo chi più può sì ne rauna.[3]

Vanno molti poveri per limosine a quello che le dispensa, facciendo calca. Poi che l'ha date IL SINISCALCO *dice:*

19
Andate, poltronieri, a lavorare!
Ciò che si dona a voi gittato è via.

As they approach the King of Hungary with his bride, the KING *comes to meet Guglielma and takes her hand and says:*

17

O my sweetheart, my belovèd spouse,
More than a thousand times you're welcome here;
Every desire of mine is fixed on you,
O you surpassing refuge of my life.
If anything should please you, ask for it;
At your command is everything of mine.

GUGLIELMA *answers her husband:*

I wish naught else—unless I ask for grace
That I, my lord, may here perform your will.

At this point, celebrations are held and the nuptials completed. The KING *addresses Guglielma and the barons and says that alms should be distributed, and that they should go to the temples to give thanks to God:*

18

Now since our wedding festivals are done,
Our joyous nuptial rites, it's fitting that,
With worthy offerings and observances
Divine, we visit holy temples, and,
So that these days may prove propitious, give
Donations to God's servants. Certainly,
These riches come from fortune to those who
Can in the world amass the most of them.

Many poor persons go for alms to the one who distributes them. They crowd around him. After he has distributed the alms, the SENESCHAL *says:*

19

You lazy louts get out of here and work!
Whatever one gives to you is thrown away.

UN POVERO *dice:*

La carità non si vuol rimbrottare:
ancor non sai di te quel che si fia.

IL SINISCALCO *dice:*

Brutto poltron, non ti vidd'io giucare?[4]
Tu cerchi ch'io ti cavi la pazia.

UN ALTRO POVERO *dice:*

Pazo se' tu a darci questi doni.

IL SINISCALCO:

Aspetta un po'. Tu vorrai ch'io ti suoni?

Il Re con Guglielma, levati di sedia, vanno al tempio ' adorare.
GUGLIELMA, *veduto un crocifisso, si volge al marito e dice molte cose della vita e passione di Cristo, e finalmente lo induce che vada in Ierusalem a vedere il Sepolcro:*

20
Vedi qui, sposo mio, quel Signor degno
per lo qual l'universo fu salvato,
il quale avea pel trapassar del segno
l'antico padre all'inferno dannato,
quando gustò di quel vietato legno,[5]
sendo nel Paradiso collocato,
venuto a sadisfar l'altrui delitto
come ciascun profeta aveva scritto.[6]

21
Essendo Re del cielo, in terra scese
e volse della Vergin incarnare;
sopra di sé nostre miserie prese,

A PAUPER says:

You should not with reproach give charity;
You do not yet know what's in store for you.

The SENESCHAL *says:*

You ugly loafer, didn't I see you gambling?[4]
Of that folly do you want a cure from me?

ANOTHER PAUPER *says:*

Hey, you're the mad one, giving us these gifts.

The SENESCHAL *says:*

If you'd like me to thrash you, just you wait.

The King and Guglielma, having risen from their seats, go to the temple to pray. GUGLIELMA, *on seeing a crucifix, turns to her husband and says many things about the life and passion of Christ, and in the end persuades him to go to the Sepulchre at Jerusalem:*

20
Look here, my spouse, upon that worthy Lord
By whom the universal world was saved;
He condemned to hell our primal father
For having overstepped the mark and having
Tasted the fruit of the forbidden tree;[5]
Then, though he dwelt in Paradise, he came
To make atonement for that other's sin
As the prophets had written he would do.

21
Though King of heaven, he came down to the earth
And by a virgin chose to take on flesh,
Take on himself our miseries; our thirst,

fame, sete, dolor volse gustare.
Quanto di dolce amor per noi s'accese,
povero, per far noi nel ciel posare,
peregrinando qui trentatrè anni
nel mondo e nel diserto in tanti affanni!

22
Dalla suo gregge fu il pastor tradito
e dato a quelli scribi e farisei;
fu da Erode e Pilato schernito,
battuto da que' perfidi giudei;
confitto in croce, dove fu sentito
pregare il Padre per que' falsi e rei;
sepolto, suscitò po' el terzo giorno
e tornossi nel ciel di gloria adorno.

23
Or pensa, signor mio, quel che sarebbe
veder cogli occhi quel ch'ascolti adesso!
Quanta dolceza il tuo cor sentirebbe
a baciar dove il legno fu commesso,
dove, morto, Maria nel grembo l'ebbe
e 'l munimento ove Iesù fu messo,
e queste ed altre sì mirabil cose
che per noi ingrati Cristian son nascose.

Il RE, *commosso per le parole di Guglielma, consente di volere andare al Sepolcro e dice:*

24
Tu m'hai di dolce fiamma il cor sì acceso
che quel ch'hai detto qui mi par presente;
l'animo a contemplar resta sospeso,
né altro brama o cerca la mia mente
che veder dove il corpo fu disteso
in croce per salvar l'umana gente.

Our hunger and our sorrow wished to taste.
So greatly did he burn with love of us,
To bring us rest in heaven, through the world
And through the desert he went wandering poor
For three-and-thirty years with many trials!

      22

The Shepherd, by his flock, though, was betrayed,
And given to those scribes and Pharisees;
By Herod was He scorned, and Pilate, too—
Was beaten by perfidious Jews and nailed
Upon the cross, whence to his Father he
Was heard to pray for those false, wicked ones.
Buried then, and on the third day risen,
Bedecked in glory, he returned to heaven.

      23

Now think, my lord, how it would be to see
These things that you have just been hearing of
With your own eyes. What sweetness would your heart
Know to kiss the spot on which the cross
Was raised, where Mary held him, dead, upon
Her lap, the tomb where they laid Jesus—all
These marvelous things and even more that we
Unappreciative Christians do not see.

Moved by Guglielma's words, the KING *agrees to go to see the Holy Sepulcher and says:*

      24

You have my heart so kindled with sweet flame
That what you've spoken of seems present here;
My mind is fixed in contemplation
And neither seeks nor yearns for anything
Except to see the place His body hung
Upon the cross to save the human race.

Per tanto son disposto e voglio andare,
Guglielma, il santo luogo a visitare.

GUGLIELMA, *aggiungendo, dice al Re che la lasci andare con lui:*

25
Così ti presti grazia il Signor degno,
pur che m'accetti teco in compagnia;
io te ne priego con tutto il mio ingegno
che questa grazia a me concesso sia.

Il RE *risponde a Guglielma:*

Non è lecito sol lasciar il regno,
però bisogna che in mio luogo stia;
reggerai con giustizia e con prudenza
e non ti pesi questa mia partenza.

Il RE, *volendo andare, dice al fratello come lo lascia insieme con Guglielma a governare il regno:*

26
Ascolta, fratel mio prudente e saggio,
e voi, baroni, notate il mio sermone:
avendo al luogo santo a far viaggio,
sospinto per divina spirazione
in questo santo mio peregrinaggio,
Guglielma lascio alla dominazione,
la qual in cambio mio receverete
e lei come regina ubiderete.

Il FRATELLO *del Re, veggendolo disposto ad andare, dice così:*

27
Poi che disposto se' voler andare
a noi debbe piacer quel ch'a te piace;

I'm firmly resolute, Guglielma, I
Desire to go to see the holy place.

Continuing, GUGLIELMA asks the King that he allow her to go with him:

      25
May our worthy Lord grant you grace for this;
And that I may accompany you I pray
With every faculty at my command
That you'll agree to grant this grace to me.

The KING answers:

I know it is not lawful to desert
The realm, so you must in my place remain;
With justice and with prudence will you rule;
And when I go, don't find my leaving cruel.

The KING, as he is about to depart, tells his brother that he leaving him and Guglielma to govern the realm together:

      26
Pray listen, prudent brother mine, and wise,
You barons, too, take note of what I speak:
By inspiration sacred have I been
Impelled to journey to the Holy Land;
In this my sacred pilgrimage, I leave
Guglielma my dominion; in exchange
For me receive her as your queen,
And be to her, as queen, obedient.

The King's BROTHER, seeing him resolved to go, says:

      27
Since you are resolved that you must go,
What you desire for us must please us too;

Guglielma penserén sempre onorare
benché la tua partita assai ci spiace.

Abracciando GUGLIELMA il marito, nel suo partire dice così:

Quel che degnò Tubia d'acompagnare,
lui sia tua guida e tua scorta verace.[7]

Il RE volto di nuovo a' baroni dice nel partire:

Adio, vi lascio; e sopra ogni altra cosa
vi raccomando la mia cara sposa.

Partito il Re, il FRATELLO finge di volere parlare con la Reina in camera per volere tentarla come innamorato di lei con parole simulate:

28

Glorïosa madonna, i' ho da dire
cose secrete alla tua riverenza,
le qual vorrei sol teco conferire,
se molesto non t'è darmi udienza.

GUGLIELMA, non accorgendosi dello inganno, consente d'ascoltarlo:

Andiàn, che mi fia grato di sentire
quel che mi vogli dir la tua prudenza;
più cara cosa, apresso alla corona,
non m'è che di parlar con tua persona.

Il FRATELLO del Re, come si dice di sopra, manifesta a Guglielma il suo amore, dicendo:

29

Quel ch'io t'ho a conferir, dolce mio bene,
è ch'io t'adoro in terra per mia stella;

Guglielma we shall always honor, though,
When you leave, we'll hate to see you go.

Embracing her husband at his departure, Guglielma says:

May he who went at the good Tobias' side
Be your true escort; may he be your guide.[7]

The KING *turns again to his Barons and says in parting:*

Farewell, I leave you, and, above all else,
In your safekeeping I leave my darling spouse.

After the King's departure, his BROTHER *pretends to have to speak with Guglielma in her chamber so he can tempt her as a lover with dissembling speeches:*

28

My glorious lady, secret things must I
Say to your reverence; I should like to speak
About them with you alone, if you don't object
To giving me an audience with you.

GUGLIELMA, *unsuspecting, consents to hear him:*

Let's go, for I am pleased to listen to
What in your prudence you would say to me;
Nothing's more dear to me, except the king,
Than having a conversation with yourself.

The BROTHER *of the King (as mentioned above) declares his love for Guglielma, saying:*

29

My sweet love, what I must confess to you
Is that on earth I love you as my star;

dicati amor quel che 'l mio cor sostiene,
e tu sia savia come tu se' bella.

GUGLIELMA, *accortasi del suo disonesto pensiero, adirata si volge a lui e comandagli che si parta da lei, dicendo:*

Omè, dov'è l'amor, dov'è la spene?
Se giustizia è, Giesù, difendi quella!
Guglielma al tuo fratel vuoi violare?
Fa' che sie savio e più non mi parlare!

GUGLIELMA, *partito il fratello del Re, dice seco medesima in camera sola:*

30

Tacerò, lassa, omai sì grande offesa
che la Reina sia suta tentata?
La maestà del re fia vilipesa
s'io parlo, la mia corte fia turbata.
O Dio, tu sia mia scorta e mia difesa;
Susanna so che fu per te salvata.
Io non so che mi far né che mi dire;
tacerò fin che 'l Re debbe venire.

Il FRATELLO *del Re, partito di camera di Guglielma, adirato e minacciando, seco medesimo dice:*

31

Veramente costei sol per paura
ch'io non voglia tentarla o farne pruova
si mostra così brusca e così pura;
che sien fallace non è cosa nuova.[8]
Vedrén se 'l ciel di lei ha tanta cura;
per vendicarsi la cagion si truova.
Io te ne pagherò. Fa', se tu sai,
e so che presto te ne pentirai.

Let love report to you what my heart feels,
And be as wise as you are beautiful.

GUGLIELMA, *made aware of his unchaste intentions, addresses him angrily and orders him to leave her, saying:*

Alas, where is my love? Where is my hope?
If there be justice, Jesus, guard it now!
Would you ravish your brother's Guglielma?
Be wise, and do not speak to me again!

The BROTHER *of the King having exited, Guglielma, alone in the room, says to herself:*

30

Shall I keep still, woe, now how great a wrong
That he's attempted to seduce the queen?
The king's great majesty will be disgraced.
My court will be in turmoil if I speak—
O God, you're my defender, you my guide;
Susanna was, I know, preserved by you.
I don't know what I ought to do or say;
I shall keep silent till the king returns.

The King's BROTHER, *after leaving Guglielma's chamber, enraged and making threats, says to himself:*

31

I know for sure that only on account
Of fear does she appear so brusque and pure
To one who'd tempt her, put her to the test,
For women's falsity is nothing new.[8]
We'll see how much that heaven of hers will care,
For I shall find a way to be avenged;
Do something if you dare—if you know how!
That you'll regret it soon, I'm sure right now!

Viene uno CORRIERE *a una osteria e dice, come il Re è quivi apresso che torna dal Sepolcro, che truovi mangiare:*

32

Truovaci presto da far colezioni;
tu piglierai con noi più d'un fiorino.
Hacci tu starne, pollastri o pippioni?

L'OSTE *risponde al corriere:*

Messer, ciò che vi piace e un buon vino.

Il CORRIERE *seguitando il suo parlare dice all'oste:*

Egli è qua presso, a piè per divozioni,
il signor nostro come un peregrino.
Facci goder—tu mi par uom discreto—
e serri l'uscio poi chi vien dirieto.[9]

Viene un CORRIERE *in corte e dice come il signore è quivi presso:*

33

Sappiate che 'l signore è qua vicino;
io l'ho lasciato apresso a due giornate
a piè vestito come un peregrino.
Alla Reina sua l'annunziate.

Il FRATELLO *del Re dice agli altri baroni:*

Andiàn, che noi troviàn quel pel camino.

Il CORRIERE *detto dice:*

Chi mi farà il dover, se voi n'andate?

A MESSENGER *comes to an inn and says that the King is near at hand, returning from the Holy Sepulchre, and they should prepare something to eat:*

      32

Hurry and find us something for our meal.
You'll get a florin from us, even more.
Have you some partridge? Cockerel? Some squab?

The INNKEEPER *answers:*

What pleases you is here, sir, good wine too.

The MESSENGER, *continuing to speak, says to the innkeeper:*

On foot he's coming here for piety,
For as a pilgrim does our lord approach.
A man discrete you seem; so treat us well.
And the last one in should bar the door.

A MESSENGER *comes to the court and says that the lord is nearby:*

      33

Know, all of you, our lord is near at hand,
I've left him merely two days' journey off,
On foot and as a pilgrim clothed he comes.
Announce these tidings to his royal queen.

The BROTHER *of the King says to the barons:*

Let us all go to meet him on the road.

The same MESSENGER *says:*

Who will pay what's due me if you go?

Il FRATELLO *del Re agli altri baroni dice così:*

Fategli dar quel che vuole egli stesso;
studiate, ché 'l signor debbe esser presso.

Vanno incontro al Re e, giunti all'osteria, il FRATELLO *del Re dice per tutti al fratello:*

34
Serenissimo Re, frate e signore,
quanto felice son pel tuo ritorno.

Il RE *non risponde a proposito, ma solo dimanda di Guglielma:*

Ch'è di Guglielma mia, perfetto amore?
Altro non bramo che 'l suo viso adorno.

Il FRATELLO *del Re dice al fratello:*

Guglielma ha tanto offeso il nostro onore,
che volendolo dir non basta un giorno.

Il RE *irato dice al fratello:*

Omè, fratel mio, che cosa fia?
Che vuo' tu dir della Reina mia?

Il FRATELLO *del Re, seguitando, dice al fratello:*

35
Io temo a dirti cosa sì molesta.
La vita di Guglielma scelerata,
poi che partisti, in balli, in canti e festa,
palesemente è stata riprovata,
tanto che a dirlo è cosa disonesta.
Tutta la corte tua resta infamata;

The BROTHER *of the King says to the barons:*

What he wishes, give him; it's his due;
Be quick, because the lord must be at hand.

They go to meet the King, and having arrived at the inn, the King's BROTHER *speaks for everyone and says:*

34
King most serene, my brother and my lord,
How happy I am made by your return.

The King doesn't answer directly, but asks only about Guglielma:

My perfect love, Guglielma—what news of her?
I yearn for nothing but her lovely face.

The BROTHER *of the King says to his brother:*

Guglielma has our honor much abused;
A day would not suffice to tell you all.

The angry KING *says to his brother:*

Alas my brother, what can this thing be?
What's this you're trying to say about my queen?

The King's BROTHER *continuing says to his brother:*

35
I fear to tell you what will trouble you:
Since you left home Guglielma's wicked life's
Been spent in dance and song and revelry—
Her conduct has been publicly reproached
So much that just to say it brings us shame.
On your whole court she brought dishonor too.

se non provedi colla tua prudenza,
vituperata fia nostra semenza.

Il RE *dice al fratello:*

        36
O lasso! È questo il premio e 'l grande onore
di Guglielma, alla qual tutto il mio regno
e la dominazione e la maggiore
sopra tutti lascia'la in luogo degno?
Non resterà impunito tanto errore:
fa' che di tanta offesa mostri segno;
io non vo' ritornar se a sua malizia
sadisfatto non è. Fanne giustizia!

Il FRATELLO *del Re viene in corte e comanda al Podestà che facci morire Guglielma:*

        37
Da parte del signore ecco il mandato:
ti si comanda, fa' che sia prudente,
che la Reina, quanto puoi celato,
facci d'aver a te subitamente;
sanza cercar di lei altro peccato,
falla morire, e fa' secretamente,
nel fuoco sanza aver alcun rispetto.

Il PODESTÀ *risponde, e va a Guglielma:*[10]

Sia che si vuole il farò con effetto.

Il RETTORE *va a Guglielma ad annunziargli la sua morte pigliando con lei scusa e confortandola:*

        38
Regina, il sommo Dio ti doni pace!
Duolmi sì duro caso averti a dire,

If with prudence you don't this matter face,
Our entire lineage you will disgrace.

The KING answers his brother:

> 36

O woe, is this the prize, the honor great
Of that Guglielma to whom, over all
My realm, my power and dominion I
Entrusted, left her in a worthy place?
So great a wrong will not unpunished go:
Go make example of such great offense;
Until such evil has had its reward
I shan't return! Go now! Do justice hard!

The BROTHER of the King comes to court and orders the Podestà to have Guglielma executed:

> 37

Upon our lord's behalf, behold his charge
That orders you thus prudently to act:
As secretly as possible have the Queen
At once brought to you; without asking her
About her other faults, let her be killed—
And do it secretly—by means of fire,
And with no token of respect for her.

The PODESTÀ answers:[10]

That which he wishes I shall have performed.

The PODESTÀ goes to Guglielma and tells her she must die, asks her pardon and urges her to be strong:

> 38

May highest God grant peace to you, O Queen!
I'm grieved to have to bring you such hard news,

ma poi ch'al mio signor, tuo sposo, piace,
pensa che a me è lecito ubidire.
Chi tutto vede sa quanto e' mi spiace:
sappi che mi convien farti morire.
Reggi l'animo tuo come prudente
e verso il tuo Fattor volgi la mente.

Seguita il detto RETTORE:

39

E tu, madonna, a me perdonerai
ché a me troppo molesta è la tua morte.
Nessun fuggir la può, come tu sai,
che a tutti è data al fin questa per sorte;
però l'anima a Dio rivolgerai,
che presto sarai dentro alla sua corte
a posseder quel gaudio ch'è infinito:
dunche, Guglielma mia, piglia partito.

GUGLIELMA, *piangendo seco medesima, dice:*

40

O sventurata a me, per qual peccato
debb'io sanza cagion patir tormento?
O dolce padre, dove hai tu mandato
la tua cara Guglielma in perdimento?
Ah crudo sposo, come hai sentenziato
colei che a te non fe' mai fallimento?
Per premio sarò data a tal supplicio,
sì come Isach al santo sacrificio.

Seguita GUGLIELMA:

41

O padre mio, sol pe' tua prieghi, presi
isposo, contra tutte le mie voglie.
Di viver pura e casta sempre intesi,

But since my lord, your husband, thus is pleased,
Consider that I'm bound to heed his law.
He who sees all things knows how sorrowful
I am; know that I must put you to death.
Your mind with prudence govern, and address
Your intellect to your Creator now.

The PODESTÀ *continues:*

39

And you, my lady, pray you, pardon me,
For your death is for me too great a grief,
But, as you know, no one can flee from death,
For in the end fate brings it to each one.
Your soul, therefore, address to God, for soon
Within his court you'll be, and you shall have
That happiness which always will endure.
Therefore, Guglielma, now accept your fate.

Weeping, GUGLIELMA *says to herself:*

40

O woe! Unhappy me! And for what sin
Must I endure this torture without cause?
O father sweet, why have you sent your dear
Guglielma to perdition here?
Ah, cruel spouse, why have you sentenced her
Who never once has disappointed you?
As my reward, I'm given to the fire
Like Isaac, offered on the holy pyre.

GUGLIELMA *continues:*

41

O father mine, at your request alone
I took a spouse, against my every wish.
For always pure and chaste I meant to live

a noia m'eran le mondane spoglie
per le qual or sostengo grievi pesi;
finisco la mia vita in pianti e 'n doglie.
Misera a me, perché volli seguire
il mondo, lasso, pien d'ogni martire!

Seguita GUGLIELMA:

42
Son queste le delizie e somme feste
che mi son dal mio sposo riservate?

E volta alle serve:

Rendete, serve, a lui le ricche veste
e una nera a me n'apparecchiate.

Le serve di Guglielma, udito il pianto suo, dicono, cioè la CAMERIERA:

Cara madonna, che cose son queste?
Pel tuo lamento siàn tutte turbate!

GUGLIELMA *dice alle serve:*

E' mi convien da voi far dipartita,
perché il mio sposo mi fa tôr la vita.

Le SERVE *dicono a Guglielma:*

43
Oimè, per qual cagion, madonna mia,
debbi tu esser di vita privata?
Merita questo la tua signoria
d'aver sì ben la corte ministrata?
Se non t'è a sdegno nostra compagnia,
la morte teco insieme ci fia grata.

And wearisome to me those worldly spoils
For which I now must bear such heavy grief;
My life I end in weeping and in woes.
Ah, woe is me, why did I here remain
In this world—so filled with every pain!

GUGLIELMA *continues:*

      42
Are these the solemn celebrations and
Delights my spouse has kept in store for me?

And addressing the serving maids she says

Those garments rich return to him, my maids,
And let me be arrayed in one of black.

The maid servants of Guglielma, the CHAMBERMAID *[speaking for them], having heard her great lament, says:*

What things are these, dear lady, that we hear?
 Because of your lament we're all upset!

GUGLIELMA *says to her maid servants:*

From you I must be separated, for
My spouse my execution has ordained.

Her MAID SERVANTS *answer Guglielma and say:*

      43
My lady, tell us what the reason is
That of your life you thus must be deprived.
Does your Highness really merit this
For having so well overseen the court?
If you do not disdain our company,
To die with you would welcome be for us.

GUGLIELMA *partendosi dalle serve dice:*

Dilette serve mie, restate in pace,
poi ch'io debba morire al signor piace.

GUGLIELMA, *andando alla giustizia, dice per la via seco medesima:*

44

O infinito amor, Padre supremo,
che per me in croce il tuo sangue versasti,
aiuta me condotta al passo estremo,
sì come Danïel già liberasti,
però che sanza te pavento e temo.
Pietà, Signor, di tutti e pensier casti!
Da poi ch'io sono a torto condennata,
l'anima almen ti sia raccomandata.

Giunta GUGLIELMA *al martire, inginocchiata dice:*

45

E tu Vergine madre, figlia e sposa,
s'io merito da te essere udita,
fa' che la tua pietà non sia nascosa
a chi con tutto il cor dimanda aita.
Benigna madre, io so che se' pietosa,
fa' che l'anima sia con teco unita;
ogni secreto mio conosci scôrto[11]
e come al fuoco son dannata a torto.

Seguita GUGLIELMA:

46

Difendi, Signor mio, la mia innocenza,
e in tanta infamia non lasciar morire
la serva tua, per la tua gran potenza;
degna, Signore, e mie prieghi essaudire.

GUGLIELMA, *taking her leave from her maid servants, says:*

My maids belovèd, rest you here in peace,
For I'm required to die my lord to please.

Going to her execution, GUGLIELMA *says to herself along the way:*

44

O Love unbounded, Father consummate,
Who shed your blood for me upon the cross,
Help me, guide me to the final pass,
As you, indeed, set Daniel free because
Without you I am terrified, afraid.
Have mercy, Lord, on all my spotless thoughts,
For which I, wrongly thus, have been condemned;
My soul, at least, to you I do commend.

GUGLIELMA, *having come to the place of execution and fallen to her knees says:*

45

And you, O Virgin mother, daughter, bride,
If by you I am worthy to be heard,
Let not your pity hidden from me be,
From one who asks for aid with all her heart.
I know, kind Mother, you are merciful,
Let my soul be united with your own;
My every secret you know perfectly,
And know I'm wrongly sentenced to the fire.

GUGLIELMA *continues:*

46

My innocence, my Lord, may you defend,
Don't let me die in such great infamy;
O, by your mighty power let my prayers,
Your servant's, granted be, O worthy Lord.

Avendo offeso mai la tua clemenza,
perdona a me e non aconsentire
che messa sia in questo foco ardente,
benigno Redentor, giusto e clemente.

Il CAVALIERE *udito che era innocente, la domanda della cagione perché è condennata:*

47

Dimmi, se è giusta la domanda mia,
madonna, la cagion di tal supplicio.

GUGLIELMA *risponde al cavaliere:*

Sallo colui che incarnò di Maria,
il qual può dar di me retto giudicio.

Il CAVALIERE *fa pensieri di liberarla e dice a' compagni:*

Io credo certo che innocente sia,
e però non facciàn tal sacrificio;
i' ho disposto di lasciarla andare,
e le sue veste nel fuoco abruciare.

Il CAVALIERE *volto a Guglielma dice:*

48

Perch'io conosco e veggo chiaramente
che tu se' per invidia condennata,
però disposti siàn tutti al presente
che tu sia da tal pena liberata;
ma qui bisogna che tu sia prudente,
che in questo regno mai non sia trovata,
perché, avendoti noi da morte sciolta,
per te non fussi a noi la vita tolta.

Since never have I wronged your clemency,
Forgive me and do not give your consent
That I be put into this blazing fire,
Benign Redeemer, merciful and just.

The KNIGHT, *having heard that she was innocent, asks her why she is condemned:*

47

Tell me, if my questioning is right,
My lady, for such torment, what's the cause?

GUGLIELMA *answers the knight:*

That one who took on flesh from Mary, he
Can properly give judgment in my case.

The KNIGHT *decides to set her free, and says to his companions:*

I think it's certain that she's innocent,
Let's not, then, offer such a sacrifice.
I have determined that we'll let her go,
And burn her clothing in the fire instead.

The KNIGHT, *turned to Guglielma, says:*

48

Because I know and since I clearly see
That for resentment you have been condemned,
We all here present, therefore, are resolved
That from such punishment you should be freed;
But in this case you must be circumspect,
For in this realm you never must be found,
Because, for having set you free from death,
For your sake we don't want to lose our lives!

GUGLIELMA *ringrazia Idio d'essere scampata e dice:*

49
Quanto io posso, Signor, grazie ti rendo,
con tutto il cuor e colla mente mia;
della tua carità tutta m'accendo,
campata ha' me da tal sentenzia ria.
Tutta la vita mia servire intendo
a te, mio Sposo, e mia madre Maria
fa' che sia meco, sola, sventurata,
ch'io non sia dalle fiere divorata.

Guglielma, giunta nel diserto quasi adormentata, apparisce a lei la NOSTRA DONNA *vestita come donna e non si manifesta chi sia e dice:*

50
Porgimi la tua man, figlia diletta,
e sta sicura e non temer niente
perché sia in questo bosco sì soletta;
sappi ch'io son con teco fermamente.
Tu mi se' stata sempre tanto accetta
e verso al mio figliuol tanto servente:
mal non riceverai pel tuo ben fare,
però ti vogli alquanto confortare.

Seguita NOSTRA DONNA *dicendo:*

51
Chiunche confesso fia de' suo peccati
con penitenza e vera contrizione,
di ciascun mal da te fien liberati;
questo è del mio figliuol promessione.
Col segno della croce fien sanati,
perché di tua costanza operazione
vogliàn mostri, perché 'l tempo è venuto
c'ogni tuo desiderio fia adempiuto.

GUGLIELMA *thanks God for having escaped and says:*

49

I thank You, Lord, devoutly as I can,
With all my heart and with my intellect;
Your holy love has set me all afire
And freed me from that wicked sentence dire!
And I intend, my Spouse, to serve you all
My life; and let my mother Mary be with me
And let me not—alone, unfortunate—
Be eaten by the wild and savage beasts.

Guglielma comes into a wilderness, and when she is about to fall asleep, OUR LADY, *dressed as a woman, appears to her, and not revealing who she is, says:*

50

Belovèd daughter, place your hand in mine,
And rest secure; of nothing be afraid
Because you are alone here in this wood;
Know that I am here with you steadfastly.
To me forever pleasing you have been,
And firmly in the service of my Son;
For your good deeds you'll not be treated ill,
So now I'm here to urge you to take heart.

OUR LADY *continues, saying:*

51

Whoever confessed and shriven comes to you,
With penitence and with contrition true,
By you from every ill will be set free;
This is the promise that my Son has made.
With the sign of the cross they will be healed,
For we want you to be rewarded for
Your constancy, for it is now the time
When all of your desires will be fulfilled.

GUGLIELMA *svegliata dice a Nostra Donna:*

52
Chi siete voi che in questo luogo scuro
mi visitate afflitta in tanta doglia?
Tanto nel vostro aspetto io m'assicuro
che da me s'è partito ogni mia doglia.
Ditemi il nome vostro aperto e puro
e farete contenta la mia voglia.
Siete regina o donna di barone,
la qual mi date tal consolazione?

NOSTRA DONNA *si manifesta a Guglielma dicendo, e lei non la conosce se non poi che è partita:*

53
Sappi, diletta e cara mia figliuola,
ch'io son colei che ti scampai dal foco;
in questo aspro diserto[12] non se' sola,
perch'io vengo con teco in ogni loco.
Guglielma, intendi ben la mia parola:
ogni tormento in allegrezza e in gioco
ritornerà per la tua gran costanza,
pur che nel nome mio abbi fidanza.

GUGLIELMA *si duole che questa donna sia partita da lei:*

54
Omè, diletta mia, dove se' gita?
Ove rimango in questo bosco errante?
Perché sì tosto se' da me partita
che sì benigna ti se' mostra avante?
Chi darà più conforto alla mia vita?
O benigno Iesù, fammi costante!
Qui non è cosa da poter cibare,
né dove io scampi più non so pensare.

Having awakened, GUGLIELMA *says to Our Lady:*

52

Pray, who are you that in this gloomy place
Thus visits me who suffers such great woe?
So much your countenance assures me that
My every sorrow now has fled from me.
Your name, O tell me openly and clear,
And all I wish will thus be satisfied.
Are you a queen or else a baron's wife,
Who brings such consolation to my life?

OUR LADY *reveals herself to Guglielma by speaking, but she doesn't recognize her until she departs:*

53

My cherished and belovèd daughter, know
That I am she who saved you from the fire;
In this harsh wilderness, you're not alone,
For I shall come with you in every place.
Guglielma, clearly understand my words:
Your every torment into delight and joy
Will be converted for your constancy
So great, as long as you will trust in me

GUGLIELMA *laments that this lady has departed from her:*

54

Alas, delight of mine, where have you gone?
While in this tang'ling wood I wander still?
So quickly, why have you abandoned me,
For you before revealed yourself so kind?
Who now will give me strength to carry on?
O gentle Jesus, let me constant be!
There's nothing here to eat, nor can I guess
How I can get myself out of this mess!

Partita Nostra Donna, vengon DUA ANGIOLI *a confortare Guglielma e messala in mezo dicono a lei:*

55
Dimmi, sorella mia, per qual cagione
così ti mostri afflitta e tribulata?
Dunche non credi alla promessione
della Regina che t'ha visitata?

GUGLIELMA *risponde e non gli conosce:*

I' son sì piena di confusïone,
ch'altro che morte a me non è più grata.

Dicono gli ANGIOLI *a Guglielma:*

Se t'è in piacere, insieme in compagnia
con esso noi piglierai la tua via.

Giunti a uno certo luogo, truovano uno padrone di nave con certi compagni a sedere, e UNO DI QUELLI DUO ANGIOLI *chiama il detto padrone e dice:*

56
Ascolta un po', diletto fratel mio,
da parte di Iesù nostro Signore:
questa donzella, gran serva di Dio,
fa' che tu guidi, e fagli grande onore,
dove sarà più volto il suo desio,
perché l'è donna di molto valore,
e tu sarai da lei ben premiato.

Il PADRONE *risponde a quelli angioli non gli conoscendo:*

Io l'accompagnerò s'i' son pagato.

When Our Lady has left, TWO ANGELS *come to comfort Guglielma, and putting her between them, they say to her:*

55
My sister, tell me, for what reason do
You seem so greatly troubled and distressed?
Do you not believe that promise, then,
Made by the Queen who tarried here with you?

Not recognizing them, GUGLIELMA *says:*

I am so totally bewildered that
There's nothing I would welcome more than death.

The ANGELS *say to Guglielma:*

If you would like us as companions we
Will go along with you upon your way.

When they come to a certain place, they find a ship's captain sitting with certain companions, and ONE OF THOSE TWO ANGELS *calls out to the captain and says:*

56
My brother dear, pay heed a moment, please,
On our lord Jesus Christ's behalf: please see
That you conduct this lady, who is God's
Exalted servant, and with great respect
Please treat her; take her where she most desires
To go, for she's a lady of great worth,
And she will compensate you very well.

Not recognizing the angels, the SHIP'S CAPTAIN *answers them:*

If I am paid, I'll take her, truth to tell.

GUGLIELMA *ringrazia quelli angioli e dice:*

57
O dolci frate' mie, diletti e cari,
da parte del mio Idio grazie vi rendo,
ma di che pago s'io non ho danari
e questo altro non vuol s'io ben comprendo?

UNO DI QELLI ANGIOLI *gli dona uno anello a Guglielma dicendo:*

Ricevi questi don nel mondo rari.[13]

E volto al padrone:

Con questo paga. A te padron commendo
costei, che per mio amor l'accetti e degni,
per la qual tu vedra' mirabil segni.

UNO ANGIOLO *rivolto a Guglielma dice:*

58
E tu, sorella mia, camminerai
con questa scorta e buona compagnia,
tanto che in questo bosco troverrai
onesto albergo qual tuo cor disia;
quivi lo sposo tuo presto vedrai
e 'l suo fratel sanato da te fia,
manifestando a te suo falsi inganni;
poi sarai ristorata de' tua affanni.

GUGLIELMA *si lamenta che quelli dua giovani si voglino partire da lei:*

59
Omè, misera a me, ch'io mi credetti
in castità la mia vita posare,
servendo sempre a Dio con puri effetti;

GUGLIELMA *thanks the angels and says:*

> 57
> O belovèd, cherished brothers mine,
> I thank you in the name of God, but how,
> When I've no money, shall I pay my fare?
> This man takes nothing else, if I judge right.

ONE OF THE ANGELS *gives a ring to Guglielma, saying:*

Receive the rare endowments of this ring.[13]

And, having turned to the captain, says:

With this be paid; to your safe keeping I
Entrust her, captain, for my love receive
And prize her, from whom wondrous signs you'll see.

Turning to Guglielma, an ANGEL *says:*

> 58
> And you, my sister, you shall journey on
> With this good and discerning company,
> Until in this woodland you come upon
> A dwelling chaste, the one your heart desires;
> Your husband there you very soon will see;
> His brother, once confessed his false deceits
> To you, you fully shall restore to health.
> Requited for your suffering then you'll be.

GUGLIELMA *laments that those two young men [the angels] must leave her, and she says:*

> 59
> O wretched me, for I had thought to lead
> My life in chastity and ever serve
> My God with pure affection, whereas now

or altra vïa mi convien cercare.
S'e giusti prieghi mia vi sono accetti,
non vi sdegnate a me manifestare
chi siete, e 'l nome vostro mi direte,
e di me sempre vi ricorderete.

Rispondono quelli ANGIOLI *a Guglielma:*

60
Ancor tempo non è manifestarti
il nome nostro, ma presto il saprai
e verrai ad abitar in quelle parti;
la casa nostra e 'l paese vedrai.
Piacciati sol con questi acompagniarti,
c'al fin sicura in porto arriverai;
sarà con teco l'aiuto divino.
A noi convien seguir altro cammino.

Partiti di nascoso quelli dua angioli, GUGLIELMA *dimanda il padrone e i compagni se gli hanno veduti:*

61
Misera a me, areste voi veduti
e mia diletti e cari buon fratelli?
Ecco, sanza cagion ch'io gli ho perduti!
O lassa a me, dove ritrovo quelli?
Sarebbono fra voi costà venuti?
Io sarei sol felice di vedelli.

Risponde il PADRONE:

Veduto non abbiàn se non te sola;
credi per certo alla nostra parola.

Another path I must expect to seek.
I pray you, if you find my righteous prayers
Acceptable, do not disdain to show
Me who you are; acquaint me with your names,
And forever keep me in memory.

The ANGELS *answer Guglielma:*

60

The time has not yet come for us to tell
Our names to you. But you will know them soon,
And you will come to dwell in those parts where
Our home is, for that country you will see.
Be pleased to be accompanied by these
Alone, for you will safely come to port
At last, and aid divine will be with you.
We are obliged to take another path.

The two angels having departed in secret, GUGLIELMA *asks the captain and his companions if they have seen them:*

61

Ah wretched me, have any of you seen
My brothers, cherished and belovèd? For,
Behold, I've lost them for no cause, alas!
Where can I once again recover them?
Are they to be found among you? Oh, I
Would be content to see them once again.

The CAPTAIN *answers:*

We've not seen anyone except yourself;
Our word you may most certainly believe.

Partiti gli angioli, GUGLIELMA, *conosciuto chi erano, si duole seco medesima e dice così:*

62
O divina bontà, or conosco io
chi son costor che m'hanno acompagnata!
Grazie ti rendo con tutto il cor mio,
benigna madre, o mia dolce advocata;
gli angioli santi del tuo coro pio
in questo bosco m'hanno visitata.
Benedetta sia tu, del ciel regina,
che guidi e reggi questa peregrina.

Il PADRONE *priega Guglielma che voglia sanare un suo compagno amalato:*

63
Poi che tu se' con Dio in grazia tanta,
piacciati a quel benigno supplicare
che degni, per la tua orazion santa,
questo misero infermo liberare;
e, se di tanto don tuo cor si vanta,
per tuo servo fedel mi vo' legare.

GUGLIELMA *risponde e dice:*

Se tanta grazia vuoi ch'io ti concedi,
bisogna che tu creda quel che chiedi.

GUGLIELMA *fa orazione a Dio e sana quello infermo:*

64
O gran monarca, o Signor giusto e degno,
che la tua serva già servasti in vita,
dolce avocato[14] del mio cor sostegno,
per tua somma clemenza ch'è infinita,
piacciati d'ascoltar el priego indegno

Once the angels have left, GUGLIELMA *realizes who they were, and, sorrowing to herself, she says:*

62

O heavenly Goodness, now I recognize
Just who those were who have accompanied me!
With all my heart, O kindly Mother, I
Give thanks to you, O my sweet advocate,
The holy angels of your godly choir
Have in this forest kept me company.
Ah, blessed be thou, Queen of heaven, who
Escorts this pilgrim and directs her way.

The CAPTAIN *asks Guglielma if she will heal one of his sick crewmen:*

63

Since you're so greatly favored with God's grace,
Petition, please, his great beneficence,
So, through your holy prayer he will relieve
This wretched, ailing man, and if so great
A gift your heart can claim, then I desire
To vow your faithful servant to become.

GUGLIELMA *answers:*

If you desire so great a grace to see,
You must believe that what you ask will be.

GUGLIELMA *prays to God and heals the sick man:*

64

O Monarch great, O just and worthy Lord,
Who once preserved your servant's life, O my
Sweet advocate, defender of my heart,
By your surpassing mercy infinite,
Be pleased to listen to my humble prayer:

sì che la prece mia sia essaudita;
concedi a me, Signor benigno e grato,
che questo infermo sia per me sanato.

Lo INFERMO *sanato da Guglielma dice:*

    65
Che dono è questo, immenso eterno Idio,
c'hai dimostro oggi a questo peccatore?
Quanto più posso con tutto il cor mio
io rendo grazie a te, giusto Signore;
e sol disposto è ogni mio desio
d'abandonare il mondo pien d'errore
per seguitarti, Signor giusto e degno,
poi che m'hai mostro sì mirabil segno.

Il PADRONE *dice a Guglielma che la vuole menare a uno monasterio dove lei potrà dimorare:*

    66
O venerabil donna, se t'è a grato
nel mio paese con meco venire;
un luogo molto accetto t'ho trovato,
volendo sempre al tuo Signor servire,
di sante donne, e molto nominato,
dove potra' la tua vita finire.

GUGLIELMA *risponde al padrone e vanno a detto munisterio:*

Servire a Dio è la mia intenzione
ma non costretta alla religïone.[15]

Giunti al munistero il PADRONE *dice alla badessa:*

    67
Reverenda in Iesù madre diletta,
perch'io ti porto grande affezïone,

O Lord, so that my prayer may answered be,
Benign and kindly, grant this boon to me:
That this sick man by me may be made well.

Healed by Guglielma, the SICK MAN *says:*

65

What gift this is, eternal, boundless God,
To this poor sinner you've revealed today?
As greatly as I can, with all my heart,
I render thanks, O righteous Lord, to you,
And each desire of mine is only fixed
Upon abandoning the world that's filled
With error, to follow you, worthy Lord
And just; you've shown me such a wondrous sign.

The CAPTAIN *says to Guglielma that he wants to take her to a convent where she can dwell:*

66

O reverend lady, if you will be pleased
To come along with me into my land;
I've found a very fitting place for you,
If you desire to always serve your Lord,
A place for holy women much renowned.
There you will be allowed to spend your life.

GUGLIELMA *answers the captain, and they go to the nunnery mentioned:*

To serve God is my firm intention, but
Not being pledged to the religious life.

On arriving at the nunnery, the CAPTAIN *says to the abbess:*

67

Reverend in Christ, belovéd mother, O
Because I bear you great affection, this

io t'apresento questa serva eletta
che di farti felice fia cagione,
perché l'orazion sua è tanto accetta
a Dio, che sanato ha molte persone:[16]
avendo contrizion de' lor peccati
di ciascun mal da lei son liberati.

La BADESSA *accetta Guglielma e dice:*

68
Sempre il Signor Iesù laudato sia!
Di tanto dono a te grazie rendiamo.
Se ti piace la nostra compagnia,
qui per nostra sorella t'accettiamo.
Intendi ben, dolce figliuola mia:
qual essercizio vuoi che noi ti diamo?

GUGLIELMA *risponde alla badessa:*

Io saprei Idio pe' peccator pregare,
ogni vil essercizio ministrare.

La BADESSA *dice a Guglielma:*

69
Assai mi piace, diletta sorella,
che tu sia tanto bene amaestrata,
ma che vuol dire, o qual cagion è quella,
che tu sia in queste parte capitata,
e come il nome tuo, donna, s'appella
da poi ch'apresso a Dio se' tanto grata?

GUGLIELMA *risponde alla badessa:*

Sappi ch'io son chiamata peccatrice;
altro non so di mia vita infelice.

Servant elect I shall present for she
Will be a source of your felicity
Because her prayer is so acceptable
To God; for she has many persons cured[16]
Who've felt contrition for their sins, by her
From every illness have they been released.

The ABBESS *accepts Guglielma and says:*

68

May the Lord Jesus be forever praised!
For such a worthy gift we give you thanks.
If being our companion pleases you,
We now accept you as our sister here.
My sister sweet, consider well: What task
would you prefer that we assign to you?

GUGLIELMA *answers the abbess:*

I'd like to pray to God for sinners—too,
I'd do each humble task there is to do.

The ABBESS *says to Guglielma:*

69

I'm very pleased, belovèd sister, that
You've been so well instructed, but what does
It mean, and what may be the reason that
You've turned up in these parts? And by what name,
Dear lady, are you known, that you should be
So greatly pleasing in the sight of God?

GUGLIELMA *answers the abbess:*

Know that my name is Sinner and that I
Know nothing else of my unhappy life.

Seguita GUGLIELMA *e dice alla badessa:*

70
Troppo lungo sarebbe il mio sermone,
s'i' volessi mia vita raccontare;
né della mia venuta la cagione,
la patria e 'l nome mio non ricercare.
Presto sarà di Dio promessïone
che tutte l'opre mie saranno chiare;
Iesù figliuol di Dio che tutto vede
d'ogni processo mio vi facci fede.

Vengono molti poveri amalati al munisterio a Guglielma che era alla porta guardiana, e uno povero dice a Guglielma gli dia limosina. Lei fa orazione e quivi sana attratti, ciechi e molti infermi, i quali sanati fanno festa e gettono via le grucce e UNO DI QUELLI POVERI *dice:*

71
O santa donna, per l'amor di Dio,
questo cieco ti sia raccomandato.

GUGLIELMA *risponde al povero:*

Danar non ho da darti, fratel mio;
per te pregherrò Idio che sia sanato.
Fa' che tu volga a quel ogni desio
e sia contrito d'ogni tuo peccato.

E volto al povero dice:

Benigno Idio, bench'è il mio priego indegno,
mostra per la tua serva qualche segno.

GUGLIELMA *continues and speaks thus to the abbess:*

> 70
> My discourse would be far too long if I
> Should wish to tell the story of my life,
> Not the occasion for my coming here,
> Neither my name nor homeland seek to know,
> For God has promised it will not be long
> Till every deed of mine will be made clear;
> May Jesus, the Son of God who sees all things,
> Bear witness to each action that I take.

Many poor and sick people come to the nunnery to Guglielma, for she was the gate keeper, and a PAUPER *asks Guglielma to give him alms. She prays, and there she cures the lame, the blind, and many sick persons, who, when cured, rejoice and throw their crutches away, and* ONE OF THE PAUPERS *says:*

> 71
> O holy lady, for the love of God,
> Let this blind person here implore your grace.

GUGLIELMA *answers the pauper:*

No coin have I to give you, brother mine;
I shall pray God that you may be restored.
Be sure your every wish is fixed on him,
And for each sin of yours contrition feel.

And facing the pauper she says:

Let my unworthy prayer, O God benign,
Through me your servant manifest some sign.

Il FRATELLO *del Re d'Ungheria, amalato di lebbra per giudicio di Dio, viene dinanzi al fratello così lebbroso, e mostrando la lebbra, dice così, pregandolo lo facci curare:*

72

Omè, signor, abbi di me pietate!
Vedi l'ira di Dio e 'l gran flagello:
tutte le carne mia son tormentate.
Non dispregiare il tuo carnal fratello.

Il RE *volto a' suo servi dice:*

Andate, servi mia, e raunate
de' medici il collegio e fate a quello
con diligenza il caso manifesto,
e quel che si può far, si faccia presto.

Va UNO SERVO *a chiamare molti medici e dice:*

73

A tutti voi dottor di medicina,
di comandarvi ci è stato commesso
che voi veggiate con vostra dottrina
un caso che vi fia narrato apresso:
tutto di lebbra molto repentina
il fratel del signor si truova opresso.
Venite questo caso a disputare.

Uno MEDICO *risponde per tutti gli altri:*

E' si proverà, non dubitare.

The BROTHER of the King of Hungary, fallen ill with leprosy by the judgment of God, leprous goes before his brother, and begging the King to have him cured, says:

72

My lord take pity on me, for you see
The wrath of God, the unrelenting scourge,
And all parts of my flesh tormented thus.
Your brother in the flesh, do not despise.

The KING says to his servants:

My servants go, convene the College of
Physicians and make clear to them this case
With diligence, and let whatever they
Can do be done and that immediately.

A SERVANT goes to call many doctors and says:

73

I am directed to command that all
You doctors and physicians come to see
A case, with all your learning, for to you
It soon will be explained how, all at once,
The King's own brother finds himself beset
With leprosy all over; you must come
And offer your opinions in this case.

One DOCTOR answers for all the others:

We'll find a cure for him without a doubt.

Giunti e medici dinanzi al signore, veduto il segno[17] *e guardato l'amalato, dice* UN DI LORO *allo infermo:*

74

Questo è un caso assai di grieve pondo
e bisogna proceder con lunghezza,
come Avicenna tocca nel secondo,
e Galïeno molto il caso apprezza;[18]
ma non temer, ch'al fin tu sarai mondo,
e sarai medicato con destrezza.

Un ALTRO MEDICO *dice allo amalato così:*

Maninconico sangue è questa offesa,[19]
e non si cura sanza grande spesa.

UNO SERVO *dice al Re che mandi via e medici e che meni il fratello a una donna che fa miracoli a uno munisterio, che era Guglielma:*

75

Perdonami, signor, s'i' sono audace:
e' non ci è uom che abbia intelligenza.
Questa scienza lor mi par fallace:
medicon tutti sanza conscïenza.[20]
Tristo a colui che nelle lor man giace!
Al fin la borsa n'ha la penitenza,
lunga o mortal fanno la malattia.
Credilo a me, signor, mandagli via.

Seguita il SERVO:

76

I'ho sentito, tal ch'io ne son certo,
d'una serva di Dio mirabil cose,
la quale sta vicina a un diserto,

When the DOCTORS *are assembled before the King, having looked at his specimen and examined the sick man,* ONE OF THEM *says to the stricken patient:*

74

This is indeed a very serious case,
And cautiously we must proceed, as in
His second volume Avicenna notes,
And on this problem Galen much remarks[18]—
But have no fear, you will at last be cleansed,
And will be treated very skillfully.

ANOTHER DOCTOR *says to the sick man:*

It's black bile in the blood that causes this;[19]
It can't be cured except at great expense.

A SERVANT *tells the King that he should send away the physicians and take his brother to a woman who performs miracles at a nunnery. This was Guglielma.*

75

Forgive me, Sir, if I am overbold:
None of these men has understood the case.
Their science seems entirely false to me;
For all these doctors have no knowledge, Sir,
Pity the man who falls into their hands!
His purse at last will be the penitent!
They'll make his illness fatal or prolonged.
O lord, believe me; send them all away.

The SERVANT *continues:*

76

I've heard report, and I'm quite sure it's true,
Of wondrous things a holy woman does,
who lives close to a great deserted spot,

che, con l'opere sue maravigliose,
a molti ciechi nati gli occhi ha aperto
(tanto le prece sua son graziose!),
e sordi e muti ha liberati assai.
Buon per costui se tu mi crederrai.

Il FRATELLO del Re dice al Re che lo meni a quella donna:

77

Io ti priego, signor, s'io ne son degno,
che ti piaccia menarmi al santo loco,
bench'io sia peccator, misero, indegno.
Vedi ch'io mi consumo a poco a poco.

Il RE dice al fratello:

I' son contento e vo' lasciar il regno,
pur che questo pensier tuo abbi loco.

E volto a un baron dice:

E tu reggi e governa in fin ch'io torni,
ch'a mio giudicio saran pochi giorni.

Giunti al munisterio dove era Guglielma, non la conoscendo,[21] *il RE la priega ch'ella voglia sanare il fratel lebbroso e dice così:*

78

La fama della tua gran santitate
ci ha fatti, immensa[22] donna, a te venire.
Abbi di questo mio fratel pietate,
qual è lebroso e vive in gran martire;
se tu gli renderai la sanitate,
tutti e sua dì desidera servire
a quel che in croce fu morto e deriso,
né io sarò da te già mai diviso.

And with the miracles that she performs
She's made men see who have been blind from birth
(Such is the grace contained within her prayers!),
And made the deaf to hear, the dumb to speak.
It's for his good if you'll believe me now.

The King's BROTHER *asks the King to lead him to that woman:*

      77
If I am worthy, lord, I pray that you'll
Be pleased to lead me to that holy place,
Unworthy, wretched sinner though I be.
You see how, bit by bit, I rot away.

The KING *says to his brother:*

I'll do this thing, and I shall leave the realm
So that this wish of yours may be fulfilled.

And turning to a baron he says:

You govern and command till I return—
It will be but a few days, as I think.

Having arrived at the nunnery where Guglielma was, the KING, *not recognizing her,*[21] *begs her to heal his leprous brother, and says:*

      78
The fame of your surpassing holiness
Has made us, famous lady, come to you.
For this my brother, who is leprous, have
Compassion, for he lives in fearful pain;
If you will give him back his health once more,
His every desire will be to serve that one
Who died and on the cross was crucified
And I shall never after leave your side.

GUGLIELMA *risponde al Re mostrando non lo conoscere:*

79

Io non posso per me tal grazie fare,
ma il mio Signor è ricco e sua potenza,
quando gli piace, può manifestare;
contenta son pregar la sua clemenza
che gli piaccia costui voler sanare;
ma bisogna che dica in tua presenza
se in sua vita t'avessi offeso mai,
e per mio amor tu gli perdonerai.

Il RE *dice a Guglielma:*

80

Io lo imprometto a te liberamente,
donna, di perdonargli per tuo amore.

E volto al fratello dice:

Di' su, fratel, e non temer niente;
confessa apertamente ogni tuo errore.
Parato è sempre Idio, a chi si pente,
di perdonargli come buon Signore;
se da Iesù vuoi essere essaudito,
parlerai chiaro acciò che sia sentito.

Il FRATELLO *del Re manifesta come accusò Guglielma e chiede perdono:*

81

Io non so come io debba cominciare
a far qui manifesto il mio peccato
e come tu mi possi perdonare,
avendoti, fratel, tanto ingiuriato.

GUGLIELMA *answers the King, pretending not to recognize him, and speaks thus:*

79

Such a grace I can't perform alone,
But my Lord is rich, and his power can,
When it may please him, be made manifest;
And to his clemency, I'm glad to pray
That he'll be pleased to wish to cure this man;
But in your presence he must first confess
If ever in his life he's done you wrong,
And, for my love, you then must pardon him.

The KING *says to Guglielma:*

80

I freely, lady, promise this to you,
That I shall pardon him to earn your love.

And turning to his BROTHER *he says:*

Speak up, my brother; don't fear anything,
And openly confess your every fault.
For God is always ready to forgive,
Like the good Lord he is, one who repents;
If you want Jesus to fulfill your wish,
You will speak clearly so you may be heard.

The BROTHER *of the King reveals how he had accused Guglielma and asks forgiveness:*

81

I do not know well how I should begin
To make my sin here manifest, or how
You, brother, will be able to forgive
My having done you such great injury.

Tu sai che mi lasciasti a consigliare
colla Reïna del tuo principato,
quando la Terrasanta visitasti,
e quella a me molto raccomandasti.

Seguita detto lebbroso:

82

Io finsi di voler parlar con lei
cose del regno in camera soletto;
quivi, con detti simulati e rei,
gli apersi del mio core il grande affetto.
Quella, che intese tutti e pensier miei
e lo sfrenato amor che ardeva il petto,
temendo che più oltre io non tentassi,
mi comandò che più non gli parlassi.

Seguita il FRATEL *lebbroso:*

83

Venendo incontro a te, subitamente,
mi domandasti della tua consorte;
io l'accusai d'infamia falsamente,
ch'avea vituperato la tua corte,
e tanto il mio parlar fu teco ardente,
ch'al fin mi commettesti la sua morte,
onde io, volendo al mio pensier dar loco,
quella innocente condannai nel foco.

Seguita lui detto dicendo:

84

Non si sentì già mai tal tradimento!
La giustizia di Dio quando vien tardi
par ch'ella rechi poi maggior tormento;
quel foco ch'arse lei convien che m'ardi!

You know you left the Queen and me as well
To govern your dominion when you went
And visited the Holy Land, and you
Trusted me much with her safekeeping too.

The LEPER *continues:*

      82

I feigned to want to speak with her about
State matters in her chamber privately;
Once there, with wicked and dissembling words,
My heart's great love I opened up to her.
She, who understood my every thought
And the unbridled love that burned my breast,
And fearing lest I might attempt much more,
Then ordered me no more to speak to her.

The leprous BROTHER *continues:*

      83

Soon after that I came before you, and
You asked about the welfare of your queen;
I falsely laid a charge of infamy,
And said that she had much disgraced your court;
Then too, my speech to you was so inflamed
That finally you charged me with her death;
Whence I, who wished to carry out my aims,
Condemned her, sent her guiltless to the flames.

The same man continues:

      84

Such treachery as mine was never known!
God's justice, when it comes late seems to bring
On greater suffering then; that fire that burned
Guglielma should rightly destroy me too!

Benché tardi pentuto e mal contento,
convien che tua pietate a me riguardi.

E volto a Dio dice:

E tu che vedi ogni pensier nel core,
merzé, merzé, Iesù, di tanto errore!

Il RE *stupefatto dice adirato contro al fratello:*

85

O lasso a me, che è quel ch'i' ho ascoltato!
Tanto delitto mai non fu sentito!
O disleal fratello, iniquo e ingrato,
come fusti ' accusarla tanto ardito?
Non ti bastava quella aver tentato
a te lasciata, il tuo fratel tradito,
che la sua morte ancor troppo crudele
cercasti, sendo a me stata fedele?

Seguita il RE *volgendo le sua parole a Guglielma stimando fussi morta:*

86

Omè, Guglielma mia, diletta sposa,
non volendolo far, troppo t'offesi;
sanza cercar di te nessuna cosa
tanto di sdegno e di furor m'accesi!
E, sendo stata a me sì graziosa,
a' falsi prieghi di costui discesi!

E volto a Guglielma:

Ma poi che per tuo amore i' l'ho promesso,
ogni peccato suo gli sia rimesso.

I'm penitent and sorry though it's late.
With mercy now you need to look on me.

And turning to God, the King's BROTHER *says:*

And you who see each thought within my heart,
Have mercy, Jesus, for so great a wrong!

Dumbfounded and enraged against his brother, the KING *says:*

85

O woe is me! What's this that I have heard!
I've never heard about so great a crime!
Then, wicked ingrate, tell your brother: how
Could you be bold enough to blame her so?
Make rude attempts on one left in your care?
Beyond that you betrayed your brother, too—
Too cruel! Why did you have to seek her death
Though with me she had always kept her faith?

Thinking Guglielma dead, the KING *addresses his next words to her, and says:*

86

Ah me, Guglielma, my belovèd wife,
Unwittingly I've done you such great wrong
Without inquiring anything from you,
So greatly kindled by disdain and wrath!
Though you had treated me so graciously,
I lowered myself to this man's false requests.

And turning to Guglielma, he says:

But since, at your request, I gave my word,
Let him be pardoned for these sins we've heard.

GUGLIELMA *fa orazione a Dio per detto lebbroso e sana quello infermo:*

        87
O Giesù mio, se nella tua presenza
alcun mio priego mai fu grazioso,
giunga la tua pietà, la tua clemenza,
sopra di questo misero lebbroso;
manifesta a costor la tua potenza,
o Iesù dolce, o mio diletto Sposo;
nel nome della santa Trinitate
rendi a costui la vera sanitate.[23]

Il LEBBROSO *sanato dice inginocchione verso Idio ringraziando:*

        88
O pietà grande, o carità infinita,
insegna a me ch'io ti possi laudare!
L'anima stanca e tutta la mia vita,
dolce Signor, a te vo' consecrare!
Donna, che se' con Dio tanto unita,
piacciati pel tuo servo supplicare,
sendo da tal supplicio liberato,
che di cotanto don io non sia ingrato.

GUGLIELMA *levatosi e veli di testa si manifesta al Re suo marito e dice:*

        89
Dolce speranza, o mio diletto sposo,
la tua Guglielma ha' sì dimenticato
che più non la conosci e stai pensoso,
quella ch'al fuoco per te fu dannata?
Non vuol tanto delitto star nascoso
colui che in sino a qui m'ha riservata,
il qual, veggendo me nel mondo errare,
la mia costanza sol volle provare.

GUGLIELMA *prays to God for the leper, and heals him*:

87

My Jesus, O if any prayer of mine
Was ever welcome in your presence, may
Your pity and your clemency reach out
To this wretched leper. May your power
Be manifest before this company,
O Jesus sweet, O my belovèd Spouse;
In the name of the Holy Trinity,
Restore this man to health for all to see.

The leprous BROTHER, *now healed, kneels to God and, thanking him, says:*

88

O Mercy great, unbounded Charity,
O show me how I can perform thy praise!
This weary soul and all its wayward course,
Sweet Lord, I want to consecrate to you!
O lady, as you're so at one with God,
Please, on your servant's part, beseech him that,
Released now from my agony so hateful,
For such a gen'rous gift I shall be grateful.

GUGLIELMA *having lifted the veils from her head, reveals herself to the King her husband, and says:*

89

O hope so sweet, O my belovèd spouse,
Your Guglielma have you so forgot
That you no longer know her, and grow grave;
She whom you had sentenced to the fire?
He who has kept me safe here until now
Would not wish such a felony concealed,
He who observed me wandering in the world,
Wished only to assay my constancy.

Seguita GUGLIELMA *e dice:*

90

Essendo già condotta al gran supplicio,
orando verso il ciel divotamente
che mi scampassi dal mortal giudicio,
subito il mio Signor toccò la mente
a chi doveva far tal maleficio,
onde e' mi disson che secretamente
io me n'andassi, e sol arson le spoglie,
mostrando sadisfare alle tue voglie.

Seguita GUGLIELMA:

91

Io mi partì' sanza saper la via
e molti dì pe' boschi camminai.
Quivi fu' visitata da Maria;
apresso a lei duo angioli scontrai,
i quai mi diero onesta compagnia,[24]
tanto che in questo loco capitai,
dove sanate abbiam molte persone,
tanto è piaciuto a Dio nostra orazione.

Il RE, *riconosciuto la sua sposa Guglielma e inteso come era scampata, dice seco medesimo e a' servi:*

92

Io non so s'io mi sogno o si'io son desto,
o s'i' sono smarrito per gli affanni.
O alto immenso Idio, che dono è questo!
Tu puoi in un punto ristorar molti anni.[25]
Faccisi a tutti il caso manifesto
ché più s'allegra ne' celesti scanni
d'uno spirto beato fra gli eletti
che di novanta nove son perfetti.[26]

GUGLIELMA *continues:*

90

When to that gruesome torture I'd been led,
And while to heaven I prayed devotedly
That I from mortal justice might be freed,
My Lord abruptly touched the mind of those
Who had to do an evil deed like that,
And so they said to me that, secretly,
I must go thence, and they burned just my clothes,
Pretending thus to satisfy your will.

GUGLIELMA *continues:*

91

I went from thence, though I knew not the way,
And many days I traveled through the woods,
Where Mary called upon me and where I
Then two angels met, and they became
My chaste companions until I came here
Within the walls of this place where we have
So many people healed, because our prayers
Have proved so gratifying to our God.

The KING, *having recognized his wife Guglielma, and, having understood how she escaped, says to himself and his servants:*

92

Am I awake or am I dreaming here?
Or am I quite deluded by my woes.
O thou almighty God, how great a gift!
You can, in just one blink, roll back the years.[25]
Now spread the news of this to everyone,
For the celestial choir rejoices more
For one new spirit raised among the elect
Than for the ninety-nine already saved.

E volto a Guglielma dice:

93
Perdona a me ben ch'io fussi ingannato
da questo crudo mio fratel carnale,
il qual sanza cagion tu hai sanato,
che mi fe' verso te sì micidiale.
Piacciati supplicar pel mio peccato
colla tua orazion che tanto vale.

GUGLIELMA *risponde al Re suo sposo:*

Ogni tua colpa a te perdoni Idio,
ch'io ti perdono, o dolce sposo mio.

GUGLIELMA *allegra d'avere ritrovato il marito, dice al Re e a Dio:*

94
Quanto fu trista nella mia partita
l'anima che sentì l'ultime pene,
tanto è lieta e felice la mia vita
ritrovato in un punto ogni mio bene;
e di tanta dolceza, ch'è infinita,
io rendo grazie a tue virtù serene,
o alto immenso, o increato Idio,
quanto se' tu benigno e giusto e pio!

Quel LEBBROSO, *ricognosciuta Guglielma, pigliando scusa dice:*

95
O santissima donna, onesta e degna,
come sarò con Dio giustificato
che colei ch'io tradì' oggi si degna
per la sua orazion ch'io sia sanato?

And addressing Guglielma, he says:

93

Forgive me; even though I was deceived
By this the cruel brother of my flesh
Whom you have cured— although you had no cause
Since he had made me want to murder you.
I pray you, ask forgiveness for my sins
Because the power of your prayer prevails.

GUGLIELMA *answers the King, her husband, and says:*

May God forgive your sins! I thus entreat,
For I forgive you, O my husband sweet!

GUGLIELMA, *joyful at having found her husband again, says to the King and to God:*

94

As sad at my departure was my soul
As it set out toward egregious pain,
So happy now my life, so joyful that
My every good at once has been restored;
And for such sweetness, which is infinite,
Unto your tranquil power I give thanks,
O high and boundless, O eternal God!
How just you are, how holy and how kind!

The leprous BROTHER *of the King recognizes Guglielma, and, apologizing to her, says:*

95

O you most holy lady, worthy, chaste,
How can I ever make amends with God,
For she whom I'd betrayed has been content
That through her prayer my health might be restored?

Ben ch'è la voce di parlarti indegna,
perdona a me, vil peccatore ingrato.

E volto al fratel dice:

E tu, fratel, da parte di Giesùe,
perdona a quel che sì crudel ti fue.

Il RE volto al fratel dice:

96
Poi che 'l Signore a te stato è clemente,
anch'io con teco voglio esser cortese;
e la Reïna qui benignamente
ha perdonato a te sì grande offese.

Il RE volto a Guglielma dice:

E tu, Guglielma mia, sempre ubbidiente,
per ritornarti nel nostro paese
buona licenza piglierai da quelle
benigne suore, a te madre e sorelle.

GUGLIELMA, *avendosi a partire, piglia licenza dalle monache e prima dice alla badessa:*[27]

97
Dilette suore mia, poi ch'a Dio piace
che questo sposo mio debba seguire,
sorelle e madre mie, restate in pace,
con ch'io credetti viver e morire.
So che la mia partita assai vi spiace:
a me bisogna a' sua prieghi ubidire;
bench'io parta da voi, con maggior zelo
aspetto ancor di rivedervi in cielo.

Though my voice too unworthy is to speak
With you, forgive this ingrate sinner vile.

And addressing his brother he says:

And, brother, you in Jesus' name forgive
This one who treated you so heartlessly.

Addressing his brother, the KING *says:*

96

Because to you the Lord's been merciful,
I too desire to treat you courteously;
The Queen so kindly has forgiven you,
As well, for such abominable offense.

The KING, *addressing Guglielma, says:*

And you, my ever dutiful Guglielma,
So you can go with us into our realm
Again, bid your farewells to those kind nuns,
From mother and from sisters, take your leave

Because she must leave, GUGLIELMA *turns to the abbess and bids farewell to the nuns:*

97

Belovèd sisters mine, since God is pleased
That this my husband I accompany,
My mother and my sisters, dwell in peace,
With you I'd thought to live, had planned to die.
I know my going much will sadden you,
But his requests I am obliged to heed;
Though I must leave you, yet, most ardently,
I expect in heaven we shall each other see!

La BADESSA *risponde a Guglielma dolendosi della sua partenza:*

98

Io non credetti mai che tanto amore
potessi separare altro che morte.
Tu te ne porti teco il nostro cuore;
pensa che 'l tuo partir ci è duro e forte,
ma, poi che così piace al tuo signore,
colui che regna nella eccelsa corte
ci dia perfetta e buona pazïenza,
dolce sorella, in questa tua partenza.

Ritornansi in Ungheria. Il RE *mostra Guglielma a' baroni suoi e racconta il caso avvenuto:*

99

Guardate ben, se voi riconoscete
Guglielma, che fu già vostra regina,
che fu nel foco, come voi sapete,
a torto condannata, la meschina;
cose maravigliose, sentirete,
per lei mostrate ha la bontà divina,[28]
però che chi dovea quella abruciare,
da Dio spirati, la lasciorno andare.

Seguita il RE:

100

Menando questo mio fratel lebbroso
a quella donna al santo munistero,
tanto fu il priego suo giusto e pietoso
che fu sanato per divin mistero;
sentendomi da lei chiamare sposo
e tutto il caso suo narrare intero,
subitamente risguardando quella
la riconobbi al volto e alla favella.[29]

The ABBESS, *sorrowful at Guglielma's departure, says:*

>   98
> I never thought that anything but death
> Could separate a love so great as this.
> As you go off, you take our hearts with you:
> Think, as you leave, how much it brings us woe,
> But since your husband's wish is that you go,
> We ask of him who reigns in heaven on high
> He'll give us perfect patience on this day,
> Sweet sister, as you travel on your way.

They return to Hungary. The KING *shows Guglielma to his barons and tells them all that has happened:*

>   99
> Look carefully! See if you recognize
> Guglielma, who was once your queen, indeed,
> And who, as you all know, unjustly was
> Condemned, poor woman, in the fire to burn.
> Marvelous things, as you will hear, have been
> Revealed through her by heaven's grace divine,
> For those who meant to put her on the pyre
> Were moved by God to let her flee the fire.

The KING *continues:*

>   100
> When this my leprous brother I had led
> Before that lady at the convent blest,
> Her prayer so just was and so merciful
> That he by holy miracle was healed.
> Then hearing her call me husband and her whole
> Narration of each circumstance, as I
> Was looking at her, suddenly I knew
> Her face and recognized her voice then too.[29]

E' BARONI, *faccendo festa di Guglielma, dicono a lei:*

101
Amatissima donna, onesta e grata,
O divina bontà, che gaudio è questo!
Benedetto colui che t'ha salvata!
Quanto ci fussi il tuo caso molesto,
o Regina Guglielma tanto amata,
chi tutto sa tel facci manifesto.
Di sì gran don, di tanto beneficio
faccisi a nostri templi sacrificio.

GUGLIELMA *si manifesta alle sue serve e dice:*

102
Fidelissime mie serve dilette,
ecco dinanzi alla vostra presenza
Guglielma, a chi vo' fuste tanto accette,
e che piangesti nella sua partenza.

Le SERVE, *abracciando Guglielma, con molta festa dicono:*

O Dio del ciel, qual mai di noi credette
veder cogli occhi più la tua clemenza?
Qual vive al mondo più di noi felice,
ritrovata la nostra imperatrice!

Il RE, volto a' baroni, dice che vuol lasciare a loro la signoria e fa dispensare e sua tesori e partesi con Guglielma e col fratello che fu lebbroso per andare in luoghi solitari a far penitenza pe' miracoli che ha veduti dimostrare Idio per Guglielma, massime del suo fratel lebbroso sì sanato.

103
E voi, diletti miei, grazie rendete
con meco insieme al nostro buon Signore,

The BARONS *rejoice for Guglielma, and they say to her:*

101

O gracious lady, most beloved and chaste,
O godly goodness, what a joy is this!
O blest be he who has preserved you so!
How much we suffered when we heard your fate,
O Guglielma, much belovèd Queen,
May the all-knowing one reveal to you.
For such a great gift, such beneficence,
At our temples shall we offer sacrifice.

GUGLIELMA *reveals herself to her maid servants and says:*

102

Most faithful and belovèd servants mine,
Right here before you in your presence now,
Behold Guglielma, to whom you were so dear,
And for whom you, at her departure, wept.

The MAID SERVANTS, *embracing Guglielma with great celebration, say:*

O heav'nly God! Who among us ever thought
To see with our own eyes your clemency?
Who in the world live happier than we
That once again our empress dear we see!

The KING, *addressing the barons, says that he wants to leave them to rule his realm. He distributes his treasures and leaves with Guglielma and his formerly leprous brother for a solitary place to do penance for the miracles that God has shown him though Guglielma, especially that of his brother healed in this way:*

103

And you my friends so dear, give thanks with me
Together to our good and gracious Lord,

e questi mia tesor dispenserete
a' poveri serventi per suo amore;
io son disposto, come voi vedete,
di spodestarmi del regal onore,
da poi che mi dimostra il Signor degno
di farmi ricco assai di maggior regno.

Seguita il RE:

104
E tutto il resto della vita mia
ne' servigi di Dio vo' dispensare;
con questa mia Guglielma in compagnia,
ogni diletto uman vo' disprezare.

E volto a' baroni dice:

Di voi, baron, sarà la signoria,
la qual vi piaccia in modo ministrare
ch'a mia stirpe regal facciate onore,
e che sia piacimento del Signore.

Andando pel diserto, dice con Guglielma e col fratello:

105
Questo ermo sarà il mio regal palazo,
questi cilicci fien le riche veste,
queste caverne fien nostro solazo,
le discipline fien l'ornate veste.[30]
O mondo falso, o stolto, o cieco, è pazzo
chi delle tue delizie si riveste!
Adio, vi lascio, umana pompa e gloria,
e tu, Signor, mi mostra la vittoria.

And these my treasures, please share out among
His servants poor for love of him. As you
Will see I have determined to divest
Myself of regal honors since my Lord
So worthy has revealed to me how I
May grow much richer in a greater realm.

The KING continues:

104
And all the days remaining of my life
I wish to spend in serving God with this
My dear Guglielma in my company,
And every human pleasure I'll despise.

And addressing the barons he says:

And barons, you will rule my kingdom now
And minister it well, in such a way
That you do honor to my royal line,
And in a way that's pleasing to the Lord.

Passing through the wilderness, he speaks with Guglielma and with his brother:

105
This hermitage my royal palace will
Become, let these hair shirts be my rich clothes,
These caverns, let them be our solace, and
Let us array ourselves with the marks of whips.
O false, O foolish world, O blind, one who
Arrays himself in your delights is mad!
Farewell, I leave you, pomp and human glory,
And, Lord, may you show me the victory!

Di poi entrati drento in uno romitorio, l'ANGELO *viene e dà licenza:*

106
O voi che siete in questa selva errante,
vita mortal dove non è fidanza,
vedete verso Idio chi è costante,
ch'alfin si truova certo ogni speranza,
come Guglielma fu, degna e prestante,
con sua grande umiltà, c'ogni altra avanza.
Felice chi nel mondo è tormentato
per viver poi nel ciel sempre beato!

FINIS

After they have entered a hermitage, the ANGEL *comes and dismisses the audience:*

106
O you who wander in this wayward wood,
This mortal life where nothing is secure,
Look now towards God alone in constancy,
For only there will you find certain hope,
As did Guglielma—lovely, full of worth,
And, more than any other, humble too.
Ah, they are happy whom the world's oppressed,
For they'll live on in heaven, ever blest!

THE END

La Rappresentazione di Santo Francesco

INTERLOCUTORI

[PROLOGO]
SAN FRANCESCO
UN POVERO
IL CROCIFISSO
SACERDOTE
AMICO DEL PADRE di San Francesco
IL PADRE di San Francesco
DUE UOMINI di Assisi, uno detto UN AMICO
LA MADRE di San Francesco
IL VESCOVO
SERVI del Vescovo
COMPAGNO di San Francesco
MESSER BERNARDO di Assisi
ALCUNI POVERI
IL PONTEFICE
COMPAGNI di San Francesco, poi DISCEPOLI, FRATI
SERVO del Pontefice
DUE CARDINALI
ALCUNI SARACENI
IL SOLDANO
MESSER ORLANDO
SERVO di Messer Orlando
FRA LEONE
IL SERAFINO
CONTADINO, padrone dell'asino
UNA DONNA con figlio idropico
[IL FIGLIO IDROPICO]*
UNA DONNA ROMANA, MADONNA JACOPA
IL GUARDIANO

*Presente, ma non parla.

The Play of Saint Francis

CAST OF CHARACTERS

[PROLOGUE]
SAINT FRANCIS
A PAUPER
THE CRUCIFIX
A PRIEST
A FRIEND OF THE FATHER of St. Francis
THE FATHER of St. Francis
TWO MEN from Assisi, one called A FRIEND
THE MOTHER of St. Francis
THE BISHOP
SERVANTS of the Bishop
FRIEND of St. Francis
MASTER BERNARDO of Assisi
SOME PAUPERS
THE POPE
COMPANIONS of St. Francis, later DISCIPLES, BROTHERS
SERVANT of the Pope
TWO CARDINALS
SOME SARACENS
THE SULTAN
MESSER ORLANDO
SERVANT of Master Orlando
FRA LEO
THE SERAPH
PEASANT, owner of the donkey
A WOMAN whose son has dropsy
[THE SON WITH DROPSY]*
A ROMAN WOMAN, LADY JACOPA
THE SACRISTAN

*Present, but does not speak.

[PROLOGO]

1
O Iesù mio, superno Redentore,
s'alcun mio priego mai t'è stato accetto,
per la tua carità, pel grande amore,
metti il tuo dolce foco nel mio petto,
sì che possa mostrar con gran fervore
del tuo Francesco, immenso servo eletto,
la sua storia divota e 'l gran mistero.

[rivolto al pubblico:]

State divoti ogniun col cor sincero!

2
E tu, vergine eletta in ciel Maria,
che siedi dalla destra del tuo figlio,
accendi e infiamma la mia fantasia
col tuo divino aiuto e buon consiglio,
acciò che in porto la barchetta mia
arrivar possa sanza alcun periglio,
che se' de' peccator ferma colonna
della terra, e del ciel regina e donna.

3
Perché sarebbe lungo a recitare
tutti e misteri e la sua santa vita,
vogliànne adunche una parte mostrare
e la carità sua giusta infinita,
sì come e' volse il mondo disprezare
per aver el riposo alla partita,
non curando del mondo alcun diletto,
perché avea volto a Dio ogni concetto.

[PROLOGUE]

        1

My Jesus, O Redeemer from on high,
If any prayer of mine you have approved,
Now for your charity, for your great love,
Set your sweet fire within my breast so I
Can show most fervently to everyone,
The pious story and great miracles
Of Francis, your high servant, your elect.

[to the assembled public:]

Devout, with hearts sincere, on it reflect!

        2

And, Virgin Mary, you, elect in heaven,
Who's seated at the right hand of your Son,
Inflame and set alight my fantasy
With your good counsel and your aid divine
So that, unfraught with peril, my small boat
Can reach the harbor; for all sinners you
Are the firm and steadfast column, and you are
The queen and lady of heaven and of earth.

        3

Because it would require too long to tell
His every miracle and holy life,
We therefore wish to show a part of it,
Portray his righteous, boundless charity,
The way he chose to scorn the world to have
Repose at his departure, caring not
For any pleasure of the world because he had
Devoted every thought of his to God.

Essendo San Francesco[1] al banco viene uno povero e chiede limosina e
SAN FRANCESCO, *essendo occupato, lo caccia da sé:*

        4
Messere, un po' di carità per Dio;
questo infermo ti sia raccomandato.

SAN FRANCESCO *dice:*

Non mi dar noia, deh, vatti con Dio.
Non vedi tu quant'io son occupato?

EL POVERO *dice a San Francesco:*

O sventurato a me! Morto fuss'io!
Io son da tutti in tal modo trattato.
Signor del cielo, abbi di me pietate:
rendimi almen la vera sanitate.

SAN FRANCESCO *dice seco medesimo:*

        5
Misero, perch'hai tu cacciato quello
povero infermo con tanto furore?
Sol pietà non ha' aùto di vedello?[2]
Perdonami, Iesù, dolce Signore.

SAN FRANCESCO *dice al povero:*

Tien qui, caro compagno e buon fratello,
che di cacciarti feci troppo errore.

El POVERO *dice:*

Per me, messer, te lo meriti[3] Idio,
di poi che meritar non tel poss'io.

While St. Francis[1] is at his counter, a PAUPER *comes and asks for alms, and St. Francis, being busy, chases him away.*

4

Good sir, a little charity for God,
Let this decrepit fellow thank you for.

ST. FRANCIS *says:*

Do not disturb me; may you go with God.
Do you not see how busy I am now?

The PAUPER *says to St. Francis:*

O me, unfortunate, would I were dead,
For I am treated thus by everyone.
Lord of heaven, pity take on me;
Give to me my true well-being at least.

ST. FRANCIS *says to himself:*

5

O stingy one, why did you drive away
That feeble pauper with such wrath intense?
Ah, did you not feel pity, seeing him?
Forgive me Jesus, my sweet Lord, for that.

ST. FRANCIS *says to the pauper:*

Take this, companion dear and brother good,
For I have greatly erred in ousting you.

The PAUPER *says:*

For me, may God reward you, my good sir,
Since, afterwards, I cannot pay you back.

SAN FRANCESCO *andando a San Damiano s'inginochia al crocifisso e dice:*

6

Giusto Signor, che per me se' chiovato
in sulla croce e giù veggo versare
el prezioso sangue immaculato
per me, vil peccator, voler lavare.

EL CROCIFISSO *parla a San Francesco e dice:*

Francesco, el tempio mio già rovinato
leva su presto e fallo racconciare;
metti quel ch'io ti dico a seguizione[4]
che tu sarai di molto ben cagione.

SAN FRANCESCO, *udito parlare il crocifisso, tornato in sé dice seco medesimo:*

7

Io sento nel mio cor tanta dolceza,
immenso Idio, ch'io non te lo so dire;
tu se' sanza dolor somma allegreza
che m'ha' tuo dolci don fatti sentire.
El tempio tuo racconciar con presteza
farò, perché sol te voglio ubidire.
Fammi sol camminar per la tua via
e contenta sarà la voglia mia.

SAN FRANCESCO *tornato a casa rauna pecunia nascosamente e va a San Damiano e giunto dice al sacerdote di quel tempio come lo vuole raconciare e profera a lui quella pecunia:*

8

Vita ti presti, sacerdote, Idio.
Parlar vorrei con teco se t'è grato,
che di far racconciar ho gran desio

Going to St. Damian's, ST. FRANCIS *falls on his knees before the crucifix and says:*

6

O righteous Lord, who on the cross are nailed
For me, your precious blood immaculate
I see pour down to wash me clean again,
An undeserving sinner, mean and vile.

THE CRUCIFIX *says to St. Francis:*

My temple's fallen, Francis, into ruin
Indeed; now raise it up and set it right.
Put into practice what I say to you;
For you shall be the doer of much good.

Having heard the crucifix speak, ST. FRANCIS *comes to and says to himself:*

7

Such sweetness great I feel within my heart,
O boundless God, I cannot speak of it,
For, with no grief, are you surpassing joy;
The sweet gifts of your words you've made me hear.
I shall restore your temple eagerly—
I shall because I wish to heed just you.
Pray, let me travel only in your way,
And my will shall remain therein content.

ST. FRANCIS, *having gone home, secretly gets money together and goes to St. Damian's and, once there, tells the priest of that church that he wants to restore it and offers him the money:*

8

May God prolong your life, O priest. I wish
To speak together with you, if you please,
For I long urgently to build again

questo tempio di Dio sì rovinato,
però ch'egli è voler del Signor mio
che sia per le mia man redificato.
Padre, questa pecunia piglierai
e questo tempio racconciar farai.

Il SACERDOTE *rifiutando la pecunia gli dice:*

9

O figliol mio, se 'l tuo padre sapessi
che tu volessi cotal cosa fare
e che questa pecunia io ricevessi,
e' mi farebbe di vita privare.
Non ti pensar che qui la ritenessi
per voler tale impresa cominciare.
E' mi fia grata la tua compagnia;
la pecunia io non vo'. Portala via!

SAN FRANCESCO *getta via la pecunia e dice seco medesimo:*

10

Io non aprezo, dolce mio Signore,
di questo mondo van nulla ricchezza;
io vo' sol te seguir, vero amatore,
e sopportar per tuo amor ogni aspreza.
Fami di tale impresa vincitore,
metti dentro al mio cor la tua dolceza.
Io vo' questa pecunia gittar via
che di seguirti è sol la voglia mia.

Va UNO AMICO *al padre di San Francesco e dice così:*

11

Sappi che 'l tuo figliuol testé trovai
che di molta pecunia seco avea.
Io gli andai drieto e sì lo seguitai
tanto ch'io investigai quel che facea;

This church of God, thus fallen into ruin,
Because it is my Lord's commandment that
This temple by my hands shall be rebuilt.
This money, father, take from me and see
This temple reconstructed with it, please.

Refusing the money, THE PRIEST *says to him:*

9

My son, oh, if your father only knew
That you would wish to do a thing like this
And that I took this money from you, he
Would certainly deprive me of my life.
Don't even think that I would keep it here,
For undertaking such an enterprise.
I'm very grateful for your company,
But I don't want this money. Take it hence!

ST. FRANCIS *throws the money away and says to himself:*

10

I set no value, my sweet Lord, upon
Whatever riches this vain world may own;
True lover of my soul, I only wish
To follow you and for your Love endure
Each harshness. Make me the victor in
This enterprise; your sweetness set within
My heart. I'll throw away this money for
My only longing is to follow you.

A FRIEND *goes to St. Francis's father and speaks thus:*

11

What your son has been up to you should know;
For he had with him lots of money, and
I went behind him, and I followed him,
Until I found out what he was about.

a Santo Damïan questo lasciai
ch'aconciar quella chiesa far volea.
Quel ch'i' ho visto volentier ridico,
perché tu mi se' stato sempre amico.

El PADRE *di San Francesco dice:*

   12
Oimè, misero a me, che m'hai tu detto?
Sol di farmi morir sarà cagione
questo figliuol diverso e maladetto;
di farmi questo già non ha ragione.
S'io lo posso trovare io ti prometto
di batter quello sanza discrezione;
La mia pecunia render mi faròe
e come un tristo da me il cacceròe.

El PADRE *di San Francesco, cercando di San Francesco dice:*

   13
Dove ritrovo questo scelerato
che m'ha furato la pecunia mia?
In mal punto per me fusti creato,
forsi ch'io ti guarrò[5] della pazia!
Tristo, di tanti benefici ingrato,
quel ch'io sudai vorresti gittar via.
Aspetta! Se m'arrivi nelle mani,
merito arai di tutti e pensier vani!

SAN FRANCESCO, *nascoso in una fossa, veggendo venire il padre dice così volto a Dio:*

   14
Difendimi, Iesù giusto Signore,
sì come il tuo Iacob\<be\> liberasti
da Esaù e dal suo gran furore,
e come Danïel già tu salvasti.

He left this money at St. Damian's
Because he wished to renovate that church.
What I have seen I tell you willingly,
Because you've always been my bosom friend.

The FATHER of St. Francis says:

12

Oh wretched me! Alas, what have you said?
It's just enough to be the death of me
This wayward, cursèd son of mine! No cause
Has he, indeed, to treat me in this way.
If I can find him, I give you my word,
That I shall beat him, and without restraint;
I'll make him give my money back to me,
And, like a rogue, send him away from me.

While searching for St. Francis, his FATHER says:

13

Where shall I find again this villain who
Has robbed me of my money? Who for me
Was in an evil hour born? I shall perhaps
Soon cure you of this woeful madness!
Ungrateful for so many benefits,
You'd throw away what I have sweated for.
Just wait, if I can get my hands on you,
For all your foolish thoughts, you'll get your due!

Hidden in a ditch and seeing his father coming, ST. FRANCIS, *addressing God, says:*

14

O Jesus, righteous Lord, defend me as
You did your Jacob when from Esau and
His awful wrath you rescued him, and as
You rescued Daniel, kindle me with your

Accendi me sì del tuo dolce amore
ch'io volga a te con tutti e pensier casti.
Fa' che sia scudo e sia mia scorta e guida,
dolce Signor, dove el mio cor si fida.

SAN FRANCESCO, *uscendo della fossa, torna ' Ascesi e prima dice così camminando seco medesimo:*

15

Misero, perché stai così nascoso?
D'uscir di questo luogo omai ti spaccia:
in questa vita non è il tuo riposo.
Adunche perché temi le minaccia
del padre tuo e perché stai pensoso?
Io voglio ire a trovarlo a faccia a faccia,
perché facci di me quel che gli piace.
Io cerco sol, Signor mio, la tua pace.

San Francesco, giunto in sulla piaza d'Ascesi, stimato uno stolto fu schernito da molti e UNO [di Assisi], *veggendolo mal vestito, dice così gittandogli adosso il loto e le pietre:*

16

Certo costui debbe esser impazato.
Misero a te, donde se' tu uscito?

UN AMICO *similmente lo schernisce e dice:*

Così ti giova d'essere straziato?
Ha' tu del tuo cervel preso partito?

UNO AMICO DEL PADRE *di San Francesco lo va a dire al padre:*

Oimè, che 'l padre suo n'ha ben cercato
a questi dì perché s'era fuggito;
come egli è qui gli voglio andar a dire.

Sweet love, that I turn all chaste thoughts of mine
To you. I pray that you'll become my shield—
That you will be my escort and my guide,
Sweet Lord, in whom my heart sets all its trust.

Coming forth from the ditch, St. Francis turns toward Assisi, and, as he walks, to himself says this:

        15

Wretch, why now are you staying hidden thus?
Get yourself out of here immediately!
Not to be found in this life is your rest,
So why then fear your father's threats,
And why do you remain so anxious? I
Desire to go and see him, face to face,
So he may do with me what pleases him.
I only seek, my Lord, to find Your peace.

St. Francis, having arrived at the piazza of Assisi and, being thought a fool, was scorned by many, and ONE [MAN *from Assisi*], *seeing him ill dressed and throwing filth and stones at him, says this:*

        16

He certainly must be a lunatic.
You wretched oaf! From what place have you sprung?

A FRIEND *likewise scorns him and says:*

Do you enjoy such suffering as this?
Oh, of your senses have you taken leave?

A FRIEND OF THE FATHER *of Saint Francis goes to tell his father about it:*

His father has, alas, looked everywhere
For him in these days since he fled; now that
He's here I'll go report all this to him,

Io so che lo farà di qui partire.

E giunto al padre di San Francesco dice:

17
Sappi che 'l tuo figliuolo è in sulla piaza
e di vederlo ciascuno ha piacere;
perché gli sta come una cosa paza,
molta gente v'è tratta per vedere.

El PADRE di San Francesco dice:

Se in man non mi si speza questa maza,
di tante colpe io gli farò il dovere.
Misero a me, questo è pur troppo errore:
perduta ho la pecunia ed or l'onore.

El PADRE, trovato San Francesco in sulla piaza, gli dice sospingendolo inverso casa:

18
Io t'ho pur ritrovato, o stolto e matto!
Maladetto sia il dì ch'io t'acquistai.
Tu se' pur quel figliuol che m'hai disfatto;
con tanto studio e spesa t'allevai.
Io te ne darò tante per un tratto
che giù disteso a' piè mi cascherai.
Entrami innanzi, brutto ladroncello!
Giucato ha' la mia robba e 'l tuo cervello.

Il PADRE lo mette in prigione e dice:

19
Poi ch'e' tu stesso del tuo mal cagione[6]
e che fortuna vuol che così sia,
la casa tua sarà questa prigione
mentre che durerà la vita mia.

For he, I know, will make him leave this place.

And when he has come before St. Francis's father, he says:

17

Know that your son's in the piazza now,
And everyone's amused at him because
He is behaving like a lunatic,
And many folk line up to gawk at him.

St. Francis's FATHER *says:*

If on this madman I can lay my hands,
I'll make him pay for such a grievous lapse.
Ah woe, this fault's unfortunate for me:
My money, first, my honor, now, I've lost.

The FATHER, *having found St. Francis in the square, and pushing him toward home, says to him:*

18

You fool and lunatic, I've caught you now!
Ah cursèd be the day that you were born,
For although you're my son, you've ruined me.
With much care and expense I reared you up.
With such a treatment shall I pay you back
That you will fall down prostrate at my feet.
You go in first, you ugly little thief!
My goods and your brains, too, you've fooled away.

His FATHER *imprisons him and says:*

19

Since you have brought this evil on yourself,
And fortune wishes that it should be thus,
This prison will remain your home as long
As my life shall endure. Now get inside,

Va' drento con la mia maladizione:
qui ti consuma con la tua pazia.

E volto a' sua servi dice così:

Altro che pane e acqua non gli date,
né mai di lui novelle mi portate.

La MADRE di San Francesco va alla prigione e dice così, aprendogli la prigione:

20

Io ho tanto dolor, dolce figliuolo,
perch'io ti vidi così flagellare
dal padre tuo; io porto tanto duolo
che la vita per te sento mancare.
Tu sai ben ch'i' non ho se non te solo,
però disposta son lasciarti andare.
Guarda che tu non sia, figliuol, trovato
dal padre tuo qual è tanto adirato.

SAN FRANCESCO uscendo di prigione dice alla madre:

21

Non ti dar di me pena, o dolce madre,
ch'io non aprezo questa umana vita
né le minacce che mi fa il mio padre,
perché presto farén di qui partita.
Io penso solo alle cose leggiadre
e alla somma gloria che è infinita.
Quanto sarò nel mondo più schernito,
tanto sarò nel ciel vie più gradito.

El PADRE di San Francesco torna a casa e trovando la madre averlo fatto fuggire dice a lei. E partendosi lo ritruova.

And take my curses with you; here you may,
Together with your madness, pine away.

And addressing his servants, he says:

But bread and water, nothing let him have;
And do not bring me any news of him.

St. Francis's MOTHER goes to the prison, and, opening the cell for him, says:

20

Sweet son, I feel surpassing sorrow, for
I saw your father laying on the whip.
His whipping you so causes me great grief—
Because of you, I feel life drain away.
You know, indeed, I have no one but you,
And so I am resolved to set you free.
Be careful that your father does not find
You, son, for he's exceedingly enraged.

As he comes out of prison, ST. FRANCIS says to his mother:

21

O, do not grieve for me, my mother sweet,
For by this human life I set no store,
Nor by the threats my father makes to me,
So quickly do we all depart from here.
I only think about things joyful and
About surpassing glory infinite.
As much as I'm derided in the world,
So much shall I be welcomed up in heaven.

St. Francis's FATHER returns home, and finding that his mother has let him flee, speaks to her, and as he leaves he finds him.

22

Oimè, che ha' tu fatto, stolta e matta?
Questo è l'aiuto che tu mi vuo' dare?
Non pensi alla vergogna che ci ha fatta?
Oimè, perché l'hai tu lasciato andare?
Vedi ch'egli ha la mia casa disfatta;
E' si vorrebbe fartene cercare.[7]
S'io lo posso trovar, sol per tuo amore
strazïar lo farò con gran furore!

SAN FRANCESCO *vede venire il padre verso di sé infuriato e dice:*

23

Vienne pur, padre, ch'i' non ho paura,
però che 'l mio Signor m'ha sì 'nfiammato
e la mia mente è fatta sì sicura
ch'io non mi curo d'esser tormentato.

El PADRE *dice, sendo presso a San Francesco:*

[*a sé:*]

Di me beffe si fa?

[*a Francesco:*]

Ponete cura!
In mal punto per me fusti creato!
Ribaldo, dammi la pecunia mia
e serbati per te questa pazia.

SAN FRANCESCO *dice al padre così, rendendogli la sua pecunia:*

24

Io non aprezo, padre, le richeze,
né del misero mondo argento o oro;
io penso solo alle somme dolceze

22

Alas, that you have played the fool, gone mad,
Is this the help that you would give to me?
Do you not think about the shame he's caused?
Oh, woe is me that you have let him go!
You see that he has ruined my family;
It would be right to make you search for him.
If I can find him, since you love him so,
With violent rage I'll tear him into bits!

ST. FRANCIS, *seeing his enraged father coming toward him, says:*

23

Come on, O father; I am not afraid,
Because my Lord has so inflamed me and
has made my mind feel so secure that though
I may be tortured, I am not concerned.

Approaching St. Francis, his FATHER *says:*

[to himself:]

Would he make a fool of me?

[to Francis:]

Watch out!
At my unlucky hour were you born!
You scoundrel, let me have my money back,
And only keep your madness for yourself.

Giving him his money, ST. FRANCIS *says to his father:*

24

I do not value riches, father, nor
The gold or silver of this wretched world.
I think just on the lofty sweetness of

del mio Signor che è nello etterno coro.
Quivi son tutte le somme allegreze,
quivi si trova certo ogni tesoro.
Tien qui la tua pecunia. Io te la rendo,
però che 'l mio Signor seguir intendo.

El PADRE *di San Francesco lo mena dinanzi al vescovo per fargli rinunziare la eredità e dice:*

25
Poi che così mi vuoi disubidire,
vo' che con meco al vescovo ne vegna
e vo'ti fare in sua presenza dire
come più mio figliuol tu non ti tegna.

SAN FRANCESCO *dice al padre:*

Io son molto contento di venire
e vo' far teco ogni patto e convegna
che non mi chiami mai più tuo figliuolo,
ché servir a Iesù son volto solo.

Giunti al vescovo il PADRE *di San Francesco dice come lo vuole diredare.*[8]

26
O reverendo padre, il vero Iddio
teco sia sempre. Intendi la mia voglia:
di diredar costui è il voler mio,
veramente cagion d'ogni mia doglia,
perché m'è stato sempre averso e rio,
e lui di ciò contento se ne spoglia.
Poi che così vuol la fortuna mia,
mostraci el modo tu che così sia.

My Lord who is in the eternal choir
Up there where all the highest joys abide,
Where every treasure, surely, one can find;
Take here the money I return to you,
Because I mean to follow my Lord now.

St. Francis's FATHER *leads him before the bishop to make him renounce his inheritance, and says:*

25

Since you intend to disobey me thus,
To see the bishop, I'd have you come with me,
And in his presence wish to have you say
That you no longer count yourself my son.

ST. FRANCIS *says to his father:*

I'm very happy thus to come with you,
And every pact and contract I shall make
With you that I'll no more be called your son.
For serving Jesus is my sole desire.

Having come before the bishop, St. Francis's FATHER *explains that he wants to disinherit him:*

26

May the true God, reverend father, always be
With you. Please understand my wish,
For I desire to disinherit him,
Truly the cause of every woe of mine,
Since wicked and wayward he has always been
To me, and he—content with this—divests.
Because it seems ordained by destiny,
Explain to us how this can come to be.

SAN FRANCESCO *consente e dice così al vescovo volto prima al padre:*

27
Io son contento al tutto rinunziare
a' ben paterni ed ogni mia ragione;
ogni mia eredità vo' rifiutare,
perché così è la mia intenzione.
E in tua presenza mi voglio spogliare
e tu, padre, sarai qui testimone
com'io mi spoglio d'ogni ben paterno
per acquistare il sommo regno eterno.

El VESCOVO, *partito il padre di San Francesco, mosso di lui a compassione, lo fa rivestire e dice:*

28
Sta' su, Francesco, mio figliuol diletto,
perch'io ti vo' col mio mantel coprire.
Di te m'increscie essendo giovanetto.

E volto a' sua servi dice così:

Recate, servi mia, qualche vestire.

E volto a San Francesco dice:

Tien' qui, figliuol, che tu sia benedetto,
ancor di te gran cose s'ha ' sentire.
Sèguita drieto alla tua intenzione
e vanne con la mia benedizione.

SAN FRANCESCO, *partito dal vescovo, seco medesimo dice così:*

29
Non giunse nave in porto con buon vento,
né più sicura dal nochier guidata,

ST. FRANCIS *agrees and, facing his father, speaks to the bishop thus:*

27

I'm happy to relinquish everything
Both all my father's goods and all my rights,
My whole inheritance I would refuse,
Since this is my intention and I wish
In your good presence to divest myself,
And father you will here bear witness that
I strip myself of each paternal good
To gain the highest and eternal realm.

The BISHOP, *once St. Francis's father has left, is moved with compassion for him, makes him reclothe himself, and says:*

28

Arise, O Francis, my belovèd son,
For I will with my mantel cover you.
I pity you because you're just a boy.

And addressing his servants he speaks thus:

My servants, go and bring some clothing here.

And, addressing St. Francis, he says:

Take these, my son, my blessing too, and we
Shall yet be hearing wondrous things of thee.
So follow closely your intended plan,
And with my benediction go from here.

After leaving the bishop, ST. FRANCIS *speaks says to himself:*

29

No ship has with a better wind reached port
Nor with a surer pilot at the helm

quant'io ne vo tutto lieto e contento,
poi ch'io del mondo ogni pompa ho lasciata;
e tanto gaudio drento al mio cor sento
che la mia mente è già tutta infiammata.
Del segno della croce armar mi voglio,
poi che del mondo van miser mi spoglio.

San Francesco, caminando truova UN SUO COMPAGNO, *il quale lo riveste e dice:*

30
Tu se' pur desso, o buon compagno mio!
Per qual cagion se' tu così spogliato?

SAN FRANCESCO *risponde:*

Sappi che gli è voler del vero Idio
che 'l mondo van da me sia disprezato.

Dice quel suo COMPAGNO *a San Francesco:*

Di rivestirti certo ho gran desio:
piglierai questa vesta se t'è grato.

Risponde SAN FRANCESCO:

Io la ricevo molto allegramente
e una corda mi dona al presente.

SAN FRANCESCO, *rivestito e cinto della corda, dice seco medesimo:*

31
Questa sarà la mia ornata vesta,
questa corda sarà la mia cintura;
la penitenza fia ogni mia festa,
mentre che la mia vita al mondo dura.

Than I, who joyful have become and glad,
Since every worldly pomp I've left behind;
And such great joy I feel within my heart,
That my intellect, indeed, is all aflame.
For with the cross's sign I'll arm myself,
Now poor and nude, this vain world I cast off.

While St. Francis is walking along, ONE OF HIS FRIENDS *encounters him and reclothes him, and says:*

30

O my good fellow, it is really you!
On what account are you undressed like this?

ST. FRANCIS *answers:*

Know that the true God wishes that, by me,
The foolish world should be disparaged so.

St. Francis's FRIEND *says to him:*

I greatly long to clothe you once again;
Pray, take this garment if it pleases you.

ST. FRANCIS *answers:*

Most happily do I receive it, and
I pray you, right now let me have a cord.

Reclothed and belted with the cord, ST. FRANCIS *says to himself:*

31

This will be my decorative garb,
This cord will be my belt, and penitence
My every celebration will become,
As long as in this world my life shall last.

O giusto Idio, che somma grazia è questa,
poi che la tua dolceza el mio cor fura!

E nel partire dice a quello suo compagno:

Diletto fratel mio, fatti con Dio,
tal carità per me ti renda Idio.

San Francesco, tornato ' Ascesi, veggendolo un cavalieri detto MESSER BERNARDO[9] *d'Ascesi, lo priega che vadi a stare a casa sua avendo già notizia della sua buona vita:*

32
Io ti priego di grazia singulare
ch'alla mia casa ti piaccia venire
questo giorno con meco a riposare,
ché un mio secreto ti vo' conferire.

SAN FRANCESCO *risponde a messer Bernardo:*

Tal grazia certo non ti vo' negare
pur che ne possa qualche ben seguire
e che la mia venuta sia cagione
di qualche degna e buona operazione.

MESSER BERNARDO *dice a San Francesco come spirato da Dio desidera essere religioso e suo compagno:*

33
Sappi che 'l giusto Dio m'ha tocco il core
pe' buoni essempli e per tua santa vita,
tanto ch'io son già di me stesso fore;
e però son disposto far partita
dal mondo cieco, falso e pien d'errore;
e priego sol tua carità infinita
che per vil servo suo m'accetti e degni
e di me peccator già non si sdegni.

O righteous God, what lofty grace this is,
Now that Your sweetness ravishes my heart!

And in parting he says to his friend:

O my belovèd brother, go with God,
May God reward you for this charity.

After St. Francis returns to Assisi, a gentleman named MASTER BERNARDO[9] *of Assisi, who had already had news of St. Francis's good life, when he meets him, invites him to come to stay at his house:*

32

Let me beseech you for a grace most singular:
Into my home today, please come; repose
With me because I would confer about
A private matter of my own with you.

ST. FRANCIS *answers Master Bernardo:*

I'd surely not refuse you such a grace
If some good may follow from it and if
Its wellspring may have been my coming here:
Some work worthy, honorable, and good.

MASTER BERNARDO *tells St. Francis how, inspired by God, he desires to become a religious and his companion:*

33

Know that the righteous God has touched my heart
Through good examples and your holy life
So much that I'm beside myself, indeed,
And, therefore, I've resolved to take my leave
From this blind world, so full of error, false;
And to your boundless love I only pray
That as your servant lowly you'll accept
And honor me, and not this sinner scorn.

SAN FRANCESCO *accetta messer Bernardo e dice:*

34
Tu m'hai fatto sì lieto e sì contento
col tuo parlar ch'io non te 'l posso dire,
poi che m'hai discoperto quel c'hai dentro
di volere a Iesù sempre servire;
e, se tu vuo' far questo a compimento,
sappi che ti bisogna compartire
a' poveri di Dio ogni tesoro,
se vuoi el riposo dello eterno coro.

MESSER BERNARDO *dice a San Francesco che insieme con lui distribuisca el suo a' poveri:*

35
Padre, io ti priego che in piacer ti sia
con meco insieme a' poveri di Dio
distribuire ogni richeza mia,
ché di servire a quello ho gran disio;
e vo' con teco insieme in compagnia
finir la vita dolce. O padre mio,
fa' di questa pecunia che ti piace,
perch'io vo' sol cercar la vera pace.

SAN FRANCESCO *piglia delle pecunie di messer Bernardo e dalle a' poveri per Dio dicendo:*

36
Poveri infermi, questi piglierete
per poter vostra vita sostenare.

UNO POVERO *dice:*

Padre, da Cristo merito n'arete,
e lui vel possa in ciel rapresentare.

ST. FRANCIS *accepts Master Bernardo and says:*

34

I cannot tell you how much happiness
And joy your words have given me because
You have revealed to me your inner wish
To serve forever Jesus Christ, and if
It's your desire to do this perfectly,
Then be apprised that you must parcel out
Among God's poor your every treasure if
You want the peace of the eternal choir.

MASTER BERNARDO *tells St. Francis that together they should distribute his goods to the poor:*

35

Father, I pray you, let it please you to
Distribute with me to the poor of God
My every luxury and all my wealth,
For I desire compellingly to serve
Him and go along in company with you
And sweetly end my life. O father mine,
Do with his money what you will because
My only wish is searching for true peace.

ST. FRANCIS *takes some of Master Bernardo's money and gives it to the poor of God, saying:*

36

You poor, decrepit ones, this money take
So that you can sustain your lives with it.

ONE PAUPER *says:*

For this, Christ will reward you, father,
And may he give you merit up in heaven.

UN ALTRO POVERO *dice a' sua compagni:*

Compagni mia, voi non ve n'accorgete:
io veggo qua molte carità fare.
Io voglio ir presto. Io lascio il mio barletto.[10]
Vienne, compagno, e piglia il tuo sacchetto.

UNO POVERO *dice a San Francesco:*

37
Fa', santo padre, a noi un po' di bene,
che siamo attratti, infermi, abandonati,
e finiàn nostra vita in tante pene
e siàn da tanti affanni tormentati;
a darne a questi non ha' fatto bene,
perché testé se gli aranno giucati.[11]
Piacciati, santo padre, darne a noi
e sempre pregherremo Idio per voi.

SAN FRANCESCO, *avendo già raunati dodici compagni di diversi luoghi, volto a loro dice così, amaestrandogli seguire la dottrina de l'Evangelio:*

38
Sendo già tanti insieme ragunati,
veggo che Dio ci vuol multiplicare.
O dolci figliuo' mia diletti e grati,
le vostre mente vogliate levare
al nostro Idio e già non siate ingrati
di tanti benefici lui laudare.
Con puro effetto[12] e con perfetto zelo
observerete il suo santo evangelo.

ANOTHER PAUPER *says to his comrades:*

My friends, take note of what is going on:
I see much charity in progress here,
I want to go at once and leave my cup.
Come on, my friend, and bring your little sack.

A PAUPER says to St. Francis:

37

O holy father, do us some small good,
For we're abandoned, crippled, and infirm,
And in great suffering our lives we'll end,
And be tormented by appalling woes;
In giving it to these, you've not done well,
Because, soon, they'll have gambled it away;[11]
O, holy father, please give some to us,
And we shall always pray to God for you.

ST. FRANCIS, having already gathered together twelve companions from various places, addresses them to teach them to follow the doctrine of the Gospel and says this:

38

We have so many brought together, indeed,
That I see God wants us to multiply.
Oh my sweet sons belovèd, dear to me,
Your intellects lift up unto our God,
And do not let yourselves ungrateful be,
But praise him for such generosity.
With pure affection and with perfect zeal,
His holy gospel see that you observe.

Seguita SANTO FRANCESCO:

39

La pace, figliuo' mia, predicherete,
la penitenza per rimessïone
de' peccatori, e constanti sarete
e forti in ogni vostra afflizione
e nell'orar sempre perseverete,
prudenti e saggi in ogni operazione;
e ne' vostri costumi onesti e gravi
ciascun\<o\> la conscienza mondi e lavi.

Appresso dice loro come vuole andare al Pontefice[13] a confermare la Regola[14]:

40

Diletti frati, io son da Dio spirato
che noi dobbiamo al Santo Padre andare,
perché ci sia da lui sol confermato
tutto quel che per noi s'ha 'osservare,
come ne' mia sermon v'ho dichiarato.
Dello Evangel vogliate frequentare
la gran dottrina, o dolci figliuo' mia,
e verrete con meco in compagnia.

Risponde UNO DE' SUA DISCEPOLI *per tutti gli altri:*

41

Noi siam contenti, padre, d'ubidire
alle tue voglie e far tutti e tua detti,
tanta dolceza ci hai fatto sentire
con tua santi ricordi e buon precetti;
e in ogni luogo con teco venire
vogliamo e sempre ti sarem suggetti,
che del divino amor ci hai sì 'nfiammati
che d'ubidirti ci tegniàn beati.

ST. FRANCIS *continues:*

39

His peace, my sons, you must go forth to preach,
And penitence for the remission of
One's sins, and constant you must be in your
Afflictions every one, and must be strong,
And ever in your praying, persevere;
In every work, be prudent and be wise,
And in your manner serious and chaste,
And all must clear and cleanse their consciences.

He next tells them how he wishes to go to the Pope[13] *to have the Rule*[14] *approved:*

40

My cherished brothers, I've been inspired by God
That to our Holy Father we must go;
For him alone to ratify the way
Of life that we among ourselves observe—
The way I've taught you in my sermons, for
You frequently must read the holy page,
The Gospel's lofty teachings, my sweet sons,
And come and keep me company, dear ones.

ONE OF THE DISCIPLES *answers for all the others:*

41

We are content, O father, to obey
Your will, and all you tell us to, we'll do,
Such sweetness it has given us to hear
With you the holy stories, and the precepts good;
And every place we wish to come with you
And ever be your subjects, for with love
Divine you have inflamed us so that we
Hold ourselves blessèd in obeying you.

Vanno al Santo Padre e giunti SAN FRANCESCO *gli dice così:*

42
Beatissimo padre e signor mio,
io son venuto nella tua presenza
perché tu essaudisca il mio desio.
Non ti sia grave di darmi audienza.

EL PAPA *dice:*

Misero poverel, vatti con Dio,
piglia a tua posta di partir licenza.

SAN FRANCESCO *volto a' compagni dice:*

Figliuo', non si convien di ciò turbare:
tal grazia non è tempo d'impetrare.

SAN FRANCESCO *fa orazione a Dio chiedendo che sia essaudito dal pastore:*

43
Sì come Ester d'Ansuero essaudita
fu e per lei suo popol liberato,
o giusto Idio, per tua pietà infinita
fa' che dal Santo Padre io sia ascoltato.
Certo nulla si fa senza tua aita.
Deh, non guardare al mio grave peccato;
fa' che intender mi voglia il tuo pastore
e ch'io sia di mia impresa vincitore.

IL PONTEFICE, *avendo cacciato San Francesco, si pente averlo fatto e dice così seco medesimo:*

44
A cacciar quello ho fatto troppo errore,
perché pare pur uom di santa vita.

They go to the Holy Father, and having arrived, ST. FRANCIS *speaks thus:*

42

Most blessèd father and my lord, I've come
Into your presence so you may assent
To my desire; I pray you do not be
Displeased at granting me this audience.

THE POPE *says:*

You poor dear fellow, now go you with God;
You have my leave to go back as you will.

ST. FRANCIS, *addressing his companions, says:*

My sons, we must not be upset by this.
It is not time to ask for such a grace.

ST. FRANCIS *prays to God, asking that the Pope grant his request:*

43

Just as Ahasuerus answered Esther's prayer,
And through her was the populace set free,
O just God, through your mercy infinite
Let the Holy Father hear my prayer,
It's certain, nothing's done without Your help.
You must not look upon my heavy sin;
Make your pastor understand my wish
And me the victor in my enterprise.

THE POPE, *having thrown St. Francis out, repents of what he has done and to himself says this:*

44

Too great an error, driving him away
I've made; he seems a man of holy life.

E volto a uno servo dice:

Fallo chiamar ch'i' ho fermo nel core
ch'ogni domanda sua sia essaudita.

Risponde IL SERVO *al Pontefice:*

Beatissimo padre e buon pastore,
la voglia tua sarà presto ubidita.

EL SERVO *giunto a San Francesco gli dice:*

Al Santo Padre, poverel, verrai
ed ogni grazia da lui otterrai.

Giunto San Francesco al PONTEFICE *gli dice così:*

            45
Chiedi ciò che ti piace arditamente,
perché ogni grazia da me puoi impetrare;
sappi che al tutto è ferma la mia mente
volere alle tue voglie sadisfare.

SAN FRANCESCO *priega di nuovo il Pontefice che gli confermi la Regola mostrandogliela scritta:*

O Santo Padre, io ti priego al presente
che tu ci vogli questa confermare,
ché d'osservarla è nostro desiderio,
fondata nel Vangel con gran misterio.

And turning to a servant says:

Have him called back, for in my heart I have
Resolved to grant every request of his

The Pope's SERVANT *answers:*

Most blessèd father and good pastor, I
Shall instantly obey your will in this.

The SERVANT, *having reached St. Francis, says to him:*

Poor fellow, to the Holy Father go,
And on you every grace he shall bestow.

When St. Francis reaches the Pope, THE POPE *speaks thus:*

45

Ask fervently for that which pleases you,
Since you may ask for anything you like.
Know that my mind entirely is made up
To want to satisfy your every wish.

ST. FRANCIS *again asks the Pope that he approve his Rule, showing it to him written down:*

O Holy Father, I pray you now that you
Will give us your approval for this Rule,
As it is our desire to follow it;
For on the Gospel's sacred text it's based.

El Pontefice piglia da San Francesco la Regola scritta e mostrandola a' cardinali, parendo loro che fussi troppo aspra, UNO DI LORO *dice al Pontefice che non la debba confermare:*

46

Certo tal cosa mai più fu sentita
e nessun la potrebbe mai seguire.
O Santo Padre, ell'è troppa aspra vita:
non lo voler per nulla acconsentire.

EL PONTEFICE *dice così:*

Sia che si vuol, che ferma e stabilita
sarà da me; io non gliel vo' disdire.

Risponde IL CARDINALE:

Ogni cosa puoi far come pastore,
ma guarda che non facci troppo errore.

UNO ALTRO CARDINALE *dice contrario al primo:*

47

O Padre Santo, se noi dispreziamo
la domanda di questo poverello,
guarda che 'l nostro Idio non offendiamo.
A me parrebbe di far grazia a quello
se la vita di Cristo contempliamo;
non sarà cosa grave a compiacello.

EL PONTEFICE *volto a San Francesco dice così:*

Ogni tuo desiderio sia adempiuto:
va' in pace che 'l Signor ti presti aiuto.

The Pope takes the written Rule from St. Francis and shows it to the cardinals, to whom it seems too harsh, and ONE OF THEM *tells the Pope that he should not approve it:*

46

We've never heard of such a Rule before,
We're sure no one could ever follow it.
O Holy Father, it's too harsh a life;
Do not for anything consent to it.

THE POPE *speaks thus:*

Let that be as it may, for I confirm
And approve it; I'll not deny him this.

THE CARDINAL *answers:*

You can do anything as pastor, sir,
But have a care lest you too greatly err.

ANOTHER CARDINAL *opposes the advice of the first:*

47

If we belittle, Holy Father, the
Request of this poor fellow, have a care
That we do not offend our God. It seems
To me that we would grant him his wish
Were we to contemplate the life of Christ;
It won't be wrong to grant him this request.

THE POPE, *addressing St. Francis says:*

May every desire of yours be gratified;
Go hence in peace and be the Lord your guide.

Seguita IL PONTEFICE *a San Francesco:*

48
Francesco, io ti do ancor piena licenza
che tu possa pel mondo predicare
e i peccator chiamare a penitenza.
Per te gran cose Idio vorrà mostrare;
tal divozion mi porge tua presenza.
Ciò che ti par di me puoi dispensare;
io ti concedo questa ed ogni grazia.[15]
Piacer ho sol di far tua voglia sazia.

SAN FRANCESCO *dice a' compagni che ringrazino Iddio e appresso dichiara che vuole andare a predicare al Soldano*[16]:

49
Figliuoli, al nostro Idio grazie rendete,
poi che di tanti don ci ha fatti degni,
e sua santi Vangel predicherete,
e la via da salir ne' sommi regni
apertamente a ciascun mostrerrete;
e di far questo alcun di voi si degni.
In Babillonia è la mia voglia andare,
però mi voglia un di voi seguitare.

UNO DE' SUA COMPAGNI *risponde:*

50
O santo padre, sempre ci fia grato
di poter le tue voglie sadisfare;
però sappi ch'io sono apparechiato
volerti in ogni luogo accompagnare:
d'esser con teco io mi tengo beato.
Ora a tua posta possiam camminare.

THE POPE *continues speaking to St. Francis:*

48

Full license, Francis, I give you as well
To preach throughout the world, to penitence
Its sinners call. Through you God wishes to
Make manifest great wonders, and in me
Your presence inspires such great devotion that
Whatever you wish from me you may obtain;
I grant you this, and every grace grant I,[15]
I'm only pleased your wish to gratify.

ST. FRANCIS *tells his companions to give God thanks and then declares that he wants to go to preach to the Sultan:*[16]

49

My sons, to our God render thanks because
He's made us worthy of so great a gift,
And you must preach his holy Gospels, and
Must clearly demonstrate for everyone
The way for rising to the highest realms;
And let some of you deign to do this task.
It is my wish to go to Babylon;
Let one among you go along with me.

ONE OF HIS COMPANIONS *answers:*

50

O holy father, it always gives us joy
To satisfy your wishes; therefore know
That I'm indeed prepared to go along
With you wherever you may wish to go:
I truly think myself entirely blest
To go along with you as you request.

SAN FRANCESCO *dice*:

El nostro grande Idio in compagnia
sarà, figliuolo, in questa santa via.

SAN FRANCESCO *fa orazione a Dio andando al Soldano*:

      51
O giusto Idio, piacciati d'essaudire
e prieghi del tuo indegno peccatore;
fa' che l'orazion mia possa venire
nel tuo cospetto, o Sommo Redentore.
Piacciati gli occhi della mente aprire
a questi saracin, che in tanto errore
voglion perseverar, Padre Superno:
deh, fagli degni del tuo regno eterno.

SAN FRANCESCO, *giunto in Babillonia*,[17] *dice al suo compagno, veggendosi venire incontro alcuno saracino adirato*:

      52
Fratel mio, rallegriànci nel Signore
ed infinite grazie a lui rendiamo,
e volentier pel suo pietoso[18] amore
in pace ogni tormento sopportiamo.
Veggo venir costor con tal furore
incontro a noi e però non temiamo
d'esser da lor battuti e tormentati,
perché sarem nel ciel poi più beati.

Seguita SAN FRANCESCO:

      53
Pensiam che 'l nostro Idio fu flagellato
per noi miseri ingrati peccatori,
e di crudele spine incoronato
e 'l giusto sangue per noi versar fòri,

ST. FRANCIS *says:*

Our God so great will keep us company,
Belovèd sons, upon this sacred way.

On his way to see the Sultan, ST. FRANCIS *prays to God:*

51

O righteous God, may you be pleased to grant
Your simple sinner's prayers; O may my prayer,
Redeemer in the highest, find its way
Into your presence, and may you be pleased
To open wide the eyes of all their minds
So that these Saracens, who will persist
In such great error, O supernal God,
Will be made worthy of your eternal realm.

ST. FRANCIS, *having arrived in Babylon[17] and seeing some enraged Saracens coming toward him, says to his companion:*

52

Let us, my brother, in the Lord rejoice,
And let us render him unceasing thanks,
And willingly, for his love merciful,
Every torture we'll peacefully endure.
I see them coming toward us so enraged;
But we must not, indeed, have any fear
Of being beaten or abused by them,
For we shall be more blessèd up in heaven.

ST. FRANCIS *continues:*

53

Let's think about the way our God was scourged
For us ungrateful sinners miserable,
And of the cruel thorns they crowned him with,
His righteous blood that he poured forth for us

e 'n su quel duro legno fu chiovato.
Ben sarebbono iniqui e nostri cuori
se per suo amore, o diletto figliuolo,
non portassimo in pace ogni aspro duolo

UNO SARACINO *giunto a San Francesco dice:*

54
Che fate voi tra noi, falsi cristiani?
Voi non dovete il bando aver sentito.
Noi vi strazierem sì, ribaldi cani,
che certo arete preso mal partito
a esser giunti tra le nostre mani.

[Ad altro saraceno, a parte:]

Guarda come egli sta pronto e ardito!

[A San Francesco e il suo compagno:]

Innanzi al Soldan nostro ne verrete;
d'esser venuti qui vi pentirete.

UNO SERVO *gli mena dinanzi al Soldano dicendo al signore:*

55
Io t'apresento questi malfattori
cristiani iniqui, maladetti e ingrati,
che son di nostra fé disprezatori.
Meriton certo d'esser tormentati,
perversi, maladetti ingannatori,
e quali hanno e tua bandi disprezati.
Fagli punir, qui nella tua presenza,
poi che t'hanno sì poca riverenza.

On that unyielding wood where he was nailed.
Our hearts would verily be wicked if
For love of him, O my dear son, we'd not,
Bear patiently their every torment harsh.

A SARACEN, *coming up to St. Francis, says:*

54

What are you doing in our midst, vile Christians?
The interdiction you must not have heard,
For here we torture knavish curs like you.
You certainly have made a foolish choice
In having put yourselves into our hands.

[To another Saracen, aside:]

Look you how bold and ready this one is!

[to St. Francis and his companions:]

You will be brought before our Sultan now;
That you have ever come here, you'll regret.

A SERVANT *leads them before the Sultan and says to his lord:*

55

To you these evildoers I present,
These wicked, cursed, ingrate Christians who
Are ridiculers of our faith, and who
Deserve most surely to be tortured too,
Perverse and cursed and deceitful men,
Who have ignored your interdiction, sir.
Let them be punished in your presence here,
So little deference to you they have shown.

EL SOLDANO *dice a San Francesco:*

   56
Come se' tu, poverello, arrivato
in queste parte? Dimmi la cagione.

SAN FRANCESCO *risponde:*

Sappi che un messo son da Dio mandato
a te sol per divina spirazione,
perché da me, Soldan, sia alluminato
della fé santa, acció che in perdizione
non vadi per seguir tua falsa setta,
fé di Macon, iniqua e maladetta.

Seguita SAN FRANCESCO *al Soldano:*

   57
El vero Dio creò la terra e 'l cielo
e tutto l'universo di nïente,
per la sua carità,[19] pel sommo zelo.
Abitar volle tra la mortal gente
sol per levar da noi l'oscuro velo
pel gran peccato del primo parente,[20]
che era ciascuno all'inferno dannato,
perché il vietato pomo avea[21] gustato.

Seguita SAN FRANCESCO:

   58
E volle della Vergine incarnare
per liberarci da tanto delitto,
appien colla sua voce dichiarare
ciò che ciascun profeta avea preditto;
e morte e passïon volse gustare,
e in sulla croce fu per noi confitto;

THE SULTAN *says to St. Francis:*

56
How is it that you have arrived, poor chap,
Within these parts? Explain to me the cause.

ST. FRANCIS *answers:*

Know that I have been sent a messenger,
Inspired divinely, just to you from God,
So that you, Sultan, may enlightened be
About the holy faith by me so you
Won't go to hell because you heed your sect,
Mohammed's false and wicked faith accursed.

ST. FRANCIS *continues speaking to the Sultan:*

57
From nothing did the true God make the earth,
The heavens, and all the universe, and with
His consummate zeal and out of charity.
He chose to live among us mortal folk,
Only so he could lift death's darksome veil
From us; for our first parent's heinous sin[20]
Was each of us to the inferno damned,
Because he'd tasted the forbidden fruit.

ST. FRANCIS *continues:*

58
He chose, too, from a virgin to take flesh,
And free us wholly from such evil great
And with his word proclaim what each one of
The prophets had predicted; and he chose
To taste both death and suffering upon
The cross where he was crucified for us;

risuscitò poi doppo il terzo die,
nella sua somma gloria in ciel salie.

Seguita SAN FRANCESCO *al Soldano dicendo così:*

       59
Credi, Soldan, per certo quel ch'i' ho detto,
che la fé del mio Idio è vera e certa,
e non voler seguir più Macometto,
però che la sua fede è vana e incerta;
consenti al mio Iesù Signor perfetto,
che la via di salute mostra aperta
a tutti que' che la voglion seguire;
di battezarti vogli acconsentire.

Seguita SAN FRANCESCO:

       60
Se ti pare aspro la tua fé lasciare
e credi che sia il me' quella seguire,
io ti voglio ogni dubio dichiarare:
però farai testé da te venire
un de' tua sacerdoti e 'nsieme entrare
io vo' nel fuoco, e, s'io debbo morire
pe' mia peccati imputato mi sia;
s'io scampo, credi al figliuol di Maria.

IL SOLDANO *dice a San Francesco:*

       61
Pel mio Macon, nessun non ci sarebbe
che alcun tormento sostener volessi!
Quel che tu di' veder non si potrebbe:
nel fuoco alcun non credo entrar volessi.
Sappi che grato a me, padre, sarebbe
di creder nel tuo Idio; quand'io vedessi

Then, after the third day, to new life arisen,
In his supernal glory rose to heaven.

ST. FRANCIS *continues speaking thus to the Sultan:*

59

For certain, Sultan, credit what I've said;
For my God's faith is true and is assured,
And do not longer wish Mohammed's faith
To follow, for your faith is surely vain.
Let Jesus, a perfect Lord, reveal the way
Of his salvation one open wide to all
Those who wish to follow it; therefore
Consent now to be baptized in his faith.

ST. FRANCIS *continues:*

60

If it seems hard for you to leave your faith
And you believe it's best to follow it,
I wish to clear away your every doubt,
So have a priest of yours come to this place;
With him I wish to enter into fire
And if I chance to die, impute it to
My sins, but if I should escape, then you
Must in the son of Mary put your faith.

THE SULTAN *says to St. Francis:*

61

By my Mohammed, no one would desire
To undergo any such suffering!
For what you talk about cannot be done:
No one, I think, would go into the fire.
Know, father, that I should be pleased to believe
In your God if I saw my people wished

che 'l popol mio mi volessi seguire,
piacer arei di poterti ubidire.

Seguita IL SOLDANO:

        62
Io mi sarei volentier battezato,
se non ch'io temo la persecuzione
di questo popol pazo e scelerato;
sì che per ora non è mia intenzione
di farlo, perché il tempo accomodato
non sarebbe ora, ché sarei cagione
certo della tua morte e della mia
da questa gente maladetta e ria.

Seguita IL SOLDANO:

        63
Francesco, alquanto meco ti starai,
ché di vederti io non sazio il cor mio;
veduto volentier da me sarai
ché d'udirti parlar ho gran desio.
Di questi mia tesori piglierai
e dara'ne a' tua poveri di Dio.

SAN FRANCESCO *al Soldano:*

Soldano, io non aprezo il tuo tesoro:
cerco sol quel che è nello eterno coro.

SAN FRANCESCO *volto al compagno suo dice:*

        64
O figliuol mio, noi ne possiamo andare,
poi che 'l cor di costui è sì indurato
che niente mi vale il predicare;
e forse el giusto Idio l'ha riserbato

To follow me, I'd willingly accede
To your request—be happy to obey.

THE SULTAN *continues:*

62

I willingly would baptized be, except
I am afraid of persecution by
This crazy, wicked populace so that,
For now, I don't intend to do it since
The time that would be right for doing it
Would not be now because I surely would
Bring on your murder—and bring mine on too—
By this accursèd lot, this evil crew.

THE SULTAN *continues:*

63

O Francis, long may you remain with me,
For I've not filled my heart with seeing you,
And with great pleasure would I see you, if
You linger here, for great is my desire
To hear you speak. Take these my treasures and
Pass them out among your poor of God.

ST. FRANCIS *to the Sultan:*

Your treasure, Sultan, I do not esteem;
I only seek that of the eternal choir.

Addressing his companion, ST. FRANCIS *says:*

64

O my dear son, let us depart this place;
Because his heart's so hard, my sermons don't
Avail with him at all, and it may be
That righteous God is saving him

a qualche tempo e però ritornare
io vo' tra 'l nostro popol battezato.
Spero che noi farem qualche buon frutto
coll'aiuto di quel che regge il tutto.

UNO SERVO *dice a messer Orlando[22] come San Francesco è arrivato in quel luogo, cioè, presso alla Vernia a uno suo castello:*

65
Sappi che ci è venuto quello uom santo,
il qual si fa pel mondo nominare,
che di vederlo hai già bramato tanto:
Francesco il nome suo si fa chiamare.

MESSER ORLANDO *dice al servo:*

Va', servo, e digli che gli piaccia alquanto
venirsi a star con meco a riposare,
che di vederlo arò sommo piacere.

IL SERVO *risponde a messer Orlando:*

Messer, presto fia fatto il tuo volere.

IL SERVO, *giunto a San Francesco, gli dice, pregandolo che venga a casa messer Orlando:*

66
Quel vero Idio che l'universo adora
salvi e mantenga la tua santitate.
Ciascun delle tu' opre s'innamora
per la infinita tua somma bontate.
Sappi che 'l mio messer che qua dimora
ti priega, padre, per la tua pietate
ch'alla sua casa ti piaccia venire,
ché di vederti, padre, ha gran desire.

Until another time, and so I wish
To go again amongst our baptized folk.
I hope we may produce some worthy fruit
With that one's help who governs everything.

A SERVANT tells Master Orlando[22] that St. Francis has arrived in that place, that is, near La Vernia, at one of his castles:

65

Sir, know that here the holy man has come
Who has become renowned throughout the world
And whom you have so greatly yearned to meet.
And Francis is the name one calls him by.

MASTER ORLANDO *says to the servant:*

Go, servant, tell him how he'd please me if
He came to stay and rest awhile with me,
For I shall gain great pleasure seeing him.

THE SERVANT *answers Master Orlando:*

Good sir, your will at once shall be performed.

THE SERVANT, *having come to St. Francis, speaks to him, requesting that he come to Master Orlando's house:*

66

That true God whom the universe adores
Save and preserve your holiness; each work
Of yours inspires us through your infinite,
And lofty goodness. Father, be advised:
My master who dwells here requests that you,
Out of compassion, will be kind enough
To come pay him a visit at his home
For greatly he desires to meet with you.

SAN FRANCESCO *risponde al Servo:*

67

Io verrò volentieri in compagnia
con teco insieme al tuo gentil messere;
poi che gli è grato[23] la presenza mia,
d'ubidir quello ho fermo ogni pensiere.

SAN FRANCESCO, *giunto a messer Orlando, dice così:*

Colui che incarnar volle di Maria
ti salvi e guardi, o gentil cavaliere,
prestiti lungo tempo, dolce vita
e l'etterno riposo alla partita.

MESSER ORLANDO *risponde a San Francesco e dice:*

68

Io ho più tempo già desiderato
veder cogli occhi mia la tua presenza.
O padre immenso, troppo mi fia grato
che tu degni restar per tua clemenza
alcun giorno con meco e sol beato
mi tengo perch'io t'ho gran riverenza.
Immenso padre, io te 'l chieggo di grazia
che resti qui per far mia voglia sazia.

Seguita MESSER ORLANDO *a San Francesco:*

69

Se tu volessi a mia contemplazione
restar qui, padre, nel paese mio,
un monte ho qua molto atto all'orazione
che di donarlo a te ho gran desio;
e certo, padre, io son d'oppenïone
che fia molto atto a contemplare Idio.

ST. FRANCIS *answers the servant:*

67

I willingly shall go along with you
To see your noble master; since he finds
My presence pleases him, my every thought
I shall address to doing what he asks.

Having come to Master Orlando, ST. FRANCIS *says this:*

May he who chose from Mary to take flesh
Preserve and save you, noble gentleman,
And may he grant you long and tranquil life,
And, at your parting, grant eternal rest.

MASTER ORLANDO *answers St. Francis and says:*

68

That I might see you with my very eyes
In person, father excellent, indeed,
I long have wished. You do me too much grace
That through your clemency you deign to spend
Some days with me. And since I feel so great
A reverence for you, account myself
But blest, O matchless father, grant this grace:
Stay here with me and so fulfill my wish.

MASTER ORLANDO *continues to St. Francis:*

69

It has occurred to me if, father, you
Might in my region wish to stay, I own
A mountain here quite suitable for prayer,
That I wish fervently to give to you,
And, father, my opinion surely is
That it's just right for contemplating God.

SAN FRANCESCO *a messer Orlando:*

Messer Orlando, andiamo a veder quello
ch'i' ho gran desiderio di vedello.

MESSER ORLANDO *dice a San Francesco e vanno al monte della Vernia:*

70
Volentier vo' venir, padre diletto,
con teco insieme e mostrarti la via,
e priego il giusto Idio con puro effetto
che gli piaccia essaudir la voglia mia,
e che 'l paese e 'l monte ti sia accetto;
d'esserti apresso sol mio cor desia.

SAN FRANCESCO *a messer Orlando:*

Messer, questo è un monte atto e divoto
alla orazione, perch'egli è assai remoto.

SAN FRANCESCO *dice a' sua compagni, giunto al monte della Vernia:*

71
Dolci figliuoli, io credo certamente
che ci sia stato questo aparechiato
dal nostro Redentor giusto e clemente,
e gran segno ci fia da lui mostrato:
vedi con quanta festa questa gente
c'invita che noi stiamo in questo lato.

SAN FRANCESCO, *volto a messer Orlando, dice:*

Grazia ti rendo, o gentil cavalieri,
e questo monte accetto volentieri.

ST. FRANCIS *to Master Orlando:*

Master Orlando, let's go see it for
I feel a great desire to look at it.

MASTER ORLANDO *speaks to St. Francis, and they go to Mount Vernia:*

          70
Belovèd father, willingly I'll go
Along with you and show to you the way
And I, with pure intent, pray righteous God
That he'll be pleased to grant my wish and that
You'll find both town and mountain suitable
For being near you is my heart's sole wish.

ST. FRANCIS *to Master Orlando:*

Good sir, this mountain's dedicated to
And right for prayer because it's so remote.

On arriving at Mount Vernia, ST. FRANCIS *says to his companions:*

          71
Belovèd sons, I certainly believe
This place has been prepared for us by our
Redeemer, just and merciful. A mighty sign
Has been revealed to us by him. Observe
With what festivity these people all
Invite us to remain in this locale.

Addressing Master Orlando, ST. FRANCIS *says:*

I give you thanks, O noble gentleman;
This mountain, too, I gratefully accept.

SAN FRANCESCO, *volto a fra Leone,*[24] *dice così:*

72
Da voi m'intendo, figliuo', separare
in questo monte a mia consolazione.
Guardate adunque di non vi turbare.

E volto a fra Leone dice:

Intendi la mia voglia, o fra Leone,
l'uficio verrai meco a psalmeggiare,
e quando tu mi vedi in orazione
tòrnati indrieto e innanzi non venire
e nella orazion mia non m'impedire.

SAN FRANCESCO, *stando nel monte in orazione, chiede di grazia a Dio le stigmate:*[25]

73
Due grazie ti domando, o giusto Idio,
prima ch'io facci dal mondo partita:
ch'io senta dentro al core el corpo mio
quanto fussi la tua doglia infinita,
che in sulla croce con tormento rio
sostenesti per darci eterna vita;
l'altra, ch'io sento lo eccessivo amore
che sì t'accese a portar tal dolore.

Risponde Idio a San Francesco in vece di SERAFINO, *segnandolo delle stigmate:*

74
Poi che se' stato a me servo diletto
in te vo' le mie pene rinovare,
perché servito m'hai con puro effetto
però ti vo', Francesco, dimostrare
quanto tu mi sia stato sempre accetto.

ST. FRANCIS *addresses Brother Leo,*[24] *saying:*

72

I mean to isolate myself from you, my son,
Upon this mountain to restore myself.
Take care and do not be upset by this.

And [still] addressing Brother Leo, he says:

Take heed, O Brother Leone, of my wish:
Come far enough with me to sing a psalm,
And when at prayer you see me, then turn back,
And do not come into my presence there,
And do not, in my praying, hinder me.

Upon the mountain in prayer, ST. FRANCIS *asks God for the grace of the stigmata:*[25]

73

Two favors, righteous God, I ask of you
Before I leave this world: the first, let me
Feel in my body and within my heart
How great the boundless suffering was that you
Endured with cruel torment on the cross
So you could give eternal life to us;
Then too that I might feel the boundless love
That made you burn to suffer so much pain.

God, in the form of a SERAPH, *answers St. Francis, marking him with the stigmata:*

74

Since you have been my cherished servant, I
Wish to renew in you my suffering,
Because with pure affection you have served me,
Therefore I want to show you, Francis, now
How much I have appreciated you.

Io ti vo' colle mie piaghe addornare:
nessun simile a te sarà mai stato
di sì gran don nel mondo premiato.

SAN FRANCESCO, *ricevuto le stigmate,*[26] *veduto Iddio in segno di crocifisso, ringraziandolo, dice così:*

75
Io son pien di dolore e d'allegreza,
avendoti veduto, Signor mio,
in croce sopportar tanta graveza
per me, vil peccator ingrato e rio.
Tu m'ha' sì acceso della tua dolceza,
o giusto Redentor, superno Idio.
Poi che degno m'hai fatto di tal grazia,
a lodarti non fia mie voglia sazia.

Seguita SAN FRANCESCO *ringraziando Iddio:*

76
Quanto io posso, Signor, con tutto il cuore
io rendo grazie alla tua maestate,
per tanta carità per tanto amore
che m'hai dimostro per la tua pietate
di trasformarti in me, dolce Signore,
o padre eterno, o divina bontate.
Di ringraziarti sazio mai non fia,
superno Redentor, la voglia mia.

SAN FRANCESCO *dice a' sua frati come si vuole partire per andare a Santa Maria degli Angioli*[27] *e raccomanda loro il monte della Vernia:*

77
O dolci figliuo' mia, udite alquanto:
sappiate ch'io mi vo' da voi partire.
Raccomandovi questo monte santo
che l'abitiate con sommo desire,

I wish to adorn your person with my wounds.
No one has ever been before like you—
Rewarded with such a gift as you've received.

Having received the stigmata and seen God as he was on the cross,
ST. FRANCIS *thanks him saying this:*

75

I'm full of sorrow, and I'm filled with joy,
My Lord, at having seen you bear upon
The cross for me, ungrateful sinner vile
And wicked, such affliction. O dear God,
With your sweetness you have kindled me,
Redeemer righteous, O eternal one.
Since you have made me worthy of such grace,
My will won't ever tire of praising you.

ST. FRANCIS *continues thanking God:*

76

As much as I am able, Lord, with all
My heart, I render to your majesty
My thanks for such great charity, such love
As you have shown me through your mercy, God,
In changing yourself into me, sweet Lord.
O everlasting Father, good divine,
My thirst for thanking you will not be quenched
O my Eternal Savior, Jesus mine.

ST. FRANCIS *says to his brothers that he wishes to depart to go to St. Mary of the Angels*[27] *and commends to them Mount Vernia:*

77

O my sweet sons, attend to me a while.
Know this: I'm longing to depart this world.
To you this holy mount I recommend.
Here, where such ineffable joy I have

nel quale ho ricevuto gaudio tanto,
cari figliuo', ch'io non vel posso dire.
Certo si può chiamar qui per memoria
dove el Signor dimostra la sua gloria.

Seguita SAN FRANCESCO a' sua frati:

78
Intendete, figliuo', la voglia mia
e ascoltate alquanto il mio parlare:
andare al luogo di Santa Maria
voglio al presente senza più indugiare,
però vi priego che in piacer vi sia
voler alle mie voglie sadisfare.

UNO FRATE risponde per tutti:

Presto faremo ogni tua voglia sazia
che d'ubidirti sol c'è somma grazia.

E FRATI, aparechiato uno asino, ve lo pongono su per conducerlo a Santa Maria degli Angioli e menano con loro il padr\<on\>e dell'asino, cioè uno contadino.

79
Monterai, padre, in su questo asinello
ed al nome di Dio cammineremo;
prestato ce l'ha questo poverello
el qual per nostro aiuto meneremo.

SAN FRANCESCO a' sua compagni:

Dolci figliuo', grazie rendiamo a quello
immenso Idio e in pace porteremo
questo freddo crudel sol per suo amore,
che per noi el giusto sangue versò fore.

Received, O my dear sons, also may you
Desire to spend your lives in this place too.
Surely this spot should be recalled, you see,
As the place where God reveals his majesty.

ST. FRANCIS *continues to his brothers:*

78

My sons, pray listen to my words a while
And understand that I desire to go
Unto St. Mary's place. I wish to go
At once, and with no more delay. I pray
you, therefore, that it will please you to
Desire to satisfy my will in this.

ONE BROTHER *responds for all:*

Your every wish we'll quickly satisfy,
We are most thankful only to comply.

THE BROTHERS, *having prepared a donkey, set him on it to carry him to St. Mary of the Angels and they lead along with them the owner of the donkey—that is, a peasant.*

79

Climb up, O father, on this burro's back,
And in the name of God let's take our way.
This poor chap here loaned us the use of it,
And we'll take him along to give us aid.

ST. FRANCIS *to his companions:*

Sweet sons, let us to that unbounded God
Give thanks and let us bear in peace
This cruel cold for love of him alone
Who spilled his righteous blood on our account.

QUELLO CONTADINO, *pel freddo non potendo camminare, si raccomanda a San Francesco dicendo:*

        80
Oimè, ch'io sento mia vita mancare
pel crudo freddo, misero meschino.
Per niente io non posso camminare;
la morte sento, oimè, lasso, tapino.

SAN FRANCESCO, *sceso dall'asinello, toccato con le mani il contadino subito si fu riscaldato e dice così:*

Non temer, poverel, che riscaldare
ti vo' al presente dell'amor divino.

IL CONTADINO *a San Francesco:*

Tu m'hai, padre diletto, riscaldato,
sì ch'ogni affanno da me s'è cessato.

Una donna, udendo che San Francesco passava, mena uno suo figliuolo ritruopico[28] *il quale San Francesco sanò e prima* LA DONNA *dice a San Francesco:*

        81
O giusto padre, poi ch'apresso a Dio
sì grato se' per la tua santitate,
piacciati quel pregar pel figliuol mio,
che vedi in quanta strema infermitate
sua vita tiene, in gran tormento rio.
Io te ne priego per la tua pietate.

SAN FRANCESCO *a quella donna:*

Io son contento il mio Signor pregare
che gli piaccia il tuo figlio liberare.

THAT PEASANT, *unable to walk because of the cold, entrusts himself to St. Francis, saying:*

80

Alas, I feel my life is weakening
For this harsh cold, poor wretch unfortunate.
I cannot travel on for anything;
Alas, ah me, I feel the pangs of death.

ST. FRANCIS, *having dismounted from the donkey and having touched the peasant with his hands, and immediately warmed him, says this:*

Poor fellow, do not be afraid because,
Just now I wish to warm you with God's love.

THE PEASANT *to St. Francis:*

Beloved father, you have warmed me up
So that my every pain has gone away.

A woman, hearing that St. Francis was passing, brings her son who suffered from dropsy, whom St. Francis heals, and first THE WOMAN *says to St. Francis:*

81

O righteous father, since you're near to God,
Be pleased to offer for your saintliness
Upon my son's behalf a prayer, for you
Can see with what extreme infirmity he leads
His life in wicked pain and torment harsh.
For your compassion, this I ask of you.

ST. FRANCIS *to that woman:*

I'll happily implore the Lord that he
Will be content to liberate your son.

SAN FRANCESCO *fa orazione a Dio:*

82

Immenso Padre, odi il mio priego indegno
e non guardare al mio grave peccato;
per tua somma pietà[30] dimostra segno
che questo poverel sia liberato.
Fammi, Signor, di tanta grazia degno
che mai nessuna cosa m'hai negato.
Giunga sopra a costui la tua potenza
per l'infinita tua somma clemenza.

LA DONNA *ringrazia San Francesco del suo figliuolo sanato da lui:*

83

Che dono è questo, padre giusto e santo,
che in un punto hai sanato il figliuol mio!
Io sento nel mio cor dolceza tanto,
ringraziato sia tu, Signore Idio!
El dolor m'è tornato in festa e in canto.
Diletto padre, quanto più poss'io,
Io rendo grazie a tua bontà infinita,
e tua serva sarò sempre in mia vita.

SAN FRANCESCO *giunto a Santa Maria degli Angioli dice a' sua frati annunziando loro la sua morte:*

84

La pace dello immenso eterno Idio
con voi, diletti figliuo', sempre sia.
Per certo or è contento il mio desio,
ringraziata sia tu, madre Maria.
Figliuo' diletti, udite il parlar mio:
presto debbe finir la vita mia.

ST. FRANCIS *prays to God:*

82

Immeasurable Father, hear my prayer
Unworthy, and upon my heavy sins
Don't look; through your surpassing mercy show
A sign so this poor man may be set free.
Pray make me, Lord, deserving of such grace,
For you have never anything denied
To me; then let your power descend on him
Through your surpassing mercy infinite.

THE WOMAN *thanks St. Francis for having healed her son:*

83

O just and holy father, what a gift
This is, for in a trice you've cured my son!
What great sweetness I feel within my heart!
My sorrow has been changed to feast and song.
O thou, Lord God, receive my thanks. As much,
Belovèd father, as I can, for your
Unbounded goodness I give thanks, and I
Shall be your servant all throughout my life.

Having arrived at St. Mary of the Angels, ST. FRANCIS *speaks to his brothers, announcing to them that he must die:*

84

The peace of God, eternal, measureless,
Be always with you, my belovèd sons.
For surely my desire is now fulfilled;
Thou, mother Mary, pray accept my thanks.
Ah, listen to my words, belovèd sons,
For in a short time, now, my life must end.

UNO FRATE *risponde:*

Oimè, che ci di' tu, padre diletto?
Come farem qui sanza il tuo cospetto?

Viene UNA DONNA ROMANA[30] *per divina ispirazione a San Francesco per ritrovarsi alla sua morte. Portato con seco molte cose per sepellire quello, e dice così, giunta a San Francesco:*

85
Padre diletto, il sommo Redentore
doni conforto alla tua infermitate.
Sappi ch'io son sì piena di dolore,
poi ch'io sentì' che la tua santitate
era presso al morire. El ver Signore
mel rivelò per sua somma pietate;
essendo a queste notte in orazione,
lo intesi per divina inspirazione.

Seguita QUELLA DONNA:

86
Io son venuta nella tua presenza
perché tu pigli, padre, rifriggero,
e ho portato alla tua riverenza
ciò che bisogna e quel che fa mestiero.

SAN FRANCESCO *a Madonna Iacopa:*

Madonna, la divina Sapienza
ti presti grazia, perché buon pensiero
facesti di venirmi a visitare,
e tal conforto a me poverel dare.

A BROTHER *answers:*

Alas! What are you saying, father dear?
What shall we do without your presence here?

By divine inspiration, A ROMAN WOMAN[30] *comes to find St. Francis at his death and has brought with her many substances for burying him, and, coming before St. Francis, she says to him:*

85

May our lofty Redeemer comfort you,
Belovèd father, in your frailty.
Please understand that I have been so filled
With grief because I sensed your holiness
Was nearing death—our rightful Lord
By holy inspiration from afar
Through his compassion has revealed this fact
To me while I was praying through these nights.

THAT WOMAN *continues:*

86

Into your presence I have come so that
You may take solace, father, and I have
Brought to your reverence some needful things
And those with which the rites may be performed.

ST. FRANCIS *to Lady Jacopa:*

My lady, may the Sapience Divine
Award you grace because of the kind thought
You had in paying me this visit and
In comforting a wretched man like me.

QUESTA DONNA, *abracciando i pie' di San Francesco, guardando quelle stigmate sante dice:*

87

O santi pie', dove l'antiche pene
son rinovate! O padre giusto e degno,
oimè, ch'io perdo in un punto ogni bene.
Diletto padre, del mio cor sostegno,
per me priega per tue virtù serene,
poi che sì grato se' nel sommo regno,
che gli piacci voler acconsentire
ch'io possi teco mia vita finire.

E FRATI *confortano questa donna dicendo così, e levonla da pie' di San Francesco:*

88

Madonna, non voler far tal lamento;
conforto piglierai per nostro amore.
Per certo noi restiamo in gran tormento,
ma, poi che piace al sommo Redentore,
bisogna al suo volere esser contento.
Però caccia da te ogni dolore;
spera, madonna, ancor con maggior zelo
vedere el nostro buon Francesco in cielo.

SAN FRANCESCO, *vicino alla morte, amaestrando e sua frati dice:*

89

Io son, dolci figliuo', forte aggravato;
all'ultim'ora mi sento appressare;
però il governo a voi sia commendato,
il qual vi piaccia in modo ministrare
ch'al sommo Redentor sia accetto e grato.
Vogliate sopra ogn'altra cosa amare,
figliuo' diletti, la povertà santa
che nel divin cospetto è grata tanta.

Embracing St. Francis's feet and seeing there the holy stigmata, THIS WOMAN *says:*

87

O holy feet, whereon the ancient wounds
Appear again! O father worthy and just,
Alas, that in an instant I must lose
Each good. Belovèd father, pillar of
My heart, with your calm power pray for me,
Since you're so welcome in supernal realms;
Please pray for me so that he will be pleased
To grant that I may end my life with you.

THE BROTHERS *console this woman and they raise her from St. Francis's feet, speaking thus:*

88

My lady you must not lament like this;
You must take consolation in our love.
Great torment we are suffering too, but since
Our loftiest Redeemer wishes this,
We must be satisfied that it's his will.
Cast out, therefore, each sorrow from yourself;
With fervent zeal, my lady, hope to see
In heaven our good Francis once again.

ST. FRANCIS, *nearing death and teaching his brothers, says:*

89

How deeply do I feel aggrieved, sweet sons,
That I feel my last hour pressing near;
I therefore leave the Order in your care,
Which it will please you to administer
The way our high Redeemer will find right
And pleasing; and above all else hold dear,
Belovèd sons, that sacred poverty
That is so welcome in the sight of God.

SAN FRANCESCO, *volto a Dio, dice raccomandando la sua famiglia:*

       90
A te, padre diletto, immenso Idio,
la mia famiglia sia raccomandata;
più cura aver di lei già non poss'io
per la mia infermità che a te celata
non è. Però ti priego, Signor mio,
che la sia sempre al tuo cospetto grata.
A te la lascio e sotto il tuo governo,
perché la guidi nel tuo regno eterno.

E FRATI, *dolendosi della morte di San Francesco, dicono così:*

       91
Come faranno e tua miseri figli,
o santo padre, in questa tua partenza?
Chi ci darà più aiuto o buon consigli?
Priega per noi la divina Clemenza
che insieme e tuo figliuo' diletti pigli
e guidi su nella Divina Essenza.

E volti a San Francesco inginochioni dicono così:

La tua benedizion ci lascerai;
di noi in ciel, padre, ti ricorderai.

SAN FRANCESCO, *benedicendogli, dice loro così, confortandoli e amaestrandogli:*

       92
Non vi turbate, figliuo' mie diletti,
che ciascun nasce per far cotal fine,
miseri tutti alla morte suggetti
e l'ultim ore abbiam sempre vicine;
però servite a Dio con puri effetti,
in penitenze e in sante discipline;

Addressing God, ST. FRANCIS entrusts his family to his safe keeping:

90

To you, belovèd Father, God so great,
My family I entrust; already I
Can care for them no more because of my
Infirmity—that's not concealed from you.
Therefore, my Lord, I pray that they will be
Forever welcome in your sight. To you
I now entrust them, governed by your rule,
So you will guide them to your timeless realm.

Grieving at St. Francis's coming death, THE BROTHERS *say this:*

91

O holy father, how shall we behave,
Your wretched sons, in this your passing on?
Who'll give us, any more, good counsel? help?
Now pray for us to Clemency divine
That he will gather all your cherished sons
And to the Heavenly Being lead us up.

And, addressing St. Francis on their knees, they say:

Your benediction, father, leave with us;
Remember us in heaven, too, we pray.

Blessing, comforting, and teaching them, ST. FRANCIS *tells them this:*

92

Do not distress yourselves, my cherished sons,
For each of us is born for such an end,
All wretches we and subject all to death,
And our last hour hovers always near;
Therefore with pure affection serve our God
In penance—mortify your flesh for God,

restate colla mia benedizione
e frequentate la santa orazione.

SAN FRANCESCO *dice a' frati che lo spoglino e che lo ponghino in terra:*

            93
Figliuo' diletti, in terra mi ponete,
però ch'io intendo in tal modo morire,
e questi panni presto mi traete,
perch'io vo' nudo mia vita finire.
El nostro immenso Idio, come sapete,
volse per noi tanti affanni sentire
in croce, afflitto in su quel duro legno,
per farci parte nel celeste regno.

SAN FRANCESCO, *spogliato in terra, fa orazione a Dio:*

            94
Di terra, Signor mio, tu mi formasti,
terra saran queste misere spoglie;
povero e nudo al mondo mi creasti,
nudo mi parto dalle mortal soglie.
L'anima sia di te che la mandasti,
che lieta sol dal senso si discioglie.
Signor, con umil voce, *clamavi ad te*,[31]
che per me ingrato servo fusti in croce.

IL GUARDIANO *dice a San Francesco, faccendolo rivestire:*

            95
Per santa ubidienza piglierai
questi tua panni nella mia presenza;
da' tuo figliuo' rivestito sarai,
e qua' ti porton tanta riverenza.
E però, padre, non ci turberai

And with my benediction carry on,
And dutifully attend your sacred prayers.

ST. FRANCIS *tells the brothers to undress him and place him in the earth:*

93

Belovèd sons, because I mean to die
A certain way, please lay me in the earth,
And quickly strip away from me these clothes,
For naked I would come to my life's end.
Our boundless God, as you are well aware,
For us desired to bear great suffering,
Inflicted on that hard and crooked wood
To make us part of his celestial realm.

Stripped and on the ground, ST. FRANCIS *prays to God:*

94

From earth, my Lord, you fashioned me, and now
These wretched leavings earth will be again;
You brought me poor and naked to this earth,
And naked from this mortal verge I go.
Let my soul be yours, who sent it forth to me,
Its only joy to be unchained from sense:
"I called to you, Lord,"[31] with humble voice; for me
A thankless servant, you were crucified.

Having St. Francis reclothed, THE SACRISTAN *says to him:*

95

It is your sacred duty to put on
These clothes of yours before me here, let these
Your sons clothe you again, who have for you
So great a reverence, and thus we shan't
Be troubled by your modest, holy rites

in questa santa tua degna partenza.

Risponde SAN FRANCESCO al guardiano e dice [a tutti]:

Figliuo' diletti, io vi voglio ubidire:
rimettetemi in dosso il mio vestire.

Viene L'ANGIOLO e dà licenza:

96
Deh, volgi gli occhi della mente pura,
anima che nel mondo se' smarrita,
e metti a contemplare ogni tua cura
del buon Francesco la sua santa vita,
che con le piaghe a Dio si raffigura,
tanto gli piacque sua bontà infinita,
lasciando qui di lui degna memoria.
Oggi l'ha assunto alla superna gloria.

FINIS

As you take your leave of us in dignity.

ST. FRANCIS *responds to the sacristan and says [to all]:*

Belovèd sons, I want to do your will:
So put my clothes once more upon my back.

The ANGEL *comes and dismisses the audience:*

96

Ah turn the eyes of your pure mind, O soul
That in the world is led astray, and with
Your diligent attention contemplate
The holy life of good St. Francis who,
While leaving here his worthy memory,
Bore wounds resembling God's because he had
With boundless goodness earned his maker's praise.
Today to highest glory, he was raised.

THE END

Figure 1: The Tanini house today, in Piazza San Firenze (formerly Via de' Leoni), Florence, Italy. Photograph by Elissa Weaver.

Figure 2: The floor tomb of Francesco di Antonio di Giannotto de' Tanini, in Santa Croce, Florence: "Sep. Francisco Antonii Iannocti de Taninis mercatori ex vrbe in patriam redvcto Ivlivs patri benemerenti fecit. Obiit anno salvtis 1467 die 23 avgvsti." Florence, Archivio di Stato, Ceramelli Papiani, 4556. By permission of the Ministero per i Beni e le Attività Culturali della Repubblica Italiana.

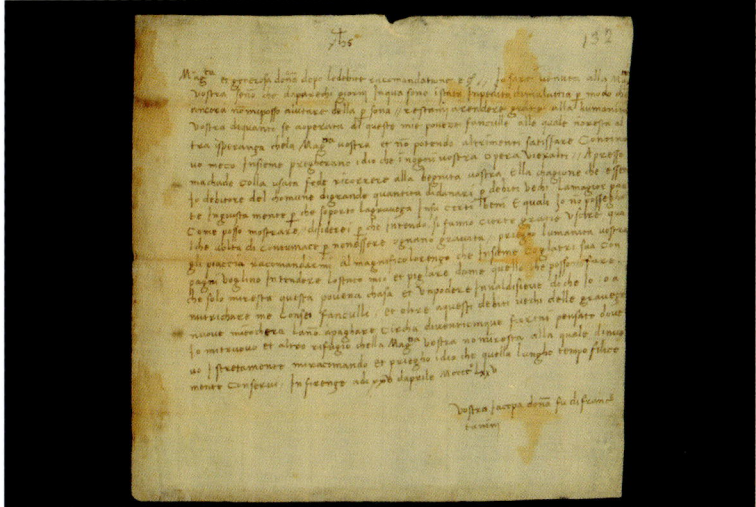

Figure 3a: Letter from Jacopa Tanini, widow of Francesco Tanini to Clarice Orsini, wife of Lorenzo de' Medici, 25 April 1475. Florence, Archivio di Stato, MAP, LXXX, fol. 132r. By permission of the Ministero per i Beni e le Attività Culturali della Repubblica Italiana.

Figure 3b: Address. Letter from Jacopa Tanini, widow of Francesco Tanini to Clarice Orsini, wife of Lorenzo de' Medici, 25 April 1475. Florence, Archivio di Stato, MAP, LXXX, fol. 132v. By permission of the Ministero per i Beni e le Attività Culturali della Repubblica Italiana.

INCOMINCIA La rapresentatione di san
cta Domitilla uergine facta & compo
sta in uersi per mona Antonia
dōna di Bernardo pulci lāno
MCCCCLXXXIII.

o   Buon iesu per la tua gran potenza
cōcedi gratia almio basso intellecto
si chio possa mostrar per tuo clemenza
lasua storia diuota elgran concepto
di domitilla pien di sapienza
che uolse uerso idio con puro affecto
christiana essendo uergine sposata
secretamente adio fu consacrata
Nipote fu questa uergine decta
del gran domitiano imperadore
fuggi losposo essendo giouanetta
& uolse lalma alsuo degno factore
& per trouar lauia uera & perfecta
daporere habitar col suo signore
cercando lacorona del martyre
alfin nel fuoco poi uolse morire
    Loimperador parla auno suo barone
chiamato Aureliano: & dice come gli
ha dato per donna Domitilla.
Aurelian perchio tho sempre amato
quanto conuiensi un buon figliuol dilecto

a i

Figure 4: *Rappresentazione di Santa Domitilla*, 1483, first edition [Florence: Antonio Miscomini, 1490s]. Florence, Biblioteca Nazionale Centrale, Banco Rari, 187a, a$_1$r. By permission of the Ministero per i Beni e le Attività Culturali della Repubblica Italiana.

COMINCIA LA RAPRESENTATIONE
DI SANCTA GVGLIELMA COMPO
STA PER MONA ANTONIA DON
NA DI BERNARDO PVLCI. ET
PRIMA VIENE LANGELO AN
NVNTIARE LAFESTA ET
DICE.

 o Giusto eterno o sommo redemptore
che per noi peccator quagiu uenisti
essendo tu del ciel padre & signore
diqueste humane spoglie riuestisti
& per tua gregge come buon pastore
in croce morte & passion sentisti
fa chio possa mostrar sol per tua gloria
di guglielma beata lasua storia
Essendo nuouamente baprezato
alla fe di iesu ilre dungheria
di torre sposa fu diliberato
& fe cerchar per ogni signoria
col gran re dinghilterra imparentato
sifu duna sua figlia electa & pia
che fu guglielma nominata quella
ornata di costumi honesta & bella
Questa guglielma molti lunghi affanni
sostenne:& fu nel mondo peregrina
& condamnata fu con falsi inganni

g i

Figure 5: *Rappresentazione di Santa Guglielma*, first edition [Florence: Antonio Miscomini, 1490s]. Florence, Biblioteca Nazionale Centrale, Banco Rari, 187g, g$_1$r. By permission of the Ministero per i Beni e le Attività Culturali della Repubblica Italiana.

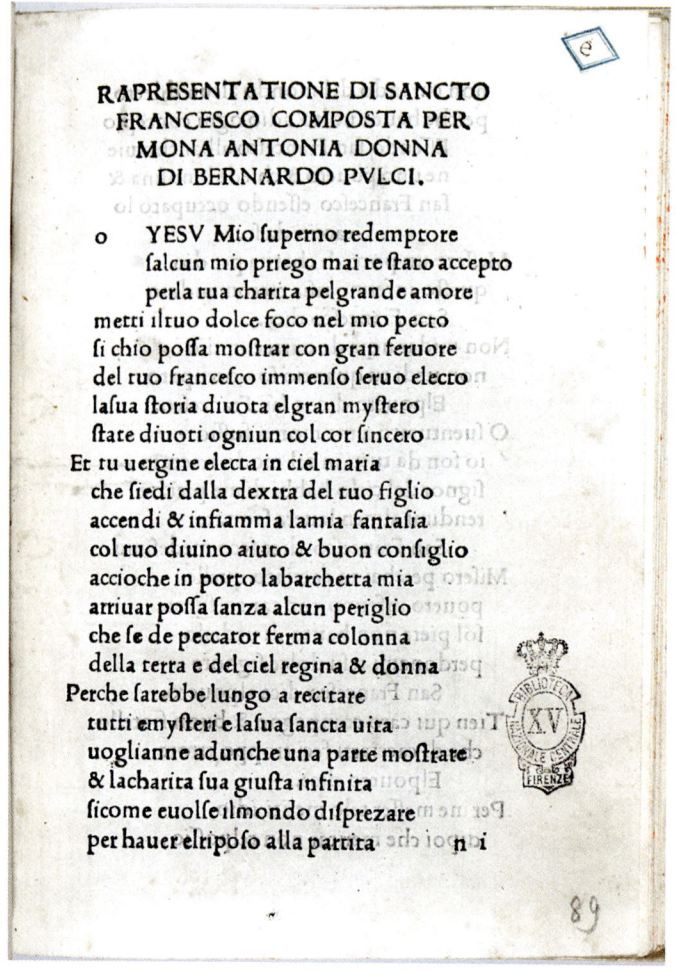

Figure 6: *Rappresentazione di San Francesco*, first edition [Florence: Antonio Miscomini, 1490s]. Florence, Biblioteca Nazionale Centrale, Banco Rari, 187e, n$_1$r. By permission of the Ministero per i Beni e le Attività Culturali della Repubblica Italiana.

Figure 7: *Rappresentazione di Santa Domitilla*, second edition [Florence: Antonio Miscomini, 1490–95]. Florence, Biblioteca Nazionale Centrale, Banco Rari, 189i, a₁r. By permission of the Ministero per i Beni e le Attività Culturali della Repubblica Italiana.

Figure 8a: *Rappresentazione di Santa Guglielma*, second edition, frontispiece [Florence: Bartolomeo de' Libri, 1490–95]. Florence, Biblioteca Nazionale Centrale, Banco Rari, 189q, a$_1$r. By permission of the Ministero per i Beni e le Attività Culturali della Repubblica Italiana.

¶ Comincia la rapresentatione di sancta
Guglielma cōposta p Mona Antonia
dōna di Bernardo Pulci. Et prima uie-
ne langelo annuntiare la festa & dice.

O Giusto eterno o sõmo redemptore
che p noi peccator quagiu uenisti
essendo tu del ciel padre & signore
di queste humane spoglie ti uestisti
& p tua gregge come buon pastore
in croce morte & passion sentisti
fa chio possa mostrar sol p tua gloria
di Guglielma beata la sua historia
Essendo nouamente baptezato
alla fe di Iesu il Re dungheria
di torre sposa fu diliberato
& fe cerchar per ogni signoria
col gran Re dinghilterra imparētato
si fu duna sua figlia electa & pia
che fu Guglielma nominata quella
ornata di costumi honesta & bella
Questa Guglielma molti lunghi affanni
sostenne:& fu nel mondo peregrina
& condānata fu con falsi inganni
nel fuoco:& quella maesta diuina
libero questa dogni insidie & inganni
p che soccorre chiunche allei si china
benche fussi nel mondo tormentata
si cõme Iob alfin fu ristorata
 Il Re dugheria uolto al fratello & a
baroni dice.
Attendi ben dilecto fratel mio
& uoi baron la mia uoglia ascoltate
di torre sposa e fermo il mio disio
& pero linghilterra ricerchate
duna che ci dimostra il nostro idio
adorna di costumi & dhonestate
Guglielma decta:del gran Re figluola

Risponde il fratello del Re.
Vbidita sara la tua parola
Il fratello del Re & i baroni giūti al re di
ghilterra dicono:& prima il fratello
La fama sereniss̃imo signore (del Re.
che della figlia tua nel mondo suona
cinduce a supplicare il tuo ualore
mandati dungheria dalla corona
che degni acompagnar con puro core
tua cara figlia colla sua persona
qual dono accepto se l consentirai
ancor lieto & felice ne sarai
Il Re dinghilterra rispōde cosi dicēdo.
I rendo somme gratie al uostro sire
che degna la mia figlia dimandare
& di piacere a quello ho gran desire
ma uo con la Reina consultare
fate Guglielma & le danoi uenire
per poter questo caso examinare
Et uolto aglimbasciadori dice.
Assai dilecta a noi uostra proposta
& presto renderem grata proposta
 Venuta la Reina & Guglielma in corte il Re dice prima alla Reina
Dilectissima mia chara consorte
a noi son dungheria messaggi degni
mandati dal signor in nostra corte
& priega ogniun di noi che nō si sdegni
di dar Guglielma allui con lieta sorte
hauendo gia cerchati molti regni
damor sospinto dabuon zelo & fama
Guglielma nostra sol ricercha & brama
Il Re uolto a Guglielma dice.
Et tu dilecta mia chara figluola
se cosi piace a quel che tutto regge
che datanto signor electa sola
nucuamente uenuto a nostra legge
non sa spect a altro che la tua parola

Figure 8b: *Rappresentazione di Santa Guglielma*, second edition, first page [Florence: Bartolomeo de' Libri, 1490–95]. Florence, Biblioteca Nazionale Centrale, Banco Rari, 189q, a$_1$v. By permission of the Ministero per i Beni e le Attività Culturali della Repubblica Italiana.

Figure 9a: *Rappresentazione di San Francesco*, second edition, frontispiece [Florence: Bartolomeo de' Libri, 1490–95]. Florence, Biblioteca Nazionale Centrale, Banco Rari, 189m, a_1r. By permission of the Ministero per i Beni e le Attività Culturali della Repubblica Italiana.

chella fie sempre alsuo subgetto grata
a te lalascio & sotto el tuo gouerno
perche laguidi nel tuo regno etterno
    E frati dolendosi della morte disan
francesco dicono cosi.
Come faranno e tuo miseri figli
o sancto padre inquesta tuo partenza
chi cidara piu aiuto o buon consigli
priega per noi ladiuina clemenza
che insieme e tuo figluo dilecti pigli
& guidi su nella diuina essenza
    Et uolti a san Francesco in gino-
chioni dicono cosi
la tuo benediction cilascerai
di noi in ciel padre tiricorderai
    San Francesco benedicendogli di-
ce loro cosi confortandogli & ama
estrandogli
Non ui turbate figluo mie dilecti
che ciascun nasce per far cotal fine
miseri tutti alla morte subgetti
& lultime hore habbian sempre uicine
pero seruite adio con puri effecti
in penitentie & in sancte discipline
restate colla mie benedictione
& frequentate lasancta oratione
    San francesco dice a frati che lospo
glino & che loponghino in terra
Figluo dilecti interra miponete
pero chintendo intal modo morire
& questi panni presto mitrahete
perchio uo nudo mie uita finire
elnostro immenso dio come sapete
uolse per noi tanti affanni sentire
incroce afflicto insu quel duro legno

per farci parte nel celeste regno
    San francesco spogliato interra
fa oratione a dio
Di terra signor mio tu miformasti
terra saran queste misere spogle
pouero & nudo almondo micreasti
nudo miparto dalle mortal sogle
lanima sia di te che la mandasti
che lieta sol dal senso sidiscioglie
clamaui atte signor con humil uoce
che per me ingrato seruo fusti in croce
    El guardiano dice a san francesco
faccendolo riueftire
Per sancta ubidientia piglerai
questi tuo panni nella mie presenza
da tuo figluo riuestito sarai
e quai tiporton tanta riuerenza
& pero padre nonci turberai
inquesta sancta tuo degna partenza
    Risponde san francesco al guardia
no & dice
figluo dilecti i uruoglo ubidire
rimettetemi in dosso ilmio uestire
    Viene langelo & da licentia
Deh uolgi gliochi della mente pura
anima che nel mondo se smarrita
& metti a contemplar ogni tuo cura
del buon francesco la suo sancta uita
che colle piaghe adio siraffigura
tanto glipiaque suo bonta infinita
lasciando qui dilui degna memoria
hoggi lha assumpto alla supna gloria
    Finita la festa di sancto francesco
composta per mona Antonia don
na di Bernardo pulci.

Figure 9b: *Rappresentazione di San Francesco*, second edition, final page [Florence: Bartolomeo de' Libri, 1490–95]. Florence, Biblioteca Nazionale Centrale, Banco Rari, 189m, a₈r By permission of the Ministero per i Beni e le Attività Culturali della Repubblica Italiana.

Figure 10a: *Rappresentazione della distruzione di Saul e il pianto di Davit*, frontispiece [Florence: Bartolomeo de' Libri, 1490–95]. Florence, Biblioteca Riccardiana, ed. R 686/17, a$_1$r. By permission of the Ministero per i Beni e le Attività Culturali.

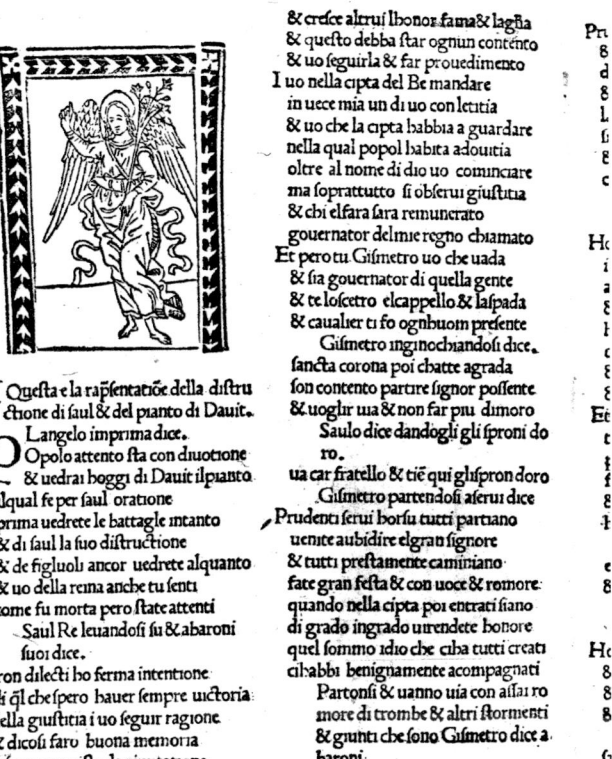

¶ Questa e la rapresentatiōe della distru‑
ctione di saul & del pianto di Dauit.
Langelo imprima dice.
Popolo attento sta con diuotione
& uedrai hoggi di Dauit ilpianto
ilqual fe per saul oratione
prima uedrete le battagle intanto
& di saul la suo distructione
& de figluoli ancor uedrete alquanto
& uo della reina anche tu senti
come fu morta pero state attenti
  Saul Re leuandosi su & abaroni
  suoi dice.
Baron dilecti ho ferma intentione
di ql che spero hauer sempre uictoria
della giustitia i uo seguir ragione
& dicosi faro buona memoria
en somma questa da riputatione.

& cresce altrui lhonor fama & laglia
& questo debba star ognun contento
& uo seguirla & far prouedimento
I uo nella cipta del Re mandare
in uece mia un di uo con letitia
& uo che la cipta habbia a guardare
nella qual popol habita adouitia
oltre al nome di dio uo cominciare
ma soprattutto si osserui giustitia
& chi elfara sara remunerato
gouernator delmie regno chiamato
Et pero tu Gismetro uo che uada
& sia gouernator di quella gente
& te loscetro elcappello & laspada
& caualier ti fo ognihuom presente
  Gismetro inginochiandosi dice.
sancta corona poi chatte agrada
son contento partire signor possente
& uoglir uia & non far piu dimoro
  Saulo dice dandogli gli sproni do
  ro.
ua car fratello & tié qui glisproni doro
  Gismetro partendosi aserui dice
Prudenti serui borsu tutti partiano
uenite aubidire elgran signore
& tutti prestamente caminiano
fate gran festa & con uoce & romore
quando nella cipta poi entrati siano
di grado ingrado uirendete honore
quel sommo idio che ciba tutti creati
cihabbi benignamente acompagnati
  Partonsi & uanno uia con assai ro
  more di trombe & altri stormenti
  & giunti che sono Gismetro dice a
  baroni.

Figure 10b: *Rappresentazione della distruzione di Saul e il pianto di Davit*, first page [Florence: Bartolomeo de' Libri, 1490–95]. Florence, Biblioteca Riccardiana, ed. R 686/17, a₁v. By permission of the Ministero per i Beni e le Attività Culturali.

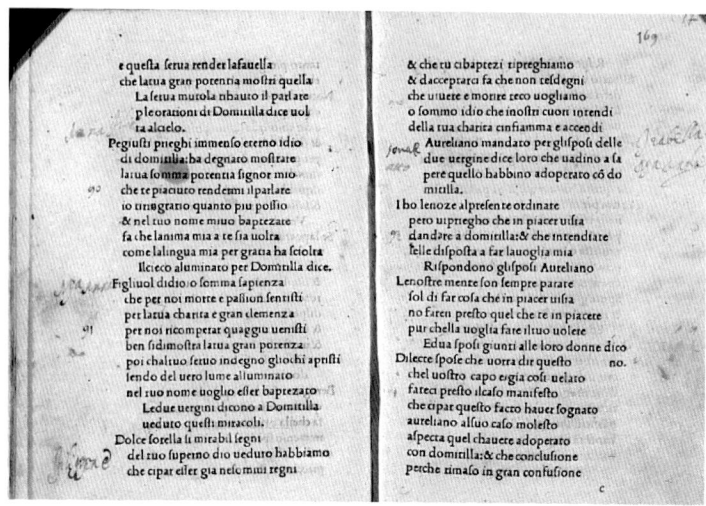

Figure 11a: *Rappresentazione di Santa Domitilla*, first edition [Florence: Antonio Miscomini, 1490s]. Two pages with names of convent actresses in the margins. Florence, Biblioteca Nazionale Centrale, P.6.37, fols. b_4v-c_1r. By permission of the Ministero per i Beni e le Attività Culturali della Repubblica Italiana, Biblioteca Nazionale Centrale di Firenze.

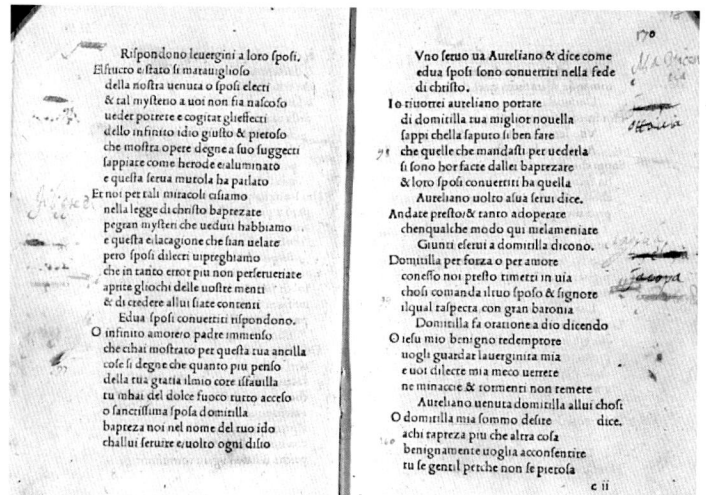

Figure 11b: *Rappresentazione di Santa Domitilla*, first edition [Florence: Antonio Miscomini, 1490s]. The two following pages with names of convent actresses in the margins. Florence, Biblioteca Nazionale Centrale, P.6.37, fols. c_1v-c_2r. By permission of the Ministero per i Beni e le Attività Culturali della Repubblica Italiana, Biblioteca Nazionale Centrale di Firenze.

Figure 12. Woodcut from the Lyons 1493 edition of the plays of Terence. Newberry Library, Vault Inc. 8602, p. 39. Courtesy of the Newberry Library, Chicago, IL.

La Rappresentatione del figliuol prodigo

INTERLOCUTORI

ANGELO
FIGLIUOL PRODIGO
RANDELLINO, amico del Figliuol Prodigo
RICCIO DEL BERRETTA, compagno di Randellino
PADRE, detto anche il MESSERE
CASSIERE del Padre
FRATELLO del Figliuol Prodigo, detto anche FRATELLO MAGGIORE e
[FIGLIUOL MAGGIORE
SUPERBIA, il Capitano dei vizi, detto anche il PRINCIPALE
AVARIZIA
INVIDIA
IRA
ACCIDIA
GOLA
LUSSURIA
MALERBA, SERVO, spenditore del Padre
UNO DEGLI INVITATI*

*Sono presenti più invitati, ma uno solo parla.

The Play of the Prodigal Son

CAST OF CHARACTERS

ANGEL
PRODIGAL SON
RANDELLINO, friend of the Prodigal Son
RICCIO DEL BERRETTA, companion of Randellino
FATHER, also called the MASTER
ACCOUNTANT
BROTHER of the Prodigal Son, also called the ELDER BROTHER and [the ELDER SON
PRIDE, the Captain of the vices, also called the LEADER
AVARICE
ENVY
WRATH
SLOTH
GLUTTONY
LUST
MALERBA, SERVANT, the Father's bursar
ONE OF THE GUESTS*

*Other guests are present but do not speak.

L'ANGELO *annunzia:,*

1
O giusto Redentor pien di clemenza,
che per noi in croce il tuo sangue versasti,
o infinita e Somma Sapienza,
più che te stesso immenso, Dio chiamasti,[1]
per la divina tua somma potenza
al ciel per tua pietà ci revocasti,
accendi il nostro cuor di sommo zelo,
che recitar possiamo il tuo Vangelo.[2]

EL FIGLIUOL PRODIGO *truova uno chiamato Randellino e dice:*

2
O Randellin, facciamo una bassetta.[3]

Risponde RANDELLINO:

Deh sì, ch'io me ne sento consumare.

RANDELLINO *dice a uno altro suo compagno:*

Hai tu le carte, Riccio del Berretta?

RICCIO *risponde a Randellino:*

Io l'ho ch'i' non saprei senza esse andare.
Chi vince vo' che paghi una mezzetta.[4]

Risponde RANDELLINO:

Cotesto in ogni modo si vuol fare.
Deh, avanziàn tempo. Orsù, che no' giochiàno.
Io alzerò poi ch' i' ho le carte in mano.

The ANGEL *heralds the play:*

            1
O just Redeemer, full of clemency,
Who spilled for us thy blood upon the cross,
O Thou surpassing Wisdom, infinite,
Exceeding thyself, thou didst call out to God
By thy divine authority, to heav'n,
Summoned us with thy pity's suffering,
Kindle our hearts so we with utmost zeal
Can here thy Gospel's sacred word reveal.[2]

The PRODIGAL SON *finds a person named Randellino, and says:*

            2
O Randellino, let's play a game of cards.

RANDELLINO *answers:*

Yes, because that's all I think about.

RANDELLINO *says to another of his companions:*

Have you the cards there, Riccio del Beretta?

RICCIO *answers Randellino:*

I have them, or I couldn't get along.
Whoever wins must buy me half a jug.

RANDELLINO *answers:*

Let that be as you wish at any rate,
Let's get a move on. Come on, now, let's play.
I'll cut because I have the cards in hand.

EL FIGLIUOL PRODIGO *a Randellino*:

                3
Io voglio essere il primo a cominciare:
Asso di tutti questi, o buon compagno.

RANDELLINO *risponde*:

Facciamo adagio. Deh, non ischerzare.
Tu se' nelle tue poste troppo magno.
Non vedi tu ch'io non ho da pagare?
Per mia fé, ch'i' non vo' far tal guadagno!

EL FIGLIUOL PRODIGO *a Randellino*:

A mezi,[5] Randellin? Non dir di no.

RANDELLINO *risponde*:

Tuo danno se tu perdi. Io alzerò.

RANDELLINO *dice*:

                4
Asso e secondo! Io te lo dissi bene:
e' non si vuol sì magne poste fare.

Risponde il FIGLIUOL PRODIGO:

Mio danno. Questo spesso m'interviene,
e par che 'l mio[6] non possa mai tornare.

E, stracciando el FIGLIUOL PRODIGO *le carte, dice*:

O asso maladetto, in tante pene
fusti sempre cagion di farmi stare!

The PRODIGAL SON *to Randellino:*

       3

I want to be the first to draw a card;
This bet says it's an ace, good buddy boy.

RANDELLINO *answers:*

Whoa, not so fast, this is no time for jokes.
Indeed, the stakes you wager are too high!
Don't you see that I can't pay or that I
Don't wish, I swear, to profit in that way!

The PRODIGAL SON *to Randellino:*

Half that, Randellino? Don't say no.

RANDELLINO *answers:*

The worse for you if you lose. Yes. I'll cut.

RANDELLINO *says:*

       4

An ace, a second! I advised you well,
It isn't good to set the stakes so high.

The PRODIGAL SON *answers:*

I've lost. This happens to me all the time!
It seems that I can't ever change my luck.

The PRODIGAL SON *tears up the cards, and says:*

O cursed Ace, you were and you are still
The reason that I suffer so much ill!

RANDELLINO *si volge a' compagni:*

Poi che m'è detto buono,[7] andiam a bere.
Io so ch'io vi farò tutti godere.

EL FIGLIUOL PRODIGO *dolendosi dice:*

       5
O maladette carte! O ria fortuna!
Iniquo, averso e doloroso fato!
Non credo che già mai sotto la luna
un uom simìle a me fussi trovato.
Di mille poste almen ne tirassi una!
Ben mi posso chiamare sventurato.[8]
I' non son ancor chiaro;[9] io voglio andare
la redità al mio padre a dimandare.

       6
Certo chi non s'arrischia non guadagna.
Io voglio andare a provar mia ventura
e pel mondo cercar ogni campagna[10]
e darmi ogni piacer senza misura.
So che la redità[11] mia sarà magna:
chi ha assai danar può ir senza paura.
Questo mondo è di chi se'l sa godere,
e vo' dar bando a ogni dispiacere.

EL FIGLIUOL PRODIGO *giugne al Padre e dice:*

       7
O reverendo mio padre diletto,
da te vorrei una grazia impetrare
<la> qual ti chieggo con benigno effetto.[12]
Deh, non me la voler per dio negare.
Sappi che in tutto fermo è mio concetto
sol di voler pel mondo a spasso andare;

RANDELLINO *turns to his companions:*

Since I've been lucky, let's go out and drink.
I'll pay the bill, we'll have some fun, I think.

The grieving PRODIGAL SON *says:*

      5
O cursèd cards! O fate malevolent!
Adverse, perverse, and sorrowful event!
I don't think that beneath the moon before
Was ever found with luck like mine a man
Who of a thousand bets could not win one!
Unfortunate I surely can be called[8]—
I'm not sure what to do. I'll take a chance
And ask my sire for my inheritance.

      6
It's sure if nothing's ventured, nothing's gained;
I want to go away and try my luck,
Go seeking through the world in every land
And revel in each joy without restraint.
I know that my inheritance is great,
And one with money travels without fear.
This world is made for those who can enjoy,
I want to banish all things that annoy.

The PRODIGAL SON *goes to his Father and says:*

      7
O venerable, beloved father mine,
I pray you to bestow a grace on me
With kind affection. That which I shall ask
Do not deny, but now fulfill my wish.
You know that I have quite made up my mind,
And all I want to do is see the world.

così disposta è la mia fantasia,
per tanto mi darai la parte mia.

Risponde il PADRE:

8

Oimè, che mi di' tu, caro figliuolo?
Come ti vuoi dal tuo padre partire?[13]
Tu m'hai messo nel core un grieve dolo;
fa' che tal cosa più non t'oda dire.
Senza pensar ti vuoi levare a volo?
Io non lo vo' per nulla acconsentire.
Pensa, dolce figliuol, di starti meco,
ché la mia vita vo' finir con teco.

EL FIGLIUOLO *risponde al Padre:*

9

O caro padre, il tempo perderesti;
non ti bisogna troppo affaticare.
Il ciel con man toccar prima potresti
che isvolgermi per certo, o il mar seccare;
però indarno ogni tempo perderesti.
Non mi voler per or più contrastare;
dammi quel che mi tocca, padre mio,
ché disposto son d'andarmi con dio.

El PADRE *dice al Figliuolo:*

10

O figliuol mio, tu se' troppo ostinato;
vogli pensar per dio quel che tu fai.
Tu sai che in tanti vezzi t'ho allevato,
alcun disagio non provasti mai.
Fusti sempre uso a esser governato;
or per le terre altrui stentando andrai.

My heart is set on this, my father dear;
Because of this, O, let me have my share.

His FATHER *answers:*

        8
Oh my, dear son, what are you telling me?
Why from your father do you desire to part?
You've set a grievous sorrow in my heart.
Don't let me hear you say such things again.
Without a thought you wish to rise in flight?
For nothing will I give you my consent.
Consider staying here with me, sweet son,
I long to be with you 'til my life's done.

The SON *replies to his Father:*

        9
O father dear, you'd be wasting your time,
You shouldn't overtax your strength so much;
You'd sooner touch the heavens with your hand
Or, surely, dry the sea than change my mind;
So all the time you spend, you spend in vain.
No longer think to try to change my mind,
My father, give me what belongs to me,
For I intend to bid farewell to thee.

The FATHER *says to the Son:*

       10
O my dear son, you are too obstinate;
Consider well the course on which you're set.
You know how comfortably I've brought you up,
You've never tasted any hardship, and
You're used to being well provided for;
Now through the world you'll go in great distress.

Misero, non voler far tale errore!
Deh, non ti lassar vincere al furore.

EL FIGLIUOLO *al Padre:*

       11
El tempo perdi e 'ndarno t'affatichi,
disposto son d'andare in altre parte.
Non bisogna che tanto mi replìchi,
certo non ti varrà tuo ingegno o arte;
non creder già, per dio, ch'io mi ridichi.
E questo puoi tener per mille carte:
consiglio non vuole uom deliberato.
Di darmi la mia parte ti sia grato.

EL PADRE *al Figliuolo:*

       12
Pel passato, diletto figliuol mio,
fusti sempre umìle e reverente;
deh, non volere acconsentir, per dio,
di partirti da me sì stranamente.[14]
Tu sai s'io t'amo con sommo desio,
certo per te il mio cor gran pena sente.
Dolce figliuol, non ti voler partire,
deh, vogli a tanti prieghi acconsentire.

EL FIGLIUOLO *al Padre:*

       13
Padre, io non vorrei tanto disputare:
dammi quel che mi tocca e resta in pace,
però ch'io son disposto così fare
e questo mi diletta e sol mi piace,
e m'è molesto il tanto tuo pregare.
Non mi voler tener più in contumace:

Poor wretch, don't think to err in such a way,
Ah, don't let anger lead you so astray.

The SON *responds:*

11

You're wasting time, and vainly tire yourself;
I am resolved to go to foreign climes.
You've no need to repeat yourself so much,
Or exercise your wit or art, for sure,
Or think that I shall reconsider this.
And mark these words, as statements sworn and true:
No guidance can a man decided bear.
So please oblige me, let me have my share.

The FATHER *to the Son:*

12

In former times, beloved son of mine,
Always you were humble and reverent—
Alas, by God, do not insist upon
Departing from me thus in this rude way.
You know with what great love I hold you dear;
My heart for you, it's certain, feels great pain.
Sweet son, do not desire to go away,
Ah, bend your will and yield to what I pray.

The SON *to the Father:*

13

My father, I don't want to argue more,
Give what is mine, and rest in peace because
I am resolved to take this step, for this
Alone can bring me pleasure and delight—
I'm irritated by your endless pleas.
Don't hold me longer so persistently;

deh, non far, padre, tanta resistenza,
perché disposto son pigliar licenza.

EL PADRE *al Figliuolo:*

       14
Deh, non mi dar figliuol tanto dolore!
Abbi pietà di me che t'allevai;
tu sai s'io t'ho portato grande amore,
più che tu stess' i' sempre mai t'amai.
Caro figliuol, conforto del mio core,
non mi voler lassare in tanti guai.
Deh, vinci, figliuol mio, tanta durezza,
pietà ti prenda della mia vecchiezza!

EL FIGLIUOLO *al Padre:*

       15
El parlar tuo non estimo niente;
tu doverresti, padre, avermi inteso,
però che in tutto è ferma la mia mente,
d'andare è la mia voglia e 'l core acceso.[15]
In questo ti sarò disubbidiente;
non ho bisogno d'esser più ripreso.
Deh, dammi il mio come per gli altri s'usa
e non ne voler far sì lunga scusa.

El PADRE *dice al Figliuolo:*

       16
Figliuol, veggo che indarno m'affatico,
poi che disposto se' voler partire;
certo a te stesso sei fatto nimico,
misero, che mi vuoi disubidire.
Di nuovo per mia fé te lo replìco:
so che di tale impresa t'hai a pentire.

Ah, father, do not so resist and grieve,
Because I am resolved to take my leave.

The FATHER *to the Son:*

        14
Oh, do not break my heart, my son, do not!
Have pity on the one who brought you up;
You know that I have loved you even more
Than you have loved yourself, I've loved you so.
Beloved son, the comfort of my heart,
Oh, do not think to leave me in such woe;
My son, control this hardness of your heart
Let pity for my age now play its part!

The SON *to the Father:*

        15
I do not hold your preaching worth a bean;
You must have, Father, understood me well,
Because my mind is all made up in this,
My will and kindled heart are set to leave.[15]
In this I shall be disobedient;
No longer do I need to be reproved.
Give me what's mine as others often do,
No long excuses! Give me what I'm due!

The FATHER *says to the Son:*

        16
I see, son, that my efforts are in vain,
Since you are quite resolved to take your leave;
You are, it's certain, to yourself a foe,
Who wants to disobey me—wretched boy!
Again, by my faith, I admonish you:
I know that you'll repent this enterprise,

Della tua parte io ti vo' contentare;
dieci mila fiorin ti farò dare.

El PADRE *si volta al Cassieri*[16] *e dice:*

17
Dagli, cassier, dieci mila ducati.
La partita a suo conto acconcerai;
fa' che con diligenza si contenti.
Misero, che per mio mal ti creai,
questi diletti mi son riservati
di te che in tanti vezzi t'allevai.

Risponde il CASSIERE:

Io gliel'andrò a contar con tua licenza;
prendi conforto ed abbi pazïenza.

EL FIGLIUOL PRODIGO *dice al Cassiere:*

18
Io gli vo'[17] veniziani e tutti a peso,
e conta adagio e guarda a non errare.

El CASSIERE *risponde:*

Deh, lassa far a me che ben t'ho inteso:
tu mi vorrai la mia arte insegnare.
Da te, per dio, non voglio esser ripreso;
avanziam tempo, comincia a contare.
Misero a te, tu farai poco bene,
al fin ne porterai poi doppie pene.

But here's your portion, as I think is fair,
Ten thousand florins—let them be your share.

The FATHER *turns to his Accountant, and says:*

17

Ten thousand ducats from the chest count out,
And for this you will debit his account.
Be sure to satisfy him diligently.
Unhappy boy, for my ill were you born,
These are the joys you have reserved for me
For rearing you in comfort and in ease.

The ACCOUNTANT *answers:*

I'll go now, by your leave, to count them out;
Bear with me sir; be patient if you can.

The PRODIGAL SON *says to the Accountant:*

18

I want Venetian ducats—all full weight,
And slowly count, be careful not to err.

The ACCOUNTANT *answers:*

Ah, let me work, for I have understood
You well; you want to teach my job to me.
I don't want to be reproved by you, for sure.
We're losing time, so start to draw your cash,
The worse for you, it won't give you much gain,
For it, at last, will buy you double pain.

El FIGLIUOL PRODIGO *dice al Cassiere:*

19
E' par che del tuo proprio m'abbi dato!
Che ti bisogna tanto borbottare?
Tu m'hai tanto il cervello aviluppato,
per fretta io non gli vo<glio> ricontare;
ma ben son certo che tu m' ha' ingannato,
alle parole tue non vuo'[18] guardare.
Io ti castigherei, pel giusto Dio,
se non fusse che stai col padre mio.

El CASSIERE *turbandosi dice:*

20
Miglior di te a riprovartel sono;
ho voglia di adirarmi, ti prometto.
Io son giusto, real, diritto e buono.
Io ti voglio scusar per giovanetto;
per amor del tuo padre ti perdono,
il qual sempre amato ho con puro effetto.
Ricontagli ch'io t'ho fatto il dovere,
sì ch'a torto di me ti puoi dolere.

El PADRE *al Figliuolo, riprendendolo, dice:*

21
Sempre cercando vai di far questione
e non si vuol così correre a furia.
Figliuol, tu se' ben fuor d'ogni ragione
a voler fare a torto a costui ingiuria.
Conosco la tua mala condizione,
misero a me, che m'ho recato auguria[19]
quel che tu hai fatto in questa tua partenza:
in te non regna senno né prudenza.

The PRODIGAL SON *says to the Accountant:*

       19
You act as if you give me your own goods!
Why do you need to grumble as you count?
You've left my brain befuddled, but I won't
Recount them, for I must be on my way.
I'm very certain you have cheated me,
And words of yours I do not mean to heed.
By God, I'd give you just what you deserve,
If it were not my father whom you serve.

Becoming upset, the ACCOUNTANT *says:*

       20
I'm better at criticizing, boy, than you;
I caution you, I'm starting to get mad.
I am trustworthy, just, correct, and good—
But I excuse you owing to your youth,
And I forgive you for your father's sake,
Whom I have always loved in simple faith.
I've done my duty; you recount each one!
You're very wrong to whine about it, son.

The FATHER, *scolding the Son, says:*

       21
You're always seeking to provoke a quarrel,
There's no point rushing into things like this.
You are indeed beyond all reason, son,
To injure wrongly my associate.
I know your bad condition, the worse for me;
What you have done in taking leave this way
Has struck me as a sign of things to come:
In you reigns neither prudence nor good sense.

El PADRE, *seguendo il suo parlare, dice:*

22

Ancor non hai di qui fatto partita
e veggo che question cominci ' fare.
Oimè, dolente e trista alla mia vita,
figliuol, tu vorrai pur mal capitare!
Per te la mente mia tutta è smarrita,
poi che tu vuoi per l'altrui terre andare.
Bisogneràtti esser più temperato:
là per mio amor non sarai riguardato.

El FIGLIUOLO, *partendosi dal Padre, confortandolo, dice:*

23

In pace resta, o mio padre diletto,
io so ch'i' troverrò molti compagni.
Deh, levati dal cuore ogni sospetto,
non vo' che per mio amor tanto ti lagni.
Io son ripien di gaudio, ti prometto,
perché spero ancor far molti guadagni.
Questo proverbio spesso dir si suole:
chi ha danari, al mondo ha ciò che vuole.

El FRATELLO, *vedendolo partire, gli va drieto dicendo:*

24

Vuo' tu, dolce fratel, così partire
e lassare il tuo padre tanto afflitto?
Certo cagion sarai farlo morire;
vedi che per dolor non può star ritto!
Misero, non volere acconsentire
che 'l padre tuo rimanga sì sconfitto.

The FATHER *continues speaking:*

22

You have not even parted yet from here,
And yet I see you start to pick a quarrel.
How sad and full of sorrow is my life,
My son, alas you'll come to no good end!
For you my mind's completely gone astray,
Since you desire to go to other lands.
You'd better learn more temperate to be,
There none will care for you for love of me.

The SON, *taking leave of his Father, comforts him, saying:*

23

Beloved father mine, O be at peace,
I know that many comrades I shall find.
Therefore, from every worry free your heart;
I don't want you, for love of me, to grieve.
So much, I'm filled with joy I promise you,
Because I'm hopeful still to earn a lot.
This proverb often one is wont to say:
'Who in the world has cash, will have his way.'

The BROTHER, *seeing him depart, follows him saying:*

24

Do you desire, sweet brother, thus to part,
And leave your father greatly stricken so?
It's certain you will be the death of him;
Behold how sorrow bows him down so low!
Ah wretched boy, do not give your consent
To leave your father vanquished by such woe.

El FIGLIUOLO PRODIGO *dice al Fratello:*

Ho io testé con teco a disputare?
Attendi a' fatti tua. Lasciami andare!

El FRATELLO *gli va drieto, dicendo:*

25
Oimè, diletto e caro fratel mio,
toccami almen nel tuo partir la mano;
di rivederti più non mi penso io.
Può esser che tu sia fatto sì strano?
Siati grato rispondermi per dio!
Deh, non aver questo mio priego in vano,
vinci te stesso sì come uom prudente.

El FIGLIUOL PRODIGO *gli risponde:*

Lassami andar! Non m'infuscar la mente.

El FIGLIUOL PRODIGO, *partendosi, dice da sé medesimo:*

26
Sempre potrò per mia fé trionfare,
e danar certo non mi mancheranno.
In verso piaza mi voglio aviare;
io so che assai compagni vi saranno
e vo'ne meco una schiera menare,
e poi si sia di chi si vuol l'affanno;
e vo' sempre pensar di stare in festa,
e non vo' che pensier mi dien molesta.

The PRODIGAL SON *says to his Brother:*

Must I now argue this with you also?
Mind your own business and just let me go!

The BROTHER *follows him saying:*

25

Alas, beloved and dear brother mine,
At least shake hands with me as you depart:
I don't think that I'll ever see you more.
So can it be you've grown so distant, strange?
You would be kind to answer me, by God!
Ah, do not let me vainly beg for this,
Master yourself as would a prudent man.

The PRODIGAL SON *answers him:*

Do not confuse me; let me go my way.

Departing, the PRODIGAL SON *says to himself:*

26

I can forever triumph, by my faith,
And certainly I'll have no lack of cash.
I want to head toward the piazza now;
I know that many comrades will be there,
And I shall lead a troop of them with me,
And let those who wish to do it toil.
I want my thoughts continually on a spree;
I won't allow my thoughts to trouble me.

*El Figliuol Prodigo giunto in piazza, se gli fa incontro sette compagnoni
e* IL PRINCIPALE [DEI VIZI] *dice:*

27
Noi siam sette compagnon, per mia fé,
e tutti verrem teco se vorrai[20]
e mai punto ci partirem da te;
come ti piace ci possederai
e amerénti più che chi ti fe'.[21]
A ogni tuo piacer sempre ci arai.

El FIGLIUOL PRODIGO *risponde al Principale di tutti:*

Vorrei saper la vostra condizione.

Risponde IL PRINCIPALE *di tutti:*

Quel che domandi è giusto e ben ragione.

Seguita il medesimo:

28
Io son di questi sette Capitano,
e Superbia mi fo chiamar per nome
e questo altro Avarizia e insieme andiàno.
Caro compagno, se vuo' saper come
hanno nome costor, di mano in mano
dirottel, ch'assai gente abbiàn già dome.
Invidia, Ira ed Accidia son chiamati,
Gola, Lussuria; or te gli ho dichiarati.[22]

La SUPERBIA *segue il suo parlare:*

29
Io ti voglio or contar la mia natura
e discoprirti in parte e miei defetti:
sopraffar vo' ciascuna creatura,

The Prodigal Son arrives at the square, where he meets seven boon companions, and the LEADER *of them says:*

27

We seven boon companions, by my faith,
Will all go with you if you so desire,[20]
And never move an inch away from you;
If you are pleased to have us for your own,
Then we'll love you more than him who made you.
You'll always have us at your beck and call.

The PRODIGAL SON *answers to the Leader of them all:*

The status of each one of you I'd know.

The LEADER *answers:*

Just and rational is what you ask, and so…

He continues:

28

I'm Captain of these seven fellows and
My name is Pride, this other Avarice;
We go together, comrade dear, and if
You want to know the names of all those chaps,
Each one in turn, I'll tell you; many folk,
Indeed, they've conquered: Envy, Wrath, and Sloth
They're named, and Gluttony and Lust.
Now I have made their natures obvious.[22]

PRIDE *continues speaking:*

29

I want to tell you of my nature now,
And to reveal, in part, my faults to you:
Far to surpass each creature is my wish.

l'ambizioso sol par che mi diletti,
e nessun vo' che di me tenga cura;
ciascun vo' superare in fatti e 'n detti
e vincitor voglio esser d'ogni impresa.
Tu hai testé la mia natura intesa.

L'AVARIZIA *si volta al Figliuol Prodigo e dice:*

30
Io son per nome chiamata Avarizia
e non penso se non di accumulare,
non riguardo parenti o amicizia,
pur ch'i' possa assai roba ragunare;
questo è mio bene ed ogni mia letizia,
me stesso offendo per meglio avanzare.
Non ho mai ben pensando nel futuro,
per far roba di mia vita non curo.

La INVIDIA *dice:*

31
O buon compagno, Invidia son chiamato
e del mal d'altri piglio gran diletto;
el cuor di tosco ho sempre avelenato,
solo ho piacer di fare altrui dispetto,
e questo m'è sopra ogni cosa grato.
Or t'ho scoperto il mio tristo concetto:
di veder male e peggio ho gran piacere,
bene a nessun non mi giova vedere.

La GOLA *dice:*

32
Poi che tu hai di questi altri notizia,
el nome mi ti vo' manifestare.
Io son la Gola piena di nequizia
che non penso se non di consumare;

Ambitious folk delight me most it seems,
And I want no one looking after me;
Each one in word and deed I would outdo,
And wish to win in every enterprise.
My nature now I trust you recognize.

AVARICE *turns to the Prodigal Son and says:*

30

My name is Avarice, and I can think
Of nothing but increasing what I own;
I value neither friendship nor my kin,
As long as I can gather many goods.
This is what I cherish, my every joy;
To prosper more, I'd even hurt myself;
I never have enough for future need;
In gathering goods, I disregard my life.

ENVY *says:*

31

O boon companion, Envy I am called
And I take great delight in others' ills;
With poison always bitter is my heart,
And only vexing others pleases me,
And this agrees with me beyond all else.
Now I have told you what my concept is:
Seeing what's bad, and worse, most pleases me,
In seeing someone's good, I find no glee.

GLUTTONY *says:*

32

Since here these others have informed you well,
My name I also would acquaint you with.
I'm Gluttony, filled with iniquity,
Who thinks of nothing else but to consume;

e carestia fo far della dovizia,
molte riccheze a basso fo tornare
e son di molta povertà cagione.
Or hai saputo la mia condizione.

La IRA *dice:*

33
So che t'è grato el mio nome sapere:
sappi che in me non regna pazïenza,
tristo a chi cerca farmi dispiacere!
Furioso senza alcuna sofferenza
son, per mia fé! Tu lo potrai vedere
a tua posta, ne fa' la esperïenza.
Ira è il mio nome, o buon compagno, detto;
sòmmi cacciar le mosche ti prometto.

La LUSSURIA *dice:*

34
Per non esser da questi altri ripreso,
el nome mio ti vo' far manifesto;
e certo so che, come l'arai inteso,
di amarmi non ti fia punto molesto.
A cavarmi ogni voglia ho il cor acceso,
senza riguardo infurïato e presto.
El nome mio si è detto Lussuria:
libidinoso a questo corro a furia.

La ACCIDIA *dice:*

35
Poi che noi siam congiunti in amicizia
io ti vo in parte dir mia condizione:
io son l'Accidia, piena di tristizia,
e spesse volte in me non è ragione;
el tedio mi diletta e la pigrizia.

I know how to have famine come of wealth,
How to have great riches turn to naught,
And I occasion direst poverty.
Now that is all you need to know of me.

WRATH *says:*

> 33

I'm sure that you'll be pleased to know my name,
Know then that in me patience does not reign.
Woe to whoever seeks to trouble me,
For violent and with no tolerance
Am I, by my faith! You can see it's so,
Try the experience of it as you please:
Wrath is my name, O boon companion true,
And I can pick a fight, I promise you.

LUST *says:*

> 34

So that the others won't reproach me, I
Will tell you what I'm called and who I am;
And when you've heard, I'm certain that you won't
Object at all to loving me full well.
My heart burns to fulfill my every wish—
All full of fury, unrestrained, in haste.
And by my name one calls me Lust; I rush
To this in frenzy and in lechery.

SLOTH *says:*

> 35

Since we in friendship are united now,
I want to tell you something of my state:
I am Sloth, one filled with wickedness,
And oftentimes I have no purposes,
For tedium delights me, laziness,

In una ora fo cento mutazione
e spesso non so dir quel ch'io mi voglia,
afflitto sempre sto in tormento e doglia.

El FIGLIUOL PRODIGO, *avendo inteso le condizioni di costoro, dice:*

36
Io ho inteso vostre condizioni
e parmi esser per certo aventurato
d'avervi qui trovato, o compagnoni.
Di venir meco ognun sia apparecchiato,
di goder sopra tutto si ragioni.
Guardate qui s'i' ho danari allato
e vo' che alla fatica diam divieto
e serri l'uscio poi chi vien dirieto.[23]

El Figliuol Prodigo se ne va con questi compagni e il PADRE *chiama el suo Figliuol Maggiore e dice:*

37
Figliuol, come tu vedi il tuo fratello
m'ha lassato sì afflitto e sconsolato
e non ispero mai più di vedello.
Perché dagli anni son forte gravato,
bisogna, figliuol mio, che tu sia quello
che mantenga e governi il nostro stato
e che di mia vecchiezza sia bastone;
certo ogni mia speranza in te si pone.

El FIGLIUOLO *risponde al Padre:*

38
Padre diletto, io priego el giusto Dio
che ti conforti e dìati pazienza;
con teco insieme gran dolor porto io
del mio fratello in questa sua partenza.

A hundred times an hour I change my mind,
And often what I want, I just don't know;
I'm plagued with torment always, and with woe.

The PRODIGAL SON, *having understood the circumstances of each of them, says:*

        36

Your circumstances I have understood,
And fortunate it surely seems to me,
O boon companions, to have found you here.
Each one, prepare to come along with me,
Above all, each intending to have fun.
Look here at all the cash I have with me,
I want us to prohibit all hard work.
And ill betide the last to come along.

The Prodigal Son leaves with these companions, and the FATHER *calls his Elder Son and says:*

        37

Your brother, son, as you perceive, has left
Me so afflicted and disconsolate.
I have no hope of seeing him again.
Because my years weigh heavily on me,
My son, it's necessary that you be the one
Who'll manage and maintain our property,
And you must be the staff of my old age.
My every hope is surely fixed on you.

The SON *answers his Father:*

        38

Beloved father, I pray to God the just
That he will give you patience, comfort you;
Together with you I bear this sorrow great
My brother's caused in leaving us like this.

Tu mi puo' comandar, buon padre mio;
sempre star voglio a tua obedienza,
e ad ogni tuo detto apparecchiato[24]
sarò, buon padre mio, sempre parato.

El PADRE *al Figliuolo [Maggiore]*:

39
A riveder le nostre possessione,
o dolce figliuol mio, si vuole andare.
Io son vecchio e bisogna far ragione
che niente per me si possa fare;
ancor questo dolor sarà cagione[25]
di far la vita mia molto affrettare.
Tu stessi[26] impara a fare e fatti tuoi
ché sei giovane, sei gagliardo e puoi.

Risponde il FIGLIUOLO [MAGGIORE]:

40
Ciò che tu di' fia fatto volentieri.
Lievati, padre, dal cuore ogni doglia:
vo' che tu viva senza alcun pensieri.
Ista' sopra di me di buona voglia;
provisto fia a ciò che fa mestieri.
La mente tua d'ogni pensieri spoglia,
e da te scaccia tanta passïone
per non esser di tua morte cagione.

El FIGLIUOL PRODIGO, *uscendo fuori*[27] *tutto stracciato, dice da sé:*

41
Come m'ha la fortuna traportato,
misero a me, come sono io condotto:
povero, infranto, nudo, abandonato,
come merito certo son ridotto.
Di ghiande sol non mi sono sfamato,

Good father mine, command me as you wish;
I'll always stay obedient to your will,
And, O good father mine, I'll ready be,
For all directives you may give to me.

The FATHER *says to the [Elder] Son:*

39

O my sweet son, it's my desire to go
To look on our possessions once again.
I'm old, and one must take into account
There's nothing any more that I can do;
My grievous sorrow yet will be the cause
Of hastening the passage of my life.
This business, yours now, must be run by you:
Learn it—you can, you're young and hardy too.

The SON *answers:*

40

What you command, that willingly I'll do,
From your heart, father, banish every woe,
From all cares free I hope that you will live,
Burden me then with anything you will;
I shall attend to what needs doing, so
Set free your mind from all anxiety,
And exile from you such great suffering
So it will not precipitate your death.

The PRODIGAL SON *enters entirely bedraggled, and says to himself:*

41

Ah how fortune has transformed me now!
Ah woe is me, for I brought myself to this:
Exhausted, naked, quite abandoned, poor,
I surely am brought low as I've deserved,
And were it not for acorns, I'd have starved,

senza vestir, tutto stracciato e rotto,
e famigli che tiene il padre mio
trionfano. Oimè così stessi io!

42
Avanzar mi solevon le vivande.
Quanti sergenti intorno aver solevo!
Ora sconto per dio le pompe grande.
Misero me, se al mio padre credevo,
io non sarei condotto a mangiar ghiande,
misero a me, se a suo modo facevo!
In questo punto a lui vo' ritornare
e merzé del mio fallo adimandare.

43
Dirogli, "Giusto padre, io non son degno
d'esser per certo tuo figliuol chiamato;
faròtti servo,[28] non mi avere a sdegno,
poich'io ti son disubidiente stato.
Della tua volontà passato ho il segno,
di accettarmi per servo ti sia grato.
Dammi del pan che avanza a' servi tuoi
per tor la fame a me, padre, se vuoi."

El FIGLIUOL PRODIGO *giunto al Padre dice:*

44
Abbi pietà di me, padre clemente,
merzé, merzé del mio passato errore.
Poi che stato ti son disubidiente,
accettera'mi[29] per tuo servidore?
So che parato è Dio a chi si pente
di perdonargli come buon signore.
Per suo amor, padre, mi perdonerrai?
Non per figliuol, per servo mi terrai?

Unclothed, all wrapped in rags, in broken health,
While servants flourish in my father's care,
Alas for me! If only I could share.

42

Of tasty dishes I once had excess.
How many servants once all round I had!
Now what a price I pay for such great pomp.
In faith, poor me, if father I had believed,
On acorns I would not be forced to feed,
Poor me, would I had taken his advice!
I want right now to go again to him,
And ask of him forgiveness for my sin.

43

"Just father," I shall say to him, "I am
Not worthy, surely, to be called your son;
I'll be your servant,[28] hold me not in scorn,
Since I have been so disobedient
And gone beyond the bounds of your good will;
Pray, as a servant please accept me now,
Give me some bread your servants leave to ease
My hunger, O my father, if you please."

The PRODIGAL SON *comes before his Father and says:*

44

Take pity on me, father compassionate,
Have mercy, mercy, for my former sins.
Since I was disobedient to you,
Will you employ me as your servant now?
I know that God is ready to forgive,
Like a good lord, one who repents. For love
Of him, good father, will you pardon me?
Keep me as your servant, not your son?

El PADRE *risponde al Figliuolo:*

45

El ben tornato sia, figliuol diletto!
Tu m'hai di gaudio il cor tutto infiammato.
Sappi che in doglia e in paura e sospetto
pel tuo partir, figliuol, son sempre stato.
Ringrazio il vero Dio con puro effetto,
poi che se' a salvamento ritornato;
e voglio far solenne e degna festa
e rivestirti d'una ricca vesta.

El PADRE *chiama uno suo Servo:*

46

Vien qua, Malerba,[30] caro servidore,
portami un vestimento ornato e bello
per questo mio caro figliuol minore,
quale è tornato così poverello.
Non fu mai tanto gaudio nel mio core:
con diligenza fa' di vestir quello.

Risponde il SERVO:

Messer, sia fatto ciò che comandate,
senza tardare appien non dubitate.

El PADRE *si volta al Figliuolo:*

47

O diletto figliuol, io ti perdono
l'offesa che m'hai fatta pel passato.
Certo umiliarti è stato buono:
fa' che mai più non caggia in tal peccato.
Vedi se stato pietoso ti sono,
ch'io t'ho liberamente perdonato

The FATHER *answers his Son:*

45

Ah, you are welcome back, beloved son!
You have inflamed my heart entirely with
Great joy. Know that in worry, woe and fear
I've always been, O son, since you left home.
With pure affection let God be given thanks
Since to safe harbor you've again returned;
I'll give a banquet and I'll entertain
And clothe you in rich vestments once again.

The FATHER *calls one of his Servants:*

46

Come here, Malerba,[30] my dear servant, bring
To me a festooned, handsome robe, for this
Is my belovèd younger son who has
Returned in so impoverished a state.
In my heart never has there been such joy;
With diligence, please, array him in good clothes.

The SERVANT *answers:*

Good sir, as you command, be sure your will,
Without delay I shall at once fulfill.

The FATHER *answers the Son:*

47

O my beloved son, I pardon you
The injury you've done me in the past.
Humbling yourself has benefitted you,
Be sure; see that no more into such sin
You fall. You see I have been merciful to you,
And I have freely pardoned you and I

e vo'ne far per dio dimostrazione,
perch'io ti porto grande affezione.

El PADRE *seguita:*

48

O benigno Signor, clemente e pio,
Tu puoi 'n un punto ristorar molt'anni!
Or mi par tu per certo il figliuol mio
poi che t'hai tratti gli stracciati panni.
Ringraziato sia tu, superno Dio,
che vivi e regni ne' supremi scanni!
Dimmi, dolce figliuol, dove sei stato
e quel che t'è pel camino incontrato.

Risponde il FIGLIUOLO:

49

Io temo, dolce padre, a cominciare
a dirti la mia vita scelerata.
Io non ho atteso se non a giocare;
accompagna'mi con una brigata
di sgherri che mi fêr mal capitare.
Tutta la mia sustanza ho consumata
in femine, in taverne, in giuochi, in feste,
in cavalli, in uccelli, in ricche veste.

50

Io menai meco sette compagnoni
di vizi pien, cattivi e scellerati,
usi al mal far, ribaldi e sgherettoni![31]
D'ogni tristizia certo eron dotati,
di pessime e cattive condizioni,
per tutto il mondo tristi nominati,
che stetton meco e mai m'abandonorno
fin che que' danar, padre, mi bastorno.

Want to make that clear to all who see,
Because I cherish you so tenderly.

And he continues:

48

O Lord most pious, merciful, and good,
You can in just one blink roll back the years!
You truly seem to me to be my son,
Now that you've shed your rags. Thanks be to thee,
Eternal God, who lives and reigns above
In Mercy's Highest throne! Tell me, sweet son,
About the many places you have been—
About those who along the road you've seen.

The SON *answers:*

49

I am afraid, sweet father, to begin
To tell you of my life so villainous.
I've not had any purpose but to play:
With ruffians did I surround myself—
A company who led me into grief.
On women, taverns, banquets, games of chance,
On horses, falcons, on rich garments new—
On these I've wasted all my substance, too.

50

With seven boon companions have I fared.
They, filled with vice and villainy, were used
To doing ill, those rascals—ruffians all!
With every kind of evil they were filled:
The worst of every sort and state! They are
Renowned through all the world for wickedness!
By me they stayed, and never left my side;
On me—while I had money—they relied.

51

El tempo ho speso in male adoperare;
per me commesso s'è ogni peccato.
Non me ne vorrei, padre, ricordare;
vita ho tenuto d'uno scelerato.
Quando danar mi cominciò a mancare
e ch'io mi vidi in sì misero stato,
feci pensieri allor pormi per servo.
Or pensa, padre, se mi parve acervo![32]

Seguita:

52

In quel paese era carestia grande.
Io m'abatte' ad un crudel padrone
che mi tenne co' porci a mangiar ghiande,
spietato senza niuna discrezione.
Quelle per certo eron le mie vivande.
Or pensa, dolce padre, s'i' ho cagione
d'essere afflitto e sì trasfigurato:
di ghiande solo mi son disfamato!

Seguita:

53

Vedendomi condotto in tanto stremo,[33]
in me tornando cominciai a pensare
—quando me ne ricordo tutto triemo—
e dissi meco stesso, "Io voglio andare
al mio pietoso padre, e già non temo
che non mi vogli per servo accettare.
So che l'umiliarmi gli fia grato
e merzé gli chiedrò del mio peccato."[34]

54

Io non dovevo in te grazie trovare
avendoti, buon padre, offeso tanto;

51

My time in ill employment have I spent,
I have committed every sin and would
Prefer not, father, to remember those;
Distinguished by infamy my life I led
Until my money started running low,
Then in such misery I found myself
That as a servant employed I thought to be—
O father, judge how bitter this seemed to me.

He continues:

52

There was great famine in that country, then,
And on a cruel master I had chanced,
Who forced me to eat acorns with the swine—
Toward me, he never felt compassionate.
Such fare became my daily sustenance.
And you know now, sweet father, why it is
That I am so afflicted and transformed:
For only eating acorns saved my life!

He continues:

53

Finding myself reduced to such a plight,
To my senses I began to come—
I tremble when I think about it now—
And to myself I said: "I want to go
Back to my father merciful, and I
Don't fear, indeed, that he will not accept
Me as a servant—my humility
Will please him—I'll beg mercy for my sin."

54

I don't deserve to find such pardon when
I've done you, father, such a heinous wrong;

per pietà m'hai voluto perdonare
e rivestirmi di sì ricco ammanto.
Non basta il basso ingegno a ringraziare,
te giusto padre, reverendo e santo,
al qual di servir sempre son disposto,
e questo è nel mio cuor fermo e proposto.

Risponde il PADRE:

55

Io son del tuo parlar forte ammirato.
Oimè, che mi di' tu, figliuol diletto?
Se pel partir tuo in doglie sono stato,
cagion n'ho aùto per quanto m'hai detto!
Dir posso che tu sia resuscitato,
dolce figliuol, che tu sia benedetto!
Non ti voler mai più da me partire,
né a tue vane voglie acconsentire!

El PADRE *al Servo dice:*

56

Odi il mio detto, caro spenditore,
e quel ch'io ti dirò appien farai:
con diligenza, fedel servidore,
un solenne convito ordinerai;
e fammi sopra tutto grande onore,
e parenti e gli amici inviterai;
e uccidete il vitel sagginato.
Fa' che 'l convito sia ricco ed ornato.

Risponde il SERVO:

57

Quel che mi di' sia fatto, o buon messere,
e saprò bene il convito ordinare.
Di buona voglia e molto volentiere

In mercy, your pardon have you granted me,
And wrapped me in so rich a cloak again.
Just father, blessed, worthy of all praise,
So greatly merciful to me; resolved
Am I henceforth to serve you always, and
My heart's purpose firm in this will stand.

The FATHER *answers:*

55

How greatly do I wonder at your words.
Oh, what are you telling me, beloved son?
If at your parting I was sorrowful,
From all you've said, I had good cause to be!
Now, I can say that you're alive again,
Sweet son, so take my blessing. Never wish
To part from me again, nor yield again
To your vain appetites nor to such sin.

The FATHER *says to a Servant:*

56

To my instructions listen, bursar dear,
And what I tell you, in full measure do:
With diligence, O faithful servant mine,
Arrange a splendid banquet, and do me
Above all else great honor, and invite
Our relatives and friends to it, and let
The fatted calf be slaughtered for the event.
Rich let the banquet be and opulent.

The SERVANT *answers:*

57

As you direct me, sir, it shall be done;
How to arrange an entertaining feast,
A banquet greatly pleasing, I know well.

farotti onor, per dio non dubitare.
Lassa far me e non ti dar pensiere:
io voglio ire il convito ’ apparecchiare.

El MESSERE *[il* PADRE*] dice:*

Fa’ che vi sia chi suoni ogni strumento.

El SERVO *risponde:*

Caro messere, io ti farò contento.

Apparecchiano il convito e, giunti quelli ch'erano invitati, el PADRE *dice:*

58
Voi siate e benvenuti tutti quanti![35]

Risponde UNO DELLI INVITATI:

Tu sia per mille volte il ben trovato!
Ringraziato sia Dio con tutti e santi,
poi che 'l tuo dolce figlio è ritornato!
In gaudio ha convertiti e lunghi pianti;
ognun di noi è molto consolato.
Da' tuoi servi chiamati, a te venuti
siam perché i detti tuoi sieno adempiuti.

Sonando e faccendo festa, el FIGLIUOLO MAGGIORE, *tornando, sente sonare e dice al Servo:*

59
Io sento tanti strumenti sonare
in casa. Or dimmi, servo, la cagione;
quel che si sia non posso interpretare.
Certo io n'ho preso grande amirazione
e stupefatto sto pur a pensare.

That I shall do you certain honor, sir,
Leave all to me; let doubt not crease your brow.
I'd like to go prepare the banquet now.

The MASTER *says:*

Have players there of every instrument.

The SERVANT *answers:*

Dear master, I shall see that you're content.

The banquet having been prepared, and those who were invited having arrived, the FATHER *says:*

      58
Ah, you are all most welcome, everyone![35]

ONE OF THE GUESTS *answers:*

And greetings to you too, a thousand times!
Let God with all his saints as well be thanked
Because returned is your belovèd son;
Long weeping has been altered into joy;
Much heartened is each one of us by this.
Called by your servants, we have come to you
At your request as you have wished us to.

While the playing and feasting go on, the ELDER SON, *coming home, hears the music and says to the Servant:*

      59
I hear playing many instruments
At home; now tell me, servant, what may be
The cause of this, for I can't fathom it.
It's certain that I wonder much at this,
Just thinking of it leaves me thunderstruck.

Parmi tal cosa fuor d'ogni ragione
perché il mio padre, quando fei partita,
di duol la mente avea tutta smarrita.

El SERVO *risponde:*

60
Sappi che gli è tornato il tuo fratello
e un magno convitto è apparecchiato;
il padre tuo, e' fa festa per quello,
ed abbiam morto un vitel sagginato.
Or vieni in casa se tu vuoi vedello;
mai non si vidde sì bello apparato.
Il padre tuo non fu mai sì contento,
per quel ch'i' ne conosco e vedo e sento.

El FIGLIUOLO MAGGIORE *al Servo:*

61
Può esser che per questo scelerato
facci il mio padre simil festa fare,
che ciò che aveva al mondo s'ha giocato?[36]
E' nol dovea per certo raccettare,
e par che con guadagno e' sia tornato,
tanti strumenti per lui fa sonare.
Per certo chi fa mal riceve bene;
io il posso dir, ché questo m'interviene.

El FIGLIUOLO MAGGIORE *seguita:*

62
Misero a me, che solo un vile agnello
si fussi un tratto ucciso per mio amore!
Per questo scelerato mio fratello,
qual è colmo di vizi e d'ogni errore,
per far più festa s'è morto il vitello.
Di doglia, per mia fé, mi scoppia il core.

My father's mind this morning when I left
Was wandering in the shadow of his grief.
A thing like this seems quite beyond belief.

The SERVANT *answers:*

60

The news is that your brother has returned,
And that, to celebrate, your father has
Arranged a splendid banquet and has slain
A fatted calf. Now come inside the house
If you desire to see it. Never did
One see such a magnificent display.
By what I know of him, and see and hear,
Your father's never been so filled with cheer.

The ELDER SON *says to the Servant:*

61

Oh, can it be that my father has prepared
A feast like this for this immoral wretch
When he's gambled away his every worldly good?[36]
He surely should not be taken back again;
It seems that he's returned with profit great,
So many instruments resound for him.
One who does evil gets good as his pay;
I see it happening here; this I can say

The ELDER SON *continues:*

62

O wretched me! They never even killed
Some measly lamb—not once—to honor me!
For this scapegrace, my brother, him who is
The very pinnacle of vice and every sin,
They've killed the calf to fatten up the feast.
With sorrow, by my faith, my heart will break;

Io non mi vo' a tal festa ritruovare,
né in casa mia più credo ritornare.

Il SERVO *lo va a riferire al Padre e dice:*

63

Sappi messer che 'l tuo figliuol maggiore
non vuol venire in casa per nïente;
di questa festa ha sentito il tinore
e pargli ch'abbi fatto ingiustamente
a fare al suo fratel sì magno onore,
perché sempre ti fu disubidiente.
È tutto afflitto e pien di passïone,
e non ci vuol venir per tal cagione.

El PADRE *va incontro al Figliuol Maggiore e dice:*

64

Dolce figliuol, per dio non ti turbare,
perché del tuo fratel facci tal festa;
ch'io non t'ami per certo non pensare.
Deh, fa che ingiuria non reputi questa!
Vienti con meco in casa a rallegrare
del tuo fratello. Non ti dar molesta
che nuovamente s'è riguadagnato:
e' dir si può che sia resuscitato.

Risponde il FIGLIUOLO *al Padre:*

65

Io ho fatto proposito e pensieri[37]
di non entrar mai più dove tu sia.
Di pregarmi per dio non fa mestieri,
così disposta è la mia fantasia,
poi che per questo tristo barattieri
tanta festa e romor par che ci sia,

Such a party I will not attend,
Nor do I mean to come back home again.

The SERVANT goes to report to the Father and says:

63

Be advised, sir, that your elder son,
On no account will come into the house.
This celebration's purpose he's perceived,
And, as it seems to him, unjustly have
You thus his brother honored splendidly,
Since that one ever disobeyed you, sir.
He's angry, sir, upset and suffering;
Such revels he won't join for anything!

The FATHER goes to the Elder Son and says:

64

Come now, sweet son, do not be so upset,
Because I have regaled your brother so;
Don't think that I don't love you, certainly.
Ah, do not be offended by this thing!
Come in with me! Your brother celebrate!
Don't be unhappy that we recently
Have got him back with us—indeed instead,
One could well say he's risen from the dead.

The [ELDER] SON answers the Father:

65

I don't intend (and I've made up my mind)
To ever enter where you are again.
Nor will entreaties move me any more,
Thus is my fantasy resolved in this,
Since for this sorry swindler so great a feast,
And such great revelry there seems to be

che tutto l'universo si rintruona,
tanti strumenti per costui si suona.

El PADRE *dice:*

       66
Figliuol diletto, umìle e reverente,
non voler più tal cose replicare;
dispoglia d'ogni invidia la tua mente,
per mio amor vogli in casa ritornare.
Pel passato mi fusti obbediente;
per l'avenir vogli ancor così fare.
Deh, sia contento rallegrarti insieme
meco del tuo fratel, mia cara speme.

El FIGLIUOLO *al Padre:*

       67
Padre, pel tuo tanto dolce parlare
disposto son di volerti ubidire;
ogni tua voglia appien vo' satisfare,
di perdonarmi vogli' acconsentire.
Misero a me, ch'io t'ho fatto turbare!
Non mi vo' più dal tuo voler partire.
Dispon, padre, di me ciò che tu vuoi:
liberalmente comandar mi puoi.

El FRATELLO MAGGIORE, *tornando in casa, abracciando il Fratello, dice così:*

       68
Caro fratello, il ben tornato sia!
Certo vederti mai più non pensavo.
Io rendo grazie al figliuol di Maria!
Dolce fratel, quando io mi ricordavo
che eri partito senza compagnia,
la notte e 'l giorno per te sospiravo.

That everywhere the sounds for him ring out,
So great a band is playing for that lout.

The FATHER *says:*

> 66
>
> Belovèd son, obedient, reverent,
> Do not desire to say again such things,
> And from your mind all envy strip away,
> For love of me, oh, do come home again,
> For you obeyed me ever, in the past,
> And in the future still so shall you do.
> Join with me now in happy celebration
> Of your brother's return to us, of his salvation.

The SON *to the Father:*

> 67
>
> By these sweet words of yours am I induced
> To want to do your bidding, father dear—
> Your every wish in full to satisfy,
> Pray pardon me, do give it your consent.
> The worse for me that I've distressed you so!
> No more do I wish from your will to part.
> Do with me, father, what you want to do,
> You're able to command me freely, too.

The ELDER SON, *returning home, embraces his Brother, and says:*

> 68
>
> Dear brother, you are welcome back again!
> I surely never thought to see you more,
> And to the Son of Mary I give thanks!
> When I recall to mind, sweet brother, how
> You had departed without company,
> By night and day I used to sigh for you.

Or sia di tutto il sommo Dio laudato,
poi che se' a salvamento tornato.

El FRATELLO *gli risponde:*

69

Fratel mio dolce, io non credetti mai
più rivederti in tempo di mia vita.
Se tu sapessi in quanti affanni e guai
istato son poi ch'io feci partita,
di me, per dio, t'increscerebbe assai.
Ma il padre mio per sua pietà infinita
m'ha voluto con gaudio raccettare
e 'l mio grave peccato perdonare.

*L'*ANGELO *dice:*

70

Grazie rendiamo a Dio con puro core,
che sempre è preparato a perdonarci.
Non è sì scellerato peccatore
che 'l benigno Iesù da sé discacci,
quantunque abbi commesso grande errore;
pur che si voglia scior da' falsi lacci
e ritornar col core umiliato
a lui, nel regno suo sarà essaltato.

Seguita ANGELO:

71

O tutti voi che la devota storia
del Vangel sacro contemplato[38] avete,
al vero Dio che è nella eccelsa gloria
con puro effetto grazie renderete;
che v'amaestri d'acquistar vittoria
in queste spoglie dove involti siete,

But now may highest God by all be praised
Because to this safe harbor you've returned.

His BROTHER *answers him:*

69

Sweet brother mine, I never believed that I
Would look on you again in all my life.
If you but knew in what great grief and woe
I've been since I departed, certainly,
How much compassion you would feel for me.
My father, though, through his goodness infinite,
Has wished with joy to have me back again,
And to absolve me of my weighty sin.

The ANGEL *says:*

70

We render thanks with upright hearts to God
Who always is prepared to pardon us;
There is no sinner who's so wicked, lost,
Whom Jesus mild will exile from himself—
Whatever sins the erring one's committed,
If he will free himself from bonds deceitful,
Return to God contrite in heart and mien,
Christ will exalt that person in his reign.

The ANGEL *continues [and dismisses the audience]:*

71

O each of you, who has considered well[38]
The sacred Gospel's history devout,
Give thanks with pure affection to the true
God, who reigns above in lofty glory,
So how to gain the victory he may
Teach you, though you are wrapt in earthly flesh,

acciò che al fin di questa breve vita
vi sia concessa la gloria infinita.

IL FINE

So, when this fleeting, earthly life is done
Unending, surpassing glory you'll have won.

        THE END

La Rappresentazione della distruzione di Saul e del pianto di Davit

INTERLOCUTORI

ANGELO
SAUL RE
BARONI di Saul
GISMETRO, barone di Saul, poi PODESTÀ del Be [Bet-Sean]
SERVI di Gismetro
BARONI del Be
DISNUDO RE dei Filistei
BARONI del Re dei Filistei
CARFASE, PRIMO TURCO [filisteo], anche PRIMO BARONE dei Filistei
MELINO, servo di Disnudo, il Re filisteo
REINA dei Filistei
CLARETA, FIGLIUOLA del Re e della Reina filisti
GINIERI, SECONDO TURCO [filisteo], poi alla fine KING GINIERI
PODESTÀ del Be
UN UOMO* della città del Be
UNA FANCIULLA, della città del Be, sorella dell'uomo
GIONATAS, figlio di Saul, PRIMO FIGLIUOLO
UNA DONNA della città del Be
UN UOMO che fuggì dalla città del Be
AMINADAB, secondo figliuolo di Saul
MELCHI, terzo figliuolo di Saul
REINA, moglie di Saul
UOMO D'ARME dell'esercito di Saul
VIANDANTE
GENTE DEI PAGANI*
DAVIT
BRAMETTO, giustiziere
TERZO TURCO [filisteo]
ANGIOLI**
COMPAGNE di Clareta
GUARDIA

The Destruction of Saul and the Lament of David

CAST OF CHARACTERS

ANGEL
KING SAUL
BARONS of Saul's kingdom
GISMETRO, a baron, later PODESTÀ† [governor and chief magistrate]
SERVANTS of Gismetro [of Be (Beth-Shan)]
BARONS of Beth-Shan
DISNUDO, King of the Philistines
BARONS of the Philistines
CARFASE, FIRST TURK [Philistine], also called the FIRST BARON of
MELINO, servant of Disnudo, King of the Philistines [the Philistines
QUEEN of the Philistines
CLARETA, DAUGHTER of the Philistine King and Queen
GINIERI, SECOND TURK [Philistine], and, at the end, KING GINIERI
PODESTÀ† of Be [of Be
A MAN* from Be
A GIRL, his sister, also from Be
JONATHAN, son of Saul, also called FIRST SON
A WOMAN from Be
A REFUGEE, a baron from Be
AMINADAB, second son of Saul
MELCHI, third son di Saul
QUEEN, Saul's wife
SOLDIER in Saul's army
WAYFARER
PAGANS*
DAVID
BRAMETTO, executioner
THIRD TURK [Philistine]
ANGELS**
COMPANIONS of Clareta
GUARD

BARONI* della corte di Carfase, nuovo Re

*Sono presenti ma non parlano.
**Cantano ma non parlano.

L'ANGELO *in prima dice:*

      1
Popolo, attento sta con divozione,
e vedrai oggi di Davit il pianto,
il qual fe' per Saul orazïone.
Prima vedrete le battaglie intanto,
e di Saul la suo distruzïone,
e de' figliuoli ancor vedrete alquanto;
e vo' della reina anche tu senti
come fu morta, però[1] state attenti.

SAUL RE *levandosi su e a' baroni suoi dice:*

      2
Baron diletti, ho ferma intenzione
di quel che spero aver sempre vittoria.
Della giustizia i' vo' seguir ragione
e di così farò buona memoria;
e 'n somma questa dà riputazione
e cresce altrui l'onor, fama e la gloria
e 'n questo debba stare ognun contento;
e vo' seguirla e far provedimento.

      3
I' vo' nella città del Be[2] mandare
in vece mia un di vo' con letizia,
e vo' che la città abbia a guardare
nella qual popol abita a dovizia.

BARONS* of the court of the newly appointed KING CARFASE

† The Podestà, the chief administrative and judicial official (both governor and chief magistrate), has no good equivalent in English. We use the Italian term.
*Present but do not speak
**They sing but do not speak

First an ANGEL *speaks:*

      1
O people, with devotion close attend,
And David's lamentation you will see—
That David who once prayed for Saul. First bend
Your gaze on battles, though, and you will see
King Saul's destruction. You'll observe the end,
As well, that Saul's sons suffered. Finally
I want to tell you too about the queen--
How she was slain, so closely watch the scene.

KING SAUL, *rising to his feet, says to his barons:*

      2
Beloved barons, I always firmly mean
To be victorious where I set my hope.
I want to follow justice's proper path,
And be remembered well in consequence;
On this, in the end, one's reputation rests—
One's honor, fame, and glory likewise grows.
So everyone must be content with this;
I want to follow through and make my plans.

      3
To Beth-Shan City I intend to send—
Delightedly—in my place one of you
One who will take the city in his care
And oversee its thriving populace.

Oltre, al nome di Dio vo' cominciare,
ma soprattutto si osservi giustizia
e chi el farà sarà remunerato,
governator del mie regno chiamato.

4

E però tu, Gismetro, vo' che vada
e sia governator di quella gente;
e te' lo scetro e 'l cappello[3] e la spada
e cavalier ti fo ogn'uom presente.

GISMETRO, *inginochiandosi, dice:*

Santa Corona, poi ch'a te agrada,
son contento partir signor possente
e vogl'ir via e non far più dimoro.

SAULO *dice, dandogli gli sproni d'oro:*

Va', car fratello, e tien qui gli spron d'oro.

GISMETRO, *partendosi, a' servi dice:*

5

Prudenti servi, orsù, tutti partiàno.
Venite a ubidire el gran signore
e tutti prestamente caminiàno.
Fate gran festa e con voce e romore.
Quando nella città poi entrati siàno,
di grado in grado vi rendete onore.
Quel sommo Idio che ci ha tutti creati
ci abbi benignamente acompagnati.

[Cambiamento di scena: vanno alla città del Be, cioè, a Bet-Sean]

Moreover, in God's name, I wish to start,
But justice, above all, must be observed,
And he who does so will be well rewarded
And will be named the governor of my realm.

4

Gismetro, therefore, I want you to go,
Be governor of that populace and lord;
Take now this scepter, diadem, and sword,
I knight you in the presence of these men.

GISMETRO, *kneeling down, says:*

O Holy Crown, since you're pleased it is so,
I'm happy to depart a powerful lord,
And now I want to leave without delay.

SAUL, *handing him golden spurs, says:*

Take these gold spurs, dear brother, go thy way.

GISMETRO, *on leaving, says to the servants:*

5

Come, prudent servants, let us all depart;
Come, let us do the will of our great lord,
And rapidly upon our road let's start.
With voice and music sound a joyful chord.
Then when we reach the city, let all men
Do honor to each other, great and small.
And that great God who made each one of us—
His blessings go with us upon our way.

[*The scene moves to Beth-Shan*]

Partonsi e vanno via con assai romore di trombe ed altri stormenti e, giunti che sono, GISMETRO *dice a' baroni:*

6
Prudenti giudici, a tutti rammento,
ed a vo' come a capi principali,
di far giustizia è proponimento
e sopra tutto gastigar gli uom mali.
La piatà[4] sia con voi, e son contento,
sì come fanno e dotti[5] ufficiali
e l'alto Dio della superna gloria;
ce ne risulterà maggior vittoria.

[Nel campo dei Filistei]

Ora essendo uno RE DE' FILISTEI, *cioè infedele, a' baroni dice:*

7
Onorevoli e dotti servi miei,
i' vo' che tutti in arme ci mettiàno;
aiuto ci daranno e nostri dei,
e però tutti quanti gli preghiàno.
Or per contarvi a pien quel ch'io vorrei,
contra a lui[6] tutti quanti n'andiàno
e vo'gli tôr per forza la corona
e farlo servo della mie[7] persona.

8
E però vi comando a tutti e dico:
tutt'i paesi sua vo' saccheggiate,
perch'i' l'ho spressamente per nimico.
Fate che la suo gente gli ammaziate
e non pigliate da' prigioni un fico:
uomini e donn'e fanciulli straziate.

They depart amidst the din of trumpets and other instruments, and when they have arrived GISMETRO *says to the barons:*

6

O prudent judges, let me remind you all
And you, our foremost chieftains, bear in mind
That doing justice is my purpose here—
Especially to punish evil men.
Show mercy, and I shall be pleased with you:
This, skillful officers are wont to do,
So too the great God of highest glory;
From this will spring a greater victory.

[Now in the Philistine camp]

Now one who is KING OF THE PHILISTINES, *that is, of the infidels, says to his barons:*

7

O honorable and skillful servants mine,
I want you to equip yourselves with arms;
Our gods will give us aid, and everyone
Of us must therefore pray to them for help.
Now, to tell you fully what I'd say,
Let every one of us oppose Saul's arms,
I'll seize from him his royal crown by force
And make of him a private slave of mine.

8

And therefore I command and tell you all:
I want you to lay waste to all his lands
For he, especially, is my enemy.
Make sure his people perish at your hands—
And take no prisoners, not even one:
Men, women, children—massacre them all.

PRIMO TURCO *dice:*

E' basta un cenno solo, alto sire,
e tutti no' sì ti vogliàn seguire.

El RE, *volendosi partire, chiama un servo e dice:*

9

Or va', Melin, per la reina presto
e di' che venga a me senza indugiare—
e per segnale tu gli porta questo[8]—
e ch' i' gli vo' testé un po' parlare.

MELINO *servo dice:*

Santa Corona, i' v'andrò, ch'è onesto,
e vo', come m'ha' detto, irla a trovare.

El RE *dice:*

Camina presto, orsù, oltre[9] va' via
e di' che meni la figliuola mia.

MELINO *truova la Reina e dice:*

10

Magnanima Reina, i' son mandato
dal mie signor. E' vuol ch'a lui venga
e ch'i' t'arechi questo[10] me l'ha dato,
che Giove nel suo stato lo mantenga!
e di suo propria bocca m'ha parlato.
Vien tost' acciò che scandol non avenga;
e colla figlia tuo vi debbi andare
e che a tutti dua vuol parlare.

The FIRST TURK *says:*

We only need your signal, mighty lord,
And eagerly we'll follow at your word.

The KING, *getting ready to depart, calls a servant and says:*

9

Now, Melin, go hence quickly to the queen;
Tell her to come to me, without delay,
My royal seal, this symbol take to her;
An urgent word to her I need to say.

MELINO, *the servant, says:*

O Holy Crown, since it is proper, I
Shall go to find her as you've told me to.

The KING *says:*

Get going, quickly, now, be on your way!
That she should bring my daughter, also say.

MELINO *finds the Queen and says:*

10

Most gracious queen, my lord has sent me, and
He wishes you to come to him; he gave
To me this sign to give to you—
May Jove preserve him in his high estate!—
And with his own lips thus he spoke to me.
Come quickly so we'll not offend the king;
And with your daughter you must also go
For he desires to speak with both of you.

La REINA *alla Figliuola dice:*

11

Andiàn, figliuola mia, a ubidire
el mie caro marito e tuo car padre.
I' non so già quel che si voglia dire.

La sua FIGLIUOLA *dice:*

Andiàn dove tu vuoi, o cara madre,
ch'i' son disposta volerti seguire.
Che Giove ci acompagni e le suo[11] squadre!
E vo' venite meco, damigelle.

La REINA *dice:*

Andiàn, che Dio ci die buone novelle!

Partonsi tutti e vanno via cantando e, giunti, la REINA *segue:*

12

Salviti Giove, con Ascrepio e Marte
e quel[12] Minerva ch'è tanto paziente,
che ti donin del ciel la prima parte
e fàccinti più grande e più possente;
ed adoperin tanto la lor arte
che contento ti faccino al presente.[13]
Melin dalla tuo parte m'ha richiesto;
quel ch'è tuo voglia, dichiàramel presto.

El RE *dice:*

13

Forza mi è di chiararvi la mie voglia
ed or, Reina, i' tel vo' dichiarare.

The QUEEN *says to her Daughter:*

11

My daughter, let us go; we must obey
My husband dear and your dear father. I
Have no idea what he wants to say.

The DAUGHTER *says:*

Wherever you wish, let's go, O mother dear,
I willingly will go along with you
May Jove and his companions go with us!
O damsels, if you please come with me now.

The QUEEN *says:*

Let's go, and may God have good news for us!

They all leave, singing as they go, and when they arrive, the QUEEN *continues:*

12

Let Jove with Asclepius and Mars keep you!
And with Minerva, ever patient, too,
May they give you the finest part of heaven,
And make you greater and more powerful;
And may they exercise their arts so well
That at this moment they may make you glad.[13]
Melin has called me here on your behalf;
O, quickly tell me what it is you wish.

The KING *says:*

13

I have to tell you both what I desire
And now, O queen, I shall explain to you.

Benché lasciarvi e' me ne sia gran doglia,
sappi, in altro paese i' voglio andare.

La REINA *dice:*

Omè, ch'i' triemo tutta come foglia.

La sua FIGLIUOLA *dice:*

Doh! Caro padre, vuo'ci tu lasciare?

El RE *dice:*

Reina, sie contenta a questa chiesta,
ch'i' tornerò con allegreza e festa.

14

I' ti lascio lo scetro e 'l segno e 'l regno
e fa' di governarlo con amore.
Giustizia osservi perch' è 'l primo segno
e sopra tutto fa' d'avere onore!

La REINA *dice:*

Bench'a pigliarlo mi sie grande isdegno,
va' pur contento e non ti dar dolore.

El RE *dice:*

Orsù, partiànci tutti, o frati miei!

La REINA *dice:*

Acompagnivi Giove e gli altri dèi!

Though parting from you brings me great distress,
I mean to travel to another land.

The QUEEN *says:*

Ah me! I'm trembling like a quaking leaf!

The DAUGHTER *says:*

Oh! Do you wish to leave us, father dear?

The KING *says:*

My Queen, please be content with this request,
For I'll come back with feasting and with zest!

14

My scepter, seal, my realm I leave with you,
And please be sure to govern it with love.
Rule here with justice; that's the foremost sign,
And, most of all, earn honor for yourself!

The QUEEN *says:*

Though taking over grieves me greatly, go;
Be full assured, let it not worry you.

The KING *says:*

Let's go now, let's depart, O brothers mine!

The QUEEN *says:*

May Jove and all the gods be at your side!

Dice el RE:

                15
Innanzi ch'i' mi parta, franca gente,
i' vo' che tutti orazion facciàno;
e tutti quanti oriàn devotamente
e nostri dei. A lor c'inginocchiàno.

El PRIMO TURCO *dice:*

Facciàn quel che tu vuo', signor possente,
che sa' per loro la forza portiàno.

El RE *dice:*

Or prieghiàn tutti Giove e la suo gloria
che della 'mpresa ce ne die vittoria.

TUTTI *ad una voce dicono:*

                16
O Giove, che la terra ha' fatto e 'l mare,
o sommo Apollo, che 'l nome ha' creato,
e tu, Marte, che 'l mondo ha' fatto fare,
e tu, Minerva, c'ha' 'l parlar trovato,
Ascrepio, tu c'ha' fatto germinare
gli uomini e gli animali c'hanno arato,
aiuto gli chiegiàn che qua giù in terra
ci diate la vittoria della guerra.[14]

El RE *dice:*

                17
Orsù, mettiànci tutti a caminare
che Giove ci darà buona ventura;
e tu, Carfase, presto abbi a passare
con una schiera per questa pianura

The KING *says:*

               15
Before I take my leave, staunch countrymen,
I ask that every person say a prayer,
And all of us, let's pray devotedly
And fall upon our knees before our gods.

The FIRST TURK *says:*

We'll follow your command, O mighty lord;
You know that from them we derive our strength.

The KING *says:*

Now, let's all pray to Jove in all his glory
That in this exploit we'll gain victory!

ALL *together they say:*

               16
O Jove, thou who hast made the earth and sea,
O highest Apollo, thou who created words,
And thou, O Mars, who made the world bring forth,
And thou, Minerva, who created speech;
Asclepius, who made those seeds bear fruit
That men and animals sowed with the plough,
Give victory in this war to those of us
Who here below on Earth invoke your aid.[14]

The KING *says:*

               17
Let's go now, let us all be on our way,
For Jove will bring good fortune to us all.
Carfase, you must march across this plain
In haste with your battalion; in your hand

e teco el gonfalon abbi a portare
e non temer e non aver paura!

CARFASE, *Primo Barone, dice:*

Lascia pur fare a me, caro signore;
i' ho pensier che noi aréno onore.

Vanno via. Giunti alla terra [Bet-Sean], dice:

18
O tu, Ginier, colla tuo squadra piglia
e passi acciò che gnun[15] possa scampare;
A questa volta la mente assottiglia
ed i' starò di qua anche a guardare.
Se noi l'abbiàn, i' ti prometto mie figlia
e po' questa città per dota dare.[16]

GINIERI, *Secondo Turco, dice:*

Fatto sarà il tuo comandamento
e vo'gli far morir tutti di stento.

El PODESTÀ *del Be [Gismetro], vedendo assediata la terra, dice:*

19
Oimè, fuggiàn! Che romor sarà questo?
E' mi par qua e demon tutti quanti!
Oimè, quanto possiàn, fuggiànci presto!
Idio ci aiuti e lievi questi pianti,[17]
perché questo sarà l'utim e 'l resto.[18]
Oimè ch' i' mi stimavo stare in canti!
Dacci, Signor, aiuto e 'l tuo governo.
E' mi par qua veder tutto l'inferno.

Our standard you must carry forth with you.
You must dread nothing; do not be afraid!

CARFASE, *the First Baron, says:*

Leave everything to me, dear noble lord;
I think that we'll gain honor with the sword.

They leave and when they arrive at the city [of Be] he says:

18

Your squadrons' tactics manage deftly, O
Ginieri, so no person can escape;
At this time you be vigilant, and I
Shall stay and keep my watch from here.
I pledge my daughter to you if we win;
You'll have this city as her dowry too![16]

GINIERI, *the Second Turk, says:*

Your order shall be carried out, and I
Shall see that they all suffer and all die.

The PODESTÀ *of Beth-Shan [Gismetro], seeing his city besieged, says:*

19

Good heavens! Let us flee! What clamor's this?
It seems that all hell's demons are at hand!
Oh woe! Let's flee away fast as we can!
May God assist us and stop these horrid cries,
For that is where our only chance now lies.
I thought life here would be a song, alas!
Grant us your aid, O Lord, and guide our way;
It seems all hell has broken loose today.

E scende della sedia e fuge e CARFASE, *Primo Turco, lo piglia e dice:*

20
Sta' saldo, traditor, non mi fugire,
che or non puo' scampar dalla mie mano!
A questa volta e' ti convien morire.

<El> PODESTÀ *dice:*

Lasciami stare, o tristo can villano!

CARFASE, *Primo Turco, dice:*

Chiama soccorso a te, se può venire.
Di' che ti venga ' atar[19] lo die[20] tuo vano,
e chiama di Saul el suo soccorso.

El PODESTÀ:

A tempo ti parrà ch'e' t'abbia morso.

Morto che l'ha, DISNUDO *piglia la signoria e dice:*

21
Or ch' i' ho presa la gran signoria,
i' vo' che tutti quanti 'nanzi andiàno.
Ma prima fate tutti scorreria
e fate una gran preda in questo piano!
Adoperate vostra gagliardia!

CARFASE *dice:*

Adesso, signor nostro, cominciàno
e vo' pigliare in questo giorno el regno,
che Giove me n'ha mostro oggi gran segno.

He descends from his throne and flees, and CARFASE, *the First Turk, captures him and says:*

20

Stand still, you traitor, don't you flee from me;
You cannot get away now from my hands!
Now is the time that you must meet your death!

The PODESTÀ *says:*

Let me alone, you vile and evil dog!

CARFASE, *the First Turk, says:*

Call out for help—if any help can come.
Call on your impotent god to come to you,
And call on Saul and his assistance too.

The PODESTÀ:

In due course you'll find out how Saul's bite smarts.

DISNUDO, *having killed him, takes command of the city, and says:*

21

Now that I've seized the city's high command,
It's my desire we all should go our way.
But first you all should carry out some raids:
Ravish and lay waste across the plain!
Now put your manly vigor to good use!

CARFASE *says:*

At this time, O my lord, let us begin;
I want to seize the realm this very day,
For Jove showed me a mighty sign today!

E fanno una grande scorreria e Carfase piglia uno ed amazalo ed UNA FANCIULLA, *sirochia di quello ch'era morto, dice, piangendo:*

22
O pessimo tiranno, lascia stare
el mie caro fratello, omè dolente!

CARFASE, *dando a colui, minaccia la fanciulla e dice:*

I' ti farò altrimenti gridare!
Lascia che morto sia costui presente.

E correndogli adosso la FANCIULLA, *dice:*

Oimè, oimè, oimè, <oimè>, non fare![21]
Non vedi tu ch'i' muoio, oh Dio clemente!

E, mortala, CARFASE *dice:*

Or grida, paza, e chiama, se tu puoi,
Saul<lo> vostro venga ' aiutar voi.[22]

[*Fuori il campo di Saul*]

E fugendo l'altra gente, GIONATAS, *andandosi a spasso, e vede una donna che fugge e, dimandandola, dice:*

23
Onesta donna, questo che vuol dire
che tu ti fuggi e piangi così forte?

La DONNA *dice:*

Sappi che oggi s'è aùto a scoprire
uno crudel, e no' fugiàn la morte;
el mie marito, ognun, n'ebbe a ferire.
Vengol ' annunziar a vostra corte.

They mount a great foray throughout the land, and Carfase seizes a man and kills him, and A GIRL, *the sister of the dead man, says in tears:*

22
O worst of tyrants! Leave that man alone,
He is my brother dear; I suffer so!

CARFASE, *adding more blows, threatens the girl and says:*

For other cause I'll make you scream aloud!
Leave him now, with Death for company.

And running after him, the GIRL *says:*

No! No! Oh no! Oh no! Oh, don't do that!
I'm dying; don't you see? Oh merciful God!

CARFASE *kills her, then says:*

Now shriek, you crazy woman, try and call,
And see if any help comes from your Saul!

[Outside Saul's camp]

While the other people are fleeing, JONATHAN *comes along and sees a woman who is fleeing and asks her:*

23
O worthy lady, tell me why it is
You flee so fast, and why so sorely weep?

The WOMAN *says:*

Take heed, sir, that today we came to know
A cruel man, and we are fleeing death;
That man wounded my husband!—everyone!
I've come here to report it to your court.

Dice GIONATAS:

Di che paesi sono o che confini?

La DONNA:

E' gridan tutti forte "Filistini!"

GIONATAS *si parte e va a Saul, suo padre, e dice:*

24
Padre mie caro, egli è una piatade[23]
a veder qua tanta gente fugire.
E' dicon fugon per la crudeltade
d'un gran signore e che gli fa morire,
sì che ripara, padre, in caritade.
E' non v'è gnun che sappi el nome dire.
Dicon che "Filistini" gridan forte
e che fan di crudele ed aspre morte.

UNO *che scampò della corte di Gismetro giugne e dice:*

25
Serenissimo Re, i' vengo a dire
come la gente tua ha 'vuto morte.
Ma prima vollon della terra uscire
e non trovòr né riscontràr le porte;[24]
primo Gismetro fu ch'ebbe a morire
ed i' fugito son in vostra corte.
Però ripara, o Re dell'alto seggio:
non lo faccendo, e' seguirebbe el peggio.

SAUL, *adolorato, dice:*

26
Oïmè, figliuo' mia, che caso è questo?
Che vi parrebbe a voi di voler fare?

JONATHAN *says:*

From what precincts or regions do they come?

The WOMAN:

They split our ears by bellowing "Philistines!"

JONATHAN *leaves and goes to his father Saul and says:*

24

O father dear, it is a piteous thing
To see so many people fleeing there;
They say they're fleeing from the cruelty
Of a great lord and that he's killing them.
Defend them, father, show your charity!
There's no one who can tell us that lord's name;
They say his troops shout "Philistines" aloud
And that they deal out harsh and cruel death.

A REFUGEE *from the court of Gismetro comes and says:*

25

O most serene King, I have come to tell
You how your subjects have been massacred.
At first they wanted to vacate the town
But found themselves prevented at the gates;
Gismetro was the first to meet his death,
And I have run away here to your court.
O King of this high throne, therefore take steps;
If you don't act, the worst is yet to come!

SAUL, *grief-stricken, says:*

26

How dreadful! In this circumstance, my sons,
What does it strike you that you ought to do?

GIONATAS, *primo figliuolo, dice:*

A me parrebbe tutti quanti presto
no' ci dovessin fortemente armare.

AMINADAB, *secondo figliuolo, dice:*

Ed a me par che questo sia onesto
e che no' dobbiàn tutti insieme andare.

SAUL *dice:*

Ed i' vo' le mie arme sien trovate.

MELCHI, *terzo figliuolo, dice:*

Ed i' venir vo' se vi contentate.

SAUL *si volge alla Reina e dice:*

27

Vedi, Reina, abbi pazïenza!
E' mi convien co' mie figliuoli andare.
Làscioti el regno, e fa' con diligenza
e la giustizia abbi a governare.
Tien qui lo scetro, adopera prudenza,
tanto che nel mie seggio abbia ' tornare;
e rimanti, che Dio ti presti vita
e voglio far da te or la partita.

La REINA *dice:*

28

Or va' che Dio ti mostri buona via!
Gionatas<se> ti sia raccomandato,
i' te ne priego dalla parte mia,
e anche Melchi, che m'ha amor portato,

JONATHAN *the first Son says:*

It seems to me we all must take up arms
As quickly and as staunchly as we can.

AMINADAB *the second son says:*

To me as well the honorable course.
And all together we must sally forth!

SAUL *says:*

I want my weapons found and brought to me.

MELCHI *the third son says:*

I too would like to come if you'll agree.

SAUL *turns to the Queen and says:*

27

See here, O Queen, bear this with patience!
For I must ride along beside my sons.
This realm I leave you; rule with diligence
And govern justly. Take the scepter here,
And, until the time that I once more assume
My throne, employ great prudence, and may God
Be with you and protect your life; from you
I must depart right now and say adieu.

The QUEEN *says:*

28

Go now: may God show you the safest way!
For my sake, I implore you, take good care
Of Jonathan—Melchi too—for they
Have loved me even though they're not my sons;[25]

benché nessun di lor mie figlio sia;[25]
Aminadab ti sie ramentato,
perché gli stimo come mie figliuoli.
Or va' con lor, perché non vadin soli.

SAUL, *avendo un bastone, dice:*

29

O Gionatas\<se\>, mie primo figliuolo,
tien qui el bastone e governa mie gente.

GIONATAS *dice:*

Ma benché di tal guerra mi sie duolo,
accettol, padre mie, benignamente.
Andiàn, frategli, a ritrovar lo stuolo
e partiànci di qui or al presente!

AMINADAB *dice:*

I' son contento, fratel mio, venire.

MELCHI *dice:*

Ed i' anch'i' di qui mi vo' partire.

SAUL *dice:*

30

O figliuo' mia, innanzi ci partiàno,
facciàn prima orazion all'alto Dio;
tutti divotamente lo preghiàno
to\<l\>ga la forza a quel can tristo e rio[26]
che c'è venuto con armata mano.

Aminadab, as well, please bear in mind,
For I esteem them all as if they were
Sons of mine in fact. Now go with them
So that they will not make their way alone.

SAUL, *holding a staff, says:*

29

O Jonathan! My dearest firstborn son,
Take here this staff and lead my army well.

JONATHAN *says:*

Although I deeply grieve about this war,
With good will, father, I accept command.
Let's go, my brothers, forth to find the foe,
And on the instant let us leave this place!

AMINADAB *says:*

My brother, I agree to come with you.

MELCHI *says:*

And I desire to leave this place, I too!

SAUL *says:*

30

O, my dear sons, before we take our leave,
Let's offer first to God on high a prayer;
To him devoutly let us pray that he
Will sap the strength from that evil, wicked dog
Who has attacked us with his armored fist.

MELCHI *dice:*

Deh! Sta contento, caro padre mio,
perché ho sopra lui buona intenzione
e fie[27] perdente. Or facciàn l'orazione.

Ed inginochiati TUTTI *a una voce dicono:*

          31
O grande Dio, po' che tu ci ha' creati,
preghiànti sommamente, Re di gloria,
che da costui tutti ci abbi scampati
e contra lui che tu ci die[28] vittoria
com'altre volte tu ci ha' liberati,
sì che di questo poi facciàn memoria.
Non fie la nostra mente già mai sazia,
se al presente non ci dai la grazia.

SAUL *dice:*

          32
Cari signori, andiàno alla battaglia,
ma prima udite quel che vi vo' dire:
s'i' fussi morto da questa canaglia,
statevi in pace, pon fine al morire.

GIONATAS *dice:*

I' non gli stimo, padre, un fil di paglia,
e vo'gli andare a trovar con ardire.
Orsù, andiàno tutti quanti avanti,
i' non gli stimo se fussin duo tanti!

[Partono e vanno verso il Monte Gielbé (Gilboa)]

MELCHI *says:*

Ah! Rest assured my father dear, because
I'm resolutely set against him. And
He will surely lose. Now let us pray.

And ALL *together, on their knees, they say:*

31

O Great God, since you have created us,
We solemnly entreat you, Glory's King,
Oh, from that enemy deliver us,
And over him give us the victory
As you have set us free in former times,
So may we hold this too in memory.
Our minds will never more find rest or peace
If now you do not grant to us this grace.

SAUL *says:*

32

My lords, let's now go forth into the fray,
But listen first to what I have to say:
If I should perish at this rabble's hands,
Then you must keep the peace: let dying end.

JONATHAN *says:*

I don't think, father, that they're worth a straw;
With courage I intend to seek them out.
Now everyone, let's go; march forward there!
If they were twice as many, I'd not care!

[They leave and proceed toward Mount Gilboa]

E partonsi con assai romore e strepito di trombe e, giunti al luogo diputato,[29] GIONATAS *segue:*

        33
Aminadab, caro mie fratello,
togli el tuo corno e va' sopra quel monte
e chiama alla battaglia quel can fello,
ed i' ti verrò drieto chiara fronte;
e tu, Melchi, caro amor mie bello,
 riman col padre nostro in questo ponte.

AMINADAB *dice:*

Padre, mi parto col nome di Dio.

SAUL *dice:*

Prima ti vo' toccare, o figliuol mio.

AMINADAB *a' frategli dice:*

        34
O tu, Melchi, rimanti, alla buon ora!
Se più non ti vedessi, ti ramento
che facci vezi al nostro padre ancora,
e tu, Gionatas, istarai contento:
vogli bene a Saul e sì l'onora.

GIONATAS *dice:*

Vatti con Dio perché gran romor sento.

AMINADAB *dice:*

Partir mi voglio e non vo' far più crollo.[30]

And they depart with much fanfare and a flourish of trumpets, and, when they have reached the appointed place, JONATHAN *continues:*

33

Aminadab, my brother dear, go up
Onto that mountain; summon with your horn
That villainous dog to battle in the field,
And I shall come behind you, unafraid;
And you, dear Melchi, beloved brother mine,
Stay with our father here upon this bridge.

AMINADAB *says:*

O father, in God's name, I say adieu.

SAUL *says:*

Let me embrace you, son, before you do.

AMINADAB *says to his brothers:*

34

And lastly, O dear Melchi, you stay here,
And bear in mind, should I not see you more,
That you treat our father kindly as before,
And, Jonathan, your happy lot will be
To love our father Saul and honor him.

JONATHAN *says:*

May God go with you; I hear horrendous noise.

AMINADAB *says:*

I wish to leave now—hesitate no more.

MELCHI *dice*:

Prima ti vo' gittar le braccia al collo.

Aminadab si parte con assai romore e, giunto in sul monte Gielbé, suona el corno e GIONATAS *dice*:

    35
Da po' che Aminadab\<be\> s'è partito
ed i' voglio anche caminar vie presto;
egli ha sonato el corno, i' l'ho sentito:[31]
i' voglio andar a veder che fie questo.

SAUL *dice*:

O sommo Dio, abbi 'l priego essaudito,
deh, non voler che questo sie 'l mie resto![32]
Vatti con Dio, che sie benedetto
per quante volte i' ho parlato e detto.

E va via GIONATAS *e, giunto al fratello, dice*:

    36
Non sono ancor compariti costoro:
e' si saran forse a drieto fuggiti.
Se ciò è stato, e' s'è fatto per loro
perché gli aran nostri romor sentiti,
o forse han fatto per campar tesoro.
Sare' lor forse buon sott'esser iti.[33]

AMINADAB *dice*:

E' me gli par sentir da quella costa.

GIONATAS *dice*:

I' son in punto. Venghin a lor posta!

MELCHI *says:*

I want to embrace you warmly ere you go.

Aminadab departs amidst great din, and, when he arrives on Mt. Gilboa, he blows his horn and JONATHAN *says:*

35
Since Aminadab has set out on his way,
On my way I would also quickly go;
His horn he sounded; I have heard it blow.[31]
I want to go and find out what this means.

SAUL *says:*

O God on high, please, to my prayer pay heed,
Don't let this lad be all that's left to me!
Go thou with God, and may your name be blessed
For as many times as I have uttered it.

And JONATHAN *leaves, and, when he reaches his brother, he says:*

36
They haven't put in their appearance yet;
Perhaps they've all turned tail and run away.
If that's the case, they've run away because
They heard our noise, or maybe it's because
They wanted to preserve their plundered pelf.
'Twere better had they fallen in the field!

AMINADAB *says:*

It seems to me I hear them on that hill.

JONATHAN *says:*

I'm all prepared. Let them come on at will!

[Nel frattempo alla corte di Saul]

MELCHI, *volendo partire, dice:*

37
Padre, dammi la tua benedizione
ch'i' vogl'ir a veder la cruda guerra.

SAUL *dice:*

Che tu vi vada non è mie intenzione;
se tu vi va', me n'anderò sotterra.

MELCHI *dice:*

Deh, fallo, padre mie, con devozione:
al mie fratel vo' ir, se 'l dir non erra.

SAUL *dice:*

Benedetto sie tu col tuo parlare,
per quante stelle in ciel e pesce in mare!

Partesi Melchi e SAUL, *piangendo, dice:*

38
Signore, in questo mondo tu m'ha' dato
tre figliuoli, però gli abbi ' aiutare;
fa' ch' in un punto non sie abandonato.
Deh, fagli sani e salvi a me tornare;
ognun divotamente t'ha pregato.
Deh, fa', Signor, le spade lor tagliare.
I' te ne priego, Dio giusto e possente,
che di tal guerra li faccia vincente.

[Meanwhile at Saul's court]

MELCHI, *wanting to leave, says:*

37

Give me your blessing, father, for I wish
To go and look upon this cruel war.

SAUL *says:*

It isn't my intention that you go;
If you leave, it will send me to my grave

MELCHI *says:*

Oh, father, with your blessing let me go;
I'd join my brother, if saying so's not wrong.

SAUL *says:*

As oft may you and your words blessed be
As there are stars in heaven, fish in the sea!

Melchi leaves and SAUL, *weeping, says:*

38

Lord, in this world you've given me three sons;
Accordingly, please help them; at one stroke,
Oh, do not let me be deprived of them.
Ah, keep them safe and sound and bring them back
To me. Each one has prayed devotedly.
Ah, make their swords slice deeply, Lord; O just
And powerful God, this is my prayer for them:
That you will give them victory in this war.

MELCHI, *giunto a' frategli, dice:*

39
Vo' siate ben trovati, frate' mia
Ès<s>' ancor la battaglia cominciata?[34]

GIONATAS *dice:*

Per mille volte il ben venuto sia!
No' abbiàn qui già tre ore aspettato,
ma i' mi stimo nella fantasia
che gli arà la suo gente rasettato.
Aminadab<be>, suona ancora el corno
acciò che venga, che se ne va el giorno.

[Al campo dei Filistei]

Aminadab suona e sonato, DISNUDO *alla gente sua dice:*

40
I' ho udito più volte sonare
un corno ed "A battaglia!" gridar[35] forte.
E' fie Saul che ci verrà ' assaltare
ed uscito sarà fuor delle porte.
Andiànlo tutti presto a ritrovare!
I' v'imprometto a chi tocca la sorte
ch'egli amazi Saul, i' gli daròne
la suo corona e gran re lo faròne.

41
E così chi amaza gnun di loro,
cioè figliuoli e 'l suo fratel carnale,
per uno arete cento libre d'oro,
ma di ciascun vo' avere el segnale.

MELCHI, *reaching his brothers, says:*

39

My brothers, I am glad to find you here;
And has the battle yet got under way?

JONATHAN *says:*

Melchi, A thousand times you're welcome here!
Three hours we've already waited now,
But in my mind I judge that he will have
Regrouped his forces. Now, Aminadab,
Let your horn once more sound so he will come,
For now the day is drawing to its close.

[At the Philistine camp:]

Aminadab blows his horn, and, once he has, DISNUDO *says to his men.*

40

I've several times heard someone blow a horn
And to the battle heard him loudly call.
It will be Saul who's mounted this attack
On us and come forth through his city's gates.
Let us all go quickly now to meet his force!
I promise you that he whom fate selects
To cut Saul down—to him I'll give Saul's crown,
And I shall make that man a mighty king.

41

Likewise, whoever butchers any one
Of Saul's sons or his brother, as I mean—
Will have a hundred pounds of gold, though I
Must have for each some token as a proof.

CARFASE *dice:*

Orsù, andiàn senza far più dimoro!
In questo giorno vo' far tanto male
e di Saul ti vo' recar la testa
e la corona e la suo ricca vesta.

[I Filistei incontrano gli Ebrei al campo di battaglia]

E partonsi e giunti, MELCHI, *vedendogli, pauroso dice:*

    42
Oimè, fuggiàn, ascondiànci in eterno!
Cognoscete, vo' frate', quella gente?
E' mi par certo el diavol dell'inferno
quel con quella corona là presente!

AMINADAB *dice:*

Aiuta ' servi tua, Signor superno!

GIONATAS *dice:*

Andiàn, compagni, a lor liberamente,
ed entriàn tutti quanti arditi al campo!

Uno UOMO D'ARME *di Saul dice:*

Ed infra tutti lor vo' menar vampo.

E fanno la battaglia e, rotta la gente di Saul e morti e sua tre figliuoli, uno UOMO D'ARME *va a Saul e dice:* [ottava 43] *E coloro, cioè la gente de' pagani, tornono alla città del Be.*

    43
Oimè, Saul, fuggiàn per la più corta,
perché gli è morto il nostro Capitano,

CARFASE *says:*

On now! Let's go! No more must we delay!
I mean to do great harm upon this day,
And mean to bring you back the head of Saul
And bring his crown and his rich robes as well.

[The Philistines meet the Hebrews on the battlefield.]

And they depart and on seeing them MELCHI *is afraid and says:*

42

Oh woe! Let's flee—forever hide ourselves!
My brothers, do you know those people there?
That one who wears the crown appears to me
To be the very devil out of hell!

AMINADAB *says:*

Come to your servants' aid, almighty Lord!

JONATHAN *says:*

Let's go, my comrades, at them with a will,
Let each one boldly into battle charge!

ONE OF SAUL'S SOLDIERS *says:*

In the midst of them I'll vent my rage!

They do battle and Saul's army is defeated and his three sons are killed; a SOLDIER *goes to Saul and reports to him:*[octave 43] *And they, that is, the pagan troops, return to the City of Beth-Shan.*

43

Woe to us, Saul! Let's flee by the shortest way
Because your son, our Captain, lives no more;

Aminadab è morto, or ti conforta,
e Melchi, ognun morì coll'arme in mano.[36]
El campo è rotto. Che vuo' far? Comporta!
E Re Disnudo gli amazò, 'l villano.
A me valse le gambe e 'l correr forte,
sì mi volsi scampar da quella morte.

SAUL *adolorato dice:*

44
O Dio, come ha' sofferto tanto errore
e dato tal balìa a questi cani
che gli abbin morto chi ti port'amore?
Come farò scampar dalle lor mani?
Di mie persona e' non aranno onore[37]
e vo' cavarmi fuor di tanti affanni.
O pur Signor, ti sien racomandati
e mie figliuoli e che gli abbi degnati.

45
O Gionatas, ov'è la forza tua
che tu solevi forte adoperare?
Aminadab\<be>, la bellezza sua,
che facie[38] tutto 'l mondo inamorare?
E' parevono dèi tutti a dua.
O Melchi, che per forza volle andare!
O quanto eran gentili, savi e forti!
Ed ora insieme voi iacete morti!

46
O uomo d'arme, sciogli el tuo coltello,
priegoti che la morte m'abbi a dare,
perch'io non vo' morir da quel can fello.
La mie corona te la vo' donare.

Aminadab's dead too— now brace yourself—
And Melchi; they all died with swords in hand.
The camp is razed! Bear up! Nought can be done!
And that villain, King Disnudo, slew them all.
My legs and speedy running rescued me,
So much I wanted to elude that death.

SAUL, *grief-stricken, says:*

44

O God, how did you tolerate such wrong
And leave us at the mercy of these dogs
Who slaughtered those that love and worship you?
And how shall I escape out of their hands?
For my person they'll have no respect
And I would spare myself such suffering.
O purest Lord, now I commend to you
My sons, and pray you've found them worthy too.

45

O my Jonathan, where now is your strength
That you were wont to put to such good use?
And where Aminadab, whose beauty caused
The whole wide world to fall in love with him?
And both of them like gods they seemed to me.
O Melchi, who insisted that he go!
Oh, how noble, wise, and strong they were!
And now, together, you're all lying dead!

46

O soldier, please, unsheathe your knife; I pray
That you will kill me, for I do not wish
To have that evil dog do me to death.
I want, as well, to leave my crown to you.

L'UOMO D'ARME *dice:*

Oimè, Saul, ti tengo per fratello
e vengo qui per volerti aiutare.
Sappi ch'i' nol farei che non son degno
amazar un tant'uom di sì gran regno.

SAUL *dice:*

       47
Da poi che tu non vuoi aconsentire,
faròllo di mie man. Piatà, Signore!
Misericordia, Dio, del mie morire!
Vedi ch'i' son condotto a l'ultime ore.
O ferro, sia pungente el tuo ferire
e non mi far patir troppo dolore!
Mondo, se' pien d'ogni mal costume!
Sie maladetto el dì ch'i' ebbi lume![39]

*E [Saul] gittandosi in sul suo coltello e morto, l'*UOMO D'ARME *adolorato dice:*

       48
Oimè, del cuore mi s'è fatto un nodo;
esser non può iguato,[40] egli è pur vero.
Per forza mi convien far questo modo,
s'i' non contavo e dicevo lo 'ntero.
O traditor, pien di malizia e frodo,
dond'è uscito questo diavol nero![41]
Anch'i' vo' far questa morte isgraziato;
so ch'i' sarei altrimenti straziato.

The SOLDIER *says:*

Oh no, Saul, I consider you a brother,
And I've come here as I wish to give you aid.
Please know I am not worthy—could not slay
A man so great, king of so great a realm.

SAUL *says:*

47

Since you will not consent to do the deed,
With my own hand I'll do it. Mercy, Lord,
In this, my hour of death, O pity me!
You see now that my time to die has come.
O sword of steel, let your keen edge wound deep,
And do not make me suffer too much pain.
O world! You're filled with every evil blight!
Cursed be that day when I first saw the light![39]

When he [Saul] has thrown himself upon his blade and died, the SOLDIER, *grieving, says:*

48

What a shame! My heart has turned into a knot;
I cannot bear to look and yet it's true.
Oh, I am duty bound to act this way,
I had to tell him all, recount the truth.
O traitor, filled with malice and with fraud,
From whence has this black devil sprung?[41] I too
Desire to die this death in my disgrace;
I know that torture, otherwise, I'd face.

E, gittandosi sopra el suo coltello, e' [l'uomo d'arme] amazòssi. El pagano RE, ritornato con la baronia nella città del Be, dice:

49
Ecci nessun di voi ch'abbia veduto
Saùl\<lo\> Re che i' vi nominai?
O, se c'è gnun che l'avessi tenuto
nella battaglia, vedestil vo' mai?

GINIERI, *Secondo Turco, dice:*

Forse che 'l vidi, non l'ho conosciuto;
e pur un de' suo figli gli ammazai.

El TERZO TURCO *dice:*

Ed i' amazai Melchi, suo figliuolo,
qual era 'l terzo ch'entrò nello stuolo.

El Primo Turco CARFASE *dice:*

50
O be', sì, ho là mort' el capitano,[42]
ch'era di costor dua carnal fratello,
e Gionatas\<se\> si chiamò, l'uom vano;
avia gran forza e fra gli altr'il più bello.[43]

El RE *dice:*

I' v'atterrò quel che dissi nel piano
quando vidi la gente d'Israello.
Tornate a' corpi morti, con amore
cercate di Saul, ch'era 'l maggiore.

And throwing himself upon his blade, he [the soldier] killed himself. The pagan KING, *having returned to the city of Beth-Shan with his barons, says:*

49

Is there not one among you who has seen
That Saul, the king I named? Not one who has
Encountered him upon the battlefield;
Has no one ever even seen him, then?

GINIERI, *the Second Turk, says:*

Perhaps I saw him, but I knew him not.
I did, however, kill one of his sons.

The THIRD TURK *says:*

And I killed his son Melchi, who was third
To take up arms and enter in his ranks.

The First Turk CARFASE *says:*

50

Well now, I was indeed the man who slew
The one who was the brother of those two:
And "Jonathan" that haughty man was called,
The strongest of them—the most handsome too.

The KING *says:*

I reaffirm what I said upon the plain
To you when I beheld the Israelites.
Return among the dead; and seek out Saul
With diligence; he was greatest of them all.

Partonsi e, mentre che vanno, uno VIANDANTE[44] *giugne al padiglione di Saul e, vedendolo morto, si rallegra e dice:*

51

Or vedra' che ventura sarà questa
e s'i' aricchirò pur qui 'n un tratto.
I' vo' cavargli questa sopravesta
e la corona e caminar vie ratto.
Or poss'i' stare in allegreza e festa.
I' la vogl'ir a vender or di fatto,
ma, s'i' la vendo, mi fie forse tolta;
m'are' perduto i passi a questa volta.

E' toglie le dette cose e va via e segue:

52

Io ho pensato un altro buon disegno.
Sarò forse per questo un gran signore,
ma presto vo' passar di questo regno
e ir via a salvamento e con l'onore.
So ch'è Davit\<te\> collo gran\<de\> isdegno
e, come vedrà questo, tal tinore
dirò: ch'i' l'abbia morto col mie brando.
Gran tesoro daràmmi al mie comando.

In questo stante che costui va via, e tre turchi vanno a' corpi morti e 'l TERZO TURCO *a' compagni dice:*

53

No' siàn tre solamente in compagnia,
andiàn po' che Disnudo ci ha pregato.

El Secondo Turco GINIERI *dice:*

Avanziàn tempo, mettiànci per via
che, se tre milia n'avessi trovato,

They depart and while they are on their way, a WAYFARER[44] *comes to Saul's tent, and, finding him dead, rejoices and says:*

51
Now you will see what good luck this may be
And see if I'll grow rich here all at once.
I shall relieve him of this cloak of his,
And of this crown and hurry on my way.
Now I can rejoice and celebrate.
I want to go and sell this now, in fact,
But, if I do, it could be snatched from me;
My coming here this time would go to waste.

He takes the things mentioned before and leaves and continues:

52
Another good plan has just occurred to me.
By this one, perhaps, I'll be a mighty lord,
But quickly I must get out of this realm—
Escape to safety, keep my honor too.
I know that David harbors great disdain
So when he sees these, this is what I'll say:
With my sword I struck down Saul today.
Great treasure he will place at my command.

At this moment as he is leaving, the three Turks go looking for the dead bodies, and the THIRD TURK *says to his companions:*

53
We are just three here in this company,
But let's go since Disnudo asked us to.

The Second Turk GINIERI *says:*

Time's very short, so let's be on our way,
Faith! Should I find three thousand of the foe,

i' non gli stimo un fico, in fede mia,
quanto uom al mondo fu mai generato!

CARFASE, *Primo Turco, dice:*

Ed i' son di tuo voglia, caminiàno,
e di Saul prestamente cerchiàno.

[Al luogo dove stava Davide, lontano dalla sede di Saul][45]

In questo tempo che vanno, quello VIANDANTE *giugne a Davit e dice:*

54
Salviti quel Signor che ci ha creato.
I' t'areco, Davit, una novella;
non credo po' che fusti generato
tu n'avessi una tanto me' di quella.[46]
Tu sa' che Re Saul t'ha superato;
per te vendetta ha fatto la coltella
e dettigli la morte al campo strano,
perch'era tuo nimico el can villano.

55
Tu sa' che Re Disnudo era venuto
coll'essercito suo per dargli morte;
e come fu nel paëse veduto
Saùl uscì co' figliuo' delle porte.
Ma, come gli è all'alto Dio piaciuto,
tutta la gente sua ebbe la morte
e mort'i tre figliuol e le suo squadre.
Ecco qui la corona del lor padre.

I'd not give a fig for them, nor
For any man born ever in this world!

CARFASE *the First Turk says:*

And I agree with you; now, let's go all
And quickly undertake our search for Saul.

[Far from Saul's court, the place where David has taken refuge][45]

While they are on their way the WAYFARER *finds David and says:*

54

May the Lord who gave us being save you, sir.
I bring you news, O David; I don't believe
That you've heard better news than this I bring
Since you were born. You know that King Saul has
Defeated you; on your behalf a knife
Has taken vengeance—I have struck him down!
I slew him in your adversary's camp
Because the wretched cur was now your foe.

55

You know that King Disnudo had arrived
With his armed forces to destroy them all;
And then, when he was seen within the land,
Saul came forth from the gates with all his sons.
But, as it pleased our God on high to do,
All his army met their deaths, and dead
Are his three sons and their battalions too.
Here is their father's royal crown, my lord.

DAVIT *adolorato, piangendo e pichiandosi le mano a palme, dice:*

56
Oimè, oimè, piatà, piatade!
Misericordia, Dio giusto Signore,
perc'ha' lasciato far tal crudeltade?
Non ebbi mai in mie vita tal dolore!
Abbia compassione in caritade
di questi che son morti per tuo amore;
vedi che la tuo fede ha un gran morso.
Perché non desti lor qualche soccorso?

57
E tu c'ha' queste cose qui narrato,
di chi se' nato, dimmel al presente,
e di' 'l tuo nome, nol tener celato,
e donde se' tu, dillo prestamente!

El VIANDANTE *dice:*

Sappi ch'i' son d'un poveretto nato;
d'Amalechite sono, re possente.

DAVIT *con superbia dice:*

Deh, come avestù mai sì grande ardire
di fare un re per le tuo man morire?

58
Tu debbi esser per cert'un ladroncello
e vuo'mi mostrar qui 'l bianco pel nero.
Farotti dir a punto, felloncello,
come la cosa è ita. Dimmel vero!
Se tu nol di', morirai di coltello;
e d'ogni cosa dira'mi lo 'ntero.

DAVID, *disconsolate, crying, and, beating himself with the palms of his hands, says:*

56
Oh no! Oh no! Compassion, Pity, Oh!
Have mercy on us righteous Lord; O why
Have you allowed a cruel deed like this?
I've never felt such sorrow in my life!
In charity may you show compassion toward
Those that have met their deaths for love of you;
With what an onerous bit does your faith guide!
Why did you not rise up and aid provide?

57
And you who have reported these things here,
Tell me at once whose son you are, and tell
Your name—do not keep it concealed—and where
You come from; tell me all this instantly!

The WAYFARER *says:*

Know that I am a poor man's son born in
The clan of Amalechite, a mighty king.

DAVID *says haughtily:*

Ah! How did you ever have the impudence
To put a king to death with your own hand?

58
You must be certainly a little thief
Who wants to prove to me that that black is white.
I'll make you tell the story straight. Be brief
You felon, what really happened. Tell the truth
If you don't want a knife to cut you down;
So tell me everything that happened there.

El VIANDANTE *dice:*

O Re, non ti voler ancor turbare,
udira'l fatto come gli ebbe ' andare.

59
Sappi, Davit\<te\>, ch'io passavo via
e 'n Amalchite ne volevo andare;
i' senti' gridar forte, in fede mia,
i' mi rivolsi intorno e ebbi a guardare.
Viddi Saul e disse, "In cortesia,
deh, vien qua ' me," e cominciò a gridare
e disse, "I' vo', fratello, che ti piaccia
che tu m'amazi," ed i' lo guarda' 'n faccia.

60
E vidilo turbato a mal colore,
sì che conobbi non potè campare
perché Disnudo venia con furore.
Piatà mi venne, corsilo ' amazare
e leva'gli dal cuor tanto dolore
de' figliuo' morti, ch' i' t'ebbi a contare;
e vedi la suo vesta e la corona
che mi donò con suo propria persona.

DAVIT *dice:*

61
Doh, come fustù mai cotanto ardito
a dar la morte a quel degno signore?
Tu non se' degno d'averlo ferito;
ma tu ara' la morte, traditore.
Non ha' tu mai ricordare udito
che chi amaza merta tal dolore?
Però, Brametto, fa' che tu l'occida,
ché 'l corpo di Saul vendetta grida.

The WAYFARER *says:*

O King, do not let this upset you more.
You'll hear about the facts just as they were.

59

Know, David, as I went along my way,
To the realm of Amalechite I meant to go;
I heard loud shouting, by my faith, and turned
Around to see what was occurring there.
I saw Saul there, and he said, "If you please
Ah, come to me here," and he began to scream
And said to me, "Ah, brother, will you please
Here take my life." I looked him in the face.

60

And I saw him upset and deathly pale,
So then I knew that he could not survive,
For raging close, Disnudo was at hand.
Then pity seized me and I ran to slay him
And lift the awful sorrow from his heart
For those dead sons I told you of before:
You see his garments and you see the crown
That he has given me with his own hands.

DAVID *says:*

61

Oh, how were you ever so brazen as to put
That worthy lord to death? For you are not
Of worth enough to have even wounded him;
But, you traitor, you've merited your death.
Don't you remember ever having heard
That he who murders earns himself such woe?
Therefore, Brametto, put him now to death,
For the corpse of Saul cries out to be avenged.

BRAMETTO *giustiziere dice:*

        62
Ubidito sarà, signor, tuo detto;
però, fratel, racomandati a Dio.

El giovane [VIANDANTE], piangendo, dice:

Non far, Davit, che sie benedetto!
È questo 'l premio che meretavo io?
O monte Gielbé,[47] che sia maladetto!

DAVIT *dice:*

Di far giustizia ho fermo il disio.

BRAMETTO *giustiziere dice:*

Perdonami e tu piglia conforto,
chiedi perdono 'nanzi che sie morto.

E dàgli ed amazalo e, morto [il viandante], DAVIT *dice:*

        63
Or va' ' acusarti da te, peccatore,
e sopra te è tornato el peccato.
Oimè, baroni, i' triemo di dolore!
O Re Saul, che cosa ha' tu fato?
Non ebbi mai al cuor pena magiore.
Guarda chi s'è del regno incoronato!
Benché mi fusse nimico mortale,
e pur m'incresce del suo brutto male.

        64
Come fus'tu, coltel, tanto villano
che 'l gran Saul tu l'abbi distrutto?

BRAMETTO, *the executioner, says:*

62
Your wishes, mighty lord, will be obeyed;
Therefore, brother, commend yourself to God.

Weeping, the young man [the WAYFARER*], says:*

Don't do it, David, and may God bless you!
Is this the recompense that I have earned?
O Mount Gilboa, cursèd may you be!

DAVID *says:*

To render justice is my firm desire.

BRAMETTO, *the executioner, says:*

I ask for your forgiveness. Now take heart
And seek the Lord's forgiveness ere you die.

And he strikes and kills him, and, once he [the wayfarer] is dead, DAVID *says:*

63
Go now, you sinner self-accused, upon
Your own head has your sin returned again.
With sorrow I am quaking, barons, woe!
Alas, King Saul, what is it you have done?
My heart has never suffered greater pain.
Observe the one who crowned himself the king!
Although Saul was my mortal enemy,
Yet I feel sorry for his dreadful pain.

64
O knife, how could you be so villainous
That you destroyed the life of great King Saul?

Signore Dio, maladisci quel piano!
Grazia ti chiego non vi nasca frutto,
e così 'l poggio dov'è quel pagano
che ' tre figliuoli ha morto e 'l popol tutto.
Qual fu quel ferro che fu tanto forte
ch'a Gionatas mio desti la morte?

65

Chi fu quel crudo e quel superbo cane
che amazò Aminadabbe bello,
e quel ch'uccise Melchi colle mane,
che fu gentile, costumato e snello?
Abbi, Signor, dell'alme lor piatane,
dico di que' del popol d'Israello.[48]
Sa' che per te sofferto han questi torti;
perdona lor po' che son per te morti.

Uno BARONE, *confortandolo, dice:*

66

Confortati, Davit, e sta' contento,
guardiànci dalla turba di coloro;
pensiàn di far un buon provedimento
e non guardiàno 'n ispender tesoro,
perché mi pare un re pien d'ardimento.

DAVIT *dice:*

Così si faccia e non far più dimoro!
E se ci viene, senza far contese,
usciàn di fuori e stiàno alle difese.

[La scena torna al campo di battaglia, dove i filistei cercano Saul]

Lord God, pray, curse that plain! I beg you, grant
That there no crops will ever grow again!
Nor on the slope, too, where the pagan king
Killed Saul's three sons and all their soldiers too.
What kind of steel was strong enough to slay
My Jonathan, who met his death that day?

65

Who was that haughty cur, that cruel dog
That slew Aminadab, who was so fair?
And at whose hands did Melchi die, the one
Who was so slender, noble, courteous?
And Lord, have mercy on their souls, that is,
Upon the souls of Israel's children all.
You know they've suffered these grave ills for you;
Forgive them, Lord, because for you they died.

A BARON, *urging him to be strong, says:*

66

David, be strong and set your mind at peace
Against their rabble, let us be on guard.
Let's think about some working strategy
And take no keep of how much wealth we spend,
Because it seems to me their king fears naught.

DAVID *says;*

Pursue this course at once, without delay!
And should he come to us, with no more talk
We'll go out on the plain and make our stand.

[The scene returns to the battleground where the Philistines are looking for Saul]

E tre turchi, avendo cerco e non conoscendolo, CARFASE *dice:*

67
Compagni mia, avetel vo' trovato?
I' n'ho cercato, non so che mi dire.

GINIERI, *Secondo Turco, dice:*

Ed i' per tutto 'l campo n'ho cercato;
per certo non dovette qui morire.

El TERZO TURCO *dice:*

E' si fie nella terra ritornato
quando la gente sua vide ferire.

CARFASE, *Primo <Turco>, dice:*

Or facciàn presto, omai, di qui partita,
diréno al Re come la cosa è ita.

E giunti al Re, segue:

68
O magnanimo Re, no' siàn tornati
del campo 'l qual ci mandasti a cercare;
e corpi tutti noi abbiàn voltati
e ma' quel Re Saul s'ebbe a trovare.

Dice el RE:

Or tutti quanti siate preparati
e vo' nella suo terra presto entrare;
e tu, rimani a guardia della terra
ed i' vogl'ir a finir la gran guerra.

[I capitani filistei ritornano al campo di battaglia]

The three Turks having looked and not found him [Saul], CARFASE *says:*

67

Ho, my companions, have you found him yet?
I've searched for him; I don't know what to say.

GINIERI, *the Second Turk, says:*

And I've looked everywhere across the field;
It's certain that he was not killed out here.

The THIRD TURK *says:*

He must have gone back to the city when
He saw the slaughter of his fighting men.

CARFASE, *the First Turk, says:*

Now, let's be quick; at once let's quit this place
Let us report to the King how things have gone.

And when he reaches the King, he continues:

68

O King magnanimous, we have returned
From the battlefield you sent us out to search;
We turned the corpses over, one and all,
But never found the body of King Saul.

The KING *says:*

Now make your preparations, all of you;
My plan is to attack his town at once;
And you, remain and guard inside the town,
And I will go to finish this great war.

[The Philistine leaders return to the battleground]

E partonsi e vanno via con assai romore e strepito di suoni e fanno scorreria. E la Reina di Saul, udendo el romore, si mette a fugire e CARFASE, *Primo Turco, la piglia e dice:*

69

Sta' salda, pazerella, non fugire,
ché tu non puo' scampar dalla mie mano!

La REINA *dice:*

Lasciami stare! O tu ha' tanto ardire
che a una reina ponghi mano!

CARFASE *dice:*

A questa volta e' ti convien morire,
come alla gente tua fatto abbiàno.

El Re, essendo in su la sedia, CARFASE *gli mena la Reina innanzi e segue:*

Ecco qui la Reina, car signore.

El RE *dice:*

Sta molto ben. Fategli tutti onore!

Di subito la lasciorno stare e 'l RE *la dimanda e segue:*

70

Dimmi, Reina, di Saul el vero
e dov'egli è tu mel debbi insegnare.
Avanza tempo e presto di' lo 'ntero,
se non, i' ti farò martoriare;
e, s'i' lo so, pel nostro Giove altiero,
darotti el regno e lascerotti stare;

They leave, departing with great noise and clamorous uproar and begin their raid. And, hearing the noise, Saul's Queen tries to escape, but CARFASE, *the First Turk, captures her and says:*

69

Don't move, mad woman; do not try to flee!
For you cannot escape out of my hands!

The QUEEN *says:*

Leave me alone! Oh you are very brash
To dare to lay your hands upon a queen!

CARFASE *says:*

At this moment your time to die has come,
As all your people have already done.

The KING *is seated on his throne when Carfase brings the Queen before him and says:*

Dear lord, before you here behold the Queen.

The KING *says:*

This is well done, my brothers. All honor her!

They immediately release her, and the KING *interrogates her as follows:*

70

Tell me, O Queen, the truth about King Saul;
You must report to me his whereabouts.
Time's wasting; I must know where he has gone
At once, if not I'll make you suffer, but, if so,
By our high Jove above, if I do know,
I'll give the realm to you and let you be;

e, s'i' non saperrò dov'è 'l tuo sire,
con aspra morte ti farò morire.

La REINA *dice:*

71
A tuo dimanda i' non so dar risposta
né dirti di Saul dove si sia;
per certo è strana questa tuo proposta,
non l'ho veduto po' che gli andò via.

El RE *dice:*

Deh, non mi far ancor sì bella mostra,
che i' ti giuro per la fede mia ...
Deh, non mi far, Reina, più parlare,
voglimi presto Saul insegnare.

La REINA *dice:*

72
Di suo persona i' non ne so niente,
quand' i' nol so, che tel posso insegnare?
Ma se 'l vi fussi per certo al presente,
verre'ti voglia di lasciarmi stare?
Ma l'alto creatore omnipotente
di tante ingiurie te n'arà ' pagare.
Priegol mi cavi fuor di tanti angosci
e che perdoni a te, che non conosci.

CARFASE, *Primo Turco, dice:*

73
Non sa' tu che le donne son di pruova
e sempre le si fan pregare assai?
Ora una scusa ed or un'altra truova:
gli è 'l più bel dondol ch'i' vedessi mai

But if I don't learn your lord's whereabouts,
Then I shall make you die a cruel death.

The QUEEN *says:*

> 71
>
> I don't know how to answer your demand
> Nor tell you where King Saul may be; for sure
> This question that you pose is very strange;
> I have not seen him since he went away.

The KING *says:*

Oh, don't you play this lovely role with me!
For here upon my faith I swear to you...
No, do not make me ask again, O Queen.
Now, tell me quickly, where has King Saul gone?

The QUEEN *says:*

> 72
>
> Where he might be, I do not have a clue;
> If I know nothing, how can I tell you?
> But if I did know surely where he was,
> Would you then truly let me be in peace?
> But the high, omnipotent Creator, he
> Will make you pay for such great injury;
> I pray he'll rescue me from such great pain,
> And that he pardon you who know him not.

CARFASE, *the First Turk, says:*

> 73
>
> Don't you know how trying women are?
> They always make you ask repeatedly;
> One pretext first, another then she brings;
> At changing things she surely takes the prize,

e sempre le bugie ella rinuova.
Oh, s'a mie modo di questo farai,
dara'li mort' e non cercar più nulla!
Non vedi tu com'ella ti trastulla?

El RE *dice:*

74

Or oltre presto, senza più indugiare,
dapoi che voi volete, son contento.
Andatela a un albore ' attacare
per le suo chiome, ognun con ardimento!
E vo' con verghe l'abbiate a frustare,
poi agli ucelli la lasciate al vento!

La REINA *dice:*

Perché mi fa' tu far, Disnudo, questo?

El TERZO TURCO *dice:*

E la risponde!
      [alla Regina]:

      Deh, camina presto!

[La scena si sposta. Vanno fuori, verso il luogo del supplizio]

Partonsi e vanno via e, giunti, la REINA *dice:*

75

S'i' potessi da voi grazia impetrare,
cari frategli, tutti ve ne priego
ch'i' potessi al mie Dio un po' adorare;
di questo gnun di voi mi de' far niego.

But always she renews her pack of lies.
Indeed, if you will do what I advise,
You'll kill her now and let this quiz be through.
Do you not see the game she plays with you?

The KING *says:*

74

Now, speedily, with no more dithering,
Since that is what you wish, I am content.
Go all of you and take her to a tree and by her hair
With stout determination hang her there!
And I want you to thrash her there with rods,
Then leave her twisting in the wind for birds!

The QUEEN *says:*

Why, Disnudo, are you doing this to me?

The THIRD TURK *says:*

She answers back!
        [to the Queen]

        Bah! On your way at once!

[Change of scene. They leave this city and proceed to the place of execution]

They leave. When they reach their destination, the QUEEN *says:*

75

O, if I may implore one grace from you,
Dear brothers, I beg this from all of you,
That I may pray a little to my God;
For none of you should deny me this request.

El Primo Turco, cioè CARFASE, *dice così:*

Orsù fa' presto, non ci fare stare,
vedi ch'a te tutto quanto mi piego!
Avanza tempo e fa' l'orazion vostro,
perché presto torniàno al signor nostro.

La REINA *s'inginochia e dice:*

76
O Sommo Imperio d'ogni altro signore,
priegoti che mi debbi rivelare
di Saul, ch'era pien d'ogni valore:
'nanzi mie morte mel debbi insegnare.
O grande Dio, fammi questo onore,
l'anima pur ti vo' raccomandare!
Contenta muoio per te al presente;
non lasciar d'Isdrael morir la gente!

E turchi, cioè e filistei[49] *cascono tutti adormentati.* L'ANGELO *viene e dice:*

77
El padre eterno m'ha a te mandato,
e come gli è suo voglia sta' contenta.
Perché tu l'ha' degnamente pregato,
e' di Saul<lo> vuol che tu ne senta.
Fu suo promissïon di quel ch'è stato,
e per disubidir ti rapresenta:
Saul<l>o è morto, che promisse Dio.
Tien qui la palma! Ferma 'l tuo disio!

L'Angelo si parte. E filistei si risentono e CARFASE, *Primo <Turco>, dice:*

78
Ha' tu tanto grachiato, berghinella?[50]

CARFASE, *the First Turk, answers:*

Be quick about it; don't make us stand around;
You see how I grant fully your request!
It's getting late, so say your prayers because
We must return at once unto our lord.

The QUEEN *kneels and says:*

76

O highest Power, above all other lords,
I pray you to reveal Saul's whereabouts
To me—Saul filled with every valor, for
Before my death I need to learn of this.
O my great God, this honor grant to me
Before I recommend my soul to thee!
Contented now, my death for you I cherish,
But do not let the folk of Israel perish!

The Turks, that is the Philistines,[49] *all fall asleep. An* ANGEL *appears and says:*

77

Our heavenly Father has sent me to you
And as it is his will be satisfied.
Because you prayed so worthily to him
He wishes you to hear some news of Saul.
What God foreordained has come to pass,
And for Saul's disobedience, I report,
Saul has been killed as God said he would be.
Here take the martyr's palm. Hold fast your faith!

The angel departs. The Philistines awake and CARFASE, *First [Turk], speaks:*

78

Have you chattered on enough, you hag?

La REINA *dice:*

Gran mercé, sì. Fate l'officio vostro.
Del ciel si muov'a piatà ogni stella[51];
dolce Signor, mettimi nel tuo chiostro.

CARFASE, *Primo Turco, dice:*

Guarda che cos'è questo! E la favella!

GINIERI, *Secondo Turco:*

Facciàn quel che c'impose il signor nostro.

El TERZO TURCO *dice:*

Or caviànne le man ché gli è sera;
la grachierebbe insin a primavera.

[*Arrivano al campo di battaglia, ora luogo del supplizio*]

E dov'era stata la battaglia v'era un albero ed a uno ramo l'attacorno per le chiome e poi la stanno a guardare e la REINA *dice:*

79

Oimè, oimè, vedi ch'i' stento,
O giusto Dio, mandami la morte!
Deh, trâmi fuora di tanto tormento
e mena la mie alma alla tuo corte;
di questa grazia tu ne sia contento.
Oimè, quest'albor tira così forte!
Mancami e sensi e la voce e l'ardire.
Piatà, Signor, chiego del mie finire!

The QUEEN *says:*

I thank you, yes. Perform your duty now.
Sweet Lord, let every heavenly star be moved
With grief and in your cloister shelter me.

CARFASE, *the First Turk, says:*

Now look at this, will you! She babbles on!

GINIERI, *the Second Turk:*

Let's carry out the order of our king.

The THIRD TURK *says:*

It's evening now; come on, let's do this thing,
For she could gabble on until next spring.

[They reach the battleground where they will execute the Queen]

And where the battle took place a tree stood, and they hanged her to a branch by her hair. As they stand guard, the QUEEN *says:*

79

What pain! Oh, woe! Look how I'm suffering!
O just God, pray, send my death to me!
Release me, ah, from such great misery
And lead me to your heavenly court on high;
Be pleased, O Lord, to grant me this request.
This tree pulls with such force! Oh my!
My senses, voice, and courage fail me now.
Take pity, Lord; I pray you, let me die.

E, morta, e filistei cascano adormentati e viene[52] gli angioli e portono via el corpo suo ed acompagnono l'anima sua a Limbo, cantando, e, partiti, e filistei si risentono e CARFASE *dice:*

80
Dov'è ita costei ch'i' non la veggio?
Son pure stato tutta via presente.

GINIERI, *Secondo <Turco> dice:*

Istiànci cheti e ritorniàno al seggio,
diren ch'ella sie morta certamente;
ed altrimenti dir faremo el peggio
ch'una femina fuga tanta gente.

El TERZO TURCO *dice:*

Questo mi piace, così si vuol fare;
andiànci al signor nostro a presentare.

[Ora, tornati alla sede del Re Disnudo]

E vanno e, giunti dinanzi al Re, CARFASE, *Primo <Turco>, dice:*

81
Salviti Giove tuo persona cara.
No' abbiàn fatto la tuo voglia a pieno.

El RE *dice:*

Or va, Reina, a le tuo spese impara!
Dov'è la tuo persona e 'l tuo veleno?
Udite, la mie lingua vi dichiara,
di quel ch'i' dico nulla fate meno.
Cercate di Saul con ardimento,
dategli morte e la polvere al vento!

Upon her death, the Philistines fall asleep and angels come and carry the body away, and, singing, they accompany her soul to Limbo. When they have gone, the Philistines awaken and CARFASE *says:*

80
I do not see her. Where could she have gone?
And yet the entire time I've been right here.

GINIERI, *the Second Turk, says:*

Let's keep this quiet; we'll go back to the throne
And tell the king that she is surely dead,
For otherwise we'd have to tell the worst:
That this mere woman has escaped and fled.

The THIRD TURK *says:*

That suits me fine; it's what we ought to do.
Let's go before the King and follow through.

[Again, back at the court of King Disnudo]

They go. When they appear before the King, CARFASE, *the First Turk, says:*

81
May Jove preserve your royal person, sire.
We have entirely carried out your will.

The KING *says:*

And so, proud Queen, at your expense you've learned!
Where are you now? What has your poison earned?
You three, hear my instructions from my tongue
And then perform exactly my command:
Go seek Saul out assiduously; put him
To death; his ashes scatter on the wind!

82

Tempo mi par ch'i' debbi ritornare
nel regno mio; or mettiànci in camino!
E tu riman questa terra a guardare
e tièlla 'nsin ch'i' mand' al tuo dimino,[53]
e ch'i' t'arà questo segno ' arrecare,
dàgli la terra per Giove divino.
Orsù, partiàn con allegrezza e festa!
Duolmi non porto di Saul la testa.

E partonsi con assai romore e, giunti che sono, el RE segue:

83

Giove che m'ha condotto a salvamento
ti salvi, cara sposa, con amore!

La REINA dice:

Sie 'l benvenuto, mie contentamento!
Di tuo tornata m'allegro, signore!

El RE, postosi a sedere, dice:

Dov'è la figlia mia ch'i' non la sento?
Tu, presto va' per lei a tal tenore;
di' che le vo' parlar. Va via destro!

MELINO servo con riverenzia risponde:

E' sarà fatto e tornerén qui presto.

E partesi. In questo che pena a giugnere[54] a Clareta, el RE a' baroni dice così:

84

Com'io vi dissi, franchi cavalieri,
vo' meritar[55] quel che fu mie disegno:

82

It seems to me high time that I return
To my own realm; let us be on our way!
And you remain to safeguard here this land;
And hold it till I send someone to you
Who bears this seal, and to that person hand
This country's rule, by Jove's divine command.
Away! Let's go with joy and gaiety.
I'm grieved that I don't take Saul's head with me.

And they depart with great fanfare, and when they arrive [home] the King [says]:

83

May Jove, who's brought me safely home to you,
O my dear wife, preserve you with his love!

The QUEEN *says:*

You are most welcome home, my happiness!
You coming home delights me, O my king!

The KING *takes a seat and says:*

Where is my daughter whom I do not hear?
Go get her quickly; tell her what I say:
Tell her I wish to speak with her. Make haste!

The servant MELINO *answers respectfully:*

It will be done, and we shall be right back.

And he leaves. And while he goes to get Clareta, the KING *says to his barons:*

84

As I told you, O daring cavaliers,
I wish to carry out the plan I made:

Venga, Carfase, sopra gli altri fieri,
dòtti mie figlia e di Saul el regno.
E tu, vien qua, o franco mio Ginieri,
la città del Be per tuo prezo[56] assegno;[57]
e tu, che desti a quel Melchi la morte,[58]
ti fo 'l primo baron della mia corte.

MELINO *giugne a Clareta e dice così:*

85
Clareta, il tuo padre m'ha mandato
a te che tu lo venghi or a vedere.

CLARETA *dice [alle sue damigelle]:*

Compagne mie, quel che m'è comandato
dal padre mio, i' gliel vo' compiacere.
Venite meco e Giove sie laudato,
che come gran signor si fa temere.
Andiàno a ubidir Disnudo grande,
el qual pel mondo la voce si spande.

Partonsi e vanno via cantando e, giunte, CLARETA *segue:*

86
E grandi dèi che t'hanno conservato
compi la voglia tua, caro signore.

El RE *dice:*

Sappi, figliuola, ch'io t'ho maritato.
Carfase è qui tuo sposo, car mie amore.
Se' tu contenta di quel c'ho parlato?

Come here, Carfase, fiercest knight of all,
I give to you my daughter and Saul's realm.
O brave Ginieri mine, you come here, too,
The city of Beth-Shan will be your prize;[57]
And you that slaughtered Melchi,[58] I make you
The first among the barons of my court.

MELINO *finds Clareta and says:*

85

Your father, O Clareta, has sent me
To say that you must come to see him now.

CLARETA *says [to her attendants]:*

O my companions, what my father has
Commanded me I'm glad to do for him.
Come with me and let Jove be praised; a lord
As great as he commands respect and fear.
Let's go obey Disnudo the Great's command;
His fame is spread abroad through every land.

They set out singing as they go, and when they have arrived, CLARETA *continues:*

86

May the great gods who have preserved your life
Grant every wish of yours, O my dear lord.

The KING *says:*

Know, my daughter, that I've betrothed you to
Carfase. Here, dear love, your plighted spouse!
Are you pleased with what I've told you?

CLARETA *vergognosa dice:*

Messer sì, padre mio, pien di valore.

El RE *dice:*

Vien qua, Carfase, come gli è usanza,
e vo' sonate e fate qualche danza.

E fanno le noze e ballano e cantano e di poi CARFASE, *volendosi partire, dice:*

87

Temp'è, Disnudo, ch'i' debbia partire
e vo' nella mie terra presto andare.

GINIERI, *Secondo Turco, dice:*

Ed i' con teco anche ne vo' venire.
Di' se tu vuo', signor mio, comandare.

El RE *dice:*

Andate in pace, state con ardire
e nostri idei fate a tutti adorare.
E tu, figliuola, vanne col tuo sposo.

CLARETA *dice:*

Rimanti a dio, padre, con riposo.

[La scena cambia. Si va alla città del Be (Bet-Sean).]

CLARETA, *modestly, says:*

Yes, sir, I am, most worthy father of mine.

The KING *says:*

Come here, Carfase, as our custom is.
Let music strike up; let the dance begin!

They celebrate the wedding and dance and sing, and then CARFASE, *anxious to depart, says:*

87

It's time, Disnudo, that I must depart;
I wish to hurry along to my own land.

GINIERI, *the Second Turk, says:*

There, I also along with you would go,
My lord, command me if you wish it so.

The KING *says:*

Go ye in peace; remain courageous, both
Make every subject there adore our gods.
And you, my daughter, go now with your spouse.

CLARETA *says:*

May God be with you, father, and give you peace.

[Scene change. They go to the city of Beth-Shan]

Partonsi e due re con festa e, giunti nella città del Be, CARFASE *dice così:*

88
Rimant'al regno tuo, fratel\<lo\> mio,
ch'i' vo' da te oggima' far partenza.[59]

GINIERI RE *lo licenzia e dice:*

Va' coll'aiuto di Giove alto dio,
da che tu vuo' da me pigliar licenza.

El RE CARFASE *dice:*

Adempi di Disnudo el suo disio
ed osservi giustizia con prudenza.
Andiànne, servi, e vo' trombetti, innanzi!
Fate ognun festa, com'io dissi dianzi!

[La scena cambia. Si va alla sede del regno di Saul]

*E, giunto al regno, [*CARFASE*] mostra el segnale e segue:*

89
Ecco 'l segnal del nostro gran signore
ed a me propio ha donato la terra.

Quello ch'era rimasto a guardare [la GUARDIA*] dice:*

Sta' molto ben, tièlla di buono amore!

CARFASE RE *dice:*

E così credo far, se 'l dir non erra,
e tu del regno sie governatore

The two kings depart in great celebration and, when they have reached the city of Beth-Shan, CARFASE says:

88

Remain here in your realm, my brother, for
This very day I'd take my leave of you.

KING GINIERI *bids him adieu, saying:*

Go with the support of our great god, Jove,
Since now you wish to take your leave of me.

KING CARFASE *says:*

Fulfill Disnudo's wishes and observe
Justice with prudence. Servants! Trumpeters!
Come on! Get going! You must lead the way!
Let's all make merry, as I said before!

[Scene change. They go to Saul's seat of power]

On arriving at his kingdom, he [CARFASE] *displays the seal of his office and says:*

89

Behold here our great lord's insignia;
He's given the land alone to me to rule.

The OFFICIAL [GUARD] *who had been left to guard the land says:*

Ah, very good! May you rule with diligent love!

KING CARFASE *says:*

And so I mean to do; if I don't err
In saying so; and you're the governor

e della gente mia, ch'i' vo' far guerra.

La GUARDIA *dice:*

I' ti ringrazio, Re di valimento,
e sono al tuo voler sempre contento.

El RE CARFASE *dice:*

90
Baroni ed altra gente di mie corte,
vo' questi d'Israel perseguitare,
e voglio a tutti quanti dar la morte
ed aspramente fargli tormentare;
se n'entra ma' nessun drento a mie porte,
voglio tutti a l'un l'altro dar mangiare.
Se fussin, che non son, dieci cotanti
dispost'ho di distrugger tutti quanti.

L'ANGELO *dà licenza e dice:*

91
Licenza diàno a vo' con divozione,
perch'el dì passa e la sera ne viene.
O buona gente, ognun fate orazione,
vedete questo mondo pien di pene.
Veduto avete a l'onor del Grifone;[60]
è pel disubidir quel che contiene.
Saul non ubbidì el comandamento
del gran Signor. Vedete che l'ha spento.

FINITA LA RAPPRESENTAZIONE DELLA BATTAGLIA DE' FILISTEI E DELLA DISTRUZIONE DI SAUL.

Here now for I am going off to war.

The GUARD *says:*

I thank you, O my worthy sovereign, and
I'm always ready to serve at your command.

KING CARFASE *says:*

90

Barons and other members of my court,
I want to continue pursuing these Israelites,
And I want to put them all to death
And to make them suffer bitterly;
Should any of them come within my gates,
I'd want to make each one devour the other.
Were there (but there are not) ten times more men,
I'd be determined to destroy them all.

The ANGEL *dismisses the public, saying:*

91

Most devoutly, we give you leave to go
For day is done; the evening draws nigh,
O you good people, pray—do say a prayer!
You see this world is full of suffering!
Thanks to the Gryphon,[60] you have witnessed here
The dire outcomes of disobedience.
Our lofty Lord's commandment, Saul defied;
See that God slew Saul; see the way he died.

END OF THE PLAY ABOUT THE BATTLE WITH THE PHILISTINES AND THE DESTRUCTION OF SAUL.

Endnotes

Domitilla

1. *barone*: baron, an anachronism typical of Italian fifteenth-century religious drama and narrative poetry, especially the *cantari* tradition. See also, Dante, who uses the term for the apostle St. James the Greater (*Paradiso* 25, l. 17. and cf. l. 42).

2. A Florentine popular form of *visitare*.

3. I use a spaced apostrophe here and throughout to indicate the absorption of either the preposition *a*, as in this case, or of the article *i*.

4. *Perciò*: therefore.

5. *discipline*: harsh self-punishment, usually meaning self-flagellation.

6. Both A and B have *del*, which I have corrected to *ché*. In a manuscript hand these two forms are easily confused, and the meaning of this passage, as I understand it, requires *ché*.

7. *mi ha avuto*.

8. On taking the veil (mentioned here and again in 33.7, 40.6, 45.2 and 8, 94.2, 96.4, and also the "veil" used metaphorically in 85.2), see Introduction, n92.

9. The preposition *a* that governs *servire* is absorbed into the final *a* of *apparecchiata*. The absorption of *a* is typical of Tuscan syntax and characteristic of this text.

10. "Per noi si mostra," is shown by or through us. Latinate syntax: passive verb + *per* to express agency. See Dante, *Inferno* I, l. 126: "non vuol che 'n sua città per me si vegna," and other occurrences in *Inferno* 26, l. 84 and *Purgatorio* 25, l. 109. For another example in this text, see below, octave 34.4, and in the *Rappresentazione di Santa Guglielma*, 99.6.

11. "che per noi si crede," in whom we believe, lit., who is believed by us. Latinate syntax, see above, n10.

12. The governing clause, an anacoluthon, begins in line 1 and is completed in line 6. The message Domitilla sends to Aureliano is expressed in lines 2–5.

13. Obsolete form of *poniàn* (*poniamo*).

14. There is something wrong with this sentence: there is incorrect agreement of two masculine adjectives, *falso* and *riprovato*, with the feminine noun *opinion*, yet *riprovato* rhymes with *parlato* and *trovato* and is clearly not a transcription error. The use of the adjective *semplice* is also odd in this context. What could it mean to say here that the opinion is simple? We believe we have captured the meaning by translating it as: A false opinion, merely, is that view—/And one disproved and quite rejected, strange (51, lines 4–5, in the English trans.).

15. Lines 1–4 must refer to the Emperor's appeal in 52.7 ("Credi a chi t'ama e che non parla in vano") that she listen to one who loves her and who has her interests at heart, one whom she understands, however, to be Christ (as she explains in 53. 4–6 and in 54.1–2).

16. Both readings in A ("Po tuto adopera più chel tuo imperio") and B ("Po tutto adopera più chel tuo imperio") must be the result of a transcription error in which the abbreviation sign for a final *r* on *adopera* has been lost. I have made this correction.

17. The Sibyls were mythical prophetesses, readers of oracles. They accompany the Old Testament prophets in some of the Florentine *sacre rappresentazioni*; in convent theater they replace the prophets.

18. Virgil, *Aeneid* 7.803; 11.539–828: Camilla is a Volscian maiden, huntress of Diana, who fought with the forces of Turnus and was killed in battle.

19. The reference is to Atalanta, who takes the epithet Calydonia from the country in central Greece ruled by Meleager; there in the mythological account she killed a monster boar. It is in Jerome's *Adversus Jovinianum* that Pulci found her cited as an example of chastity (I thank Emanuela Carney for this reference).

20. The story of Claudia Pulchra, a courageous vestal virgin, who saved her father from an assailant interposing herself between the two, is narrated by Boccaccio in *De mulieribus claris*, LXII, very likely Pulci's source. Claudia is also mentioned in Valerius Maximus' *Factorum ac dictorum memorabilium* (Book 8, chapter 1).

21. I have reversed the lines of the final couplet as they are found in both of the fifteenth-century editions (and in all subsequent ones consulted): "di Calidonia si scrive e postilla,/ la vergine vestale amò già Roma,/e Claudia, che fra noi tanto si noma." Since I find no reference to a vestal virgin Calydonia, it seems to me that the expression "la vergine vestale" that follows mention of her should follow, instead, the reference to Claudia (see above, n20). Entire lines of poetry were set at a time, and it would have been easy for a typesetter to reverse the final rhyming lines of the octave.

22. Ponza.

23. *avevate*. Rohlfs, *Morfologia*, § 550, p. 287; Nannucci, *Analisi*, 144–45, 495. Mentioned also in Manni, "Ricerche," 163. Form common in the Tuscan vernacular, e.g., Machiavelli, *Decennale* I, l. 112: "Voi vi posavi qui col becco aperto"; I, l. 244: "E voi vi ritrovavi in gran timore" (N. Machiavelli, *Tutte le opere*, edited by Mario Martelli, Florence: Sansoni, 1971, 942, 944).

24. Insult, typical of chivalric poetry. See Luigi Pulci, *Morgante*, for example: "O Macometto, becco can ribaldo." (18.101.7), "dunque tu m'hai condotto, can ribaldo/ traditore, a combater con Rinaldo." (22.184. 7–8).

25. *Cavaliere*, knight, like *barone*, baron, used earlier, is an anachronism typical of the genre.

26. B: "Il cavaliere gli mena dinanzi agl'idoli e dice."

27. Euphrosina e Theodora, according to the *Legenda Aurea*, foster sisters of Domitilla, sent to induce her to change her mind, but whom she converted. In one copy of the play (BNCF, Banco Rari 187a, fol. b$_6$v) the two names are hand-written in the left margin.

28. *conoscessi* and *credessi* are second person plural here. This is common in Tuscan of the period, for example in Machiavelli, *Arte della guerra*, I (Sansoni edition, M. Martelli, ed. p. 312b): "Faresti voi differenza di qual arte voi li *scegliessi*?" See Manni, "Ricerche," 163–64; Rohlfs, *Morfologia*, § 561, p. 304.

29. *morta'*=*mortai, mortali*. Elsewhere: *frate'*=*fratei, fratelli* (67.1, 71.1, 74.7; see also *Saul e Davit*, 39.1; *Guglielma* 57.1).

30. A: *chella orazion*. I have adopted the reading in B.

31. B: "Le due vergini veduti questi miracoli dicono a Domitilla." I have accepted the reading in A("veduto questi miracoli"), since in the vernacular of the time there is often no agreement when the referent follows the past participle, as it does here. See Gianfranco Folena, "Appunti sulla lingua," in *Motti e facezie del Piovano Arlotto*, ed. G. Folena (Milan-Naples: Riccardo Ricciardi, 1995), 376–77. For another instance of this syntax, see the stage directions that introduce octave 104.

32. See above, n8.

33. What looks to a reader at this point as a lack of temporal and spatial realism would not necessarily have the same effect in performance; the scene could be dramatized in a different part of the stage or on a different stage.

34. B: "Il cavaliere mena Domitilla agl'idoli e prima che uccida lei e le altre dice." I have accepted the reading in A ("menato Domitilla"). See above, n31.

35. *Usciamone*: lit., Let's get out of here! meaning let's get on with it!

36. *consumare*: waste his pay. The executioner also complained earlier that the delay was costing him: "Andianne! Ch'i' ho già tanto aspettato / ch'io m'ho mezo il guadagno consumato!" (77.7-8).

37. The author, through the angel, indicates that the audience of the devout story dramatized in the play will not have been simply entertained by it but will have given its message serious consideration, pondered the meaning it has for their lives. She uses the same expression, "contemplato avete," (considered well) in the envoy of the play of the *Figliuol prodigo* (see *Figliuol prodigo*, 71.1-2 and n38).

Santa Guglielma

1. In the second edition, B, attributed to the publisher Bartolomeo de' Libri, the form in 9.2 is *piata*, i.e. *piatà*, a common form in the fifteenth-century Florentine vernacular. This form is also found twice in the second edition of the *San Francesco* (at 52.3 and 82.3). In the other nine occurrences of the term in the *Santa Guglielma* and the other seven in the *San Francesco* we find instead *pieta, pietate, pietoso,* or *pietosi*. The vernacular form is instead the one used throughout the *Saul and David* play, also attributed to Bartolomeo dei Libri, where it occurs eight times. Neither edition of the *Santa Domitilla* includes this form, only variants of *pieta, pietoso*, and both editions of this play are attributed to the publisher Antonio Miscomini.

2. *Guglielma* a [ha a] *ubidire*: Guglielma must obey.

3. *rauna, raduna*: gathers.

4. On gambling, see also the reference in *S. Francesco*, 37.6, *S. Domitilla* 35.4, and the card game that opens the *Figliuol prodigo*, 2-6.

5. Here the author echoes the language Dante attributes to Adam when he meets him in *Paradise* 26, ll. 115-17: "Or, figliuol mio, non il *gustar del legno/* fu per sé la cagion di tanto esilio, / ma solamente il *trapassar del segno*" ("Now, son of mine, the *tasting of the tree* / Not in itself was cause of so great exile, / But solely the *o'erstepping of the bounds*" [Longfellow trans.], italics mine). It is noteworthy that Pulci, who in her *Rappresentazione di San Francesco* (*Play of St. Francis*), oct. 57, ll. 6-8, lays the blame for original sin on him ("pel gran peccato del primo parente," "for our first parent's heinous sin,"l. 6) and not on Eve, here puts Adam in Hell for his act. That Adam's was a sin of pride (*passer il segno*) is in the *Summa* of Thomas Aquinas (II. II, 163, 1 ff.)

6. The syntax of this period is made difficult by the embedded reference to Adam's fall ("… pel trapassar del segno/ l'antico padre all'inferno dannato,/ quando gustò di quel vietato

legno," ll.3–15). The other dependent clauses refer to "Signor degno": Signor degno per lo qual ..., il quale ..., sendo ..., venuto a sadisfar....

7. "Quel che degnò Tubia d'acompagnare" ("He who went at good Tobias's side") is the archangel Raphael, who in the biblical account (Tobit 3:16–12:22) accompanies, protects, and instructs Tobias on his journey to Media.

8. Pulci attributes to the king's brother this commonplace of male psychology: she only refuses him and feigns being chaste and offended out of fear that he is testing her; it is all an act he has seen before (see line 4, "che sien fallace non è cosa nuova," an accusation of all women).

9. D'Ancona explains in a note that this is what one says when one wants to do something without worrying about what might follow (something like 'and the devil may care'). He cites similar usage by Fagiuoli and in the *Vocabolario* of Fanfani. (see the note to the *Rappresentazione del figliuol prodigo*, 36.8, where the prodigal son uses the same expression).

10. Podestà and Rettore are two terms for the same judicial authority. Having found no good English equivalent for this word, we use Podestà exclusively in the English translation. The Podestà answers the King's brother, then he goes to Guglielma, presumably to render judgment, but that scene is not dramatized. In the English transltion we have omitted the reference to it.

11. *conosci scôrto*: you know clearly, *scôrto* is the past participle of *scorgere*, to discern, recognize.

12. The "aspro diserto" is simply a bitter and deserted, lonely place; in 52.1 it is called a "luogo scuro," a dark place, and in 54.2 below it is called a "bosco," woods or forest.

13. Only a ring is mentioned in the stage directions, but the angel refers to "doni," gifts in the plural. Nerida Newbigin suggests (personal communication) that this is a magic ring and the "doni" represent its powers. This may certainly be implied, and we have translated "the rare endowments of this ring." The ring is probably an element taken from her sources which Pulci simply leaves undeveloped. The notion of the gift, however, has a central importance in this play and could be seen as a leitmotif. There are many references to gifts (*doni*) in the play. First it is Guglielma, a much treasured gift to the King of Hungary (in octaves 5 and 13), then there is reference to gifts thrown away when given to beggars (the opinion of the seneschal in octave 19). Following the gift of the ring to Guglielma, the term refers to her gift of healing, seen both as her power and its effects, the healing of the sick (octaves 63, 65, and 88). There is also a return to the initial meaning of the gift, that of Guglielma: when she arrives at the convent the abbess refers to her as a gift (68); and when she is reunited with her husband (92) and returned to their kingdom (101), her incredible salvation and return is seen as a gift to those who thought they had lost her.

14. A: *auocata*. B: *aduocata*. Both D'Ancona (*Sacre rappresentazioni dei secoli XIV, XV, and XVI*, Florence: Le Monnier, 1872, vol. 3) and Banfi (*Sacre rappresentazioni del Quattrocento*, Turin: UTET, 1974; hereafter D'Ancona, Banfi) have *avocata* in their editions of the play, and in octave 62, line 4, "dolce advocata" refers to Our Lady, but this prayer seems entirely addressed to God. According to St. Paul, Christ is our advocate with God. The OVI gives a reference to this in Domenico Cavalca's *Specchio de' peccati* [1340] (ed. Francesco Del Furia, All'insegna di Dante, Firenze 1828, Ch. 6, p. 47): "Chiunque ha peccato, pensi ch' egli ha avvocato appo Dio Iesù Cristo giusto: ed egli è propiziatore per li peccati nostri. (whoever has sinned, let him know that he has an advocate before God, Jesus Christ the just one: and he is the propitiator for our sins.)" I have substituted the masculine form "*avocato*."

15. Without taking religious vows.

16. With a jump in time typical of the genre of *sacra rappresentazione* we are informed that Guglielma has by now cured many people, while only one example was presented (in octave 64). There has been no explicit indication of the passing of time, however, it is assumed. See also below, n25.

17. The "segno" is a medical term used at the time to indicate a urine sample. In Machiavelli's *Mandragola*, Act 2, Callimaco, feigning to be a physician asks for Lucrezia's urine sample in order to determine the cause of her infertility: "Io credo che bisogna che voi veggiate il segno" (sc. ii, see also scs. iv, v, and vi). Boccaccio, *Decameron* 2.8: "Avvenne che … egli infermò, e gravemente; alla cura del quale essendo più medici richiesti e avendo un segno e altro guardato di lui e non potendo la sua infermità tanto conoscere, tutti comunemente si disperavano della sua salute." We have chosen to translate it as "specimen," which in English also has that connotation.

18. Avicenna and Galen, famous physicians of antiquity, considered the most important authorities on medicine until the sixteenth century. Avicenna (Arabic Ibn Sina, 980–1037), born in Asia Minor, was famous for his *Canon of Medicine*, which was particularly influential in Europe from 1100 to 1500. Galen (c. 130–c. 200), Greek physician from Pergamum, author of many medical treatises (credited with 500, of which circa 80 are extant), who moved to Rome and was physician to several emperors.

19. Melancholy (mélas 'black' + chol 'bile') was one of the four humors (blood, phlegm, choler, and melancholy) that, according to ancient medicine, determined a person's state of health and temperament.

20. *Conoscenza*: knowledge (of their science).

21. This unrealistic detail, the failure of the king and his brother to recognize Guglielma since they believe her to be dead, is typical of romance literature (see, for example, Boccaccio, *Filocolo* IV. 67.19–21 and *Decameron* X, 4. 32–33). There is, however, in this text a

belated attempt to rationalize the failure to recognize Guglielma in the stage directions preceding octave 89, where we learn that Guglielma was wearing a veil: "Guglielma levatosi e veli di testa si manifesta al Re suo marito.." (Guglielma, having lifted the veils from her head, reveals herself to the King her husband…")." See also octave 100 and n29.

22. Very great, excellent and renowned (Luigi Banfi, annotation to his edition of *Santa Guglielma*).

23. Both A and B have: "Rendati la vera sanitate," an obvious error. D'Ancona and Banfi correct the text, perhaps following a later edition. I have adopted their reading.

24. A and B: "i quali mi dierono onesta compagnia," but the line is hypermetric. I have accepted the correction proposed by D'Ancona and Banfi.

25. Another indication of the indifference of the genre to temporal realism. The same line appears in the *Rappresentazione del figliuol prodigo*, octave 48, line 2. There too it serves to indicate that many years have passed, since that would not seem to be the case, judging from the sequence of actions alone. See also above, n16.

26. In A the line is lacking a syllable: "che di novanta nove perfetti." B has: "che di novanta nove son perfetti." D'Ancona, in his edition of the play cites in a note the biblical reference to Luke 15:7 "Dico vobis quod ita gaudium erit in caelo super uno peccatore poenitentiam agente, quam super nonaginta novem iustis, qui non indigent poenitentia," I say unto you that likewise joy shall be in heaven over one sinner that repenteth, more than over ninety and nine righteous persons, who need no repentance (King James Version). I have accepted the correction proposed by D'Ancona (and in Banfi, who reproduces D'Ancona's text).

27. The passage is not clear, but "prima dice alla badessa" perhaps means "rivolta alla badessa," that is, turning [lit., turned] to the abbess (*badessa*), since she represents the convent. This would make sense of the plural address to the group of nuns ("Dilette suore mia") that follows and the response to it on the part of the abbess alone. I thank Nerida Newbigin for this interpretation.

28. Passive form, Latinate construction: "per lei" expresses agency: Divine Goodness has shown marvelous things through (by means of) her. See *Rappresentazione di Santa Domitilla*, notes 10 and 11.

29. This is the third attempt to explain the implausible situation in which neither the King nor his brother recognize Guglielma when they first see her at the convent. Here the King says he recognized her face and voice only when she called him her "sposo," spouse, and told him her story.

30. The word "ermo" is the syncopated form of *eremo*, hermitage; "cilicci" are hair shirts; and "discipline," whips for self-flagellating. The repetition of "veste" in rhyme is curious. D'Ancona corrects the first occurrence to read "feste" to avoid the repetition (Banfi follows D'Ancona), but it makes little sense to call "cilicci"(hair shirts) "feste" (entertainments); had he made the substitution of "feste" for "veste" in line 4 (the "discipline," or self-flagellation, as entertainment), it would fit better in the pattern of paradoxes expressed in this octave. However, the recurrence of the term also in line 6 in the verb "riveste" would seem to indicate intention. Could it be that the play was written to be performed at a clothing ceremony, "vestizione," and the repetition meant to underscore the occasion? See Weaver, *Convent Theatre in Early Modern Italy*, especially 60–61, 194–96, for performances on such convent occasions.

Santo Francesco

1. Francesco (1181 or '82–1226), son of Pietro di Bernardone, a cloth merchant from Assisi, and Giovanna (Pica), was the founder of the Franciscan order. Canonized in 1228, his feast is celebrated on October 4th.

2. *hai avuto di vederlo*. A: *hauto di vederlo*; B: *hauuto di vedello*.

3. *ricompensi*: compensate, repay.

4. *metti … a esecuzione*: carry out.

5. Future of *guarire*, to cure: *guarirò*, with syncopation of the weak pretonic vowel.

6. *Poi ch'e'* [e'=ei, from Lat. es. See G. Rholfs, *Grammatica storica della lingua italiana e dei suoi dialetti. Morfologia* (Turin, Einaudi, 1968), §540, p. 269; V. Nannucci, *Analisi critica dei verbi italiani* (Florence: Felice Le Monnier, 1843) 432–33]. Since you are the cause of your own trouble.

7. You should have to go find him.

8. *diseredare*: disinherit.

9. Bernardo di Quintavalle, a well-to-do merchant from Assisi, was Francesco's first disciple.

10. *barletto*, or *barletta*: a small container usually attached to the belt for travel. Here it is probably a beggar's cup.

11. On gambling, see also the reference in the *Santa Guglielma*, 19.5, *Santa Domitilla*, 35:4, and the card game that opens the *Figliuol prodigo*, 2–6.

12. *effetto* for *affetto*: common early usage, occurs again in 70.3, 74.3, and 92.5, and appears in the *Santa Guglielma* and in the *Figliuol prodigo* (see n12). Cfr. I *Fiori di. San Francesco*, 33 "... il Papa desiderava con grande *effetto* di udirla" (*Vocabolario della Crusca*, see Opera del vocabolario italiano at http://tlio.ovi.cnr.it/voci). The emphasis is mine.

13. Innocent III, pope from 8 January 1198 until 16 July 1216.

14. The *Regola*, Rule, the rules by which the religious order must live, including the observance of chastity, poverty, and obedience, and in the case of the Franciscans, with special emphasis on poverty.

15. The first Rule of St. Francis was probably written in 1221 (some sources speak of an earlier version written in 1209); it was approved orally by Pope Innocent III, but it was not submitted then for approval to the Roman Curia. In 1223 Francis submitted a new text of the Rule to the Roman Curia and it was officially approved by Pope Honorius III (*Il grande libro dei santi. Dizionario enciclopedico*, ed. Elio Guerriero and Dorino Tuniz. Cinisiello Balsamo [Milan]: Edizioni di San Paolo, 1998.I, 207).

16. al Malik al-Kāmil (1180–1238), Ayyūbid Sultan of Egypt, Palestine, and Syria (from 1218). *Encyclopaedia Britannica Online*, s.v. "al-Malik al-Kāmil," http://www.britannica.com/EBchecked/topic/310638/al-Malik-al-Kamil (accessed April 25, 2009). In 1219 Francis joined the crusaders at Damietta where he met with the Sultan. The early sources say that the meeting was cordial.

17. Egypt.

18. The form is *piatoso* in B, the edition attributed to the publisher Bartolomeo de' Libri; and *piata* appears again in B in octave 82, line 3 (see *Santa Guglielma*, n1). This form appears frequently in the only fifteenth-century edition of *Rappresentazione della distruzione di Saul e il pianto di Davit*, which is attributed to the same publisher.

19. I have corrected the obvious error in A: "la tua carità" to read "la sua carità." Toschi, in his edition of the play (in P. Toschi, ed. *L'antico dramma sacro italiano*, 2 vols., Florence: Libreria Editrice Fiorentina, 1926–27), has substituted the invariable possessive of popular speech "la suo carità" probably following the second edition, B, which has "la tuo carità."

20. It is probably significant that the author uses "primo parente" ("first parent") in the masculine singular, blaming Adam and not Eve. See also a similar accusation of Adam in the *Santa Guglielma* 25.3–5. The defense of Eve against the accusations of Church Fathers was a standard argument in the defense of women tradition, beginning with the earliest Italian women humanists. See, for example, the dialogue of 1451 by Isotta Nogarola, "Dialogue on Adam and Eve," in *Complete Writings*, ed. and trans. Margaret L King and Diana Robin (Chicago: University of Chicago Press, 2004), 138–58.

21. B: *havie*, and again in 58.4.

22. Count Orlando di Chiusi, nobleman, who in 1213 gave Francis the mountain of Verna, in Southern Tuscany.

23. It is characteristic of the language of these plays, and common in the period, to forego accord when the referent follows the adjective. Both A and B: "gli è grato la presenza mia."

24. Fra Leone, Brother Leo, (died 1271) was not one of Francis's original disciples. He was with Francis when the Rule was approved by Honorius III and remained close to him for the rest of his life. He wrote an account of the miracle of Francis's receiving the stigmata. *The Catholic Encyclopedia*, s.v. "Brother Leo," http://www.newadvent.org/cathen/09173a.htm (accessed April 25, 2009).

25. The wounds of the Passion of Christ on the hands, feet, and side.

26. Another instance of lack of agreement when the referent follows the modifier. See also above, n23.

27. Church in the plain beneath Assisi, at Porziuncola, the site of the first Franciscan settlement, consisting of several huts. It served as the central church of the order during Francis's lifetime.

28. *idropico*: suffering from dropsy.

29. B: *piata*. See above, n18.

30. Jacopa da Settesoli, a noble Roman woman of the Frangipani family and longtime friend of St. Francis. The account of her visit to Francis as he lay dying is reported in the *Fioretti*. See "Introduction," xx and n129 and on the *Fioretti* episode, E. Palandri, "Rappresentazioni sanfrancescane," 429–30.

31. From Psalm 118:146: "Clamavi ad te, salvum me fac: ut custodiam mandata tua," "I called (or cried out) to you, Lord."

Figliuol Prodigo

1. Difficult verse, probably to be understood as follows: *più che te stesso immenso*, greater yet than thyself, exceeding your own greatness, *Dio chiamasti*, you called to God, a reference, it seems, to Christ's show of humility (through which he shows the magnitude of his greatness) when, on the cross, he called out to God the Father.

2. The performance of the play is here called the recitation of the Gospel, an acknowledgement of the Biblical source of the story, the parable of the Prodigal Son, told in the Gospel of Luke 15:11–32. The appeal to God for help to recite the Gospel parable with a heart inflamed underscores the association of this literary form and prayer. This notion is reinforced in octave 71, which concludes the play (see note 38 below). Piero di Mariano Muzi's opening octave of the *Rappresentazione del vitel sagginato* concludes similarly: "Ciascun stia a udire con buon zelo/ come Gesù si parla nel Vangelo" (each of you listen [with good zeal] to what Jesus says in the Gospel).

3. Ancient card game. The game "bassetta" (from *basso*, low) was played with the low cards of the deck, five and below according to Paolo Orvieto, in a note to Lorenzo de' Medici's "Canzona de' confortini," l. 15, Lorenzo de' Medici, *Tutte le opere*, ed. P. Orvieto (Rome: Salerno Editrice, 1992), 2: 776.

4. Small pitcher of wine.

5. *A mezzi (a metà), Randellino?*: Will you cut that in half? I believe "mezzi" refers to "tutti questi (soldi/denari)" in line 2 above, the money being waged. I have found only one similar use of *a mezzi*: "la chioma dell'oro pendeva infino *a mezzi* gli omeri," in the *Metamorfosi d'Ovidio volgarizzate*, translation by Arrigo Simintendi da Prato (1333) of Ovid's *Metamorphosis*, Book 12, ll. 395–6: aurea/ex umeris medios coma dependebat in armos (*Opera del vocabolario italiano*. http://artfl.uchicago.edu/cgi-bin/philologic/search3t?dbname=ovi2006r1&word=a+mezzi [accessed July 11, 2009]).

6. *il mio*: what's mine.

7. *dire buono*: to be lucky in games of chance. See Giovan Battista Gelli, *La Sporta*, Act III, sc. 7 "…che ognuno par che giuochi bene, quando gli dice buono," …winning makes it look like you know how to play, G. B. Gelli, *Opere*, ed. A. C. Alesina (Naples: Fulvio Rossi, 1970), 455.

8. The prodigal son loses at cards and loses the money he has wagered, an indication from the beginning of the play of his sinful nature. On gambling, see also *Santa Domitilla*, 35.4, *San Francesco*, 37.6, and *Santa Guglielma*, 19.5, for references to this sin as characteristic of beggars.

9. I'm not clear [about what to do] Cfr. Cellini, *Vita*, Book II, ch. 82: "… io fui chiaro di che sorte si è la fede dei mercanti, e così malcontento me ne ritornai a Firenze."

10. The early editions have a hypermetrical verse, "& poi pel mondo cercar ogni campagna." I have corrected the line, eliminating "poi," which is probably a misreading of the manuscript.

11. All three sixteenth-century editions have "rendita" (income) but the sense here indicates a reference to the "redità" (inheritance) mentioned in the previous octave. I have made this correction.

12. Obsolete form meaning *affetto*, affection. It is used in the expression "puro effetto" in 20.6, 45.5 and 71.4, in *Santa Guglielma*, at 37.8 and 59.3, and also in *San Francesco*, where it appears four times (see there n12). In *Santa Domitilla*, 1.6 we find instead *affetto*, whereas *effetto* is used instead in its current meaning of result, effect. This line is hypometric in the early editions; I have corrected it adding the article "la."

13. This line is identical to Piero di Mariano Muzi, *La rappresentazione del vitello sagginato*, l. 66 (octave 9, line 2). The Newbigin edition of the play (in *Nuovo corpus*, 29–55) numbers the lines consecutively and does not number the octaves.

14. *sì stranamente=inconsueto*, so unusual, unnatural behavior.

15. Cfr. Muzi, *Rapp. del vitello sagginato*, ll. 121–24: El parlar vostro niente stimo o curo./ Voi mi dovresti pur avere inteso./ e del fare a mio modo starò duro./ All'andar presto ho il core acceso (I neither esteem nor care what you say. / You must have understood me, / And I will hold fast to do as I wish. / I have my mind set on leaving right away).

16. Sixteenth-century editions have *cassieri* (*-ieri*, singular ending, popular Tuscan form now obsolete), however, all other occurrences of the term in the text employ the ending *-iere* (*cassiere*). There are three more examples of singular *-ieri* in octave 65, lines 1, 3, and 5.

17. The sixteenth-century editions have *voglio*, which makes the line hypermetrical. To preserve the meter I have substituted *vo'*, a form that Pulci uses more often than *voglio*.

18. *voglio*

19. Plural of *augurio*: signs, forewarning.

20. Cfr. Muzi, *Rapp. del vitello sagginato*, ll. 193–94: Siàn sette compagnon che veren teco:/ andianne tosto che siàn volentieri (We are seven companions who will come with you: / let's get on our way and go willingly).

21. *fece*.

22. Cfr. Muzi, *Rapp. del vitello sagginato*, ll. 209–16: Io sono el capitan della brigata:/ Superbia da ciascuno i' son chiamata./ Questa è l'Avarizia nominata,/ questa è la 'Nvidia, andrà in ogni lato,/ questa è la Gola che è molta amata,/ quest'è l'Accidia che le sta al lato,/ e quest'è Ira che verrà con furia,/ questa che dà piacer si è Lussuria (I am the captain of this group: / everyone calls me Pride. / This is one called Avarice, / this one is Envy—she goes everywhere,

/ this is Gluttony, who is much loved, / alongside her is Sloth / and this is Anger, who will come in fury; / this one who gives pleasure is Lust).

23. Pietro Fanfani, *Vocabolario dell'uso toscano* (Florence: Casa Editrice Le lettere, 1976, 2 vols.; facsimile of 1863 edition), in the entry for 'uscio' explains the expression *Chi è addietro serri l'uscio* to mean figuratively that if you are slow or careless you shouldn't be surprised to see that others take advantage or get ahead.

24. The line is hypometrical, lacking one syllable. It is, in all the early editions: "& ad ogni tuo decto apparecchiato." The only way to read it as metrical is to transcribe "&" as "ed," which, because of the cacophony it produces, is unlikely, or "et"; perhaps Pulci intended it to be read as "et".

25. All three sixteenth-century editions have *maggiore*, an obvious error of logic and rhyme. I have substituted *cagione*.

26. The form *stessi* appears with singular pronouns in the fourteenth- and fifteenth-century Tuscany, for example: "vattene in zambra e pigliane *tu stessi*," or "tu fusti come giovane ignorante/ e furioso; or lo piangi *tu stessi*"(Luigi Pulci, *Morgante*, II. 83. 2 and XXII. 108.5–6), and "Addoppia quello spaghetto e fa' nel capo *tu stessi* un nodo scorritoio…" (Franco Sacchetti, *Il Trecento novelle*, 166 §45).

27. Perhaps a stage direction. *Uscir fuori* can mean "enter stage." There is a similar case in the *Distruzione di Saul e il pianto di Davit*, in the stage direction that precedes octave 33 which refers to the "luogo diputato" (*Saul e Davit*, 33 and n29).

28. A passage taken from the Biblical text of the Parable of the Prodigal Son, Lk 15:18–19: "Pater, peccavi in caelum, et coram te, iam non sum dignus vocari fiulius tuus: fac me sicut unum de mercenariis tuis" ("Father, I have sinned against heaven and before you; I am no longer worthy to be called your son; treat me as one of your hired servants"). Part of this passage is echoed in the liturgy of the mass just before communion when the celebrant asks that, despite his sinful nature, he be united with God, saying *Domine, non sum dignus*. This familiar phrase calls attention to the allegory of the parable and the lesson to be learned through the play.

29. I have adopted the text of A: *accetterami*. A is an undated and incomplete sixteenth-century edition, which may be anterior to B (c. 1550) and C (1572), both of which have the obviously incorrect *accettarmi*.

30. Malerba, lit., bad grass, weed. Attributing a name with negative connotations to a servant is a sign of class distinction common in theatrical texts.

31. *sgherettoni*: villains, thugs, from *sgherrettare* (*sgarrettare*), to hamstring. The term would mean men capable of villainous actions (such as to cut someone down from behind, as one might hamstring an animal).

32. *acerbo*: bitter, harsh.

33. A, B and C share the common error *stratio*. I have substituted *stremo*, a reading found in later editions (e.g., in Florence: Heirs of Jacopo Tosi, 1620).

34. B: *chiedero*: C: *chiedro*. A is incomplete, interrupted after octave 51.

35. Line identical to Muzi's l. 377.

36. Another reference to gambling, but here it is a figure of speech meaning that the prodigal son has 'thrown away' his inheritance.

37. As in the earlier case of the form *cassieri* (see above, n16), here again, now in rhyme position, we find three instances of —*ieri* (singular): *pensieri*, *mestieri*, and *barattieri*.

38. The audience is said not only to have witnessed the enactment of the parable on stage, but to have given considerable thought ("contemplato avete") to the meaning of the Biblical text, an indication that the author expects her audience to be actively engaged in interpreting and taking to heart the meaning of the sacred story. The experience of the play should be transformative. Pulci uses the same expression in the final octave of the *Santa Domitilla*: "O tutti voi che contemplato avete/ di Domitilla la divota storia" (106.1).

Saul e Davide

1. *però=perciò*: therefore, here and throughout the text.

2. Beth-Shan or Beth-Shean (Ital. Bet-Sean).

3. Crown.

4. *pietà*: Throughout this text alongside *piata* (seven occurrences) we also find *piatade* (two occurrences), never *pieta* or *pietate*. See *Santa Guglielma*, n1.

5. *dotti*: expert, experienced, or well-trained. The term is used again in the same sense in the next octave: *dotti servi miei*. For this use, see Luigi Pulci, *Morgante*, 16, oct. 109, l. 3: "Baiardo …prese in aria un salto,/ onde il pastor, ch'a l'arte non è dotto, / si ritrovò di fatto in su lo smalto / e del petto due costole s'ha rotto."

458 *Endnotes*

6. Referring clearly to Saul, implying that the conversation has been about him and there is no need to mention his name.

7. *mie*, like *suo* in the next octave, 8, line 6, and *tuo* in 10, line 7, are invariable possessive adjectives, popular Tuscan spoken forms. While the variable forms are also employed, the invariable possessives appear frequently in this edition, attributed to the publisher Bartolommeo de' Libri, and only rarely in those attributed to Antonio Miscomini.

8. *per segnale*: perhaps a reference to the *segno*, royal seal or other symbol of his status, that the king gives to the queen together with his scepter, when he leaves her in charge of the kingdom (see below, oct. 14, line 1). Here it serves to authorize Melino to enter the queen's chamber and deliver the king's message.

9. *oltre* is a synonym of *orsù* and serves here as an intensifier. See L. Pulci, *Morgante*, 6, oct. 41: "Oltre, proviànci colle lance in mano!" The 1547 edition incorrectly amends the early edition to read: "Chamina presto horsu presto va via."

10. Edition A has *questa*, but the referent must be the *segnale*, or insignia of the king that gives Melino access to the queen's quarters.

11. See above, n7.

12. Unless this is a transcription error of some sort, the author seems to think that Minerva is a god and not a goddess.

13. See octave 16 and note 14 for the attributes of these Greek gods as Pulci understands them.

14. The confusion of this list of the attributes of Greek gods cannot be ascribed to transcription error. Jove as creator of land and sea is the only one that follows tradition. Here Apollo is said to have invented language, Mars, the "mondo," the world (perhaps she has in mind the Mars of early Roman religion, a spirit [*numen*] of vegetation), and Minerva, the spoken language. Asclepius may here be confused with Cadmus, who planted dragon teeth from which grew men and the house of Thebes. The line, whose syntax is not at all clear, says that Asclepius generated men and the beasts that have plowed the fields. The period seems to be an anacoluthon: it begins invoking the gods and concludes addressing the assembled members of the court ("aiuto gli chiegiàn…" we ask their help…).

15. *gnuno*: from *niuno*: obsolete forms meaning *nessuno*, 'no one.'

16. There is a discrepancy between the promise Disnudo makes here to Ginieri of his daughter in marriage and rule of Beth-Shan, as her dowry, if Ginieri in battle takes the city

from the Hebrews, and octave 84, 3–6, where he, instead, gives his daughter in marriage to Carfase and only the city of Beth-Shan to Ginieri.

17. A has "I dei ci aiuti & lievi questi pianti." I have corrected "I dei" with "Idio," since it is the cry of the Podestà of Beth-Shan, a Jewish city, and the verbs are singular.

18. A: *lutimelresto: l'ultimo e il resto*, all we have left, all that is left for us (*l'ultima cosa che ci resta a poter fare*).

19. *atar: aitare, aiutare*, to help.

20. *die: dio*, god.

21. Hypometric line which I have corrected by adding an additional exclamation.

22. [*che*] *il vostro Saul venga ad aiutar voi.*

23. *pietà*: a piteous thing.

24. A has: *e lor trovor neriscontrar le porte*. I have corrected it to read: *e non trovòr* (trovorno) *né riscontràr* (riscontraro) *le porte*.

25. The Reina (Queen) and wife of Saul was Ahinoam. She is mentioned by name in the Bible only once (1 Sam. 14:50). According to the Biblical text Saul had two wives and a concubine (1 Sam. 14: 49–50 and 2 Sam. 3:7 and 21:8). Jonathan, Abinadab and Malcheshua are not the sons of either Ahinoam or of the concubine, so they are presumably the sons of the unnamed other wife of Saul.

26. *can tristo e rio*, language of insult taken from chivalric poetry, as is *canaglia* (32.3), "I' non gli stimo, padre, un fil di paglia,"(32.5), *can fello* (33.3), *can villano* (54.8), etc.

27. *fie: fia, sarà.*

28. *die: dia.*

29. *luogo diputato*: May be a stage direction. Rather than meaning simply "the agreed upon place," it may mean the stage or the place on stage where the next action will be performed. See also *Prodigal Son*, the stage direction before octave 41 which uses the term *uscir fuori*, the technical term for "to enter stage": "*El figliuol prodigo uscendo fuori tutto stracciato dice da sé.*" See also Figliuol prodigo, n27.

30. Cfr. L. Pulci, *Morgante Maggiore*, 19.46.3 and 5, for *collo* and *crollo* in rhyme; and again in 19.110.3 and 5.

31. This action seems dependant upon the story of Roland, the hero of the French epic poem, the *Chanson de Roland*, who, with his horn, calls in vain for help in battle against the infidel. There is no mention of this in the Biblical account. See L. Pulci, *Morgante Maggiore*, 27.69.

32. The demonstrative pronoun *questo* seems to refer to Melchi, who would be Saul's only surviving son, if Gionatas, who now leaves, and Aminadab, who has blown the horn, do not return. The prayer is for the departing son, Gionatas.

33. *sott'esser iti*: to have gone down in battle, to have succumbed.

34. A: *Esancor*: Ès<s>' ancor, that is, Èssi (Si è) ancora. The form is enclitic, but the "s" has not been doubled here. *Si è ancora cominciata la battaglia?* Has the battle already begun?

35. A: *grida forte*. It could mean "loud cries of 'On to battle!'" but I think rather that this is an error and that an *r* has been lost. I have substituted *gridar* for *grida*.

36. I have corrected the obvious error in A: *ognun morì colla mie mano*.

37. Here I have corrected the reading in A: *amore*. I see no justification for a repetition of the rhyme word in line 3, and I believe the sense here requires *onore* (honor), easily an error of transcription from the manuscript.

38. *Faceva*: The form *facie* is a third person singular imperfect form. In certain areas of Tuscany the third person *ia* and *iano* became *ie* and *ieno*, e.g., in Cecco Angiolieri we find *facien* (*facevano*), and in Dante *faciènsi* (*facevano di sé*, Par. 18, 77). See G. Rohlfs, *Morfologia*, §551, pp. 288–89.

39. It is perhaps worth noting here the theme of *contemptus mundi*, central in all the plays of Antonia Pulci; however, it is also a common theme of the genre of *sacra rappresentazione* (especially in the martyr plays), and it is the main theme, as well, of Bernardo Pulci's *Barlaam e Iosafat*.

40. A: "esser non puo iguato eglie pur uero." It is possible, though not entirely convincing, to read "iguato," as *guato* with the Tuscan prothetic *i*, in which *guato* is the strong form of the past participle of *guatare*, meaning "looked upon." The passage would mean that the sight of the dead king was unbearable, so painful that it could not be looked upon. This reading is in keeping with the second half of the octave in which the soldier laments Saul's death and decides to kill himself, to die alongside his king. I have adopted this reading, not wishing to intervene heavily in the text; however, it may be that "iguato" is a transcription error, perhaps for "iquale," or "equale."

41. The "diavol nero," black devil, must refer to King Disnudo who killed Saul's sons. See oct. 43,6: "E Re Disnudo gli amazò, 'l villano," ("And that villain, King Disnudo, slew them all.")

42. There is an obvious transcription error in A which has: "O bestiola mortel capitano:" I read *bestiola* as "be', sì, i' ò là." It seems clear that Carfase is saying that he has killed Jonathan, the Captain of Saul's army. This follows the claims of Ginieri to have killed one of Saul's sons (49, 5–6) and of the Third Turk to have killed Melchi (49, 7–8), claims that contradict 43, 6. I thank Nerida Newbigin and Francesco Bruni for their help sorting out this syntax.

43. Here "he was" is understood: "avia gran forza e fra gli altr'[era] il piú bello."

44. In the various English translations of the Biblical text he is called either a "sojourner" or a "foreigner."

45. In the Biblical account David fled to Gath and the King of Gath gave him one of the country towns, Ziklag, as his residence (1 Sam. 27: 1–6).

46. I have corrected the obvious error in A: "...tanto dime quella."

47. A, B (Florence, 1547) and C (Florence, 1559): *Glielbe*.

48. A: "di ciò di que del popol disraello." The expression "di ciò" makes no sense here; I believe it is a transcription error for "dico" and have made this correction in the text.

49. See Introduction, pp. 56–57, on the anachronism of calling the Philistines Turks.

50. A rather strong insult for a queen, *berghinella* means a woman of low class and comportment. The unusual term is found also in a ballad written by a close friend and sometime literary collaborator of the Pulci brothers, Bernardo Giambullari (Florence 1450-ivi 1529). It occurs in the final stanza of ballad 25, known as the "Ballata delle comari pettegole": "Attendete, o smemorate,/ o cicale, o *berghinelle,*/ a non far tante novelle,/ e stiesi ognuna nel suo lato (B. Giambullari, *Rime inedite o rare*, ed. Italiano Marchetti, Florence: Sansoni Antiquariato, 1955 stanza 7, lines 5–8, italics mine), *Biblioteca Italiana*, s. v. Bernardo Giambullari, *Rime inedite o rare*, http://www.bibliotecaitaliana.it/xtf/view?docId=bibit001393/bibit001393.xml&chunk.id=d6481e2739&toc.depth=1&toc.id=d6481e631&brand=default (accessed June 29, 2009).

51. A: *tela*, an obvious error for *stella*. I have also corrected *favela*, in line 5. Both are in rhyme with *berghinella* (l.1).

52. It is normal in texts of this period to find lack of agreement in cases like this one in which the subject follows the verb. See Gianfranco Folena, "Appunti sulla lingua," in *Motti e facezie del Piovano Arlotto*, ed. G. Folena (Milan-Naples: Riccardo Ricciardi, 1995), 376.

53. Obsolete form of *dominio*.

54. *pena a giugnere, ci mette tanto a giungere*, it's taking him time to get there.

55. *meritar*: transitive use of the verb. "to reward," as in his plan, as he planned to.

56. *prezo* [*prezzo*] from *pretiu(m)*, obsolete for *premio*, prize, reward.

57. Inconsistent with the offer King Disnudo made to Ginieri in octave 18. 7–8. See above, n16.

58. "Il terzo turco" (the third Turk) claims to have killed Melchi (49.7–8), however, earlier a soldier tells Saul that King Disnudo killed his three sons (43,6). Perhaps we are to understand Disnudo as metonymy, the leader standing for his troops.

59. *oggimai, ormai*, now, at this time.

60. The *licenza* (envoy) seems to refer to a performance by a company or confraternity called the Grifone. I have not been able to identify it.

Appendix 1

Inventory of the Tanini house in Via de' Leoni
(today Piazza San Firenze)
Translation by Elissa Weaver

ASF, Notarile antecosimiano 389, fol. 84[1]

(84r)
Inventario di più chose: [Inventory of many items]

Una chasa posta nel popolo di san Pulinari chon suo chonfini, cioè da un lato Francho Sacchetti et dall' altro lato Mariotto degl' Asini e frategli e dinanzi e di dreto via pubricha; et in detta chasa sono più maserizie, cioè:
[A house located in the parish of St. Apollinaris bordered on one side by Franco Sacchetti and on the other side by Mariotto degli Asini and his brothers and at the front and back public streets; and in that house are a number of furnishings, that is:

una pancha in sul terazo: [a bench on the terrace]

In chamera di sopra: [in the upstairs *camera*[2]]
uno letto cholle chasse panche [a bed with chests]
uno sachone [a stuffed cloth sack to support a mattress]
una materassa [a mattress]
una choltrice [a bed (or mattress) cover]
2 pimacci [2 feather cushions]
uno paio di chortine di tovagle intorno a letto [a pair of cloth curtains around the bed]

---

1. In editing this text I have preserved the orthography of the original. I have reproduced only the inventory of the house and not the final notes that refer to property in the Mugello (a *podere*) owned by the family or to the indication of two accounts, one owed to the family and the other, which is unclear, but which seems to be a debt they have yet to pay.

2. A *camera* was a bedroom but also a place for various household activities and for receiving guests.

uno choltrone [a blanket]
una sargia biancha [a white bedspread]
4 ghuanciali [4 pillows]
uno choltrone di bambagia [a cotton blanket]
uno lettuccio chon chapellinaio [a high-backed wooden bench (*lettuccio*) with overhanging cornice[3]]
uno materassino da llettuccio [a small mattress for the *lettuccio*]
una choltre biancha da llettuccio [a white quilt for the *lettuccio*]
una Nostra Donna [an image of Our Lady]
uno forziere dorato [a gilded chest]
uno altro forziere dorato [another gilded chest]
uno paio d' alari [a pair of andirons]

In chamera della sala principale: [in the *camera* of the main *sala*[4]]
uno letto chon chassapancha [a bed with a chest]
uno sacchone [a stuffed cloth sack to support a mattress]
una materassa [a mattress]
una choltrice [a bed (or mattress) cover]
una sargia gialla [a yellow bedspread]
2 pimacci [2 feather cushions]
uno paio chortine di tela lina chon sopra <cielo> [a pair of linen bed curtains with a <canopy>[5]]
uno ghuanciale [a pillow]
uno lettuccio chon chapellinaio [a *lettuccio* with overhanging cornice]
uno materasino [a small mattress]
una Nostra Donna di rilievo [an image of Our Lady (sculpted) in relief]
uno descho da schrivere [a writing desk]
6 chucchai d' ariento [6 silver spoons]
4 forchette d' ariento [4 silver forks]
uno forziere dipinto [a painted chest]
uno mantello di rosato [a cloak of rose-colored cloth]

3. The overhanging cornice of a *chapellinaio* was often equipped with hooks for hanging things.

4. A *sala* was a large space that served as living, dining, and reception room

5. I thank Brenda Preyer for suggesting that the missing word is probably *cielo* and that the reference is to a bed canopy.

uno ... foderato di rasetta [a ... lined in coarse wool]
uno sargetto (?) di velluto nero [a little black velvet drape (?)]

Nell' antichamera: [in the *anticamera*[6]]
uno letto chon chassapancha [a bed with chest]
uno sachone [a stuffed cloth sack to support a mattress]
una materassa [a mattress]
una choltrice [a bed (or mattress) cover]
una sargia rossa [a red bedspread]
uno panno d' arazzo grande a figure [a large figured tapestry]
uno altro panno d' arazzo a figure [another large figured tapestry]
2 spalliere d' arazzo a mezura [2 pieces of tapestry fitted[7] and affixed to the wall]
uno portiere d' arazo [a tapestry door curtain]
una choltre di panno lino da lletto [a linen bed quilt]
2 pimacci [2 feather cushions]
una chopertura da chassa [a chest cover]
una sargia rossa [a red bedspread]

In sala principale: [in the main *sala*]
la pancha intorno [the bench going around the room]
una chassetta da pane [a bread box]
2 tavole chon trespoli [2 tables with trestles]
4 deschetti [4 small tables]
4 segiole [4 chairs]
uno sechione [a large pail]
2 bacini cholle <mesci>robe[8] [2 basins with pitchers]
7 chandellieri d' ottone [7 brass candlesticks]

---

6. The *anticamera* was a small, elaborately decorated room that followed the *camera*, and, like the camera, had various uses.

7. *a mezzura*: probably a *misura*, meaning made to fit to the wall area.

8. I thank Brenda Preyer for suggesting that the letters I was unable to read were *mesci*, that the object in the list is a *mescirobe*, a pitcher, and that this item, the, *bacini*, *sechione*, and the *candellieri* were part of an *acquaio*, a wall fountain, probably a decorative one, a standard feature of the Florentine *sala* (see B. Preyer, "The Florentine *Casa*," p. 38, and "The *Acquaio* [Wall Fountain] and Fireplace in Florence," in *At Home in Renaissance Italy*, ed. M. Afmar-Wollheim and F Dennis, 284–87).

una choltelliera [a knife-box]

In chamera della fante: [In the domestic servant's room]
uno letto chon chasapancha [a bed with chest}
uno sachone [a stuffed cloth sack to support a mattress]
una materassa [a mattress]
una choltrice [a bed (or mattress) cover]
uno pimacco [a feather cushion]
uno chopertoio azurro [a blue cover]
uno panno rosso [a red cloth]
una madia da pane [a kneading tub for bread]
uno botticino da aceto [a little vinegar jug]

In chucina: [in the kitchen]
10 piattegli di stangno grandi [10 large tin plates]
5 piatelletti di stangno [5 small tin plates]
12 schodelle di stangno [12 tin bowls]
21 schodelline di stangno [21 small tin bowls]
12 quadretti di stangno [12 square tin plates]
2 paiuoli di rame [2 large copper pots]
uno orc<i>uolo di rame [one copper jug]
2 padelle di rame [2 copper frying pans]
3 teghie di rame [3 copper baking pans]
una gratichola [a grill]
una grattugia [a grater]

(c. 84v)
3 palette di ferro [3 iron fire shovels]
3 paia di molle [3 pairs of fire tongs]
una forchetta [a fire fork][9]
uno schaldaletto [a bed warming pan]
2 mortai [2 mortars]
3 treppie [3 trivets]
uno paio d' alari [a pair of andirons]
2 mestole di rame forate [2 perforated copper ladles]

9. Again I thank Brenda Preyer for pointing out that the *palette, molle,* and *forchetta* are all commonly found at the fireplace.

uno paio di stadere [a pair of scales]
uno paio di secchie al pozzo [a pair of buckets at the well]
4 lucerne [4 lamps]
3 orci da olio [3 terracotta jugs for oil]

In chamera terrena: [on the ground floor]
uno letto chon una chassapancha [a bed with a chest]
uno sachone [a stuffed cloth sack to support a mattress]
una materassa [a mattress]
una choltrice [a bed (mattress) cover]
2 pimacci [2 feather cushions]
uno coltrone [a blanket]
una sargia biancha [a white bedspread]
4 ghuanciali [4 pillows]
uno lettuccio chon chapellinaio [a *lettuccio* with overhanging cornice]
uno materassino [a small mattress]
una Nostra Donna [an image of Our Lady]

In chamera del famiglo: [in the *camera* of the male servant]
uno letto [a bed]
uno sachone [a stuffed cloth sack to support a mattress]
una choltrice [a blanket]
una choltre a foglami [a quilt with a leaf pattern]
una pancha [a bench]

In terreno le panche intorno [in a covered area on the ground floor, benches around][10]
più pezzi ... avanzati [several pieces ... left over]

Nella volta: [in the cellar]
13 botte tra grandi e pichole [13 casks, some large, some small]
3 barili [3 barrels]
una pevera [a wooden wine funnel]
uno chatino di rame [a copper basin]

---

10. Brenda Preyer informs me that the *terreno* would have been a covered area that opened onto a court. While no court is mentioned in here, there was a court, which is described in one of the archival documents regarding this house, see my Introduction, note 15.

Appendix 2

Letter from Jacopa Tanini, widow of Francesco Tanini to Clarice
Orsini, wife of Lorenzo de' Medici, 25 April 1475
(ASF, MAP, LXXX, fol. 132)[1]

Translation by Elissa Weaver

Mag[nifi]ca et generosa donona [sic], M[adonn]a Clarice di Lorenzo de Medici, a Careggi, etc. (fol. 132v)

(132r)
Mag[nifi]ca et generosa donna. Dopo le debite racomandatione et cet[era] cet[orum], io sarei venuta alla Ma[gnificen]tia vostra sennò che da parechi giorni in qua sono istata inpedita di malattia, per modo che ancora non mi posso aiutare della persona. Restami a rendere gratie alla humanità vostra di quanto s'è adoperata di queste mie povere fanculle alle quali non resta altra isperanza che la Mag[nificen]tia vostra; et non potendo altrimenti satisfare, continovo meco insieme pregheranno idio che in ogni vostra opera vi exalti. Apresso m'achade colla usata fede ricorrere alla be<ni>gnità vostra; e·lla chagion è che esser io debitore del Chomune di grande quantità di danari per debiti vechi, la magior parte ingiustamente, perché soporto la graveza insù certi beni e quali io non possegho, come posso mostrare. Disiderei, perché intendo si fanno cierti gratie, uscire qualche volta di contumace per non essere ogn'ano gravata. Priegho l'umanità vostra gli piaccia racomandarmi al magnifico Lorenzo che insieme cogli altri sua conpagni voglino intendere lo stato mio et piglare da me quello che posso fare che solo mi resta questa povera chasa et un podere in Val di Sieve di che io ò a nutrichare me con sei fanculli; et oltre a questi debiti vechi, delle graveze nuove mi tocherà l'ano a paghare circha di venticinque fiorini. Pensate dove io mi truovo et altro rifugio che·lla Mag[nificen]tia vostra non mi resta alla quale di nuovo istretamente

---

1. I have not altered the orthography of this text except to introduce modern punctuation and diacritical marks, to resolve abbreviations (in square brackets), and to make one correction (be<ni>gnità).

mi racomando et priegho idio che quella lungho tempo filicemente conservi. In Firenze a dì xxv d'aprile Mccccºlxxv.

Vostra Iacopa donna fu di Franc[esc]o Tanini

Magnificent and generous lady, Madonna Clarice di Lorenzo de' Medici, at Careggi.

Magnificent and generous lady, after the required recommendations, etc. I would have come to your Magnificence if not that for the last several days I have been impeded by illness so that even now I cannot manage on my own. I still have to thank you in your humanity for all you have done on behalf of these poor daughters of mine for whom there is no other hope except Your Magnificence; and, not having any other way of repaying, they pray to God constantly with me that he will exalt you in all your endeavors. Next I must, with my usual trust, turn to your kindness. The reason is that I am in debt to the Comune for a large amount of money for old debts, most of which unjustly, because I am taxed on certain properties which I do not possess, as I can demonstrate. Because I hear that certain debts are being forgiven, I would like to clear myself of this obligation, so as not to be taxed each year. I ask you in your humanity to recommend me to the Magnificent Lorenzo that he and his other companions will understand my situation and take from me what I can give, since all that I have left is this poor house and a farm in the Val di Sieve with which I have to feed myself and six children; and besides these old debts I will have new taxes this year to pay of about twenty-five florins. Think of where I find myself and I have no resort left except your Magnificence, to whom again I strongly recommend myself and I pray to God that he keep you happy for a long time. In Florence, the 25th day of April 1475.

Yours, Jacopa, widow of Francesco Tanini

Appendix 3

Fra Antonio Dolciati's Introductory Letter of Dedication of his *Esposizione della Regola di Sant'Agostino* (Detailed explanation of the Rule of Saint Augustine) to the nuns of the Convent Founded by Antonia Tanini.[1]

Pistola de l'autore

Frate Antonio Dolciati fiorentino eremita augustiniano della observanza della congregazione di Lombardia alle venerande madre e sorelle dilettissime in Cristo del monasterio della Assunta[2] fuori della porta di San Gallo di Firenze del medesimo ordine, congregazione ed observanza, in Cristo salute.

  Costretto dallo obligo ed amore che porto a questa mia santa religione, onorande in Cristo madre e sorelle carissime, dalla quale in sino dal principio della mia adolescenza sono stato già per otto lustri insino al dì di oggi nutrito; e di quelle poche littere che ho imparate istrutto e di tanti buoni ed ammaestramenti ed essempli informato, che beato a me se la metà ne avessi osservati. Imperoché, avendo puerilmente e tre primi lustri di mia vita nel seculo consumati uno e mezo non so in che; e l'altro e mezo in sino in quindici anni (imperoché un lustro è lo spazio di cinque anni) imparare i primi rudimenti grammaticali ed e principii delle ragioni del canto con e mia coetanei cherici nella scuola del nostro duomo di Firenze, dove *etiam* imparai l'ordine de' divini offizi, di poi, essendo di età di quindici ani mesi otto e dì tredici, cioè, a dì 19 di maggio nel 1492, el sabbato precedente

---

1. Florence, Biblioteca Laurenziana, ms. Gaddi 132, cc. 2r-4v. The text of the letter of dedication reproduced here is also available, but in a heavily modernized form, in the Bandini catalogue of the Biblioteca Laurenziana: Angelo Maria Bandini, Supplementum catalogus codicum latinorum Bibliotecae Medicae Laurentianae, II (Florence: Typis Regis, 1797), cols. 144–48. In editing this text I have followed the criteria outlined on pp. 63–64 in the section entitled "Note on Editing the Italian texts."
2. The official name of the convent was Santa Maria della Misericordia, but it is often referred to in the documents as the "Assunta."

la quarta domenica doppo la Pasqua (imperoché io nacqui a dì 6 di settembre nel 1476) detto matuttino in questo convento di San Gallo (del quale oggi corre el decimo anno che non per mia meriti, ma per voluntà d'Iddio e de' mia padri, sono indegnmente priore), presi l'abito di questa santa religione, e insino al dì presente ho portato anni trentasei, mesi tre, infruttuosamente. E insino al fine della vita mia desidero con salute della anima portare. Per l'obligo adunque, dico, e per l'amore che porto e son tenuto portare a questa mia sacra religione, doppo molte e diverse cose da me scritte, e in latino e in vulgare, son costretto a scrivere qualche cosa di quella la quale abbia ad accendere ad amore e devozione di essa quegli che la leggeranno. Né voglio più tardare a fare questo imperoché gli anni mia e le lunghe, varie e grave infermità mi ammoniscono che io presto di questa vita debbo far partita. Non ho voluto ancora questa opera scrivere in lingua latina, come ho scritte le prediche per tutto l'anno *de tempore* e *de sancti*[3] ed el trattato *Della correzione del modo del celebrare le feste mobile* [*De reformatione ritus celebrationis festorum*], e *El millenario*, delle *Inquisizioni sopra e libri de' Re e del Paralipomenon* ed el *Psalmista mutato in laude di Nostra Donna* e altre più nostre operette. Ma l'abbiamo scritta in vulgare volendo così giovare a più persone semplici e idiote e devote. E perché la dedico al vostro devoto collegio el quale quanto è meno di gramatica instrutto tanto è più di devozione ed altre innumerabili virtù ornato.

E così per le vostre fervente orazioni dalla divina grazia aiutato nel scrivere e racorre questa opera de' detti di diversi dottori, farò dua effetti: ed a dua oblighi satisfarò a un tratto. Prima a quello el quale (come ho detto) ho con questa sacra religione e secondariamente a quello che ho con el vostro prefato venerando collegio: al quale più e più anni sono ho desiderato della mia povertà fare qualche presente, quale a tutte voi e a qualunche persona lo leggessi fussi testimonio del mio amore verso di voi. E perché son povero frate e non ho alcuna cosa terrena e materiale sustanza la quale vi possa conferire, voglio che la mia oblazione sia spirituale: cioè la scienza delle cose scritte in questo libro, la quale spero vi debba esser molto più utile, e dare assai maggiore consolazione che se vi offerissi gran sustanza temporale, perché la scienza delle cose spirituale vince ogni temporale richeza.

3. The *Prediche per tutto l'anno* and the *Sermones de Sanctis*.

E se Dio ottimo per sua pietà e vostre devote orazioni mi presterrà vita e sanità, spero in breve farvi un altro presente molto maggiore ed assai più utile che questo, cioè delle prediche che ho raccolte sopra gli Evangeli di tutto l'anno, le quali intendo per vostro amore vulgarizare. A che mi induce prima el massimo amore della buona memoria della prima mia e poi vostra veneranda madre suora Antonia de' Tanini, della quale io nella mia fanciulleza fui maestro, insegnandogli ordinare l'offizio del Signore e lei a me fu madre e maestra nella via d'Iddio, inducendomi continuo al servizio di quello e al disprezo del mondo. Né mai cessò insino a tanto che mi ebbe condutto a questa sacra religione nella quale di grazia ottenne che mi fui posto el suo nome.[4] Imperoché io nel battesimo fui chiamato Francesco.

Questa quasi come una nuova Santa Judith, quanto al Vechio Testamento, o vero quanto al Nuovo, come un'altra Santa Monica, era vedova e in casa di sua madre, madonna Jacopa, e del suo fratello Nicolò Tanini, nella superiora parte di quella si aveva religiosamente e poveramente ordinata una cameretta con el suo oratorio e più libri devoti, e in quella, standosi quasi sempre sola, dì e notte si essercitava in orazioni e sacre lezioni, castigando el suo corpo con assidui digiuni, discipline, vigilie e lacrimose contemplazioni. Continuo sulle sue pudicissime carni portava uno aspro cilizio e sopra quello una dura camicia di stame di che *etiam* erano e sua lenzuoli posti sopra un grosso sacone di paglia. Spesse volte con molta devozione e lacrime si comunicava e molto più spesso si confessava qui nel nostro convento di San Gallo dal padre frate Lattanzio, nobile e gentile uomo sanese della magnifica casa de' Piccolomini, dal quale, essendo lui del detto convento vicario, ed essendo el Reverendo priore frate Benigno da Genova ito a capitulo a Crema, io ricevetti l'abito di questa sacra religione. E perché aveva grande notizia della Bibblia e singulare grazia in fare versi vulgari in rima, compose[5] più e più devote laude di diversi santi, tra le quali è quella devotissima del Corpo di Cristo, la quale lei soleva dire con grande devozione prima che si comunicassi. Questa di sua propria mano scritta io ho ancora appresso di me e come un

---

4. In the right margin is written in red "Suora Antonia de Tanini: & sua vita religiossima" (Sister Antonia de' Tanini: and her very religious life), a rubric that indicates the point in the text at which Dolciati begins to recount her life.

5. In the right margin, written in red: "Opere di quella" (Her works).

gioiello di mia cara madre tengo. Compose *etiam* molte belle e devote rapresentazioni, di Joseph, di David e Saul, del figliuolo prodigo e assai altre delle quali ora non mi ricordo, emperoché sono più di trentasei anni non le ho vedute. In questo fu da Santa Monica differente che non fece mai figliuoli corporali, ma bene (come ho detto) me spiritualmente a Cristo rigenerò nella religione, benché in quella poco bene abbia fatto.

Di poi, non potendo patire di stare tra seculari, avendo già per più anni prima ricevuto l'abito delle mantellate di Santa Monica per le mani del reverendo padre maestro Mariano, predicatore eccellentissimo e fundator del detto nostro convento di San Gallo; e in quello a sue spese fabricata una cappella intitulata alla prefatta Santa Monica, cominciò a ragunare alcune devote donne a servire a Dio nel detto abito con le quale religiosamente visse alquanto tempo nel venerabile monasterio di Annalena di Firenze, insino a tanto che riscossa la sua dota, di quella comperò la casa ed el terreno nel quale voi abitate, e in essa entrò ad abitare con le sua compagne el dì di Berlingaccio nel 1501, che fu quello anno a dì 18 di febraio.⁶ Costì visse con gran fervore di spirito insino a dì ventiuno di settembre del medesimo anno, nel qual dì, lasciando a tutte le sue figliuole e compagne grande essemplo di santità, dall'ottimo Iddio rimuneratore di tutte le opere buone (come per le sue buone opere credere possiamo e dobbiamo), commutata la presente morte con la futura vita, fu in cielo beatificata e in terra el suo corpo con molte lacrime e reverenzia fu sepulto in San Gallo, nella predetta cappella di Santa Monica. Doppo la sua morte, a poco a poco, più in bontà ancora che in numero (quantunche ancora in gran numero come si vede), per grazia d'Iddio di dì in dì insino al dì d'oggi in grande osservanza con molta umiltà, obbedienza, povertà, castità, devozione, carità, e altre assai virtù cotesto vostro convento è cresciuto per le quale diverse virtù molte delle vostre sorelle già son fatte beate, le vestigie delle quali, come voi avete cominciato a seguire così vi essorto quanto posso a perseverare, acciochè al fine meritate con quelle da Dio in cielo esser glorificate. Per eccitarvi dunche a questo, la presente mia opera vi ho voluto dedicare [...].⁷

6. See Introduction, n80.

7. The rest of the prefatory letter presents an outline of the work that follows, including important aspects of the history of the Augustinians and a study of the Rule of Saint Augustine.

Scritto nel convento di San Gallo nella cella del Priore a dì 19 di agosto 1528 a ore dodici.

Translated by Elissa Weaver

(2r–4r)
Author's Letter

  Fra Antonio Dolciati, Florentine, Observant Augustinian Hermit of the Congregation of Lombardy, to the most dear reverend mothers and sisters in Christ of the convent of the Assunta, outside the Gate of San Gallo in Florence, of the same order, congregation and observance, greetings in Christ.

  Most dear reverend mothers and sisters in Christ, I am obliged by the bond and love that I bear to this holy religious order of mine, by which I have been nourished for well eight lustrums, from my earliest adolescence until today, and I am armed with that little smattering of letters that I have gained, and informed by so many good lessons and examples that I would be happy had I observed the half of them. Since I have consumed the first three lustrums of my life in the world in childish things, one and a half doing I know not what, and the other and a half until I was fifteen (since a lustrum is the space of five years) in learning the first rudiments of grammar and the principles of the systems of singing with the other clerics of my age in the cathedral school in Florence, where I also learned the order of the divine office, then, at fifteen years, eight months, and thirteen days, that is, on 19 May 1492, the Saturday before the fourth Sunday after Easter (since I was born on 6 September 1476), that morning in this convent of San Gallo (of which, today marks the tenth year, not for my merits but by God's will and that of my fathers, I am the unworthy prior), I took the habit of this sacred religious order, and I have today worn it thirty-six years, three months, fruitlessly, and which until the end of my life I wish to wear in spiritual health. Then, for the bond, I say, and for the love that I bear and am held to bear for this holy religious order of mine, after many and diverse things I have written, in Latin and in the vernacular, I am obliged to write something about it which will inflame readers with love and devotion for it. Nor do I wish to delay any longer doing this, since my years and long, various, and grave illnesses warn me that soon I must depart from this life. Nor did I want to write this work in the Latin language, as I have written my sermons for the entire year *de tempore* and *de sancti* and the treatise on the correction of the time to celebrate the moveable feasts, and *The Millennium, Inquiries into the Books of Kings and Paralipomenon*, and the *Psalmist Rewritten as Hymns to Our Lady*, and other little works of ours. But we have written it in the vernacular, wanting in this way to be of benefit to many simple, unlettered, and devout persons. And because I dedicate it to your devout college which, for all that it is without Latin learning, it is all the more adorned by devotion and innumerable virtues.

And so, because of your fervent prayers, I have received divine aid in writing and putting together this work composed of that of diverse doctors [of the Church], I will achieve two effects and will satisfy two obligations at the same time. First, that which (as I have said) I owe this holy religious order and, in the second place, that which I have with your aforementioned venerable college, to which I have for many years desired to offer some gift, which to all of you and to any other person who read it, might bear witness to the love I have for you. And because I am a poor friar and have no earthy and material goods to give you, I want my offering to be spiritual, that is, the knowledge provided by the things written in this book, which, I hope, will be of much greater use to you and give you much greater consolation than if I were to offer you a great amount of temporal goods, because the knowledge of spiritual things is far better than any temporal wealth. And if the mercy of our great God and your devout prayers will earn me life and health, I hope in a short time to offer you another much greater and more useful present than this, that is, some sermons that I have collected on the Gospels for the entire year, which I intend to translate into the vernacular out of love for you. First of all I am induced to do this because of the greatest love I have for the dear memory of first mine and then your venerable Reverend Mother Antonia de' Tanini, whose teacher I was in my youth, instructing her in the Lord's holy office, and she to me was mother and teacher in the way of God, urging me continuously to serve Him and to disdain the world. She did not cease until she had led me to this holy religious order in which, in thanks, I was able to take her name, since my baptismal name was Francesco.

Like a modern Saint Judith, if we consider the Old Testament, or another Saint Monica, if the New, she was a widow. In the house of her mother, Madonna Jacopa, and her brother Niccolò Tanini, on the upper floor she had set up a small room, a poor and a spiritual place, with an oratory and many devotional books, and there, almost always alone, day and night she dedicated herself to prayer and reading religious works, castigating her body with strict fasting, corporal punishments, vigils, and tearful contemplations. On her most chaste flesh she continually wore a harsh hair shirt and over it a rough blouse of wool, and of this her sheets were also made, which were put on a large sack of straw. Often, with much devotion and tears she took communion, and even more often she went to confession here in our convent of San Gallo to Father Fra Lattanzio, a noble Sienese gentleman of the magnificent house of the Piccolomini. And it was from him, since he was vicar of that convent and since the Prior, Reverend Fra Benigno da Genova, was away at the chapter meeting in Crema, that I received the habit of this holy religious order. And because she knew the Bible very well and wrote verse in the vernacular with singular grace, she wrote many, many devout *laude*, to various saints, among which there is a most devout one on the Body of Christ [*Corpus Christi*], which she used to recite with great devotion before taking communion. I still have this one with me, in her own hand, and I keep it as one of my dear mother's jewels. She also composed many beautiful and devout plays [*rappresentazioni*] on Joseph, on David and Saul, on the Prodigal Son, and many others which I do not now recall, since it has been more than thirty-six years since I have seen them. In one thing she was different from Saint Monica: she never gave birth to children, but she did (as I have said) cause me to be reborn spiritually to Christ in my religious order, even though I have achieved little of worth.

Then, unable to suffer living among lay persons, and, having earlier received the habit of the *ammantellate* of Saint Monica from the hands of Reverend Father *maestro* Fra Mariano, most excellent preacher and founder of our aforementioned convent of San Gallo, there, at her expense, she built a chapel dedicated to the above-mentioned Saint Monica. She began to gather around her some devout women to serve God in that habit, and with them she lived religiously for some time in the venerable convent of Annalena in Florence, until when, having gotten her dowry back, she bought with it the house and land where you live; and there she entered to live with her companions on the day of Berlingaccio 1501, which that year was on 18 February. There she lived with great fervor of spirit until on 21 September of the same year, that day, leaving her daughters and companions a grand example of sanctity, she was repaid by the highest God who repays all good works, (as for her good works we can and must believe) she exchanged the present death for the future life and was blessed in heaven, and on earth her body, with many tears and reverence, was buried in San Gallo in the aforementioned chapel of Saint Monica. After her death, little by little, greater in goodness than in number (yet still in good number as we see), by the grace of God, from day to day until this day, in great observance, with much humility, obedience, poverty, chastity, devotion, charity, and many other virtues that convent of yours has grown. Because of their many virtues, many of your sisters have been rewarded in heaven, and, as you have already begun to follow their paths, I exhort you to persevere, so that in the end you will, with them, be rewarded by God with glory in heaven. Thus, in order to inspire you to this end, I have decided to dedicate this work to you [...]

Written at the friary of San Gallo in the Prior's cell, on 19 August 1528, at the twelfth hour. [...]

(Fra Antonio Dolciati, 19 August 1528)

Editor's Bibliography

Primary Texts

Dolciati, Antonio (Fra). *De tribus regulis S. Augustini* [*Esposizione della Regula di S. Agostino*]. Florence, Biblioteca Laurenziana, manuscript Gaddi 132. Florence, 19 August 1528.

Muzi, Piero di Mariano. *Rappresentazione del vitello sagginato*, in *Nuovo corpus*. Edited by Nerida Newbigin. Bologna, Commissione per i testi di lingua, 1983, 29–55.

Pulci, Antonia Tanini. *La rapresentatione di Sancta Domitilla* [Florence: Antonio Miscomini, ca. 1490].

———. *La rapresentatione di Sancta Domitilla* [Florence: Antonio Miscomini, ca. 1495].

———. *La rapresentatione di Sancta Guglielma* [Florence: Antonio Miscomini, ca. 1490].

———. *La rapresentatione di Sancta Guglielma* [Florence: Bartolomeo de' Libri, ca. 1495].

———. *La rapresentatione di Sancto Francesco* [Florence: Antonio Miscomini, ca. 1490].

———. *La rapresentatione di San Francesco* [Florence: Bartolomeo de' Libri, ca. 1495].

———. *La rapresentatione della distructione di Saul & del pianto di Davit*. [Florence: Bartolomeo de' Libri, ca. 1495]

———. *La rapresentatione della distrutione di Saul e del pianto di Davit*. Florence: per Zanobi Tozi da Prato, May 1547.

———. *La rapresentatione della distruttione di Saul e del pianto di Davit*. Florence: Giunta, 1559.

———. *La rapresentatione del figliuol prodigo*. [Florence, ca. 1550].

———. *La rapresentatione del figliuolo prodigo*. n.p., n.d.

———. *La rapresentatione del figliuol prodigo*. Florence: ad istanza de Iacopo Chiti, 1572.

Pulci, Bernardo. *La rapresentatione di Barlaam e Iosafat*. [Florence: Antonio Miscomini, ca. 1490].

———. *La rapresentatione divota di Barlaam e Iosafat*. [Florence: Antonio Miscomini, ca. 1495].

———. *La rappresentatione di Barlaam e Josafat.* Florence: Tubini e Ghirlandi: per Francesco di Giovanni Benvenuto, 24 March 1516.

———. *Passione di Cristo.* Florence: Francesco Bonaccorsi, 1490.

———. *Passione di Cristo.* n.p., n.d. [incunable].

———. *Passione di Cristo* with *Il pianto di Maria Maddalena.* Bologna: Bartolomeo Bonardo, 1551.

Linguistic Resources

Accademia della Crusca. *Opera del vocabolario italiano.* http://tlio.ovi.cnr.it/voci.

———. *Vocabolario degli accademici della Crusca.* Florence: Tipografia Galileiana di M. Cellini e comp., 1863–1923.

Alighieri, Dante. *La commedia.* Edizione critica. Edited by Giorgio Petrocchi. 4 vols. Milan: Mondadori, 1966–67.

[Battaglia, Salvatore]. *Grande dizionario della lingua italiana.* Turin: UTET, 1961–2004.

Biblioteca Italiana. http://bibliotecaitaliana.it. Rome: University of Rome, La Sapienza.

Boccaccio, Giovanni. *Tutte le opere.* Edited by Vittore Branca. Milan: Mondadori, 1964–.

Cellini, Benvenuto. *La Vita, scritta per lui medesimo.* 2 vols. Ed. Enrico Carrara. Turin: UTET, 1926–27.

Fanfani, Pietro. *Vocabolario dell'uso toscano.* 1863. A facsimile. Florence: Casa Editrice Le lettere, 1976.

Gelli, Giovan Battista. *Opere.* Ed. A. C. Alesina. Naples: Fulvio Rossi, 1970.

Giambullari, Bernardo. *Rime inedite o rare.* http://www.bibliotecaitaliana.it.

Liber Liber. Biblioteca digitale (2006 version). http://wwww.liberliber.it.

Machiavelli, Niccolò. *Tutte le opere.* Ed. Mario Martelli. Florence: Sansoni, 1971.

Macinghi Strozzi, Alessandra. *Lettere di una gentildonna fiorentina del secolo XV ai figliuoli esuli.* Ed. Cesare Guasti. Florence: G. D. Sansoni, 1877. http://colet.uchicago.edu.proxy.uchicago.edu/cgi-bin/iww.

Manni, Paola. "Ricerca sui tratti fonetici e morphologici del fiorentino quattrocentesco." *Studi di grammatica italiana* 8 (1979), 115-71.
Medici, Lorenzo de'. *Tutte le opere*. Ed. Paolo Orvieto. Rome: Salerno Editrice, 1992.
Nannucci, Vincenzio. *Analisi critica dei verbi italiani*. Florence: Felice Le Monnier, 1843.
Piovano Arlotto [Arlotto Mainardi]. *Motti e facezie del Piovano Arlotto*. Ed. Gianfranco Folena. Milan-Naples: Ricciardi, 1953.
Pulci, Luigi. *Morgante e lettere*. Ed. Dominico De Robertis. Florence: Sansoni, 1962.
_____. *Opere minori*. Ed. Paolo Orvieto. Milan: Mursia, 1986.
Rohlfs, Gerhard. *Grammatica storica della lingua italiana e dei suoi dialetti. Morfologia*. Third edition, rev. and enl. Turin, Einaudi, 1968.
Tavoni, Mirko. *Storia della lingua italiana. Il Quattrocento*. Bologna: Il Mulino, 1992.

Works Consulted

Acta Sanctorum. Paris, V. Palmé, [etc.], 1863–.
Baccini, Giuseppe. "I poeti fratelli Pulci in Mugello e il *Driadeo d'amore*." *Giotto* 2 (1903): 352-63, 371-82; *Giotto* 3 (1904), 405-11.
Banfi, Luigi. *Sacre rappresentazioni del Quattrocento*. Turin: UTET, 1963.
Belcari, Feo, Lorenzo de' Medici, Francesco D'Albizzo, Castellano Castellani, et al. *Laude spirituali*. Florence: Presso Molini e Cecchi dietro il Duomo, 1863.
Beltrami, Pietro G. *La Metrica italiana*. Bologna: Il Mulino, 1991.
Bertoli, Gustavo. "Documenti su Bartolomeo de' Libri e i suoi primi discendenti." *Rara Volumina* 1 (2001), 19-56.
_____. "Per la biografia di Bartolomeo de' Libri," in A. Tura. *Edizioni Fiorentine*. Appendix 2: 77-83.
Biblioteca agiografica italiana (BAI): repertorio di testi e manoscritti, secoli XIII-XV. Ed. Jacques Dalarun et al. 2 vols. Florence: Edizioni del Galluzzo, 2003.

Bibliographia augustiniana cum notis biographicis Scriptores Itali. 4 vols in 1. Florence: Typis Florentinis Librariae aeditricis, 1929–37.

Black, Nancy B. *Medieval Narratives of Accused Queens.* Gainesville: University Press of Florida, 2003.

Bonfadini, Antonio. *Listoria de Santa Guglielma fiola delo Re dangalterra, et moglie delo Re dungaria* in *Vite di S. Guglielma regina d'Ungheria e di S. Eufrasia vergine romana scritte da frate Antonio Bonfadini.* Ed. G. Ferraro. Scelta di Curiosità letterarie inedite o rare dal secolo XIII al XVII in appendice alla Collezione di Opere inedite o rare, 159. Bologna: Gaetano Romagnoli, 1878, 1–67.

Bonfantini, Mario, ed. *Le sacre rappresentazioni italiane. Raccolta di testi dal secolo XIII al secolo XVI.* Milan: Bompiani, [1942].

Bongi, Salvatore, ed. *Lettere di Luigi Pulci a Lorenzo il Magnifico e ad altri.* Second edition enl. Lucca: Tipografia Guasti, 1886.

Böniger, Lorenz. "I primi passi della stampa a Firenze: nuovi documenti d'archivio," in A. Tura. *Edizioni fiorentine*, Appendix 1, 67–75.

Bruni, Francesco. *L'Italiano. Elementi di storia della lingua e della cultura.* Turin: UTET, 1984.

Bryce, Judith. "'Or altra via mi convien cercare': Marriage, Salvation, and Sanctity in Antonia Tanini Pulci's *Rappresentazione di Santa Guglielma*" in *Theatre, Opera, and Performance in Italy from the Fifteenth Century to the Present: Essays in Honour of Richard Andrews.* Ed. Brian Richardson, Simon Gilson, and Catherine Keen. Occasional Papers, 6. Leeds: The Society for Italian Studies, 2004, 23–38.

_____. "Adjusting the Canon for Later Fifteenth-Century Florence: The Case of Antonia Pulci," in *The Renaissance Theatre. Texts, Performance, Design.* Ed. Christopher Cairns. 2 vols. Burlington, VT: Ashgate, 1999, 1:133–45.

_____. "Les livres des Florentines: Reconsidering Women's Literacy in Quattrocento Florence," in *At the Margins: Minority Groups in Premodern Italy.* Ed. Stephen J. Milner. Minneapolis: University of Minnesota Press, 2005, 133–61.

Callahan, Leslie Abend. "The Torture of Saint Apollonia: Deconstructing Fouquet's Martrydom Stage." *Studies in Iconography* 16 (1994), 119–38.

Capelli, Adriano. *Cronologia, cronografia e calendario perpetuo.* Fifth edition rev. Milan: Hoepli, 1983.

Cardini, Franco. "La figura di Francesco d'Assisi nella 'Rappresentatione di Sancto Francesco' di Antonia Pulci," in *Il Francescanesimo e il teatro medievale.* Atti del convegno nazionale di studi, San Miniato, 1982. Castelfiorentino: Società storica della Valdelsa, 1984, 195–207.

Carnesecchi, Carlo. "Per la biografia di Luigi Pulci. *Archivio Storico Italiano.* Fifth series, 17 (1896), 371–79.

Carney, Emanuela. "Antonia Pulci's *Rappresentazione di Santa Domitilla* and the Defense of Virginity in Quattrocento Florence," in *Scenes from Italian Convent Life: An Anthology of Theatrical Texts and Contexts.* Ed. Elissa B. Weaver. Ravenna, Italy: Longo Editore, 2009, 11–36.

The Catholic Encyclopedia. http://www.newadvent.org/cathen/

Carrai, Stefano. *Le muse dei Pulci: studi su Luca e Luigi Pulci.* Naples: Guida Editore, 1985.

Cattaneo, Enrico, S. J. "L'interpretazione di Lc 15, 11–32 nei Padri della Chiesa," in G Galli, ed. *Interpretazione e invenzione*, 69–96.

Cicali, Gianni. "L'Occultamento del principe. Lorenzo il Magnifico e il *Barlaam e Josafat* di Bernardo Pulci." *Quaderni d'Italianistica* 27:2 (2006), 57–70.

Cionacci, Francesco. "Sopra le rime sacre del magnifico Lorenzo de' Medici ... osservazioni," in *Rime sacre del magnifico Lorenzo de' Medici.* Second edition. Bergamo: Pietro Lancellotti, 1760, v–xxvii.

Cioni, Alfredo. *Bibliografia delle sacre rappresentazioni.* Florence: Sansoni Antiquariato, 1961.

Colomb de Batines, Paul. *Bibliografia delle antiche rappresentazioni sacre e profane stampate nei secoli XV e XVI.* 1852. Rpt. Milan: Görlich, ca. 1958.

Cox, Virginia. *Women's Writing in Italy 1400–1650.* Baltimore: Johns Hopkins University Press, 2008.

Crabb, Ann. "'If I could write:' Margherita Datini and Letter Writing, 1385–1410." *Renaissance Quarterly* 60:4 (2007), 1170–1206.

d'Alençon, Èdouard. *Frère Jacqueline, recherches historiques sur Jacopa de Settesoli, l'amie de Saint-François*. Paris: Société et Librairie Saint-François d'Assise, 1927 and Rome: Postulation Générale des f.f. m.m. Capucins, 1927.

Dalle Celle, Giovanni. *Lettere, Giovanni dalle Celle, Luigi Marsili*. Ed. Francesco Giambonini. 2 vols. Florence: Olschki, 1991.

D'Ancona, Alessandro. *Origini del teatro italiano*. 2 vols. 1891. 2nd edition, rev. and enl. A facsimile. Rome: Bardi Editore, 1971.

D'Ancona, Alessandro, ed. *Sacre rappresentazioni dei secoli XIV, XV e XVI*. 3 vols. Florence: Successori Le Monnier, 1872.

Dominici, Giovanni. *Regola del governo di cura familiare*. Ed. Donato Salvi. Florence: Garinei, 1860.

_____. *Regola del governo di cura familiare, parte quarta, On the Education of Children*. Trans. Arthur Basil Coté. Washington, DC: The Catholic University of America, 1927.

Dizionario biografico degli Italiani. Rome: Istituto della Enciclopedia italiana, 1960–

Dizionario degli istituti di perfezione. Rome: Edizioni Paoline, 1974–2003.

Doglio, Federico. *Teatro in Europa*. Milan: Garzanti, 1982–

Eisenbichler, Konrad. *The Boys of the Archangel Raphael: A Youth Confraternity in Florence, 1411–1785*. Toronto: University of Toronto Press, 1998.

_____. "Confraternities and Carnival: The Context of Lorenzo de' Medici's Rappresentazione di SS. Giovanni e Paolo," in *Medieval Drama on the Continent of Europe*. Ed. Clifford Davidson and John H. Stroupe. Kalamazoo: Medieval Institute Publications-Western Michigan University, 1993, 128–39.

_____. "From *sacra rappresentazione* to *commedia spirituale*: Three Prodigal Son Plays." *Bibliothèque d'Humanisme et Renaissance* 45 (1983), 107–13.

Encyclopaedia Britannica Online. http://www.britannica.com.

Falvey, Dávid. "A Lady Wandering in a Faraway Land: The Central European Queen/Princess Motif in Italian Heretical Cults." *Annual of Medieval Studies at CEU* 8 (2002), 157–79.

———. "Santa Guglielma, regina d'Ungheria: Culto di una pseudo-santa d'Ungheria in Italia. *Nuova Corvina: Rivista di Italianistica* 9 (2001), 116–22.

———. "Szent Erzsébet, Szent Vilma és a magyar királyi származás mint toposz Itáliában (Saint Elizabeth, Saint Guglielma and the Hungarian Royal Origin as a Topos in Italy, with English summary). *Aetas* 1 (2008), 64–76.

Francis of Assisi, St. [attr.]. *Fioretti, di S. Francesco*. Ed. Guido Battelli. Turin: UTET, 1929.

Ferrigni, Mario. "San Franceco e il teatro." *Nuova Antologia* 63 (1928), 207–20.

Flamini, Francesco. "La vita e le liriche di Bernardo Pulci." *Il Propugnatore*. New Series, 1 (1888), 217–48.

Fusco, Vittorio. "Narrazione e dialogo nella parabola detta del figliol prodigo (Lc 15, 11–32)" in G. Galli, ed. *Interpretazione e invenzione*, 17–67.

Galli, Giuseppe, ed. *Interpretazione e invenzione. La parabola del Figliol Prodigo tra interpretazioni scientifiche e invenzioni artistiche*. Atti dell'ottavo colloquio sulla interpretazione. Macerata, 17–19 marzo 1986. Genoa: Mariotti, 1987.

Gehl, Paul. "Watermark Evidence for the Competitive Practices of Antonio Miscomini." *The Library*. Sixth series, 15 (1993), 281–305.

Ghinassi, Ghino. *Il volgare letterario nel Quattrocento e le* Stanze *del Poliziano*. Florence: Felice Le Monnier, 1957.

Giorgi, Emilio. "Le piú antiche bucoliche volgari." *Giornale storico della letteratura italiana* 66 (1915), 140–52.

Il Grande libro dei santi. Dizionario enciclopedico. Ed. Elio Guerriero and Dorino Tuniz. 4 vols. (dir. Claudio Leonardi, Andrea Riccardi, and Gabriella Zarri). Cinisiello Balsamo (Milan): Edizioni di San Paolo, 1998.

Gutiérrez, p. David, O.S.A., "Testi e note su Mariano da Genazzano." *Analecta augustiniana* 32 (1968), 117–204.

Heiserman, Arthur R. *The Novel Before the Novel: Essays and Discussions about the Beginnings of Prose Fiction in the West*. Chicago: University of Chicago Press, 1977.

Herlihy, David. "Tuscan Names, 1200–1530." *Renaissance Quarterly* 41:4 (1988), 561–82.

Hirsh, John C., ed. *Barlam and Iosaphat: A Middle English Life of Buddha, edited from MS Peterhouse 257*. Oxford: Oxford University Press, 1986.

Jerome, St. *A Select Library of Nicene and Post-Nicene fathers of the Christian Church*. Ed. Philip Schaff and Henry Wace. 2nd series, vol 6. New York: The Christian Literature Company, 1890–1900.

Jacobus de Voragine. *The Golden Legend. Readings on the Saints*. Trans. William Granger Ryan. Princeton: Princeton University Press, 1993, 1: 308–09.

Kent, F. W. "New Light on Lorenzo de' Medici's Convent at Porta San Gallo." *Burlington Magazine* 124 (1982), 292–94.

Kirshner, Julius. "Pursuing honor while avoiding sin: the Monte delle doti of Florence." *Studi Senesi* 87 (1977), 175–256.

———. "The Morning After: Collecting Monte Dowries in Renaissance Florence," in *From Florence to the Mediterranean and Beyond: Essays in Honor of Anthony Molho*. Ed. Diogo Ramada Curto, Eric R. Dursteler, Julius Kirshner and Francesca Trivellato. Florence: Leo S. Olschki, 2009, 1: 29–61.

Kirshner, Julius and Anthony Molho. "The Dowry Fund and the Marriage Market in Early Quattrocento Florence." *Journal of Modern History* 50 (1978), 403–38.

Klapisch Zuber, Christiane. "The Name 'Remade': The Transmission of Given Names in Florence in the Fourteenth and Fifteenth Centuries" in *Women, Family, and Ritual in Renaissance Italy*. Trans. Lydia G. Cochrane. Chicago: University of Chicago Press, 1985, 283–309. Originally published as "Le nom 'refait': La transmission des prenoms à Florence (XIVe–XVIe siecles)." *L'Homme* 20:4 (1980), 77–104.

Lommatzsch, Erhard, ed. *Beiträge zur älteren Italianischen Volksdictung untersuchungen und texte*. N. 17. Band IV. 2 teil: *Sacre Rappresentazioni*. Berlin: Akademie Verlag, 1963.

Lowe, Kate (K. J. P.). "Female Strategies for Success in a Male-ordered World: the Benedictine Convent of Le Murate in Florence in the Fifteenth and Sixteenth Centuries." *Studies in Church History* 27 (1990), 209–21.

―――. "Patronage and Territoriality in Sixteenth-century Florence." *Renaissance Studies* 7 (1993), 258-71.

―――. *Nuns' Chronicles and Convent Culture in Renaissance and Counter-Reformation Italy.* Cambridge: Cambridge University Press, 2003.

Lumini, Apollo. *Le sacre rappresentazioni italiane dei secoli XIV, XV e XVI. Saggio critico.* Palermo: Tipografia di Pietro Montana & Comp., 1877.

Mancini, Andrea. "Francesco nella lauda e nella sacra rappresentazione," in *Il Francescanesimo e il teatro medievale.* Atti del convegno nazionale di studi, San Miniato, 1982. Castelfiorentino: Società storica della Valdelsa, 1984, 135-47.

Martelli, Mario. *Letteratura fiorentina del Quattrocento. Il filtro degli anni Sessanta.* Firenze: Casa Editrice Le Lettere, 1996.

Martines, Lauro. *Strong Words: Writing and Social Strain in the Italian Renaissance.* Baltimore: Johns Hopkins University Press, 2001.

Menichetti, Aldo. *Metrica italiana. Fondamenti metrici, prosodia, rima.* Padua: Antenore, 1993.

Molho, Anthony. "Names, Memory, Public Identity in Late Medieval Florence" in *Art, Memory and Family in Renaissance Florence.* Ed. Giovanni Capelli and Patricia Rubin. Cambridge: Cambridge University Press, 2000, 238-50.

―――. *Marriage Alliance in Late Medieval Florence.* Cambridge, MA: Harvard University Press, 1994.

Molinari, Cesare. *Spettacoli fiorentini del Quattrocento. Contributi allo studio delle sacre rappresentazioni.* Venice: Neri Pozza, 1961.

Mombritius, Boninus. *Sanctuarium seu Vitae Sanctorum.* Hildesheim: Georg Olms Verlag, 1978.

Najemy, John. *A History of Florence, 1200-1575.* Oxford: Blackwell Publishing, 2006.

Neri, Ferdinando. "Studi sul teatro antico italiana. Le parabole." *Giornale storico della letteratura italiana* 65 (1915), 1-44.

Newbigin, Nerida. *Nuovo corpus di sacre rappresentazioni fiorentine del Quattrocento.* Bologna, Commissione per i testi di lingua, 1983.

―――. "Plays, Printing and Publishing, 1485-1500: Florentine sacre rappresentazioni." *La Bibliofilia* 90 (1988), 269-96.

———. "Agata, Apollonia, and Other Martyred Virgins: Did Florentines Really See These Plays Performed?" in *European Medieval Drama 1997. Papers from the Second International conference on 'Aspects of European Medieval Drama,'* Camerino, 4–6 July 1997. Ed. Sydney Higgins. Camerino: Centro Audiovisivi e Stampa Università di Camerino, 1998, 175–97.

———. "'Word Made Flesh.' The *Rappresentazione* of Mysteries and Miracles in Fifteenth-Century Florence," in *Christianity and the Renaissance: Image and Religious Imagination in the Quattrocento.* Ed. Timothy Verdon and John Henderson. Syracuse: Syracuse University Press, 19942.

———. *Feste d'oltrarno: Plays in Churches in Fifteenth-Century Florence.* 2 vols. Florence: Olschki, 1996.

Newman, Barbara. "The Heretic Saint: Guglielma of Bohemia, Milan, and Brunate." *Church History* 74:1 (2005), 1-38.

Nigro, Salvatore S. "Pulci e la cultura medicea," in *Il Quattrocento.* Bari: Laterza, 1972, 5–89.

Nogarola, Isotta. "Dialogue on Adam and Eve," in *Complete Writings.* Ed. and trans. Margaret L. King and Diana Robin. The Other Voice in Early Modern Europe. Chicago: University of Chicago Press, 2004, 138–58.

Orvieto, Paolo. "Luigi Pulci," in *Storia della letteratura italiana. Il Quattrocento.* Rome: Salerno Editrice, 1996, 3: 405–55.

———. "Lorenzo de' Medici e l'umanesimo toscano," in *Storia della letteratura italiana. Il Quattrocento.* Rome: Salerno Editrice, 1996, 3:295–403.

Paatz, Walter and Elizabeth. *Die Kirchen von Florenz: ein Kunstgeschichtliches Handbuch.* 6 vols. Frankfurt a. M.: V. Vestermann, 1952–55.

Paci, G. "Domenico Cavalca, volgarizzatore della *Legenda maior*." *Italia francescana* 44 (1969), 322–28.

Palandri, Eletto, don. "Rappresentazioni sanfrancescane" *Studi francescani* 23. New series, 12 (1926), 413–28.

Pellecchia, Linda. "Untimely Death, Unwilling Heirs: The Early History of Giuliano da Sangallo's Unfinished Palace for Giuliano Gondi." *Mitteilungen des Kunsthistorischen Institutes in Florenz* 47 (2003/1), 77–117.

Perini, Davide. *Un emulo di fra Girolamo Savonarola: fra Mariano da Genazzano.* Rome: Tipografia dell'Unione Editrice, 1917.

Poli, Liliana. "Contributi sopra Bartolomeo de' Libri." *La Bibliofilia* 61 (1949), 1: 9–27.

Ponte, Giovanni. *Attorno a Savonarola. Castellano Castellani e la sacra rappresentazione fiorentina tra '400 e '500.* Genoa: Fratelli Pagano Tipografi Editori, 1969.

———, ed. *Sacre rappresentazioni fiorentine del Quattrocento.* Milan: Marzorati Editore, 1974.

Preyer, Brenda. "The Florentine *Casa*" and "The *acquaio* (Wall Fountain) and Fireplace in Florence," in *At Home in Renaissance Italy.* Ed. M. Afmar-Wollheim and F. Dennis. London: V & A Publications, 2006, 34–49; 284–87.

Procacci, Ugo. *Studio sul Catasto fiorentino.* Florence: Leo S. Olschki Editore, 1996.

Pulci, Antonia. *Florentine Drama for Convent and Festival.* Trans. James Wyatt Cook and ed. James Wyatt and Barbara Collier Cook. The Other Voice in Early Modern Europe. Chicago: The University of Chicago Press, 1996.

Pulci, Luigi. *Morgante e lettere.* Ed. Domenico de Robertis. Florence: Sansoni, 1962.

———. *Morgante. The Epic Adventures of Orlando and His Giant Friend Morgante.* Trans. Joseph Tusiani, ed. Edoardo A. Lebano. Bloomington and Indianapolis: Indiana University Press, 1998.

Pullia, Anna. "Due Guglielme per una drammaturga. Guglielma d'Ungheria e Guglielma la Boema nell'ottica teatrale di Antonia Pulci." Tesi di laurea, University of Florence, 2005.

Quadrio, Francesco Saverio. *Della storia e della ragion d'ogni poesia.* Vol. 3. Milan: Francesco Agnelli, 1744.

Repetti, Emanuele. *Dizionario geografico fisico-storico della Toscana.* 6 vols. Florence: Allegrini e Mazzoni, 1833–46.

Richa, Giuseppe. *Notizie istoriche delle chiese fiorentine.* 10 vols. Florence: Stamperia di Pietro Gaetano Viviani, 1754–62.

Rhodes, Dennis. *Gli annali tipografici fiorentini del XV secolo.* Florence: Olschki, 1988.

———. *La stampa a Firenze 1471–1550, omaggio a Roberto Ridolfi.* Ed. Dennis Rhodes. Florence: Olschki, 1984.

Ridolfi, Roberto. *La stampa in Firenze nel secolo XV.* Florence: Olschki, 1958.

Rossi, Vittorio. *Il Quattrocento.* Third edition, rev. Milan: Vallardi, 1938.

Sonet, Jean. *Le roman de Barlaam et Josaphat, I: Recherches sur la tradition manuscripte latine et française.* Namur: Bibliothèque de la Faculté de philosophie et lettres de Namur and Paris: Édition J. Vrin, 1949.

Stallini, Sophie. "Du religieux au politique: la *Sacra Rappresentazione* chez Antonia et Bernardo Pulci." *Arzanà. Cahier de littérature médiévale italienne* 11 (2005). Special issue *La poésie politique dans l'Italie médiévale.* Ed. Anna Fontes Baratto, Marina Marietti and Claude Perrus, 327–76.

Strocchia, Sharon. *Nuns and Nunneries in Renaissance Florence.* Baltimore: Johns Hopkins University Press, 2009.

———. "Naming a Nun: Spiritual Exemplars and Corporate Identity in Florentine Convents, 1450–1530," in *Society and Individual in Renaissance Florence.* Ed. William J. Connell. Berkeley: University of California Press, 2002, 215–40.

———. "Taken into Custody: Girls and Convent Guardianship in Renaissance Florence." *Renaissance Studies* 17:2 (2003), 177–200.

Testaverde, Anna Maria and Anna Maria Evangelista. *Sacre rappresentazioni manoscritte e a stampa conservate nella biblioteca nazionale central di Firenze, Inventario.* Florence: Giunta Regionale Toscana Editrice Bibliografica, 1988.

Tornabuoni, Lucrezia. *Le laudi di Lucrezia de' Medici.* Ed. Guglielmo Volpi. Pistoia: Flori, 1900.

———. *Poemetti sacri.* Ed. Fulvio Pezzarossa. Florence: Olschki, 1978.

———. *Sacred Narratives.* Ed. and trans. Jane Tylus. The Other Voice in Early Modern Europe. Chicago: University of Chicago Press, 2001.

Toscani, Bernard, ed. *Le laude dei Bianchi.* Florence: Libreria Editrice Fiorentina, 1979.

Toschi, Paolo. *L'antico dramma sacro italiano.* 2 vols. Florence: Libreria Editrice Fiorentina, 1926–27.

Trexler, Richard. "Ritual in Florence; Adolescence and Salvation in the Renaissance," in *The Pursuit of Holiness in Late Medieval and Renaissance Religion*. Ed. Charles Trinkaus and H. A. Obermann. Leiden: Brill, 1974.

———. "Florentine Theater, 1280–1500. A Checklist of Performances and Institutions." *Forum Italicum* 14 (1980), 454–75.

———. *Naked Before the Father: The Renunciation of Francis of Assisi*. New York: Peter Lang, ca.1989.

Trovato, Paolo. *Con ogni diligenza corretto: la stampa e le revisioni editoriali dei testi letterari italiani (1470–1570)*. Bologna: Il Mulino, 1991.

———. *L'Ordine dei tipografi: lettori, stampatori, correttori tra Quattro e Cinquecento*. Rome: Bulzoni, 1998.

Tura, Adolfo, ed. *Edizioni fiorentine del Quattrocento e primo Cinquecento in Trivulziana*. Milan: Comune di Milano, 2001.

Ulysse, Georges. "Un Couple d'écrivains: les sacre rappresentazioni de Bernardo et Antonia Pulci," in *Les femmes écrivains en Italie au Moyen âge et à la Renaissance*. Ed. G. Ulysse. Aix-en-Provençe: Publications de l'Université de Provençe, 1994, 177–96.

Valerius Maximus. *Factorum et dictorum memorabilium, Libri IX*. English and Latin. Ed. and trans. D. R. Shackleton Bailey. Loeb Classical Library. Cambridge, MA: Harvard University Press, 2000.

Ventrone, Paola. *Gli araldi della commedia. Teatro a Firenze nel Rinascimento*. Pisa: Pacini Editore, 1993.

———."La sacra rappresentazione fiorentina: aspetti e problemi," in *Esperienze dello spettacolo religioso nell'Europa del Quattrocento*. Atti del XVI convegno del Centro Studi sul Teatro Medioevale e Rinascimentale, Roma, 17–21 giugno 1992. Ed. M. Chiabò and F. Doglio. Rome: Torre di Orfeo, 1993, 67–99.

———. "Feste e spettacoli nella Firenze di Lorenzo il Magnifico," in *Le tems revient. 'L tempo si rinuova. Feste e spettacoli nella Firenze di Lorenzo il Magnifico*. Catalogo della mostra Firenze, Palazzo Medici Riccardi, 8 aprile–30 giugno 1992. Ed. Paola Ventrone. Cinisello Balsamo (MI): Silvana Editoriale, 1992, 21–53.

_____. "Per una morfologia della sacra rappresentazione," in *Teatro e culture della rappresentazione. Lo spettacolo in Italia nel Quattrocento.* Ed. Raimondo Guarino. Bologna: Il Mulino, 1988, 195–225.

Verde, Armando. *Lo Studio fiorentino 1473–1503 ricerche e documenti.* 5 vols. Florence: Olschki, 1973–1994.

Vespasiano da Bisticci. *Lamento d'Italia per la presa d'Otranto fatta dai Turchi nel 1480* in *Vite.* Ed. Ludovico Frati. Bologna: Romagnoli dall'Acqua, 1892–93, 3:306–25.

Villari, Suzanna. "Una bucolica 'elegantissimamente composta': il volgarizzamento delle egloghe virgiliane di Bernardo Pulci," in *Filologia umanistica per Gianvito Resta.* Ed. Vincenzo Fera and Giacomo Ferraú. Padua: Editrice Antenore, 1997, 3:1873–1937.

Volpi, Guglielmo. "Luigi Pulci. Studio biografico." *Giornale storico della letteratura italiana* 22 (1893), 1–63.

Weaver, Elissa. *Convent Theatre in Early Modern Italy: Spiritual Fun and Learning for Women.* Cambridge: Cambridge University Press, 2002.

_____. "Antonia Pulci e la sacra rappresentazione al femminile," in *La maschera e il volto. Il teatro in Italia.* Ed. Francesco Bruni. Venice: Fondazione Giorgio Cini: Saggi Marsilio, 2002, 3–19.

_____. "Antonia Tanini (1452–1501), playwright, and wife of Bernardo Pulci (1438–1488)," in *Essays in Honor of Marga Cottino-Jones.* Ed. Laura White, Andrea Baldi, and Kristin Phillips. Florence: Edizioni Cadmo, 2003, 23–37.

Weddle, Saundra. "'Women in wolves' mouths': Nuns' Reputations, Enclosure and Architecture at the Convent of Le Murate in Florence," in *Architecture and the Politics of Gender in Early Modern Europe.* Ed. Hellen Hills. Burlington, VT: Ashgate, 2003, 115–29.

_____. "Enclosing Le Murate: The Ideology of Enclosure and the Architecture of a Florentine Convent, 1390–1597." Ph.D diss., Cornell University, May 1997.

Wogan-Browne, Judith. "Saint's Lives and the Female Reader." *Forum for Modern Language Studies* 27 (1991), 314–32.

Zaccaria, Raffaella. "Antonio Dolciati," in *Dizionario Bibliografico degli Italiani*. Rome: Istituto della Enciclopedia italiana, 1991, 40: 433–35.

Zafarana, Zelina. "Per una storia religiosa di Firenze nel Quattrocento. Una raccolta privata di prediche." *Studi medievali*. New series 9:2 (1968), 1017–1113.

Zanetti, Guid'Antonio. *Nuova raccolta delle monete e zecchi d'Italia*. Bologna: Per L. dalla Volpe, 1775–89.

Zorzi, Ludovico. *Carpaccio e la rappresentazione di Sant'Orsola. Ricerche sulla visualità dello spettacolo nel Quattrocento*. Turin: Einaudi, 1988.

———. *Il teatro e la città. Saggi sulla scena italiana*. Second edition. Turin: Einaudi, 1977.

Index

Accarigi, Francesco di Tommaso, 26–27n79
Achilleus. *See* Nereus and Achilleus
Adam (*l'antico padre, primo parente*), 160–61 (oct. 20), 276–77 (oct. 57), 447nn5–6, 452n20
Ahasuerus (*Ansuero*), 264–65 (oct. 43)
Ahinoam, 55n143, 59, 459n25
Alamanni, Domenico, 27
Albizi, Lucrezia degli, 18n46
allegory, 50, 52–53, 456n28
alms (*limosine*), 42, 42n118, 45, 90–93 (octs. 34–35), 158–61 (octs. 18–19), 200–1 (octs. 70–71), 224–27 (octs. 103–4), 234–35 (octs. 4–5), 258–61 (octs. 34–37), 280–81 (oct. 63)
Ambrose, St., 35, 35n102
ammantellate (also *mantellate*), 3–4, 26, 473, 476
Annalena, convent of. *See* San Vincenzo
annunziazione. *See* prologue
anthology (attr. to Antonio Miscomini), 2n1, 3, 3n3, 18n47, 19, 22–23, 30–31, 37, 44, 61–62
Antonio (Maestro), 29
Apollo, 376–77 (oct. 16), 458n14
Asclepius (*Ascrepio*), 372–73 (oct. 12), 376–77 (oct. 16), 458n14
Asini, Mariotto degli, 463
Atalanta. *See* Calydonia

Avicenna, 204–5 (oct. 74), 449n18
Babylon (*Babillonia*), 45, 58n, 270–73
Baccini, Giuseppe, 15n38, 16n39, 25nn72–73
Banfi, Luigi, 38n, 451n30
Bartolomeo de' Libri, 21n58, 23, 44, 48, 54, 60n, 62–63, 447n1,.452n18, 458n7
bassetta, 310–11 (oct. 2), 454n3
Benazzi, Paola, 16n41
Benigno (Fra) da Genova, 472, 476
Bernardo di Quintavalle, 45, 451n9
Bettini, Piero di Francesco, 15n38, 25
Black, Nancy, 39
Boccaccio, Giovanni, *De mulieribus claris*, 445n20
Bonaventure, St., *Legenda maior*, 44, 44n126,
Bonfadini, Antonio, 40
Bozzi, Tanino, 9
Bryce, Judith, 2–3n2, 9n19, 14n32, 34n100, 41–43

Calydonia, 106–7 (oct. 57), 445n19, 445n21
Camilla, 37, 106–7 (oct. 57), 445n18
Canto dei Cartolari, 21
Cardini, Franco, 42n118, 44–45
Carney, Emanuela, 34–35, 61n, 445n19

Carrai, Stefano, 16n41
Castellani, Castellano, 23,
  23n66, 24n68, 47n133,
  *Rappresentazione del figliuol
  prodigo*, 47–48, 48n135, 53–54
Cavalca, Domenico, 44, 449n14
Chanson de Roland, 460n31
charity. *See* alms
Cioni, Alfredo, 3n3, 47n131, 62
Claudia, 106–7 (oct. 57), 445nn20–21
clothing ceremony (*vestizione*),
  451n30
Colomb De Batines, Paul, 3n3, 8,
  31n92, 43, 47n131
Compagnia della Purificazione,
  19n51, 47n132
Compagnia di San Gerolamo della
  Costa di San Giorgio, 47n133
constancy (*costanza*), 38, 43, 88–89
  (oct. 29), 98–99 (oct. 43), 108–9
  (oct. 59), 118–19 (oct. 73), 138–
  39 (oct. 103), 184–85 (oct. 51),
  186–87 (oct. 53), 214–15 (oct.
  89), 228–29 (oct. 106), 262–63
  (oct. 39)
contemplation (*contemplare*), 13n31,
  53, 142–43 (oct.106), 162–63
  (oct. 24), 268–69 (oct. 47),
  284–85 (oct. 69), 306–7 (oct.
  96), 358–59 (oct. 71), 447n37,
  457n38, 472, 476
contemptus mundi, 43, 45, 226–27
  (oct. 105), 232–33 (oct. 3),
  246–47 (oct. 21), 254–55 (oct.
  30), 256–57 (oct. 33), 404–5
  (oct. 47), 460n39

convent theater, 23n59, 30–31,
  30–31n91, 31n92, 45, *figs. 11a
  and 11b*, 445n17, 451n30
Cox, Virginia, 2n1
Crabb, Ann, 2–3n2

dalle Celle, Giovanni, *Vita di Santa
  Domitilla*, 34
D'Ancona, Alessandro, 8, 38n107,
  39n109, 448n9, 450nn23–24,
  450n26, 451n30
Daniel, 180–81 (oct. 44), 240–41
  (oct. 14)
Datini, Margherita, 2n2
Davanzati, Bartolomeo di Mariotto,
  20
Davanzati, Mariotto d'Arrigo, 2, 20
Dei, Bartolomeo, 48n135
Della Robbia, Luca, 29
De Robertis, Dominico, 20
Diana, 37, 106–7 (oct. 56), 445n18
Dolciati, (Fra) Antonio, 12n27, 15,
  15n37, 23–26, 27n80, 30, 30n88,
  46, 48, 54; *Esposizione della
  Regola di Sant'Agostino*,15n37,
  24–25, 470–77, 472n4, 473n7;
  other works, 471, 475
Dominici, Giovanni, 35n102
Domitian, 33
Domitilla. *See* Flavia Domitilla
dote. See dowries
dowries, 2, 11–12, 14, 15, 15n38, 17,
  378–79 (18.6), 458n16, 473, 477
dowry fund (Monte delle Doti), 14,
  14–15n35

Eisenbichler, Konrad, 47n133

endecasillabo [hendecasyllabic verse], 24n68, 33, 33n97
envoy. *See licenza*
Erode. *See* Herod
Esau, 240–41 (oct. 14)
Ester, 264–65 (oct. 43)
Euphrosina and Theodora, 36, 446n27
Evangelista, Anna Maria, 3n3.
Eve, 5, 447n5, 452n20

Falvay, Dávid, 40
Fanciulle della Concezione, 28
Fanfani, Pietro, 456n23
Fedele, Cassandra, *Oratio pro Bertucio Lamberto*, 2n1
Festa del vitello sagginato, La. *See* Muzi, Piero di Mariano
Fioretti, 44, 44n126, 57–58n148, 453n30
Flamini, Francesco, 8–9, 8n17,16n39, 19n50, 20n53
Flavia Domitilla, 33, 34n99
Francis of Assisi, St., painted by Giotto, 44–45, 57–58n148, 451n1, 452n16. *See also* Bonaventure, St., *Legenda maior* and *Fioretti*

Galen, 204–5 (oct. 74), 449n18
gambling (*giucare, giocare*), 48, 48n136, 53–54, 92–93 (oct. 35), 160–61 (oct.19), 260–61 (oct. 37), 310–15 (octs. 2–6), 344–45 (oct.49), 352–53 (oct. 61), 447n4, 451n11, 454n8, as metaphor, 244 (oct. 18), 352–53 (oct. 61), 457n36

Genazzano, (Fra) Mariano da, 26, 26n77, 473, 476
Ghirlandaio (?), 28–29
Giambullari, Bernardo, 461n50
giannizzero (Janissary), 57
Giannotti family, 8
Giove. *See* Jove
giucare, giocare. *See* gambling
grain market, 7
Guglielma of Hungary, 39–40
Guglielma of Milan, 39–40

Herlihy, David, 9–10n20, 44
Herod (*Erode*), 162–63 (oct. 22)
Honorius III, 452n15, 453n24

Innocent III, 452n13, 452n15
Isaac, 176–77 (oct. 40)

Jacob (*Iacob*), 240–41 (oct.14)
Jacobus de Voragine, *Legenda aurea* (*Golden Legend*), 34–35, 34n99, 446n27
Jacopa da Settesoli, 44–46, 453n30
Jerome, St., 35, 35n102, 445n19
Jove (*Giove*), 370–73 (oct. 10–12), 374–77 (octs.14–17), 380–81 (oct. 21), 422–23 (oct. 70), 432–35 (octs. 81–83), 436–37 (oct. 85), 440–41 (oct. 88), 458n14

Kirschner, Julius, 14n35

Landino, Cristoforo, 60n
Lapo (convent of Santa Maria del Fiore), 27
laude, 3, 21n56, 24, 472, 476. *See* Pulci, Antonia, *Corpo di Cristo*

Leone (Fra), 453n24
licenza (envoy), 32, 53, 55, 462n60
limosine. *See* alms
Lommatzsch, Erhard, 54n142
Lottini, Apardo di Niccolò, 6n10
Lottini, Niccolò, 6n10, 11n24
Lowe, K . J. P (Kate), 13n30
Lumini, Apollo, 38n
luogo deputato, luoghi, 32–33,
    32n95, 36, 56, 456n27, 459n29

Macinghi Strozzi, Alessandra, 2n2
marriage vs. virginity, 33, 35–38,
    35n102, 43, 71 (octs. 1–2), 77–
    88 (octs. 11–30), 102–3 (octs.
    49–51), 104–7 (octs. 55–57),
    150–53 (octs. 9–11), 176–79
    (octs. 41–42)
Mars (*Marte*), 104–5 (oct. 54),
    372–73 (oct. 12), 376–77 (oct.
    16), 458n14
Medici, Lorenzo (de'), 12, 14–16,
    15n36, 18, 22, 60n, 454n3,
    468–69
Mercury (*Mercurio*), 104–5 (oct. 54)
Minerva, 372–73 (oct. 12), 376–77
    (oct. 16), 458n12, 458n14
Miscomini, Antonio, 60n,
    Florentine press of, 2n1, 3n3,
    13n31, 17n44, 21n58, 22–23,
    60n151, 62–63, 447n1, 458n7.
    See also anthology
Mombritius, Boninus, *Sanctuarium
    seu Vitae Sanctorum*, 34–36
Montici. *See* Pulci family properties
Mugello, 6, 5–6n6, 15n38, 16–18,
    20, 25, 463n1

Murate, Le (convent of Santissima
    Annunziata), 8n18, 13,
    13nn30–31, 27–28
Muzi, Piero di Mariano, *La festa del
    vitello sagginato* (the fatted calf
    play), 47–54, 47n132, 454n2,
    455n13, 455n15, 455n20,
    455n22

Nasi, Jacopo, 17n43
Nasi, Lena di Jacopo, 17n43
Nereus and Achilleus, Sts., 33–34
Neri, Ferdinando, 47n133
Newbigin, Nerida, 23, 23n66, 36,
    36n103, 42n117, 47n133,
    448n13, 450n27, 455n13
Newman, Barbara, 39nn108–9, 40
Nogarola, Isotta, 452n20

Orlando (Count) of Chiusi, 453n22
Orsini, Clarice, 12, 14, 18, 468–69,
    figs. 3a and 3b
Ortensio, 36n103
Orvieto, Paolo, 17n44, 454n3
ottava rima (octaves, eight-line
    stanzas), 3, 5, 16n40, 20, 33

Palagio, il. *See* Pulci family
    properties
Palandri, Eletto, 8n18, 13n31,
    22n60, 43n122, 44n126, 453n30
Pellecchia, Linda, 7n12, 7n15
Peter, Saint (*Pietro*), 136–37 (oct. 84)
Piccolomini, Latanzio (Fra), 472,
    476
Pilate (*Pilato*), 162–3 (oct. 22)
Pius II, 57

Poliziano, Angelo (Angelo Traversari), 26n77, 60n
Ponte, Giovanni, 47n133
Ponza (Pontine Island, *Isola di Ponzio, Isola Ponziana*), 36–37, 108–9, 124–25, 445n22
Preyer, Brenda, 7n14, 464n5, 465n8, 466n, 467n
printers, Florentine, 21, 21n58; *See also* Miscomini, Antonio and Bartolomeo de' Libri
prologue (annunziazione), 31–32, 48, 55
Pulci, Antonia (Antonia Tanini), 472–73, 475–77; dowry, 2, 11, 14, 15, 15n36, 15–16n38, 17; identity, 8–10, 8nn17–18; marriage, 2, 12, 15–18; portrait, 29; religious vocation, 3–4, 17, 26; versification, 33; will, 9–10, 10n22, 24, 26–28; works: *Corpo di Cristo*, 24, 24n68, 472, 476. *See Rappresentazione del figliuol prodigo, Rappresentazione della distruzione di Saul e il pianto di Davit, Rappresentazione di Santa Domitilla; Rappresentazione di Santo Francesco*, and *Rappresentazione di Santa Guglielma*. *See also* Santa Maria della Misericordia and San Gallo, chapel of St. Monica
Pulci, Bernardo, 2, 5–6n6, 12–20, 14–15n35, 22–23, 22n60, 25–26, 44, 46, 47n133, 53; *camerario*, 18; lyric poetry, 17, 20; *Provveditore degli Ufficiali* (of the Studio), 16n39, 18–19; will, 15n38, 25; works: *Passione di Cristo*, 8n18, 13, 13n31, 17, 20; *Il pianto di Maria Maddalena*, 20; *Resurrezione di Cristo*, 17, 20; translator of Virgil's *Eclogues*, 17, 17n44, 20, 22, 35; *Vita della gloriosa Vergine Maria*, 20. *See also Rappresentazione di Barlaam e Josafat* (*Play of Barlaam and Josafat*)
Pulci, Costanza, 20
Pulci family, 2–3, 16, 21, 461n50; properties, 15n38, 16–21, 25
Pulci, Jacopo, 16
Pulci, Lisa, 2, 20
Pulci, Luca, 2, 14–15n35, 16–18, 16n41, 53, 58; works: *Ciriffo calvaneo*, 20; *Driadeo d'Amore*, 20; *Pistole*, 20, 22
Pulci, Luigi, 2, 14, 16–18, 18n46, 20, 25; works: *Ciriffo calvaneo*, 20, *La Giostra di Lorenzo de' Medici* (The Joust of Lorenzo de' Medici), 22; *Morgante*, 16, 20, 20n55, 53, 58, 446n24, 456n26, 457n5, 458n9, 459–60nn30–31
Pulci, Raffaello di Luca, 17, 17n42
Pullia, Anna, 39n108

querelle des femmes, 5

Raphael (Archangel), 448n7
Rappresentazione del figliuol prodigo (Play of the Prodigal Son) [by Antonia Pulci], 4, 23–24, 31–32, 46–54, 62, 448n9, 450n25

Rappresentazione del figliuol prodigo (Play of the Prodigal Son) [by Castellano Castellani]. *See* Castellani

Rappresentazione della distruzione di Saul e il pianto di Davit (Play of the Destruction of Saul and the Lament of David), 4, 23–24, 31, 46–47, 54–62, 452n18, figs. 10a and 10b

Rappresentazione dell'Angelo Raffaello e Tobia,19n52

Rappresentazione di Barlaam e Josafat (Play of Barlaam and Josafat), 4n4, 19, 42–43, 460n39

Rappresentazione di Joseph, di Jacob e de' fratelli, 4n4

Rappresentazione di Joseph, figliuol di Jacob, 4n4

Rappresentazione di Santa Domitilla (Play of St. Domitilla), 2n, 4, 18–19, 22–23, 31–37, 43, 43n121, 62, figs. 4, 7, 11a and 11b

Rapprezentazione di Santa Guglielma (Play of St. Guglielma), 4, 19, 19n52, 22–23, 31–32, 37–43, 48n135, 54–55, 55n145, 61–62, figs. 5, 8a and 8b

Rappresentazione di Santo Antonio Abbate (Play of Saint Anthony Abbot), 4

Rappresentazione di Santo Francesco (Play of St. Francis), 4, 22–23, 31–32, 42–47, 48n135, 54, 57n148, 61–62, figs. 6, 9a and 9b

Regola. *See* Rule

Richa, Giuseppe, 11–12, 12n27, 15–16n38, 25–29, 27n80,

romance tradition, 5, 20, 38, 38n, 43, 54–58, 449n21; Greek romance, 38

Rule (*Regola*) of St. Francis, 45, 262–63, 266–69, 452nn14–15, 453n24

Sacchetti, Franco, 21, 463

sacre rappresentazioni (miracle and mystery plays), 3–5, 32–33, 39, 42, 47, 54, 446n33, 449n16, 450n25, 460n39; virgin martyr plays, 5, 33, 36–37, 36n103, 54, 59. *See also* romance tradition.

San Clemente, 25, 28, 30

San Damiano, 45–46, 236–37, 238–39 (oct. 8), 240–41 (oct. 11)

San Gallo, 4, 26–28, 30, 471–74; chapel of St. Monica, 473, 476

San Marco, 19n51, 47n132

San Simone (parish), 6n10, 11n24

Santa Caterina al Monte (at San Gaggio), 31n91

Santa Croce, 9, 14, 25, 44–45, 476–77, fig. 2; Giotto frescoes, 44–45

Santa Maria degli Angioli, 45, 290–293, 292 (oct. 78), 296–97, 453n27

Santa Maria della Misericordia (convent, also called the "Assunta") , 26–27n79, 28–30, 28n84, 30n88, 470, 470n2; foundation of, 4, 15, 15–16n38, 24–27, 27n80, 470, 473, 476

Sant'Apollinare (San Pulinare), 6n10, 7, 11n24, 19n52, 463
Santissima Annunziata. *See* Murate, Le
San Vincenzo ("Annalena"), 26, 26n78, 27–28, 473, 477
Scarperia, 6, 5–6n6, 6n7, 9, 12
Sibyls (*Sibille*), 37, 106–7 (oct. 57), 445n17
Strocchia, Sharon, 13n30, 26–27n79
Strozzi, Ridolfo di Filippo, 26–27n79
Sultan of Egypt, 452n16
Susanna, 168–69 (oct. 30)

Tanini, Antonia. *See* Pulci, Antonia
Tanini: family of Francesco d'Antonio, 2, 5–15, 5n, 17; house, 7–8, 21, 25, 463–67; Annalena (suor), 8n18, 13, 13n31; Antonia (Antonina, 'Ntonia). *See* Pulci, Antonia; Cornelia, 11–12, 11n24; Costanza, 11–12, 14–15; Francesco d'Antonio di Giannotto (de'), 5–7, 6n10, 9–12, 9–10nn19–20, 10n22, 11n24, 12n27, 14, 44, 46; Girolama, 11–12, 17n45; Giulio, 9, 11, 14; Lisabetta, 11–12; Lucrezia, 11–12; Niccolò, 10–11, 12n27, 14, 72, 472, 476; Tita (daughter of Francesco), 11–12, 14–15; Tita (mother of Francesco), 11; *See* Pulci, Antonia (Antonia Tanini) and Torelli, Jacopa di Torello di Lorenzo

Tanini: family of Lotto di Tanino Tanini: 9, 9n19; Agostino di Lotto (de'), 9; Girolamo di Lotto (de'), 17n43
Testaverde, Anna Maria, 3n3
Theodora. *See* Euphrosina and Theodora
Tobias (*Tobia, Tubia*), 19n52, 448n7
Torelli, Jacopa di Torello di Lorenzo, 5–7, 10–12, 12n27, 14, 14n32, 18, 46, 468–69, 472, 476, figs. 3a and 3b
Tornabuoni, Lucrezia, 2–3nn1–2, 16, 16n40, 20–21; *laude* and narrative poetry, 21n56
Toschi, Paolo, 43n122, 452n19
Tosigni, Francesco di Ranieri, 14n34
Trexler, Richard, 30n91, 47n132
Trovato, Paolo, 30, 63n155
Turan, Ebru, 57n146
Turks, 57
Turnus (*Turno*), 106–7 (oct. 57), 445n18

Ulysse, Georges, 37, 38n, 45n, 53

Valerius Maximus, *Factorum ac dictorum memorabilium*, 445n20
veiling ceremony, 31n92
Verde, Armando, 16n39, 19, 19n50
Vespasiano, da Bisticci, 57, 57n147
vestizione. *See* clothing ceremony
Vignamore. *See* Pulci family properties
Villani, Tedice di Ludovico, 20
Villari, Susanna, 17n44

virginity. *See* marriage vs. virginity
virgin martyr plays. See *sacre rappresentazioni*
Visconti family, 40
Visdomini, Roberto, 12, 17n45,

Weddle, Saundra, 13n30